Geir Lundestad (ed.)

The Fall of Great Powers

Peace, Stability, and Legitimacy

Scandinavian University Press

Oxford University Press

Scandinavian University Press (Universitetsforlaget AS),
P.O. Box 2959 Tøyen, N-0608 Oslo, Norway
Distributed world-wide excluding Norway by
Oxford University Press, Walton Street, Oxford OX2 6DP

Oxford   New York   Toronto   Dehli   Bombay   Calcutta   Madras
Karachi   Kuala Lumpur   Singapore   Hong Kong   Tokyo   Nairobi
Dar es Salaam   Cape Town   Melbourne   Auckland   Madrid
and associated companies in   Berlin   Ibadan

Oxford is a trade mark of Oxford University Press

Published in the United States
by Oxford University Press Inc., New York

© Universitetsforlaget 1994

ISBN 82-00-21922-4
ISBN 82-00-03947-1 pbk

British Library Cataloguing in Publication Data
Data available

Library of Congress Cataloguing in Publication Data
Data available

Printed in Norway by A/S Foto-Trykk, Trøgstad, 1994

CONTENTS

CONTRIBUTORS

Professor J. F. Ade Ajayi is professor of history emeritus at the University of Ibadan, Nigeria. His most recent publications are *People and Empires in African History*, ed., London, 1992, and *Africa in the Nineteenth Century until 1880s*, ed., Oxford, 1989.

Professor A.O. Chubarian is director of the Institute of Universial History, the Russian Academy of Science, Moscow. His most recent publications are *Allies at War*, New York, 1993, and *Wars and Peace in the 20th century*, ed., Moscow, 1990.

Professor Istvan Deak is professor of history at the Institute of East Central Europe, Columbia University, New York. His most recent publications are *Beyond Nationalism*, New York, 1990, and *The Lawful Revolution*, New York, 1979.

Professor Michael W. Doyle is professor of political science at the Center of International Studies, Princeton University, Princeton, New Jersey. His most recent publications are *Empires*, Ithaca, 1986, and *Escalation and Intervention*, ed., Boulder, 1986.

Professor Aaron L. Friedberg is professor of politics and international affairs at the Center of International Studies, Princeton University, Princeton, New Jersey. His most recent publication is *The Weary Titan: Britain and the Experience of Relative Decline 1895–1905*, Princeton, 1988.

Professor John Lewis Gaddis is professor of history and director of the Contemporary History Institute at the University of Ohio, Athens, Ohio. His most recent publications are *The United States and the End of the Cold War: Implications, Reconsiderations, Provocations*, New York, 1992, and *The Long Peace: Inquiries into the History of the Cold War*, New York, 1987.

Professor Imanuel Geiss is professor of history at the University of Bremen, Germany. His most recent publications are *Europa.*

Vielfalt und Einheit. Eine historische Erklärung, Mannheim, 1993 and *Der Hysterikerstreit: Ein unpolemischer Essay*, Bonn, 1992.

Professor Robert Gilpin is professor of international affairs at Princeton University, Princeton, New Jersey. His most recent publications are *The Political Economy of International Relations*, Princeton, 1987, and *War and Change in World Politics*, Cambridge, 1981.

Professor Wang Gungwu is Vice-Chancellor of the University of Hong Kong, Hong Kong. His most recent publications are *The Chineseness of China*, Hong Kong, 1991, and *China and the Chinese Overseas*, Singapore, 1991.

Professor Paul Kennedy is professor of history at Yale University, New Haven, Connecticut. His most recent publications are *Preparing for the Twenty-First Century*, New York, 1993, and *The Rise and Fall of the Great Powers*, New York, 1987.

Professor Geir Lundestad is director of the Norwegian Nobel Institute in Oslo and adjunct professor of history at the University of Oslo. His most recent publications are *East, West, North, South. Major Developments in International Politics 1945-1990*, revised edition, Oslo, 1991, and *The American "Empire" and Other Studies of US Foreign Policy in a Comparative Perspective*, Oxford, 1990.

Professor William H. McNeill is professor of history emeritus at the University of Chicago, Chicago, Illinois. His most recent publications are *A History of the Human Community*, 4th ed., Englewood Cliffs, New Jersey, 1993, and *The Global Condition*, Princeton, 1992.

Professor Wolfgang J. Mommsen is professor of history at the Heinrich Heine Universität, Düsseldorf, Germany. His most recent publications are *Das Ringen um den nationalen Staat. Gründung und Ausbau des Deutschen Reiches unter Bismarck 1850–1890*, Berlin, 1993, and *Grossmachtstellung und Weltpolitik. Die Aussenpolitik des Deutschen Reiches 1870-1914*, Berlin, 1993.

Professor Alex Nove is professor of economics emeritus at the University of Glasgow, Scotland. His most recent publications are

Policial Economy and Soviet Socialism, London, 1979, and *Stalinism and After*, London, 1975.

Dr. Carol R. Saivetz is a research fellow at the Russian Research Center, Harvard University, Cambridge, Mass. Her most recent publications are *The Soviet Union in the Third World*, ed., Boulder, 1989, and *The Soviet Union and the Gulf in the 1980s*, Boulder, 1989.

Professor Zara Steiner is professor of history at New Hall College, Cambridge, England. Her most recent publications are *The Times Survey of Foreign Ministries of the World*, ed., London, 1982, and *Britain and the Origins of the First World War*, London, 1977.

Professor Susan Strange is professor of political economy emeritus at the London School of Economics, London. Her most recent publications are *International Monetary Relations*, London, 1976, and *Sterling and British Policy*, London, 1971.

Professor Immanuel Wallerstein is professor of sociology and director of the Fernand Braudel Center for the Study of Economics, Historical Systems, and Civilizations at the State University of New York at Binghamton, Binghamton, New York. His most recent publications are *Geopolitics and Geoculture*, Cambridge, 1991, and *Unthinking Social Science*, Oxford, 1991.

Vladislav M. Zubok is presently a senior fellow at the Norwegian Nobel Institute. His most recent publications are *A Forest and the Trees: Outlines of Three National Ways of Life*, Moscow, 1991, and *Political Parties and Executive Elites in the United States* (with Yu. Abranov) Moscow, 1990.

INTRODUCTION

Geir Lundestad

From 31 July to 4 August 1993, the Norwegian Nobel Institute held a Nobel Symposium in Tromsø in Northern Norway under the title "The Fall of Great Powers, Peace, Stability, and Legitimacy". The word "symposium" is derived from the Greek and quite literally it means "drinking together", but within the Nobel family, as in modern usage generally, a symposium does not particularly emphasize the drinking, but rather denotes the gathering of scholars for the discussion of a given topic.

At its most recent symposiums the Norwegian Nobel Institute focused in 1988 upon human rights[1] and in 1991, at the celebration of the 90th anniversary of the Nobel prizes, upon old and new dimensions in international relations after the end of the Cold War.[2] The 1993 symposium brought some of the world's leading historians, political scientists, and political economists to Tromsø, reflecting the fact that much of the most exciting research in international relations takes place on the borderlines between disciplines. In order to provide as much of a common approach as possible, it was deemed generally desirable that the analyses were set in a historical-political context. The participants presented their initial papers at the symposium, but the many lively sessions in Tromsø have led to substantial revisions in almost all of them. The present book consists of these revised papers.

In its symposiums the Norwegian Nobel Institute tries to focus upon topics which are both politically meaningful in the sense that they are of interest to the Norwegian Nobel Committee that each year awards the Nobel peace prize, and academically stirring in the sense that sound and stimulating research can be presented. In this respect, few subjects can be as relevant as the one we dealt with in Tromsø.

The rise and, particularly, the fall of great powers and civilizations has been a topic of enduring academic and, even more, popular interest, as witnessed by, for instance, the works of Edward Gibbon and Arnold Toynbee. The immediate background to this Nobel symposium was, however, constituted by two important events, one on the academic side, the other on the political: the publication of Paul Kennedy's *The Rise and Fall of the Great Powers*[3] in 1987 and the collapse of the Soviet Union a few years later.

Many of the themes presented by Paul Kennedy in his best-selling book were not entirely new. Thus, in 1981 Robert Gilpin had touched upon several points later made notable by Kennedy: the parallels between earlier empires and post-1945 USA, the historical importance of uneven growth rates, the significance of the discrepancy between commitments and resources, and the general mechanisms that lead to cycles of rise and fall.[4] What Kennedy did, however, was to sketch in considerable detail how, over 500 years, powers had come and gone, how they became great because they were technologically and organizationally advanced; how, with a certain time lag, they would then take on military commitments and expand; and how this expansion was bound to end in "imperial overstretch" and thus represent a handicap in the ever-continuing economic competition and therefore contribute to the decline of the power in question.

Kennedy's interpretation could be perceived as somewhat crude, as he, himself, had feared,[5] but it was an account that was to have a most dramatic impact on both the academic community and at the popular level. Numerous supporting statements and even more rebuttals were published and detailed studies of some of his key points undertaken.[6] In the US electoral campaign of 1988, not only the presidential candidates, but also many voters felt that they had to address the question whether the US was declining or not. Was it true, as Kennedy had argued, that "it simply has not been given to any one society to remain *permanently* ahead of all others, because that would imply a freezing of the differentiated pattern of growth rates, technological advance, and military developments which has existed since time immemorial."[7] Would the USA really go the same way as the Habsburg and the British empires?

Much of both the academic and the popular fascination with Kennedy's book had undoubtedly to do with the future of the United States, a question about which no historian can really claim to be an expert. And it was highly questionable whether the United States, and, even more, Britain in the nineteenth century, actually conformed to the closest Kennedy himself came to a precise definition of "overstrech": that "a particular nation is allocating *over the long term* more than 10 percent (and in some cases – when

it is structurally weak – more than 5 percent) of GNP to
armaments...".[8]

There could be no doubt, however, that the Soviet Union met
this definition of "overstretch" and that "overstretch" was at least
one important dimension behind its collapse. While the debate was
raging about whether the United States was declining or not, the
other superpower was actually falling apart before our very eyes. It
took Kennedy, like most of us, som considerable time to understand
the depth of the Soviet crisis and what would prove the outcome of
Mikhail Gorbachev's policies.[9]

After the dismantling of the Soviet outer empire in the
exhilarating months of 1989, from the elections in Poland in June to
the fall of Ceausescu in Romania in December, the turn came to the
inner empire. In 1991 the Soviet Union was dissolved; 15 new states
emerged and a Commonwealth of Independent States provided only
for the loosest and most transitory forms of cooperation among
most of those states. In 1993 several of the new states, including
Russia, were themselves in serious danger of fragmenting.

In the West, the wildest of hopes had, in one way, suddenly
come true. But it soon became evident that the consequences of the
Soviet collapse were not exactly those hoped for. Self-determination for Eastern Europe and the Soviet republics was indeed fine,
but on the ruins of the collapsed Soviet structure emerged not peace
and stability, but age-old conflicts and violence.

The contributions in this book, as did the discussion in Tromsø,
focus on three broad sets of problems. First, as a starting point, we
address the question about which Paul Kennedy's *The Rise and Fall
of the Great Powers* had done so much to create such strong
interest: Why did great powers fall? Since the fall part was to
represent only one of the dimensions of the symposium, the papers
had to concentrate on broad categories of explanation. The decision
was made to study great powers of the twentieth century only since
a selection had to be made and there were many advantages in
having the studies drawn from roughly the same historical period
and then from the most contemporary one. Thus, Britain, Austria-
Hungary, Germany, the Soviet Union, and the United States were
the powers chosen. The Ottoman empire, China, France, and Japan
were obvious additional candidates, but primarily for reasons of
space they were left out. (On the substance side, the roots of the
decline of the Ottoman empire and of China went back many
centuries and had little to do with the twentieth century more

specifically; France's role was in many ways similar to that of Britain, with the emphasis on empire and relative economic decline; Japan's omission was more serious, but its fall had much to do with the outcome of the Second World War and in that respect it paralleled the fall of Germany.)

Second, we wanted to move from the discussion about the reasons for the fall of great powers to the question of what the consequences of these falls were for peace and stability. What kind of stability had the power in question provided for whom and at what price? How did the fall of this power affect its own behavior, relations among the great powers, and stability in the various areas which the great power had controlled? In sum, did the fall of the great power in question lead to a more stable and peaceful world?

Third, it seemed important to keep in mind that peace and stability, crucial as they are, are not the only dimensions that should be connected with the fall of great powers. Thus, while the fall of the Soviet Union soon led to the flare-up of many local conflicts in Eastern Europe and in the old Soviet territory, this fall should also be seen as a great victory for the self-determination of the peoples concerned. So, the fall of the great powers affected not only peace and stability, but also legitimacy.

"Legitimacy" became a much used word and a much discussed concept at the symposium in Tromsø. The various chapters in the present book reveal that not all the contributors felt equally convinced about the meaningfulness of this concept. What did "legitimacy" really mean? How was it different from acceptance, the simple fact that some regimes are accepted, others are not? How did one address the problem that legitimacy, if it existed at all, existed at several different levels? (The three most obvious ones seemed to be the international systemic level, the relationship between the great powers and the areas they controlled, and inside the various states and territories.)

Nevertheless, most participants clearly felt that legitimacy was a useful concept which could help to address a significant dimension of the fall of great powers. Legitimacy is here defined as "in accordance with established rules, principles, or standards", in other words that a certain state of affairs "can be justified".[10] Thus, legitimacy added a moral dimension to the simple fact of acceptance. For instance, the Soviet position in Eastern Europe was accepted as a matter of fact, but this did not necessarily mean that it was seen as morally right or legitimate, at least not by most of the local populations. Acceptance came more easily if a certain regime was also seen as legitimate. The definition of what constituted legitimacy certainly changed over time and each of the levels had their separate, although related, bases of legitimacy. Yet these complications did not mean that legitimacy as such was not a useful concept, only that the term had to be put into a specific context when used.

The most dramatic long-term change in the relationship between great powers and small powers was probably the change from empire to nation states. As William McNeill argues in his contribution, the traditional "norm for civilized governance was laminated polyethnic empire." Gradually, that norm changed to that of the nation state, just as the norm in the relationship between ruler and ruled changed from absolutism to some form of popular rule. The norms changed, i.e., the definition of what was legitimate changed, and these changes certainly affected the fall of the great powers.

The choice of any one overall perspective means that other perspectives can not be given equal attention. In analyzing the relationship between the fall of great powers, peace, stability, and legitimacy, this book is generally, but not entirely, set within a state system dominated by military and political considerations. This outcome flows from the overall framework and from the choice of scholars represented. Economic factors in the form, for instance, of technology and organization, multinationals and interdependence have certainly been given some attention, but not the kind of attention that would have followed from the choice of other perspectives and other contributors. Demographic and environmental factors have been taken into account even less. Such results are unavoidable. As editor, I do not claim that the contributors cover every relevant angle, but I do claim that almost everything written is relevant to the topic chosen.

In analyzing the three sets of problems mentioned, the contributions are grouped into six basic parts. In part one, William McNeill and Imanuel Geiss deal with the role of great powers and peace, stability, and legitimacy in the long-term historical perspective, or, as McNeill defines his task: to set "contemporary political phenomena in a larger time frame than that provided by the past five hundred years."

In part two the studies of the relationship between the fall of specific great powers and peace, stability, and legitimacy are presented: Zara Steiner's on the fall of Great Britain, Istvan Deak's on Austria–Hungary, Wolfgang Mommsen's on Germany, the three studies on the Soviet Union – the case that inspired much of the entire effort – by Alec Nove, Alexandr Chubarian, and Vladislav Zubok, and, finally, the opposed interpretations of Aaron Friedberg and Susan Strange on whether the United States has been experiencing a "fall".

In part three the perspective is reversed and we move away from the point of view of the great powers and to what, for lack of a better word, can be rather broadly termed the "local level." Since, in this case, this level encompasses most of the southern half of world, a selection had to be made. J.F. Ade Ajayi analyzes the colonial and Cold War orders from the point of view of an African with regard to peace, stability, and legitimacy, while Wang Gung-wu does the same from an Asian point of view. Carol R. Saivetz deals with the extent to which, first, the Cold War and then, the end of the East–West confrontation, enhanced or dampened conflict in the most volatile region of all, the Middle East.

In part four Michael W. Doyle examines the relationship between peace and one basic element of modern legitimacy, democracy. How have political theorists seen this relationship and is there really, as Doyle himself has argued earlier, not a single example of a democracy going to war against another democracy? (There are many examples of democracies conducting colonial wars and going to war against dictatorships.) If this kind of close relationship does indeed exist, there would seem to be reason for considerable optimism in that democracy has never been stronger internationally than today.

In part five, Robert Gilpin, Immanuel Wallerstein, and John Lewis Gaddis speculate about what the future might hold. Robert Gilpin reviews what he terms the "Post-Cold-War International Disorder." Immanuel Wallerstein describes quite concretely the new superpower structure he sees emerging and the consequences of this structure for "peace, stability, and legitimacy, 1990-2025/2050." John Gaddis focuses on the long-term tension between the economic integration and the political fragmentation of the world. What will be the consequences for peace and stability when a rapidly increasing number of new states discover that their choices are economically ever more circumscribed?

While the discussion in Tromsø revealed surprisingly broad agreement on many important points, no effort was made to reach any academic consensus. In part six Paul Kennedy and the editor therefore sum up the findings of the eight country studies and the nine more general chapters in their own personal ways. Kennedy, whose *The Rise and Fall of the Great Powers* provided so much of the original intellectual inspiration for the symposium, does this by relating the contributions in part to the great power perspective of the earlier book, in part to the much broader transnational issues he deals with in his *Preparing for the Twenty-First Century*. The editor, in turn, tries to explore some of the relationships between the key concepts at the symposium, i.e., between the fall of great powers and legitimacy at various levels, and between legitimacy and stability.

I hope that this book will, firstly, represent a useful summing-up of where we stand today in our research on the basic relationship between the fall of great powers and peace, stability, and legitimacy, a topic of great importance for both scholars and practitioners. Secondly, I hope that the book will stimulate further inquiries into these crucial issues. If, in answering some questions, the book has created new ones, this can only be welcomed. In fact, such is the very nature of research.

The editor wishes to thank all those who made this volume possible: the academically so distinguished and personally so agreeable participants at the symposium and contributors to this book, the various branches of the Nobel organization involved: the Norwegian Nobel Committee under Francis Sejersted that agreed to the original idea of having a symposium on this topic, the Symposium Committee under Michael Sohlman that financed the symposium, and the many staff members at the Norwegian Nobel Institute who did all the work, with Sigrid Langebrekke taking special responsibility for the organizational details. I thank Teis Daniel Kjelling for having prepared the index. We had a great time at 70 degrees north, way inside the Arctic circle!

Notes

1. Asbjørn Eide and Bernt Hagtvet, eds., *Human Rights in Perspective. A Global Assessment* (Oxford: Blackwell 1992).
2. Geir Lundestad and Odd Arne Westad, eds., *Beyond the Cold War: New Dimensions in International Relations* (Oslo–Oxford: Scandinavian University Press 1993).
3. Paul Kennedy, *The Rise and Fall of the Great Powers. Economic Change and Military Conflict from 1500 to 2000* (New York: Random House 1987).
4. Robert Gilpin, *War and Change in World Politics* (Cambridge: Cambridge University Press 1981), particularly chapters 4 and 5.

5. Kennedy, op. cit. (see note 3), p. xxiv.

6. For further comments on this debate, see my *The American "Empire" and Other Studies of US Foreign Policy in a Comparative Perspective* (Oxford-Oslo: Oxford University Press–Norwegian University Press 1990), pp. 31–141, particularly pp. 85–87.

7. Kennedy, op. cit. (see note 3), p.533.

8. Kennedy, op.cit. (see note 3), p. 609, note 18. The emphasis is Kennedy's own. For indications of how low British defense spending actually was, see Paul Kennedy's own "The Costs and Benefits of British Imperialism 1846-1914", *Past & Present*, Number 125, November 1989, pp. 186-192. In his newest work, *Preparing for the Twenty-First Century* (New York: Random House 1993) Kennedy is somewhat less insistent about the negative effects of moderate defense spending on economic growth. See particularly pp. 293-294.

9. In addition to *The Rise and Fall of the Great Powers*, pp. 488–514, see Paul Kennedy, "Grand Strategies and Less-than-Grand Strategies: A Twentieth-Century Critique" in Lawrence Freedman, Paul Hayes and Robert O'Neill, eds., *War, Strategy, and International Politics. Essays in Honour of Sir Michael Howard* (Oxford: Clarendon Press 1992), pp. 227–242.

10. *The Random House College Dictionary* (New York: Random House 1984), p. 765. *The Advanced Learner's Dictionary of Current English* (London: Oxford University Press), p. 558.

Part I

The Fall of Great Powers in a
Long-Term Historical Perspective

1

Introductory Historical Commentary

William H. McNeill

Our task, I take it, is to throw what light as we are able on contemporary international politics by analyzing comparable, or seemingly comparable, circumstances in the past. Since the other contributors will deal with the decay of particular great powers within the context of the European state system and some of the recent consequences of these changes elsewhere, my most appropriate role is to take a longer view, setting contemporary political phenomena in a larger time frame than that provided by the past five hundred years. This may be useful inasmuch as political patterns of recent centuries cannot, in the nature of human things, be eternal. Just as the idea and practice of state sovereignty within a context of other sovereign states arose in Western Europe, beginning about 1450 and attaining full theoretical and institutional expression by 1650, so we, in the second half of the twentieth century, may be witnessing the initial stages of the unravelling of that system as subsequently projected upon the entire globe. It is too soon to be sure; but, in any case, awareness of how other, older political systems once worked ought to be part of our intellectual armament when attempting to appraise the phenomena around us. Let me therefore remind you of some political patterns of the deeper past.

From Polyethnic Empire to Nation States and back?

One such pattern commands special attention because of its precision. In at least eight important instances, to wit, in the ancient Near East, in the classical age of Mediterranean, Chinese and Indian civilizations, and again in more modern times in pre-Columbian Mexico and Peru, as well as in Italy and again in Japan, a plurality of warring states was transformed when one of them achieved hegemony over the others and then established a bureaucratic empire that dominated the whole territory where warring states had formerly exercised a divided sovereignty. Boundaries were often vague; and populations within imperial borders sometimes escaped effective taxation by being too poor, too isolated or too formidable. But throughout the civilized area in question urban centers and settled agricultural populations surrounding the cities did pay taxes and sustained the resulting empires – sometimes for centuries, sometimes for much shorter periods of time.

Reasons for the instability of empires are not far to seek. Taxing conquered and resentful subjects was inherently difficult, especially when the governing elite constituted a minority whose morale, cohesion and cooperation with a distant monarch were all liable to erosion. Assimilation between conquering and conquered populations (which always occurred, though with differing degrees of reluctance) cut two ways. On the one hand, it might diminish the conquerors' cohesion, as happened for instance when Germanic chieftains who had invaded the western Roman empire dismayed their followers by aping Roman landowners. On the other hand, assimilation sometimes allowed a ruling elite to recruit from below, and thus prolong its power. But even when such recruitment was effective – as happened for instance in the Roman, Ottoman and Manchu empires – territorially far-flung conquest states remained comparatively fragile structures, perpetually liable to revolt from within and assault from without.

Yet the fact remains that once imperial state structures had arisen in the Middle East, Eastern Europe, India and China, recurrent revolts and invasions could disrupt them – sometimes for more than a century at a time – only to see new imperial regimes, much resembling their predecessors, regularly emerge from the resulting turmoil. State boundaries fluctuated quite drastically, but the sociological character of successive empires remained substantially the same, comprising a ruling elite of a particular ethnic background that presided over a multiplicity of other peoples who labored in the fields and jostled one another for niches in urban society under the always distrustful eyes of the rulers.

One must therefore conclude that the norm for civilized governance was laminated polyethnic empire. This was true in pre-Columbian America as well as in Eurasia and Africa. Ethnically uniform and more or less egalitarian polities – the erstwhile norm for modern democratic nation states – were characteristic of barbarian populations and only manifested themselves marginally and ephemerally in civilized landscapes. Perhaps the European nation states of recent centuries may, on an appropriately extended time scale, also prove to be marginal and ephemeral, as were the ancient Greek poleis, the Roman republic, Indian aristocratic polities of the sort into which Gautama Buddha was born, and the city states of renaissance Italy. In these cases, and many others about which we know far less, ethnically uniform states, emerging from barbarian simplicity, were supplanted by large polyethnic empires within a few generations, or, sometimes, centuries.

The Biblical account of the Kingdom of Israel under Saul and David offers a particularly vivid and familiar example of how rapidly (and irresistibly) polyethnic empire could evolve from tribal simplicity. Empire had been endemic in the Middle East for more than a millennium when Saul set out to rally the semi-barbarous Hebrew tribes against their enemies. But after a mere fifty years of warfare and state building, Saul's successor, King David, emerged as ruler of a small but authentically polyethnic empire, complete with ruthless tax gatherers and professional warriors like Uriah the Hittite. David's imperial kingdom did not last long; and its remnants were, of course, eventually incorporated into far vaster imperial structures: Assyrian, Babylonian, Persian, Macedonian, Roman, Arab, Ottoman and, most recently, British. But the Biblical story of the Hebrew kingdom makes clear both how inescapable, and how unstable, the imperial pattern of governance proved to be. Incidentally, it is worth pointing out that the state of Israel reconstituted a traditional polyethnic empire in parvo after winning independence in 1947 by treating the Moslem and Christian Palestinians, who came under its jurisdiction, differently from Jews.

Should we view the modern vogue for sovereign, homogeneous, and democratic nation states as another instance of temporary departure from the laminated polyethnic norm of civilized governance? It seems a plausible hypothesis, despite the fact that a plurality of rival states has lasted far longer in Europe than in the ancient Middle East and other civilized areas. Exceptional circumstances explain Europe's persistent political divisiveness. At the start, when the Roman empire collapsed, urban life almost disappeared from the western provinces, and, as a result, efforts to revive imperial government there failed repeatedly, since an adequate tax base was lacking. That was normal enough since, in general, whenever barbarian invasion destroyed city life in formerly civilized lands, empire faded away. That is what happened to the Indus civilization, for instance; and to Minoan and Mycenaean empires in the Aegean lands.

West-European political history became aberrant from civilized norms only after about A.D. 1000, when urban life and commercial activity started to flourish anew, but imperial consolidation failed to ensue. Presumably that was because two rival bureaucracies – one papal, one imperial – struggled to assert universal jurisdiction over Latin Christendom, and, through the investiture controversy, cancelled each other out. Instead, kings and other territorial rulers made good their claim to full sovereignty, first in practice, then, beginning about 1300, in theory also.

The resulting state system even survived the invention of mobile, wall-destroying cannon, though everywhere else in the Eurasian ecumene, the gunpowder revolution had the effect of consolidating imperial power more firmly than ever before. But it so happened that the partition of the Burgundian lands after the death of Charles the Bold in 1477 divided gun-making capability almost evenly between French and Hapsburg sovereignties. And by the time strategic Hapsburg marriages threatened to tip the balance against France by adding Spain and Italy to the family's vast holdings in Germany and the Low Countries, behold, a new style of fortification, developed initially in Italy, blunted the instant, devastating effect of cannon fire on old-fashioned vertical stone fortifications. The result was that the possessor of a powerful gun park no longer had the ability to overpower local resistance merely by defeating the opposition in the field and breaching any and all fortified places where his fleeing enemies might find refuge. Instead, defeated field forces could once again withdraw into cannon-proof strongholds that were difficult and expensive to besiege. Consequently, the possibility of a swift and easy imperial unification of Western Europe disappeared after 1520 just when Emperor Charles V's enormous territorial inheritances seemed to put a real empire of western Europe within his grasp.

Thereafter, incessant warfare among rival states provoked unceasing technological advances in the use and design of weapons; and this soon allowed European armies and navies to outstrip other armed establishments. But within Western Europe itself, recurrent bouts of general war never produced a victor who could impose his will on all the other states. Political pluralism therefore survived within an undeniably civilized social context, and survives still, despite the substantial invasions of state sovereignty that NATO and the EEC have introduced since 1945.

Under these circumstances, the myth of ethnic uniformity within separate national jurisdictions took root in recent centuries when the leading nations of Europe harked back to suitably idealized and arbitrarily selected barbarian predecessors. (It is worth noting that the French and British chose Gauls and Britons as their putative national ancestors, in cheerful disregard of subsequent conquerors and invaders from whom they inherited their respective national languages.) The fiction of ethnic uniformity flourished, especially after 1789, when the practical advantages of a neo-barbarian polity in which all adult males, trained to the use of arms, united by a sense of national solidarity, and willingly obedient to chosen leaders demonstrated its power as against governments that limited their mobilization for war to smaller segments of the population.

Ancient Greeks and Romans had enjoyed this same advantage for a brief period of time when they were emerging from barbarian simplicity into the complexity of polyethnic urbanism. Classical education had long sensitized Europe's ruling classes to ideals of heroism and patriotism derived from this phase of Mediterranean history. Hence, beginning in the eighteenth century and throughout the nineteenth, the model of the Roman republic and/or the Athenian democracy, superimposed on the invented virtues of ancient Gauls, Britons, Germans, or some other barbarian ancestor, inspired modern European states to demand active loyalty from almost everyone within their boundaries.

Herein lay much of the secret of European political and military superiority to other polities in recent centuries. Yet the west-European tour de force, combining urban complexity and technological mastery with a neo-barbarian ideal of active political and military participation on the part of a presumably homogeneous citizen body, did not long escape the trammels of civilized polyethnicity. For European nations promptly used their new military and economic power to establish polyethnic empires, overseas and overland, that conformed closely to traditional patterns.

Like many other imperial systems, these colonial empires proved comparatively fragile when the latent discontent of the subjected populations was mobilized against the Hapsburg and Ottoman empires after World War I, and against the British, French, Dutch and all other European empires after World War II. Similar political mobilization is now breaking up the Russian empire before our eyes. As a result, only China and, on a lesser scale, Amharic Ethiopia, continue to preside over an old-fashioned polyethnic empire, though stirrings of discontent in Tibet and along China's inner Asian borderlands are not far to seek.

The collapse of imperial governance in our time is indeed impressive; but it does not follow that the forces that so persistently restored polyethnic empire after periods of disruption in the Eurasian past have lost their cogency. To be sure, the geographic and technological pattern of life that prevailed in Eurasia for at least 2500 years and produced recurrent conquests of settled lands by mounted nomads from the steppes disappeared as long ago as 1750. But from the point of view of Asian civilized populations, the erasure of the threat from the steppes in the eighteenth century was immediately succeeded by a new threat from the sea when European encroachment got seriously under way. Now that European empires have collapsed in their turn, should we assume that some new center of military power will not define itself and begin to subordinate other polities, as innumerable steppe conquerors in the deeper past and as European empire-builders in more recent centuries did?

Nuclear weaponry and all the other recent changes in military capability certainly altered the calculations of statesmen and therefore affect the conduct of international affairs in ways we are only beginning to get used to. But I think it is premature to conclude that aggression and conquest have been permanently foreclosed. In a global political system, abounding in nuclear warheads, risks are obviously greater than ever before. But successful conquerors have always been willing to take risks, even suicidal risks. Think of Alexander, or of Genghis Khan. It follows, I think, that the dynamic that so often produced an empire out of a system of warring states within a particular part of the world in times past might erupt anew, with or without the explosion of nuclear warheads. Any government that emerged as victor from a struggle for world mastery would speedily establish global empire by depriving all other states of weapons of mass destruction under the aegis, no doubt, of a restored United Nations. What the United States and its allies are trying to do in Iraq today constitutes a precedent for what any victorious government would surely do to secure future peace and safeguard itself from potential rivals.

When the Cold War was new, I used to think that this scenario of the future was imminent. I still think it possible, even probable, over a long enough future, since modern communications and transport make global empire feasible, and the advantages of making political management coincide with the global scope of contemporary economic exchanges might be considerable. Of course, possibilities for economic mismanagement would enlarge as well. The perils of the human condition will not be erased by any conceivable political future; and the inherent fragility of polyethnic empire implies that the emergence of a world empire would not bring an end to political and military upheaval. It would, however, change the terms of subsequent struggles by inhibiting systematic preparation for war, eliminating organized and deliberate arms races, and altering existing political alignments and identities in unpredictable ways, depending on which human group might emerge as rulers and who would turn into (presumably resentful) subjects.

So much for the most persistent political pattern of the deeper past. I merely wish to suggest that polyethnic empire has not necessarily been consigned to the dustbin of history by the contemporary vogue for national self-determination, democratic government and – most sacred of all – economic growth.

Polyethnic Empire, Demography, and Migration

A second persistent pattern of the deeper past, rooted in economics and demography, seems more immediately relevant to our contemporary situation. Not accidentally, it also acts to undermine the solidarity of separate national states, pushing society towards the civilized norm of laminated polyethnicism.

Almost always, cities were population sinkholes before the medical discoveries of the late nineteenth century made it relatively easy for public health administrators to interrupt the transmission of lethal infectious diseases. Wherever transport nets sustained a lively circulation of infections, urban deaths exceeded births, owing to the intensified exposure to diseases that concentration of human numbers in close quarters produced. Only by recruiting migrants from the healthier countryside could cities sustain themselves demographically. This meant that villagers, who had to feed the cities by parting with a portion of their harvest, also had to supply the towns with surplus sons and daughters to sustain urban civilization. New arrivals, of course, faced serious risk of infection and early death as a result of entering a more diseased environment than the one they had grown up in, so the flow from country to town had to be sustained, year in and year out, if all the nasty urban occupations were to be adequately staffed.

Not infrequently, the spontaneous flow of migrants from the countryside was insufficient. When that happened, cities regularly resorted to forcible recruitment from afar, importing slaves, often from across cultural and ethnic boundaries. The prominence of slavery in antiquity indicates the importance of this phenomenon; and the revival of slavery (and of neo-serfdom) in early modern centuries was also a response to drastic population shortages induced by disease disasters to the native populations of the Americas and across the western steppelands of Eurasia.

As a result, just as recurrent conquests of settled agricultural populations by barbarians from across the frontiers maintained polyethnicity by overlay at the top, so also the influx of enslaved outsiders at the bottom of society added another strand to the mix of peoples who inhabited Eurasian cities.

A third class of alien outsiders were engaged in long distance trade. Such persons commonly set up self-governing ghettoes in separate quarters at major trade centers, paying special taxes to local authorities for the privilege, and, incidentally, providing local ruling elites with a variety of luxury goods not otherwise accessible to them. This commercial element in the urban populations of Eurasia tended to grow across the centuries as transportation improved and as rulers became more firmly convinced of the fiscal advantages of tolerating or even of protecting trade. Trial and error established sustainable levels of protection rents; and a great variety of other customs cushioned contacts among the diverse alien communities that thus emerged in all the major cities of Eurasia.

Polyethnicity sustained by these three sorts of migration across cultural boundaries is alive and well in our world. One may discern an analogy to old-fashioned conquest in the UN peacekeeing forces that currently operate in several disturbed lands, bringing armed men of utterly alien background onto the scene to act as (presumably) temporary, surrogate rulers. Similarly, even though slavery has all but disappeared, migration into cities has assumed an increasingly massive scale. Runaway urban growth in the poor and backward countries of the world is a register of crowding on the land and the psychological impact of radio and TV that now allows even remote rural communities to glimpse the privileges of urban life. The push of overcrowding in the villages and the pull of bright lights in the cities work in tandem. Massive migration that strains the social and political order of African, Asian and Latin American countries results.

A special circumstance of our time extends the reach of this phenomenon to Europe and lands of European settlement overseas. Since World War II, some of the rich nations of the earth have ceased to reproduce themselves demographically while others have almost ceased to grow. In a sense this is nothing new, for, as I just pointed out, across millennia of civilized history urban living involved a failure of biological reproduction. But traditionally it was intensified deaths from infection that made cities inimical to biological survival. Today it is birth control, and the weakening of family ties due to separating domicile from workplace that impels the urbanized rich to spend more on themselves, and less on the nurture of children. But the effect is analogous to the older pattern of birth and death that required cities to recruit from healthier countrysides round about.

The major difference is that demographic sinkholes now embrace whole nations, rather than single cities as in times past. That is because, in the leading countries of Western Europe, in the United States, and even in Japan, the rural reservoir for urban recruitment has almost dried up. In these countries, urban patterns of life invaded the countryside, beginning about 150 years ago. Subsistence farming faded away, the market ruthlessly weeded out marginal producers, and the surviving rural population then started to enter peripherally into urban popular culture, thanks to radio and TV. But as the gap between town and country closed, recruits for nasty urban jobs had to come from further and further away, wherever peasant poverty still prevailed. Population pressure meant that such recruits came not as slaves, but of their own accord, seeking a better life than was available in their native land. Yet whenever their numbers became substantial, polyethnicity of a particularly stubborn sort established itself within west European and other rich nations.

As long as urban recruitment drew on countrysides close by, where peasants shared at least marginally in the language and culture that dominated the city itself, assimilation of newcomers to urban ways was relatively easy and assured. The experience of the United States and other lands of European settlement in the nineteenth century showed that when newcomers crossed linguistic lines the process of assimilation slowed but did not come to a halt. Religious diversity was more stubborn, since synagogues and churches struggled hard to maintain old customs and beliefs. However, when differences of physical appearance reinforced linguistic and cultural differences, assimilation became lame and partial, if it occurred at all.

The reason is that when differences of outward appearance reinforce group identities, assimilation cannot proceed imperceptibly, case by case, and individual by individual. Persons who might wish to abandon their ancestral identity and assimilate to the dominant group cannot alter their physical appearance, nor escape the stereotypes and discrimination associated with that identity. The difficulties blacks face in the United States show how problematic the ideal of assimilation becomes under such circumstances. Yet Moslem immigrants to Western Europe and Latino and Asian immigrants to the United States face comparable barriers today. Interaction and mutual adjustment is certain; but assimilation of these newcomers into a single, seamless citizen body, as called for by democratic theory, is highly improbable in the forseeable future.

Accommodation between host society and newcomers by constructing ghetto-like communities within which diverse peoples can pursue their separate ways more or less autonomously is an obvious alternative. That was the way old-fashioned polyethnic empires managed. The resulting separate and unequal communities endured indefinitely because individuals seldom abandoned the community into which they were born. This sort of cultural pluralism has been powerfully reinforced in our time by the cheapening of transport and communication. Migrants can now maintain far more intimate contacts with their homelands than was possible before, thanks to airplanes and the easy availability of long-distance telephones, FAX machines and the like. They can live simultaneously in two worlds, surrounded by an alien society, and adapting to it, while sustaining (and renewing) their own group identity through constant communication back home, wherever that may be.

These circumstances suggest, therefore, that the Eurasian style of old-fashioned polyethnicity has already begun to flourish among us, whether or not political empire ever arises again. Demographic and economic patterns that will not easily be reversed point clearly in that direction, and the rapid growth of Latino and Asian immigrant communities in the United States, and the multiplication of Moslem immigrant populations in all the West-European countries, indicates the power of the phenomenon. Only the Japanese remain almost homogeneous despite incipient demographic décay. That is because, so far, they have preferred to export capital and industrial plants to foreign soil rather than inviting alien laborers to enter Japan itself.

Obviously, a persistently polyethnic, culturally diverse society creates strains upon democratic ideals of active citizenship, national unity and equal rights. In particular, it challenges our inherited assumptions about the rational autonomy of individual voters, since group loyalty and pursuit of ethnic advantage can easily overshadow the residual and less clearly perceived common interests of all citizens.

States are weakened and Great Powers may crumble when ethnic identities, by commanding stronger loyalties and defining behavior across a greater range of circumstances, become more important than political citizenship. That was clearly the case in the Ottoman empire and many other polyethnic imperial states of the past. The United States and other countries that attract large numbers of immigrants from afar seem to be moving in that direction. Whether electoral politics, law enforcement, and the redistribution of income by bureaucratic action can cushion ethnic collisions and make citizenship emotionally valid for all concerned – rich and poor, old and new inhabitants alike – remains to be seen. This, indeed, is likely to become the most critical political question of the next century for rich nations confronting incipient demographic decay and substantial immigration of physically distinct, religiously different and (to begin with) desperately poor outsiders.

Great Powers and the Nurturing of the Young

A related and almost equally refractory problem is how to nurture the young in our cities so as to fit them for adult roles. Until quite recently, most people lived and worked at home. From infancy, children observed their parents' daily activity and began to help out at a very early age. This quickly converted children into family assets, as gradually, and without much in the way of formal education or deliberate training, they acquired adult skills and practical knowledge.

The rise of factory production and the development of other specialized workplaces outside the home in the past two or three centuries meant that family nurturing began to lose its automatic, all-embracing character. Schools took up some of the slack, teaching literacy and other skills that most people had not needed when oral instruction and simple imitation, largely within the household, sufficed for the transmission of ordinary work habits and practical knowledge. Schools also became a principal channel for the inculcation of national sentiment and other civic virtues appropriate to the participatory citizenship and national mobilization for war that European states needed in order to remain competitive after 1789. But schools did not take over the nurturing of infants; and only a few expensive boarding schools functioned around the clock.

More commonly, in the nineteenth and early twentieth centuries, the main task of nurturing among urban populations fell to women who, after marriage, were expected to keep house and look after the children. Their efforts at preparing the young for adult roles were reinforced by the survival in rural settings of the older style of life whereby men as well as women worked where they lived and therefore shared automatically in nurturing the young. Since cities drew migrants from the countryside, and, at an accelerating rate, rural families continued to feed work-ready adults into urban society. Until recent decades, this half-way house between familial and extra-familial nurturing prevailed in our cities with only sporadic signs of breakdown.

Since World War II, however, nurturing for adult roles in urban settings has weakened, especially in the rich countries of the world. Three changes undermined the nineteenth century arrangement. First was the increasing number of married women who started to work away from their homes. Second was the development of a vivacious youth culture that prized instant gratification and made ordinary adult life seem dull and unattractive. Third was the changed character of rural recruitment to the cities, analyzed above, which allowed (or even required) culturally diverse groups of new-comers to maintain their distinctiveness.

These changes make the transmission of traditional patterns of behavior across the generations far more problematical than before. Generation gaps have always become apparent, whenever an age cohort had to respond to altered conditions. But in our time diminished contact between parents and children, deeper immersion in youthful counter-cultures, and the influx of newcomers from diverse cultural backgrounds mean that old ways and habits of life lack their usual momentum. New invention has correspondingly greater scope, whether for good or ill. Social and political stability diminishes. Old institutions and political principles, even when enshrined in sacred constitutional documents, become brittle.

It follows that change, perhaps radical change, lurks near the surface of public life. Attenuation of familial nurture, which seems to have gone very far in modern cities, implies that institutions of all kinds – public and private, governmental, religious and social – have been undermined. Great Powers exist, after all, only because of the attitudes, habits and skills of the population under their jurisdiction. If continuity of attitudes, habits and skills across the generations falters, the basis of political power alters also; though in what direction and with what effect only time will tell.

How to invent more efficient arrangements for nurturing in urban settings therefore rivals the question of future relationships among different ethnic groups cohabiting a common cityscape as the most critical that our successors in the twenty-first century will have to face.

From Hunting and Gathering to Global Urbanity

I would like to try putting these twin problems of our age into the broadest of all possible historical perspectives. Indeed, let me start by going back before recorded history, when, ten to twelve thousand years ago, more and more human groups had to abandon hunting and gathering and started to cultivate the soil. The costs and strains were enormous, since the new style of life was far more laborious and required rationing consumption throughout the year, saving the necessary amount of seed, together with innumerable other adjustments that ran counter to the habits of hunters and gatherers. Nevertheless, the transition was made in different ways in different places, relying on diverse crops and modes of cultivation.

Then a few thousand years later, a second difficult adjustment had to be faced wherever villagers fell under the jurisdiction of urban tax and rent gatherers and therefore had to learn how to produce more food than they needed for their own consumption. Nevertheless, between five and two thousand years ago, a majority of the human race did learn to survive as peasants, with city folk living as parasites upon them. As such, urban society was not self-sustaining. Villages and in the ensuing millennia the great majority of human lives were shaped by the transmission of skills and attitudes across the generations that prevailed within rural communities.

This balance started to shift only after about 1000 A.D. Change proceeded slowly at first, as market relations between town and country began to supplement (and redress) the one-way flow of rent and taxes. Then, with the radical cheapening of transportation and communication that occurred in the past hundred and fifty years, it became possible to enfold villagers more and more fully into urban-based exchange systems. As a result, the world now seems well launched on the experiment of making urban-style living preponderant. Assuredly, peasants are everywhere in full retreat. Rural life is everywhere being engulfed in an exchange system that unites the globe through a flow of goods and services among individuals and groups, and projects urban attitudes and expectations to the remotest villages.

The effect on the peasant and ex-peasant populations of the earth is little short of catastrophic. Village routines and values are crumbling; yet urban delights remain largely inaccessible, even (or especially) for those who migrate to the cities. Under the circumstances, the world's peasants and ex-peasants are puzzled, angry and dismayed; yet almost everywhere remorseless population growth makes the continuation of traditional local ways increasingly impractical. At least half of the human race faces this dilemma in our time. Responses are bound to be drastic. It follows that peasant and ex-peasant discontents, mingling and intertwined with the, instabilities of urban living sketched above, will probably define the course of world history in the twenty-first century.

Adjustments required for long-term survival in a globally urban society are as drastic as the adjustments needed when hunters and gatherers first settled down to cultivate the land. And just as it took centuries to invent and routinize the skills, habits and expectations needed to sustain settled village life in neolithic times, so, in all probability, we are only at the beginning of a process that will take many lifetimes before anything like a viable, enduring definition of a new era of global urbanity emerges.

If human communities succeed in inventing appropriate responses to these new conditions of life, and if what works best eventually spreads, due to the usual human penchant for borrowing useful novelties and adjusting them to local conditions, one can believe that some centuries from now the long-standing gap between urban privilege and rural subjection will have been transcended, and more equable forms of society emerge. If ecological disaster can be avoided (or recovered from) and if population growth and decay come closer to an even balance among the diverse peoples of the earth, one might even imagine that something like the wealth and comfort now enjoyed by the rich could become general.

Yet I do not think that good will and social engineering, nor the most informed calculations of development economists are in the least likely to bring humanity to that sort of liberal Nirvana. Inventiveness, yes: but as much among the poor and oppressed as among managerial elites. Inventiveness, too, that pushes and pulls in different directions, responding to individual and group interests, or apparent interests. The result, as in all human history, will continue to be a fumbling, piecemeal process of trial and error, with ample scope for repeated error and resulting disasters. But it is only from disasters that all concerned can learn what does not work in a context of urban interdependency, just as a community that achieves some exceptional success can show the rest of the world what does work. (Think how Britain's industrialization between 1750–1850 has affected world affairs ever since; or how China's commercialization, between 1000–1400, led the rest of the world towards widened market mobilization of resources.)

Primary Communities, Territorial States, and Global Urbanity

Serious reflection on our current experiment with global urbanity should accord respectful attention to ancient precedents. Especially relevant today are the ten to twelve centuries that bracketed the Christian era, when civilized peoples of Eurasia grappled with the problem of finding a satisfactory way of living in cities that were increasing in size and importance all the way from China to Spain. Eurasian urban life exhibited localized ups and downs between 500 B.C. and 700 A.D., but generally trended upward owing to improved transport that permitted caravans and ships to connect China, India, western Asia and the coastlands of the Mediterranean more closely than ever before. Strangers met and mingled at all the way-stations of this transportation net. Ideas and practical skills spread more rapidly than ever before as a result.

By far the most conspicuous and important innovations that percolated among the urban populations of the age were the so-called higher religions. Beginning with Buddhism, and including Judaism, Christianity, Islam, Hindusim and some less successful faiths like Manichaeism and Zoroastrianism, these religions diffused along the trade routes of Eurasia, attracting converts, altering customs, and affecting daily lives in a multitude of ways. They agreed with Confucianism (a contemporary, comparable but divergent idea-system) in inculcating an individualized, universal ethic that required believers to deal justly, even with strangers and the poor and disadvantaged.

This may have softened encounters in the cities, and made personal relations among strangers a little more predictable. But the higher religions did not promise peace and justice on earth. That waited upon supernatural intervention, bringing the world to an end. In the meanwhile, believers (but not Jews and Confucians) could look forward to life after death, when suitable punishments and rewards would redress inequities and injustices on earth. Hope of Heaven (or its equivalent, e.g. incarnation as a higher form of life for Hindus) consoled sufferers, making life, and its disappointments, far more tolerable than before. As a result, the higher religions helped to stabilize urban living, despite the wide scope for injustice and inequity that inhered in the occupational differentiation among strangers that characterized urban society.

There was also another and more important way in which the higher religions stabilized urban life, for they propagated themselves by creating local meeting places where the faithful could assemble, affirm their commonality and establish a simulacrum of the sort of primary communities that had prevailed in villages since neolithic times. This, I suggest, was their most important achievement. Human beings need primary communities to give their lives meaning and value. The higher religions in effect provided a substitute for village life by creating effective primary communities even in urban contexts, where strangers abounded, inequality prevailed and outlooks differed. Although the new religions were not able to overcome injustice, their ideological and sociological innovations did make city life endurable as never before for ordinary persons, and especially for those towards the bottom of the social scale.

This in turn made civilized urbanity far more viable than before. It is not strange, therefore, that rulers of polyethnic empires swiftly discovered how such faiths helped to sustain the existing order of society. Accordingly, beginning in the third century B.C. with Asoka in India, and with the Han emperors of China, imperial rulers took the initiative in concluding an alliance of throne and altar that became universal by the time of Constantine, some five centuries afterwards. Personal conviction doubtless played a part in rulers' policies. Authentic piety was never the monopoly of the poor. But it was also the case that a shared religion, uniting rulers and subjects in a common world view, gave rulers a legitimacy that mere military force and conquest could never confer.

To be sure, the alliance of throne and altar had a seamy side. Holy war in defence of the true faith could, and often did, degenerate into sanctified brutality. In addition, priests in possession of conspicuous wealth and power were perpetually vulnerable to reproach by religious purists, and sometimes repressed their critics by force. But despite recurrent surges of reforms aiming to purify manners and restore the true faith, the fundamental idea of sanctifying secular government through alliance with an authoritative priesthood was never effectively challenged in any of the civilized societies of Eurasia from the time of Constantine until the eighteenth century, when a few French philosophers and other self-styled enlightened thinkers started to call the alliance into question.

Then in the nineteenth century secular faiths – first liberalism and then socialism – won wider followings, turning Christian teachings inside out by rejecting Heaven, and projecting hope for a better life into the terrestrial future instead. Rising material standards of consumption lent plausibility to such hopes in many parts of the world, and they remain vigorous still. On the other hand, traditional religions, often in intensified, sectarian forms, have begun to counter-attack. This may well be symptomatic of things to come. For just as the eclipse of polyethnic empire among us today may turn out to be temporary, so also I think we should recognize that our secular faiths and egalitarian doctrines have yet to prove their long-term viability.

After all, the undeniable successes of secular liberalism in the past two and a half centuries occurred under quite unusual conditions of economic expansion. How will secular recipes for social management fare if the upward creep of material consumption is reversed for most or all of the world's inhabitants? Yet, given what we know about potential ecological difficulties, and the population growth that surely lies ahead among the poor of Asia, Africa and Latin America, it is rash to assume that a rising material standard of living will be attainable for all of us in the near future.

Even among the rich, the enormous advance in living standards which took place in the last two centuries may prove impossible to sustain if market competition with poorer countries continues to nibble away at existing economic inequalities. Leveling down is just as possible a pattern for the future as leveling up. Economic theorists may have complete confidence in the ultimate advantages of free market competition across political and cultural boundaries, but ordinary people, finding themselves buffeted by changing job conditions in a world market, are usually unable or unwilling to wait.

Under these circumstances, it seems to me that our secular, liberal and democratic principles, inherited from the Enlightenment, are already in trouble. The surprising suddenness with which Russian state socialism failed is no guarantee that American principles will prevail. On the contrary, the Soviet collapse strikes me as an unusually spectacular demonstration of how fragile radically urbanized society has become, dependent as it is, on a smooth flow of goods and services among hundreds of millions of persons and across thousands of miles. The technical feat of assuring such a flow of goods and services is enormous in itself. Far more tricky is the maintenance of attitudes, habits and feelings needed for effective performance of all the diverse jobs required of the millions of persons immersed in, and dependent upon, the uninterrupted exchange of goods and services.

Inadequate nurture of the young and intensified ethnic frictions are signs that American society is not coping very well with this latter dimension of global urbanity. I very much suspect that reinvigorated primary communities, within which individuals can lead meaningful, satisfying lives, are as necessary for modern cities as they were in antiquity. But no plausible alternative to holding primary communities together by some form of religious commitment has yet appeared. Youth gangs, revolutionary parties, and sports associations usually wear out as their members mature in years; yet these are the most obvious rivals to religious sects to be found in our cities today. Still, it does not follow that revival of old religious faiths and practices is the path to the future. Invention is not dead among us. All sorts of experiments have been launched already – most of them evanescent and often silly. But combination and recombination of old and new practices and ideas are sure to continue, as indeed is already evident among the incandescent, expanding sects that have already taken the field.

There is, nonetheless, a bitter dilemma built into the project of building vivacious primary communities while continuing to participate in a world-wide, flow-through economy. The best of all possible cements for any human group is a clear and present threat from outside. By defining an enemy we define ourselves and create powerful incentives for smoothing over internal differences. Modern urban conglomerations offer plenty of diversity. Consequently, potential in-groups abound, each confonted by a variety of plausible enemies. How to moderate resulting collisions while also allowing emotionally-supportive primary communities to arise and flourish within our cities is the question.

Good answers are far to seek. In ancient, medieval and early modern times, a plurality of different religious communities, each with its own meeting places, and all subordinated to a distant imperial state, provided one kind of answer. Other rulers strove for a firmer bond between themselves and their subjects by insisting on religious uniformity. When successful, they expanded their power at home, and intensified conflict abroad by mobilizing a larger proportion of their subjects' resources for war. This was the Safavi way in Iran after 1499, and Spain's policy after 1492. A new-minted secular faith allowed France (and her rivals) to mobilize entire nations after 1789; and, with, diverse modulations in different nations, propelled western Europe's path towards world dominion. Yet, as already mentioned, the empires that secularizing Europeans built in the eighteenth and nineteenth centuries tolerated religious and ethnic diversity from the beginning; and the resulting lack of sympathy between rulers and ruled erased them from the map soon after World War II.

How to stabilize local identities and ways of life by rooting them in primary communities while allowing individual members of such communities to function effectively as citizens of territorial states and as participants in a world-wide economy is a problem we will hand down to our successors. Defining loyalties and establishing common identities has always been critical for public affairs. It is unusually critical today, when intensified contacts have weakened old identities and undermined the village communities that shaped the lives of most people ever since neolithic times.

Yet primary communities remain essential for human life. How they can thrive in our time without disrupting global urbanity or paralyzing territorial states remains to be discovered. It is a daunting task. But human beings are perpetually fated to confront insoluble problems simply because our hopes and fears always outrun reality. Surely we ought to be used to it by now, trusting that, as in times past, trial and error and the human propensity for imitating forms of behavior that produce desired results will continue to expand the scope for human life on earth.

Success, of course, simply breeds new, insoluble problems, commonly even more intractable than those of earlier ages. That is how history unfolded in the past, and the end of history is not yet at hand, even though global urbanity appears to be dawning around us. What sort, or sorts, of political configuration might fit such a society is the ultimate question behind the more specific theme of this book.

The fall of Great Powers is a particularly dramatic aspect of political change, and recent cases are well worth the careful analysis they are about to receive. The long-range context within which contemporary Great Powers and other states both rise and fall is also worth bearing in mind. At any rate, that is what I have attempted.

2

Great Powers and Empires: Historical Mechanisms of their Making and Breaking

Imanuel Geiss

"In the long run, we are all dead." (Keynes)

The sudden, apparently unforeseeable, collapse of the Imperium Sovieticum has raised new interest in the "Rise and Fall" of empires, to generalize Gibbon's famous formula. After the unthinkable has happened, it becomes urgent to analyse some historical mechanisms that make and break great powers. "Historical mechanisms" does not imply a new set of theories, but a condensation of knowledge, transcending the alleged primacy of "traditional" political or "progressive" social and economic history, of external or internal policy. Instead, the dialectics of internal and external, political and socio-economic factors are made fruitful under broader perspectives.

Taking Empirical Stock: The Imperial Balance

For the comparative study of empires, their rise and fall, history has a vast store of material.[1] It will be analysed with a macro-historic method that takes facts for granted. For the sake of legitimate simplification, "empire" and "great power" are used roughly as synonyms. The question, "What is new?" finds some answer: Historical mechanisms are not new, only the actors, their costumes and their historical ambience change. The distant past is enlisted to enlighten the present because traditional empires are easier to analyse, if only for the lack of embarrassing details. Contemporary superpowers did not (USSR) and will not (USA) escape those mechanisms.

Even a superficial look at imperial world history suggests a serious problem for modern historians. So far, traditional political history has concentrated on great powers or empires, because we know them best and the pageantry of battles and empires is easier to narrate. The chief source of our knowledge leads us back to the fountainhead of writing – civilization. If, as the French put it so charmingly about themselves, every empire has its "*mission civilisatrice*", so empire, as the highest stage of power, is wedded to civilization: Traditional and contemporary empires represent(ed) the power aspect of civilization. Civilization provides power – concentration of people, men in armed forces, economic potential in social, political and military structures.

Power, organized in great or small powers down to the level of African tribal kingdoms,[2] is applied in patterns that are universal in time and space. Hunters and gatherers in dispersion, with families and hordes as the highest form of social organization, did not have power in the strict sense. It arose only with the growth of populations and concentration of people in villages, towns, cities, kingdoms and empires, as Aristotle already observed in his *Politics*. Complex societies made for hierarchical organization, usually with a monarch at its head in the older history.

Powers, great and small, started in obscurity, unsure of themselves, then hit on some organizational novelty to give them fleeting advantages which vanished once rivals adopted, adapted and "improved" them. They startled their world by spectacular conquest, had their climax, which usually became the turning point, leading to decline, crisis, agony and the end.

For the various rises and falls there is no general relationship of time. Usually, the emergence of a power centre and its rise to regional hegemony as an empire took decades, sometimes even centuries. The climax is generally brief, lasting, perhaps, one or two generations, the decline drawn out, as of the Roman, Byzantine and Ottoman empires. Occasionally, the rise is just as rapid as the fall, as Alexander's, Napoleon's and Hitler's empires demonstrate.

Solemn discussions among historians about the causes of the end of empires create the impression that had but the one cause, singled out as the sole or supreme reason for the downfall, been avoided, that particular empire could have been saved. As German fairy tales ritually end: "Und wenn sie nicht gestorben sind, so leben sie noch heute." ("And if they have not died, they are still alive today.") No: In the long run, they are all dead.

Empires die hard or not for good. Most staged their comeback in whatever guise was appropriate for the times, in Renaissances or Restorations, from the Sumerian to Carolingian or Ottonian, or in the Middle and New Empires of both Egypt, Assyria and Persia, or the Second or Third German Empires, Tsarist and Communist

Russia. In the Old West, the geographical seat of imperial power shifted from the Ancient Orient (Mesopotamia, Egypt) westwards, via the Persian Empire and Greece–Macedonia to Rome, moved from there to the north (Portugal, Spain, France, Holland, England), crossed the Atlantic to the Far West after 1492, finally to the USA. Another line runs from the Roman Empire via Western Rome and the Medieval Roman Empire of the Germans to Austria–Hungary and two modern German Empires, via Eastern Rome/Byzantium to Russia.

Legitimacy can take three forms: 1. Success breeds booty and charisma, defeat destroys both. Failures have to go. 2. As long as an empire is a going concern, proving its superiority by success, the Gods are with it, as the inscription on the belt buckle of the German Army ran, even under Hitler – "Gott mit uns" ("God is with us"). Then, celestial and terrestial decrees were in order, success sanctified empire. Not only Chinese emperors had their "mandate from Heaven". Modern imperialism gave itself the "Dual Mandate" (Lugard) to rule over "lesser breeds" and to bring them modern (European) civilization. 3. In a more secular sense, empires often followed former empires – conquerors claiming to be the legitimate successor of the defeated monarch, e.g. as the Persian King-of-Kings, as Alexander the Great saw himself after his victory over Dareios III. Or an empire proclaims its succession to an older one, long defunct, as the Sassanids claimed to be the sole legitimate successors of the Achaemenids, so that they reclaimed all territories that had once belonged to the Old Persian Empire from upstart and usurping Rome. Legitimacy can be relative. The Greek Byzantians, to their bitter end in 1453, called themselves "Rhomaians"; the Germans also called their Empire in the Middle Ages, in the footsteps of Charlemagne, "Roman Empire", although it differed radically from the original Roman Empire in geographical basis, social structure, and ethnic composition. Napoleon I claimed to restore Charlemagne's Empire by replacing the Old Roman Empire of the Germans, in 1804, with the modern Franks, the French. After his failure in 1812–15, his nephew, Napoleon III, resumed the Bonapartiste mantle in the Second Empire.

Traditional empires expressed continuity in their official symbols. Since the Sumerians, the eagle has been the symbol of royal power, the double-headed eagle of a kind of supra-royal imperial power. There could be striking oddities. Even the otherwise practical-minded Queen Victoria was persuaded to raise her monarchical status from an ordinary Queen of England, Scotland and Ireland etc. to that of an Empress of India by taking up the crown of the deceased Moghul Empire in 1877. Apparently, she did not mind the ideological clash between adding the title of a traditional Eastern arch-despot to a modern industrial parliamentary power on its way to being a fully-fledged democracy. Similarly, the USA, the "Imperial Republic", revelled in the glory of the royal Eagle as its state symbol. America's aspiration as the future World Power was literally built into the stately architecture of her republican capital with its classicist capitol – the Fourth Rome, after the real First Rome, Constantinople the Second, and Moscow, since 1453, the Third Rome. Even ultra-progressive Albania stuck to the double-headed eagle on her official flag, pointing back to her Byzantian past.

Apart from 5000 years of imperial waxing and waning with shifting geographical settings in the West, three other notable variations of the imperial pattern represent different possibilities for the relation of power centre and power vacuum in time and space – China, India, Persia. They are useful counters to Western arrogance that recognizes only our model of empire with its many variations. A truly global view can discern their histories together. At the height of classical Eurasian antiquity, four empires between them secured some relative imperial peace and prosperity (William H. McNeill). Combined, they formed what could be called "Pax Imperialica" – "Pax Romana", "Pax Parthica/Persica", "Pax Indica" (Kushan Empire), and Han "Pax Sinica".

China's imperial history unfoldet over an ever-expanding area from one clear centre – in the north on the middle Zheng He (Huangho), where the mighty tributuary river Wei falls into the Zheng He. The usual change between power centre and power vacuum happened in the same region, but within the "dynastic cycle". A new dynasty re-unites China, puts the Imperial House in new order, expands, suffers revolts inside and invasion from outside, and is replaced by a new dynasty. Dynasties changed, but China's structural continuity is impressive, comparable to ancient Egypt. For China, imperial unity is the rule and ideal, turmoil and anarchy the exception when regional warlords took the interim place of central power. China's concept of the dynastic cycle could be fruitfully transferred to universal history – the imperial cycle of ups and downs.

India, in contrast, usually had an overwhelming plurality of empires and kingdoms, great and small. Her history is like looking into a huge kaleidoscope, where pieces are constantly changing in form, substance and colour. She had neither China's remarkable consistency of one empire with a succession of dynasties, nor precise political structures and traditions, like the European national state. The chaos of wild fluctuations was interrupted four times by conquerors who succeeded in uniting the sub-continent completely, or almost so, into one super-empire. But their feat ran so much against the grain of Indian society, based on village, caste and family, that the very success of empire-builders on the sub-continental scale produced Paul Kennedy's imperial "overstretch" almost instantly: Indian super-empires lasted only the reign of one super-Maharadj – Asoka of the Maurya Dynasty (271–231 B.C.); Ala-ud-Din of the Slave Sultanat of Delhi (1296–1316), followed by a spell of reconsolidation under Firoz Shah (1351–1388); Moghul Emperor Aurangzeb (1658–1707). The strangest conqueror of all, the British Raj, held India together for a record period of 90 years (1856–1947). India's imperial cycle was the opposite to China's: Political fragmentation was the rule, imperial unity the rare exception.

Persia offers yet another variety of the imperial cycle. The Old Persian Empire, for the first time in history, united all the civilized *oikumene* (W.H. McNeill) of the old West into one huge empire (550–330 B.C.). Twice Persia was engulfed by sudden conquest, first from the West by Alexander (334–330 B.C.). After more than 500 years of alien rule, the Persian Empire re-emerged with the Sassanids (224/7 A.D.), with the Parthians as forerunners (247 B.C. to 224/7 A.D.) – half Hellenized, half Iranian. Four hundred years later, Persia, exhausted by her struggle with Byzantium over the disputed territories, was again overrun, this time by Muslim Arabs from the South (641/51). Post-Sassanid Persian successor states arose at the periphery of the shrinking Caliphate of Baghdad; Persian civilization found its classical form and spread with Islam – from India and central Asia in the east to the Ottoman Empire in the west. It took 850 years for the Persian Empire to re-assert itself, in the New Persian Empire of the Safavids (1499/1500–1722).

Types of Empire

Apart from the kind of empire we are most used to – centralized empires in sedentary peasant and urban civilizations – other types enrich and modify the picture. Though the distinction between continental and maritime, sedentary and nomad empires may look outworn, their structures influenced even contemporary Great and

Superpowers, down to surprising after-effects of traditional long-distance trade, slave trade and slavery.

The well-known difference between land and sea power was often blurred by their co-existence in traditional and modern empires complementing each other: Persia, Rome, Byzantium, the Caliphate, the Ottoman Empire, for some time even Imperial China under the Ming dynasty (1405–33), Tsarist Russia, Imperial and Nazi Germany – all had their navies as well. Byzantium held her own against all invasions, as long as she commanded the seas around her capital, Constantinople. Still, they were all predominantly continental powers and fought according to the rules imposed by strategies of land warfare. Classical naval empires, in contrast, were fighting for supremacy on sea, thalassocracy, as the Ancient Greeks called it – Athens, Carthage, Venice, Portugal, the British Empire, although they also had their land elements. Land powers were more militaristic and autocratic, from Assyria and Sparta to (Tsarist and Soviet) Russia, more regimentated and more Spartan. Sea powers were richer, more cultured, more flexible and subtle internally and externally, but could be ruthless in crushing opposition to their vital interests.

Traditional differences between land and sea powers took a new twist in the case of modern World Powers. Tensions between the greatest modern sea power and land power, the British and Tsarist Empires, dominated the history of international relations in the nineteenth century, sharpened by their structural contrasts – Britain becoming the first industrial power, Russia remaining largely agrarian. After 1945, superpowers claim(ed), with their democratic pathos (in one form or another), to have overcome traditional empire, but still carry (carried) on some of their features. In the Cold War, the two remaining World Powers embodied different types of traditional empire on a global scale. The Soviet Union was a centralist militarist land power in the tradition of Assyria and Sparta, but with naval, air and rocket fleets, and nuclear arms. She was highly centralized, but also had autonomous adjacent vassal states (Outer Mongolia, Poland etc) and client states overseas (Cuba etc.). The USA combines the classical pattern of Athens and Venice, with a strong continental basis at home. After 1945 their "Empire by invitation" (Geir Lundestad) found its closest historical precedent in the two Athenian Sea Leagues, as long as Athens remained the naval hegemon, the leader of a coalition of equals, before she lorded it over and supressed allies as subjects. And the People's Republic of China clings to every square mile Chinese,

Mongol or Manchu emperors have conquered in the past and added to the "Middle Empire".

The second category of differences is less obvious and needs some elaboration, between sedentary, civilized and nomad barbarian empires. Classical empires had centralizing bureaucracies and clear-cut frontiers, known from historical atlases. Nomad empires, beyond the pale of settled civilization, were more fluid in forms and frontiers. Their highest political structures were tribal confederations for conquest and exacting tributes from subject peoples. Their rulers were suzerains over far-flung, ill-defined territories rather than sovereigns in a stricter sense. This type of empire also prevailed in parts of sub-Saharan Africa on the southern fringes of expanding Islam. The title of one such ruler, the Monomotapa in Eastern Africa, neatly described their main function – "He who collects the tribute". Loose tribute suzerainty is a hall-mark of nomad empires. As long as nomads stayed in their steppes and deserts they did not need professional bureaucracies.

Nomad power remained linked to sedentary empires throughout older history to the Moghuls of India (1526) and Manchus in China (1644). The most commonplace link was political: For traditional empires, nomads were decisive, overwhelmingly destructive external factors, often taking over empires by invasion. When they conquered civilized empires, they just kept the bureaucracies they found. Once nomad conquerors had assimilated themselves to sedentary civilizations, against the harsh law of nomadism, they took over the raison d'état of their new mode of existence and defended it against later-coming nomads from the steppe. Inversely, keeping barbarous nomads out from the civilized oikumene was one effect of expanding empires (W.H. McNeill).

Other links between sedentary and nomad empires, largely ignored by traditional political history, were commercial: Intercontinental long-distance trade, basically between the Far West and the Far East (China), via India, Persia, Central Asia and Arabia, provided ready cash for the great empires. Their ups and downs are correlated to the rise and fall of great traditional empires, from Han China to the Roman West. Long-distance trade, by land and sea, provided channels for the flow of goods and ideas, largely between East and West, which helped to transform the underdeveloped and peripheral Old West to the New West since 1492 that achieved world domination in the age of Imperialism.[3]

A legitimate part of traditional intercontinental long-distance trade was the slave trade, and with it, slavery became an integral part of sedentary empires. Tribute was often collected by nomads in the form of young people who were sold as slaves into the centres of civilization and power, or slaves were produced by raids (Arabic: "razzia"). Nomads were great slave hunters who collected slave labour from fragmentated (and therefore weak) peoples at great distances and funnelled them into empires, mainly of the West. India also received some black slaves from East Africa across the Indian Ocean, but was never dependent on them, because she had her pariahs and lowest castes to do the menial jobs. Theoretically, all subjects were slaves of the despotic ruler in any case, also in China, where the Emperor was the sole and absolute lord of the land, and Chinese peasant families felt only too honoured to supply servants to the Imperial household, e.g. boys to be made eunuchs.

Empires in the West, including Persia, Muslim states, and, in that respect, also Black Africa, needed slaves – males for hard labour and soldiery ("mamluk" or warrior slaves), females for household work and biological reproduction, often in harems or as concubines. Only Empires had the military means to control vast masses of slaves. Since "mamluks" could rise to the top of empires – India (1206–1398), Egypt (1250–1517) – nomads linked sedentary Empires to the barbarian periphery in that special way, from the bottom to the top of oriental societies.

Slaves were transported on the beaten paths of intercontinental long-distance trade, and were in fact an essential part of it. Black slaves came through the Sahara with camel caravans to the Mediterranean, or were shipped from the coast of East Africa over the Indian Ocean to India, Persia, and Arabia.

The regions where slaves came from also governed their positions within Mediterranean, in the Middle Ages usually Muslim, imperial societies: White slaves from the North (from the Caucasus to Slavs of the Adriatic and East of the river Elbe until the High Middle Ages) usually ranked above black slaves from sub-Saharan Africa. In times of crisis white and black military mamluk corps could clash. Tensions between white and black warrior slaves thus formed part of the general background to racism.[4]

Modern transatlantic slave trade, which provided so much of the necessary labour for the "Rise of the West" (W.H. McNeill), began as a modern extension of traditional slave trade from Africa.[5] Diverted across the Atlantic, it escalated into modern forms of proto-industrial enterprise, contributing to the sinews of the British and American empires.[6] In the New World tension between slavery, later racial discrimination, and the pathos of freedom and democracy provoked conflicts that are lying at the heart of internal troubles in the last World Power remaining after the demise of the Soviet Union. As Tocqueville shrewdly observed as early as 1831 in his great chapter on the future of the three races on the soil of America, in the first volume of his *Democracy in America*, the abolition of slavery was followed by racial discrimination. Racism is destroying the American Dream of World Domination from within, as Los Angeles 1992 has revealed. Thus, modern democratic structures are secretly, if only indirectly, linked to one aspect of traditional empires, which today is regarded as rather repulsive – slavery and slave trade. In the totalitarian USSR it strengthened structures of autocracy, in the democratic USA it bred racism – hidden or open.

Structures of Power

Empires as the highest stage of power reveal in their vicissitudes distinctive patterns. Out of the dialectics of power vacuum and power centre, new power centres arise and expand, leading to different applications of power – direct and indirect rule.

Power fluctuates through history, at times wildly, between the extremes of power centre and power vacuum. As ideal types in the Weberian sense, they can be roughly defined, although, in reality, they could be mixed. A power centre is a region with a central government, armed forces and internal peace, waging wars outside its own territories. A power vacuum is the very opposite – a region without central government and armed forces, politically fragmented, in constant warfare amongst its components (tribal or city states), the battleground of intervening and expanding powers. Fluctuations of imperial fortunes can best be illustrated by an image from meteorology – highs for power centres, depressions for power vacuums; both belong together. Usually, there can only be one or the other at a time – "hammer or anvil", as Chancellor Bülow graphically put it at the height of German imperial power before 1914.

Primary fragmentation, or, for short, "chaos", prevailed amongst hunters and gatherers ("savages" in the triad "savagery", "barbarism", "civilization", also used by the classical scholar that Marx also was) and tribes on the level of extensive agriculture ("the barbarians"). Secondary chaos arose where power centres had broken down, giving way to post-imperial successor states, or in nations during civil war or revolution. Just as nature has a *horror vacui*, so has power. Power vacuums attract intervention or imperial conquest, trying to fill the power vacuum. At times, conquerors are literally invited by one or the other party in a civil war for military help or simply as mercenaries. Or outsiders could be called in by warring parties to mediate or impose an end to civil war. This was how Europeans sometimes established their colonial rule, e.g. over the Yoruba to end century-long civil wars (1821–93), after the conquest of their Old Oyo Empire in 1821 by the extension of the Jihad of Utman dan Fodio (1804–17).

Power centres emerged from primary power vacuums in three possible ways: 1. Tribes (or city-states) were attacked from the outside, united against the common enemy, and remained so after warding off the invader. In pursuit, they become a new power centre under the hegemony, i.e. originally the military command, of the strongest in an alliance of tribes or city-states. 2. From constant infighting one emerged as the strongest and subdued other tribes or states, as in China after fragmentation before the Sui dynasty (589), or in Scandinavia to establish the kingdoms of Denmark, Sweden, and Norway (in that chronological order). 3. Or tribes (city-states, or smaller states) become tired of constant fighting for elementary goods (water, pastures, fishing rights) and unite their forces to get all those items for a better life by conquering neighbours. Tribal confederations of half-nomad peasants (e.g. Germanic) and nomads in the steppe (Indo-European, Turk–Mongolian, Arab, Berber) formed in that way and proceeded to invade sedentary civilizations.

Usually, a new power centre emerges at the periphery of the highest stage of culture in the region, often beginning as a march, a militarized border region of an empire, for the defensive *and* offensive – e.g. Assur as a military colony of Babylon; Castile for León at the beginning of the Iberian Reconquista; Austria, Saxony, and Prussia as Eastern marches of the Holy German Roman Empire, further expanding with the German drive to the East since the Middle Ages; Moscow as an advanced outpost of the Kiev Rus; the Americas with their moving "Frontier". China, after periods of turmoil, e.g. the "Fighting States", was usually reunified by new dynasties from the periphery (Ch'in, Sui, Tang; the Manchus, over-throwing the Ming). The reason for the presence of militarized borders is obvious: They combine the military potential, organization and discipline of civilization with the hardiness of the frontier. The mediating position of the imperial frontier between civilized empire and barbarian periphery also explains the ambivalent image of frontiersmen in the centres of old civilization. They were both despised for their coarsenesss and feared (or welcomed) for their military superiority when taking over centres of refined civilization, whose power had been waning: Assyrians, Romans (before they fully adopted Greek civilization themselves), Prussians compared with Bavarians or Austrians, Russians and North Americans for Europeans are cases in point.

The central purpose of empire is expansion. Power structures, large and small, followed the same pattern, the way of least resistance, like water running downhill. Filling adjacent (primary or secondary) power vacuums, empires increased their power as efficiently as possible. Generally, power centres expanded sometime after digesting their own establishment and consolidating early gains. Imperial rulers considered it their god-given duty to expand even more. To be "Mehrer des Reiches", part of the ceremonial title of German Emperors, was reality for all imperial rulers. Power wants more power. That is what the classical Greek meant by *pleonexia*. The shrinking and collapse of an empire was considered utterly abnormal.

An essential precondition for expansion is internal unity. It always preceded imperial expansion. If it broke down, imperial expansion usually stopped or was reversed. The history of European expansion overseas provides splendid examples on national scales (Portugal, France, England). Internal conflict may, on the contrary, also incite outward expansion. The (political or religious) leader, defeated at home and fleeing abroad, to seek his fortunes in the "barbarian" periphery, is a time-honoured figure in history, in particular of the East (China, India, Muslim Middle East). In Black Africa the lonely hunter, exiled from his tribe and marrying the chief's daughter to start a new tribe, is another variation of the same theme.

Early Rome provides striking examples: Changes between internal conflicts amongst patricians and plebs, internal peace and conquest wove the well-known pattern of Roman expansion abroad and social conflicts at home. During the Roman civil wars towards the end of the Roman Republic (133–130 BC), expansion went on because Rome had become so powerful that she took those internal troubles in her stride. In one instance, internal tensions even made for more conquest: Ambitious Caesar conquered Gaul, i.e. beyond the Roman periphery, to gain a powerful military basis abroad for his power struggle in Rome.

As expansion proceeded from the imperial centre to the periphery, from the imperial core to "distant provinces", power and its application diffused over the distance. The further away the Tsar, the less his commands were obeyed, the more freedom of manoeuvre opened or remained to his subjects. Thus, power was always applied with different intensity. The greatest concentration of power is to be found in the imperial core, its capital city, the royal or imperial palace with its palace guard. The capital is surrounded or protected by provinces of the imperial nation ("Reichsvolk") – Assyrian, Persian, Greek–Macedonian, Roman, Russian, English, German. Further away live relatives, cousins adopted as equals – Medes, Italians, Ukrainians and White Russians, Scots and Welsh. At even greater distance from the capital, but still within the reach of its military power, are the outer provinces. They were conquered, annexed and brought under direct rule in early stages of expansion, often the first victims of conquest. As provinces, they were without political rights. Their military potential was forcefully conscripted into the imperial army and commanded by officers from the imperial nation or its associates.

Further towards the periphery we find two kinds of areas under diminishing indirect rule – vassal and client states. For conquered peoples, vassaldom was the mildest form of alien rule. They kept their own nobility and rulers and autonomy to manage internal affairs (family and heritage laws, distribution of land, taxes, education, religion, military establishment). In return their duties were threefold: They had to supply troops to their overlord in war, in military units of their own; they had to pay tribute; they had to get a new ruler confirmed by the Suzerain, or his accession was justly notified. If they rebelled or refused to supply troops at the command of the central government, vassal states were punished by annexation, as was Serbia in the ascendancy of the Ottoman Empire (1389, 1459). In Ottoman decline, Serbia followed the opposite course, rising from a province (*pashalik*) (1459) through revolts (1804, 1815) to a vassal state (1817) as a half-way house to independence (1878).

Furthest away from the centre, client states bordered on virtual independence or near-sovereignty. Armenia used to hover between the status of an always precarious independence, as a client state of Rome/Byzantium or Persia or, when divided between them, both at the same time, and of an annexed province of either or both. A logical result of the distances of power is the difference between direct and indirect rule. It came to our European mind only at the height of the British Empire, after Captain Frederick Lugard transferred his experience from British India (direct rule) and

Princely States (indirect rule) to the freshly conquered North of Nigeria with its Sultanate of Sokoto, which was more a confederation of emirates than a closely-knit centralized empire. Beyond the narrow colonial context, the distinction, in substance, was universal and very old indeed. The new Assyrian Empire (912–612 BC) introduced it for the first time – direct rule from the imperial centre over annexed provinces, autonomous vassal states (e.g. Tyros, Sidon) to the periphery. But the practice, because of its internal logic, may have been much older.

The Rise and Fall of Empires

The regular course of empire follows from the gradations of power: first unity and consolidation, then expansion, often punctuated by internal conflicts. Initial success came from some social, political and/or military novelty in organizing society more efficiently for military success. Reforms provide more income through higher taxation, internal peace encourages economic growth, means of communications for long-distance trade are introduced or improved – roads, bridges, canals (in China). Greater wealth allows a growing military establishment; structural changes allow "better" use of manpower for military purposes: The "dynastic circle" is in full swing.

Since expansion cannot but progress from the imperial centre to the periphery, the fate of an empire is decided on its borders. From this follows the problem of how far expansion can safely go. What is the optimal size of an empire? The quest for it outside (expansion) is paralleled by the classic search for an optimal point inside – the "best state", optimal political and social structures or constitutions. Yet there is no optimal point either inside or outside. No one could ever spot it or make it permanent: "Verweile doch, du bist so schön!" (Goethe). Since all nature and history is constant change, the optimal point remains an idle abstraction. It slips through the fingers of both empire-builders and their historians.

The periphery, the extent or limit of expansion, governs the end of an empire in two ways. Since expansion is an imperial principle for its own sake, empires often lose their dynamics once they turn from the offensive to the defensive, materialized by frontier fortifications. A first example was the "Princes' Wall", erected by the Middle Egyptian Empire across the Sinai around 2000 BC. The building of the Roman *limes* was an admission that imperial expansion was no longer possible or worthwhile. A few centuries earlier, the Chinese Wall had followed a similar logic. But at the ecological frontier between nomads and sedentary civilized empire, it remained a permanent feature of Chinese history, and was even rebuilt in stone by the Ming (after 1368). For Imperial China at the peaks of her power, the Great Wall also served as a strategic basis for offensives into the steppe against nomads. But imperial fortifications functioned only as long as internal unity prevailed. If frontier troops were withdrawn to fight civil wars in the interior, *limes* or Great Walls only became a laughing stock for invading barbarians.

More often, borders limited power centres in more dramatic ways, when the ascendancy of an empire ended with a serious military defeat sometime, somewhere at the periphery. From then on the imperial cycle went into reverse gear, the relationship of internal and external factors now functioned negatively: Military defeat made for internal strife and diminished or ended profits from conquest (booty, land). The imperial army was no longer an asset but a staggering burden. Often the king or emperor, or even his dynasty, was overthrown, usually by the palace guard (praetorian guard in the Roman Empire, mamluks in the Caliphate) or by rivals within the ruling aristocracy. Rulers became puppets in the hands of the strong soldier behind the throne, who might make himself king or emperor. The army consisted of mercenaries, often foreigners, who manipulated rulers in their own narrow interest.

Failure challenged legitimacy, once the "mandate from Heaven" was withdrawn. Invasion from abroad and internal conflicts escalated crisis to agony, dissolution and downfall. Now, everything seemed to conspire against a decaying regime. Floods turned into catastrophes, e.g. in China, when in general turmoil, dams and irrigation works were neglected and fell into disrepair. The nuclear catastrophe of Chernobyl could not be hushed up, as in Tsarist Russia and the Soviet Union: "When sorrows come, they come not single spies, but in battalions" (Hamlet). Political consequences were shattering: Conquered provinces rose in revolt, client states and vassals defected, became new power centres of their own, or joined more powerful invaders. The increasing burden of taxation fell on a dwindling population. If taxed too heavily, even hitherto loyal central provinces of the imperial nation revolted – plunging into civil war.

The former power centre became a power vacuum, often filled by a conqueror from abroad. The last ruler fell, fighting on the steps of his throne or murdered by his own entourage, or fled to the

periphery of his empire, setting up new cells of resistance or imperial regeneration. The last Sassanid king of Persia reacted that way
after Arabs had destroyed the Middle Persian Empire (651). Sixty
years later, Visigoth nobles retreated from the Conquista by Muslim
Arabs and Moors of Spain in 711 to the mountains of Asturia,
preparing their Reconquista (1064–1492).

Collapse often followed after one major defeat at the periphery.
Most empires ended roughly along these lines: Assyria's loss of
Egypt (656 BC); Persian defeats at Salamis and Plataia (480, 479
BC); the battle at the Talas for T'ang China 751; the traumatic
defeat at Manzikert 1076 for Byzantium; at Legnano 1176, caused
by the rift between Frederick I and Henry the Lion, escalating to
civil war between Staufers and Welfs from 1198, for the Roman
Empire of the Germans; the defeat of the Portuguese against
Morocco at Al-Kasr al-Kabir (1578); the Spanish Armada 1588;
Vienna 1683 for the Ottoman Empire; the War of Spanish Succes-
sion (1701–1713/14) to Absolutism in France, leading to the French
Revolution of 1789; the defeat of Poltava for Sweden (1709); the
check for Napoleon I in Moscow 1812 and his First Empire;
Mexico 1867 and Sedan 1870 for Napoleon III and his Second
Empire; the Marne in September 1914 for the Second German
Empire, Stalingrad and El Alamein for the Third Reich 1942;
Guadalcanal for Japan 1942; Dien BienPhu for the IV French Republic in the First Vietnam War 1954 and the Algerian War
1954–62; the moral defeat in the Second Vietnam War for the USA
1965–75; the Afghanistan War 1979–88 for the USSR, with consequences that have become history. These and many more examples
confirm in overwhelming detail the link between defeat abroad and
conflict at home, ending in the fall of Empire.

Two exceptions are important enough to warrant a closer look –
Rome and Britain. The Roman Empire absorbed, in its long history,
several defeats at its peripheries. Its decline and fall was a gradual
process, many factors contributed to it, none was a prime cause. If
one wants to cling to one single blow, the plague of 166 might do,
which the Roman legions had brought home from a Parthian War.
From then on, heavy losses of population, income and military
power opened internal conflicts, the era of the Soldier Emperors
(235–283), exacerbated by invasions of Germanic tribes, and a
really severe defeat against the Sassanids (260). Re-consolidation
under Diocletian (284–305), repeated by another spell of imperial
unity under Constantine the Great (324–337), can also be observed
in another empire, almost simultaneously in China, where, after the

downfall of the Han dynasty (220) and the breaking up of the Chinese Empire, the Chin dynasty reunited China for a short span (280–317).

Imperial unity and strength after Diocletian was sapped by renewed conflicts, leading at first to provisional partitionings, the final one under the thrust of the Western Huns who drove before them panic-stricken Germanic tribes. Rome was unable to defend her frontiers, not even with foreign mercenaries, but had to settle invading refugees as *foederati* or client/allies with stipends in border provinces to prevent them from plundering or overrunning provinces: Proud Rome had to pay protection money, to avoid being robbed by her last defenders.

Nor did the British Empire come down after one blow on her many peripheries. Rather, it scraped home as victor in two World Wars, thanks to the help of the USA, England's most powerful western extension on her moving frontiers of imperial expansion. But the aggregate effect of Pyrrhic victories in two world wars amounted to defeat: Both world wars ruined the British Empire, as Emperor Wilhelm II in his Götterdämmerung mood on 31 July 1914 had hoped for, provoking the rise of colonial nationalism. Legitimacy of colonial rule was shaken by defeats of a different kind: Massacres at the colonial periphery – Amritsar 1919, Accra 1948[7] – denied the benevolent "Dual Mandate" arrogated by colonialism, amounting to moral defeats of the colonizers. They fit into another historical mechanism – short-term victors losing dialectically in substance to the vanquished, sooner or later. If there was really one conclusive military defeat at the periphery of the British Empire, it was the fall of Singapore at the end of 1941,[8] overrun by the Japanese onslaught after Pearl Harbour (which was the beginning of the undoing of the Japanese Empire).

The link between defeat outside and crisis inside can be made universal: the greater a defeat, the deeper the internal crisis – overthrow of a monarch, a dynasty, a civil war. The modern version of internal crisis after military defeat is revolution. The French Revolution needed 75 years to overthrow the Ancien Regime after it had lost the War of Spanish Succession. Later, revolutions punished failure more swiftly. Since the emancipation of the serfs in 1861, following Russia's defeat in the Crimean War, Bismarck expected the next revolution in Russia after her next defeat in a great war. Defeats against Japan 1904/5 instantly unleashed the first Russian Revolution; defeat against Germany in World War I triggered two Russian Revolutions in 1917.

The same chain of events struck also the next losers of the Great War – ordinary collapse revolutions in Germany, Austria–Hungary, and the Ottoman Empire after military defeat. Germany had two revolutions, oscillating between the extremes of left and right. Italy, unsatisfied with her gains at Versailles, reacted as if defeated, by going fascist. When France was defeated in 1940, she experienced that collapse which she had escaped in 1918, because she was, just as England, an exhausted victor.

Once empires disappear, the question follows: What next? Former empires are taken over by another empire, or break up into successor states to form a secondary power vacuum. They are by-products of collapsed empires, but can become breeding grounds for new empires, arising from the ashes of the successor states. First known successor states are those to the Churrite Mittani Empire (c. 1350 BC), perhaps with far-reaching consequences – one historical myth has it that the Kurds descended from the Churrites, wandering in the stateless wilderness ever since. Less far-fetched are post-Hittite successor states after the second Hittite Empire ended under the onslaught of the Northern and Sea Peoples, as the ancient Egyptians called them, around 1200 BC. As a classical precedent, they demonstrated two dimensions of successor states: Smaller Hittite principalities to the south in northen Syria, carried on direct Hittite traditions for some time. To its west, conquering barbarian Indo-European peoples founded post-Hittite successor states of their own in Asia Minor, in particular Phrygians and Lydians, whose names today mainly linger on in the names of the Church modes, Lydian and Phrygian. Fabulously rich Lydia struck coins for the first time (c. 600 BC). Before her last king, Croesus, attacked Persia by crossing the Halys in 547 BC, the Delphic Oracle had warned him: "If you cross the Halys, you will destroy a great empire." Since then, many such oracles could have warned rash imperial rulers.

The Hittite example contained a sinister precedent, which, even before the downfall of the Soviet Union, I used to cite orally in advance to illustrate one of its results: The Hittites had had the monopoly of iron technology and iron weapons. After its fall, iron weapons spread across the ancient Orient and most of the world. Similarly, nuclear weapons, which the former Soviet Union had monopolized for her sphere of direct influence, are now proliferating beyond the limits of its successor states.

Even biblical history knows successor states – Israel and Judea after the partition of the Great Jewish Empire, soon after Solomon's death (928 BC). Modern Israel is a perfect example of imperial restoration, claiming to resuscitate the Davidian Empire, spanning almost 3000 years, whereas in the very name of the Socialist "Baath" (= Rebirth) parties of Iraq and Syria the ideal of pan-Arab unity is meant to resurrect the Arab Muslim Caliphat of the Middle Ages. Also all Black Africa has her empires,[9] plus successor states that look to glorious imperial pasts for ideological inspiration.

Diadoch Empires, after the rapid breaking up of Alexander's Empire, are the better known and more classical examples of successor states. Rome started her career as a peripheral civilization at the western frontier of Mediterranean–Oriental Civilization. She succeeded in taking over the western half of the Hellenistic post-Alexandrian diadoch empires, leaving the eastern half first to Parthia, then to Sassanid Persia.

Important are post-Han Hun successor states in northern China, because the difference between them and their contemporary peers in the Far West sheds a light on the different course of imperial history in East and West: post-Roman successor states mutated to medieval proto-national monarchies and modern national states. In the Far East, however, nomad successor states absorbed the remnants of Chinese culture and developed them again to the point of becoming fully sinizized and restoring China's imperial unity by conquest from her western periphery.

Early France and Germany *in statu nascendi* passed through another empire: Both started as a proto-national *regnum*, as successor states to the Carolingian Empire. The Roman–German Empire splintered into many successor states that achieved sovereignty by 1648, though behind the facade of formal empire, until 1806. Since 1648, the Old Reich was a loose confederation, only held together by its Emperor, who drew his power from his possessions as a territorial Prince. With the end of the Holy Roman Empire of the German Nation in 1806, replaced by the First French Empire, Napoleon I opened the Pandora's Box of the German Question,[10] as the most explosive national question in Europe east of France. The Second German Empire arose by transforming the German Confederation of 1815 into a federal structure with Prussia as its hegemonial power and crushing the Second French Empire. Imperial Germany ended in defeat and revolution in November 1918 and gave rise to the unhappy interregnum of the Weimar Republic. The Third German Empire duly unleashed the Second World War, opening another round of the German Question – collapse and breakup in 1945, unification in 1990 after the breakdown of Communism in 1989/91.

Byzantium was the eastern, Greek and Orthodox continuation of Rome, after she had succumbed to the western Huns and Germanic tribes in 476. Her heirs were Arabs with their Muslim Caliphate, coming from the south; Turks, invading from the North in two waves, Seljuk and Ottoman. To its north-west, Byzantium gave birth to successor states on the Balkans – Bulgaria, Serbia, Albania. Structurally similar were neighbouring Croatia, Bosnia and Herce-govina, whose territories originally belonged to West Rome, but were claimed by East Rome. By adopting different cultures from East and West Rome, Orthodox and Latin south Slavs drifted away from each other for over 1000 years. With their dynamism, the Serbs fused them into Serbian dominated Yugoslavia, producing tensions, which are now exploding.[11] Historically, post-Yugoslav states succeed to several empires, telescoped into their present precarious "national" existence: They succeeded to East or West Rome, the Ottoman Empire, Austria–Hungary, and Titoist Yugoslavia.

Post-Soviet successor states follow several empires as well: Tsarist Russia had been the heir of three empires – Kiev Rus, Byzantium, and the nomad Empire of Genghis Khan, because Tatar indirect rule of the Golden Horde over Russia was that of a post-Genghis-Khan successor state. Moscow rose from the northern edge of the old Kiev Rus, but always remained at the end of the general slope of economic and cultural development from west to east. The Soviet Union, as a continuation or restoration of the Tsarist Empire, had inherited features of all her four preceding empires. The Afghanistan War, the Soviet Vietnam War, was the beginning of the end for both Communism and the Soviet Union.

Most post-Communist successor states had already been post-Tsarist successor states after World War I, but were recaptured into the fold of *Imperium Sovieticum* – Ukraine, Armenia, Georgia, Azerbaijan, Central Asian states by 1920, Lithuania, Latvia, Estonia by 1939/40. Central Asian states can retrace their imperial pedigree via Timurid khanats or emirates, to Timur himself, who tried to restore Genghis Khan's empire, from there to two empires of the Turks in Central Asia. Here are as many imperial traditions to be picked up at will, which makes the history and politics of Central Asia so volatile.

After the collapse of Communism, post-Communist and post-Yugoslav states follow the normal course of successor states: They are unstable inside and outside, fighting for their new identities or for their very existence, as unhappy Bosnia-Hercegovina and Armenia are painfully demonstrating. Successor states usually create a secondary power vacuum. Even their nationalisms are linked to empires in yet two other ways: They base their identities and territorial claims on some empire of their own in the past – the Great Croatian, Serbian, Bulgarian Empires of the Middle Ages, Alexander the Great for the Greeks, Georgians and Armenians, with imperial traditions of their own. Post-Communist Slovakia even goes back to the Great Moravian Empire (830–907). Usually, successor states are just as heterogeneous, ethnically or religiously, as their former empire. When unleashing an assimilationist quasi-imperial, pseudo-democratic nationalism of their own against their minorities, they reproduce *en miniature* the woes of their mother Empire in decline and agony.

Thus, successor states belong to the dialectical process of continuity and discontinuity. Although they depart in anger and conflict from their former mother-empire, they remain influenced by the imperial matrix, culturally and mentally. The same is happening in post-colonial successor states after World War II: Languages of former colonial masters – English, French, Spanish, Portuguese – are taking the role of Latin after the Roman Empire as means of communication for the intellectual elites, particularly in Africa and, until recently, on the Indian subcontinent. Or, European languages could become the language of whole populations (West Indies) or largely so (Spanish America).

In retrospect, empires were at their peak around 1900. The aggregate sum of colonial powers and national states then procured a precarious kind of civilized world peace. It broke down with the First World War, giving rise to Soviet Communism and German National Socialism fighting for world domination in the Second World War. After it, decolonization ushered in the end of colonial empires, followed by the end of the Soviet Empire. Remaining great powers of imperial stature – India, China, the USA – are under internal stresses.

The world is full of post-imperial successor states – post-colonial (Americas, since 1783, post-1945 in the Third World), post-Communist and post-Yugoslav, possibly post-Indian and post-Chinese. Most recent successor states are fighting it out in what may become the future of other successor states – national identity, frontiers drawn at the point of the Kalashnikov and the tank, guided by nationalisms that take their cues from empires long past. The New World Order after the Cold War seems to be plunging into the chaos of more post-imperial successor states. They are the stuff that dreams of empire are made of.

Notes

1. For a general survey see Hermann Schreiber, ed.: *Weltreiche*. 6 vols (Westermann: Braunschweig 1980–81).

2. After the pioneering work by Jan Vansina, *Kingdoms of the Savanna* (Madison, Wisconsin: University of Wisconsin Press 1966), see his follow up on a people of the Central African rain forest area, *The Children of Woot. A History of the Kuba Peoples* (id.: Madison, Wisconsin 1978).

3. For a first sketch see Imanuel Geiss, "The Intercontinental Long-Distance Trade. A Preliminary Survey". *Itinerario* X, 2/1986, pp. 33–51.

4. For the wider historical context see Imanuel Geiss, *Geschichte des Rassismus* (Frankfurt am Main: Edition Suhrkamp nr. 1530, [1988] 4th ed. 1993).

5. Philip D. Curtin, *The Atlantic Slave Trade. A Census* (Madison, Wisconsin: University of Wisconsin Press 1972); Peter Hogg, ed. *The African Slave Trade and its Suppression. A Classified and Annotated Bibliography.* (London: F. Cass Publishers 1973).

6. Despite all detailed criticism of the Williams thesis – Eric Williams, *Capitalism and Slavery* (Chapel Hill 1944) – the overall result will stand, if only because of the internal logic of the slave labour connection and its overall impact on Western industrialising societies. For the criticism see Seymour Drescher, *Econocide: British Slavery in the Era of Abolition.* (Pittsburgh: University of Pittsburgh Press 1977); Roger Anstey, *The Atlantic Slave Trade and British Abolition, 1760–1810* (London: Humanities Press 1975). For support of the substance of the Williams thesis see David Eltis & James Walvin, eds. *The Abolition of the Atlantic Slave Trade. Origins and Effects in Europe, Africa, and the Americas* (Madison, Wisconsin: University of Wisconsin Press 1981), especially the editors' introduction, p. 6.

7. See Geir Lundestad's contribution to this volume, p. 388–393.

8. See Zara Steiner's contribution to this volume, p. 71–72.

9. Nehemia Levetzion, *Ancient Ghana and Mali* (London: Methuen 1973).

10. For more details see Imanuel Geiss, *Die deutsche Frage, 1806–1990.* Meyers Forum no. 1. (Mannheim: Brockhaus & Meyer, 1992); also id., *Europa – Vielfalt und Einheit,* Meyers Forum no. 12 (Mannheim: Brockhaus & Meyer 1993).

11. Imanuel Geiss, *Der Jugoslawienkrieg* (Frankfurt am Main: Diesterweg 1993).

Part II

The Fall of Great Powers: Peace, Stability, and Legitimacy

3

The Fall of Great Britain: Peace, Stability, and Legitimacy

Zara Steiner

Britain's "fall" was a slow, irregular and interrupted process. Even after 1945, while not a superpower, Britain remained a power of the first rank, one of the "big three" or at least the "big two and a half". The ability of a small island state to maintain such a position, no small achievement in itself, had as much to do with the relativities of power as with the country's assets and capacity to defend them. Nonetheless, much was owed to the persistent efforts made to preserve a great power role. Influence was used first as an instrument of power and then as a substitute for strength, perpetuating British power beyond its natural limits. The efforts made to sustain a status quo that assured Britain's continuing importance contributed to the stability of successive international systems for a period of some 150 years but at a domestic price, blocking or delaying those domestic reorganizations required to prevent Britain's present relegation to an unnecessarily low position in the global pecking order. There may be, too, a principle of entropy at work which applies to great powers carrying too heavy an international burden, a running down of national energies expended on too broad a scale that leads to internal shrinkage.

Sources of Strength and Weakness

Britain's role as a great power was always a peculiar one. At her nineteenth century peak, she had the world's largest empire and fleet and was its greatest trader and banker. Even in this period, she lacked a continental territorial base comparable to that of Russia or the United States, and was never the master of Europe. The British needed allies to defeat Napoleon. The war of 1812 showed how difficult it was to fight overseas and on the continent simultaneously. If Castlereagh played a major part in the creation of the Concert of Europe at Vienna, its maintenance depended on the rough military balance between the continental states and the unwillingness of any one of them to challenge the existing equilibrium. Britain's main contribution to the stability of the new system lay in her rejection of the claims to intervention in the domestic affairs of the European states. The Concert of Europe allowed Britain to expand and consolidate her empire without increasing her continental strength. The balance of power in Europe sustained the Pax Britannica and not the other way round.

The sources of mid-century British strength were imperial and naval, commercial and financial. The ability to defend the empire at relatively low cost was due to the absence of competitors during a unique period of time. A variety of controls, formal and informal, and a small British army with modern weapons kept scattered territories under home direction. Control of the sea lanes provided protection and transportation for men, women, and goods. Britain's economic supremacy in the mid-Victorian age was equally unusual but very brief. The country's advantages owed much to an "early start". For a short period, it set the rules of international trade. The difficulties of embracing free trade lay in the inability to bargain with or retaliate against others when competitors inevitably appeared. The atomistic organization of British industry in the third quarter of the nineteenth century, when Britain emerged unchallenged in the world economy, became a source of weakness in a more competitive age. The country's much longer reign as the world's greatest importer of foodstuffs and goods was both a source of strength and weakness. It is the present view of some historians that it was Britain's financial and commercial role and not its manufacturing base that was, and remained, the real source of her wealth. The City of London played the dynamic role in overseas expansion and stood at the centre of Britain's global prestige. World trade was invoiced in pounds and financed by London. However imperfectly it functioned, the gold standard was "really a sterling standard". It allowed other states to conduct their trade in a "reasonably coherent way", though none had designed the system and no international agency directed it.

In 1852, Lord Granville boasted of Britain's ascendancy in Europe. When invited, he suggested, Britain was prepared to settle any disputes that might arise between other nations. What enabled these off-shore islands to play this arbital part? It was, in part, the domestic preoccupations of the main European players and their unwillingness or their inability to upset the status quo. Unencumbered abroad, Gladstone could eschew balance-of-power politics ("this foul idol") and defend the rights of self-determination, the freedom of small countries from the domination of the large, and the pursuit of free trade. The merging of morality with self-interest gave domestic legitimacy to a "liberal" foreign policy. "The danger (of a combination against Britain) can in practice only be averted," Eyre Crowe, a Foreign Office clerk could write in 1907, "...on condition that the national policy of the insular and naval State is so directed as to harmonize with the general desires and ideals common to all mankind, and more particularly that it is closely identified with the primary and vital interests of a majority, or as many as possible, of other nations."[1] Britain was a "liberal state", a nation dedicated to peace (navies were defensive, armies offensive), stability, and the advancement of trade. Representative government at home meant the avoidance of war abroad.

There was more dispute in the Gladstonian period about the benefits and costs of empire, a dispute still raging in the historical literature.[2] But while British rule was ultimately based on force (the Indian Mutiny was a shock), a large part of the ruling elite assumed that power was exercised legitimately and brought benefits, material and spiritual, to more backward people. Already, there had developed a preference for informal over formal rule and a willingness to consider devolution for countries of white settlement and government. Whatever the critiques of empire, more and more of the world in the Victorian period was coloured in shades of red.

By 1885, the limits to Granville's assertions of ascendancy were already becoming clear. The country played no part in the unification of Italy or of Germany. The British were forced to accept the new situation created in Europe after Prussia defeated Austria in 1866 and France four years later. "The policy of conciliation and non-commitment was arguably entirely appropriate to a situation," Agatha Ramm has written, "where military (i.e. Prussian) power and not naval (or British) power counted."[3] The British digested a major shift in the European balance of power. It was Bismarck's diplomacy after 1871 which stabilized the new balance, leaving the British free to deal with the return to a more competitive world scene, itself a product of Bismarck's manoeuvrings.

Lord Salisbury, in this more difficult time, could still use Britain's "free hand" in Europe to enlist the conservative powers to check the Russian threat to Britain's imperial interests. The prime minister had the confidence to deal with each of his extra-European crises, and they were many, on their individual merits, a confidence maintained even after Bismarck's departure and the creation of the Franco–Russian alliance. Britain could defend "against all comers that which we possess, and we know, in spite of the jargon about isolation, that we are competent to do so".[4] But if Britain was a "free rider", her freedom depended on a European balance over which she had only limited control. Given its lack of military strength, Britian's continental position was always vulnerable. As the European equilibrium became more fragile and the empire came under threat, British foreign secretaries had to face a double challenge, necessarily inter-connected. In the last two decades of the nineteenth century the cold winds were felt on every side. Germany and the United States were beginning their respective industrial ascents that would challenge British supremacy. E.E. Williams's *Made in Germany* was published in 1896; Frederick MacKenzie's book, *The American Invaders* in 1902. On 7 March 1889, George Hamilton, the First Lord of the Admiralty, almost casually proposed a standard of naval strength on "such a scale that it should be equal to the naval strength of any two other countries", a statement made in response to agitation in the popular press about the state of the fleet. The meaning of the Two Power standard, muddled from the start, was modified, abandoned, and reasserted in the next decades. By 1903–4, the British cabinet acknowledged that Britain could no longer rule all the waves. The Hay-Pauncefote treaty and the Anglo–Japanese alliance were symptoms of retreat, as were changes in the global disposition of the fleet.

From the Boer War to the Great War

The heating up of the imperial race as well as local difficulties on the periphery of the empire shook the confidence of those less sanguine than Lord Salisbury. French action in Africa, Russian pressure in Central Asia and in the Far East, and Germany's unexpected meddling in extra-European affairs appeared to require a more positive response than Salisbury's misnamed policy of "masterly inactivity". Official and public alarm at Britain's exposed position reached its height during and after the Boer War and the effects of that costly struggle, psychological as well as imperial, military and financial can hardly be exaggerated. Shock led to a period of self-examination that split parties, initiated major institutional reforms and created new, if conflicting, political agendas whose reverberations were felt far beyond Whitehall and Westminister.[5] The "trouble-makers", Gladstone Liberals and Cobdenite radicals, questioned the legitimacy of British rule and a new breed of anti-imperialists turned the economic weapon against the supporters of empire. As Lord Curzon was to write, "The pessimists are abroad in the land. We can hardly take up our morning news-paper without reading of the physical and moral decline of the race. ... beaten in cricket, then in polo. ... Every man over 50 is a Cassandra."[6]

The Boer War was won and no coalition of foreign powers isolated Britain, yet the pessimists prevailed. Between 1901 and 1905, the new foreign secretary, Lord Lansdowne, moved to defend the empire. Against Salisbury's better judgement, an arrangement was made with Germany in China, the Hay-Pauncefote agreement was concluded with the United States, and an alliance, seen as a fundamental break with the policy of isolation, was made with Japan. The Anglo-French entente, a colonial bargain, was yet an-other step in this policy of retrenchment. Good fortune as well as damage limitation policies improved Britain's strategic position. The Russian fleet was sunk at Tsushima and Japan emerged trium-phant from its war without British involvement. The Russian naval defeat restored the Two Power Standard to its "full virility". It ushered in a period of complacency; Admiral Fisher could boast as late as 1908 that the Royal Navy had attained the greatest margin of strength in its history. The United States could be restored to its position as a possible foe.

The Russian defeat made it possible to try again for a diplomatic settlement with St. Petersburg, for the importance of India, eco-nomic, military, and psychological, to Britain's well-being was beyond question. "As long as we rule India we are the greatest power in the world," Lord Curzon wrote to Arthur Balfour in 1901. "If we lose it, we shall drop straight away to a third rate power." Winston Churchill, faithful to his Edwardian past, argued the same case in 1930–31 and again in 1947. Faced with the demands of the Indian government for an army of over 100,000 men, Conservatives and Liberals alike agreed that India could not be defended against Russia. Tortuous and long negotiations in the Grey period led to the Anglo-Russian conventions. Its main focus was on the defence of India though it had a European side. After the summer of 1907, "India ceased to bulk large, indeed to bulk at all," John Gooch writes in *The Plans of War*, "in the cycles of strategic debate in England."[7] The burden of preserving stability in Central Asia fell on the diplomats.

How far did Britain's policy of re-adjustment in the period 1895–1906 contribute to the undermining of the European equilibrium? Lansdowne's diplomatic efforts were all imperially directed. Joseph Chamberlain was one of the few who saw the Anglo–French entente as an anti-German gesture. The foreign secretary hoped to reach an arrangement with the Russians and to renew the line to Berlin. Even the German testing of the entente at Morocco failed to alert Lansdowne to the possible European consequences of his imperial settlements. The voices of the Salisbury generation were still heard. "It has sometimes seemed to me that to a foreigner reading our press the British Empire must appear in the light of some huge giant sprawling over the globe, with gouty fingers and toes stretching in every direction," Lord Sanderson wrote in response to Crowe's memorandum, "which cannot be approached without eliciting a scream."[8] Others at the Foreign Office were more clear-sighted than Lansdowne and more apprehensive than Sanderson. The change in perception became far more marked under Sir Edward Grey.

"The avoidance of isolation," according to Keith Wilson, "... and his lack of confidence in Britain's ability to sustain it was Grey's only principle of foreign policy."[9] The consequence of Grey's diplomacy, dictated by fears of a Russian advance on India, was, in Dr. Wilson's view, to leave Britain's very existence as an Empire at stake. Grey's lack of flexibility and his brinkmanship in 1911 and 1912, designed to exclude the Germans from any international condominiums and to confine them to Europe, helped to undermine the peace of the continent.[10] It is true that the fear, however exaggerated, of the Russian threat to India remained as a leitmotiv in British pre-war diplomacy. But there was, too, a heightened perception of Germany as a danger to the European balance of power, which reached its height in the Grey period. Both the 1905 and 1911 crises were read as tests of the Anglo-French entente and interpreted as threats to the stability of Europe. A series of German naval building programmes provided the background for the alarms of 1908–9 and the massive British ship-building programme that followed. The Grey Foreign Office may have over-reacted to signs of German restlessness and a lack of clear direction in its diplomacy, but it is only in retrospect, viewed from the historian's chair, that Germany's pre-war policies could be characterized as conservative. Whether due to a calculated choice of options dictated by a difficult domestic situation or forced upon the government by interest groups it could not control, German actions appeared provocative. The German danger was not invented; it existed. Curiously enough, when the Berlin government turned from Weltpolitik to south-east Europe and Asia Minor, Grey, always obtuse in regard to Austria–Hungary and the balance in the Balkans, was able to take a more sanguine view of Anglo–German relations.

Greater flexibility might have helped take the edge off German frustration. Viewed from Berlin, and not just from Berlin, Britain had no "right" to enjoy the major share of the extra-European fruits. Legitimacy is in the eye of the beholder. The problem of being the late-comer in the imperial race contributed to the gap between German expectations and fulfilment, but the sources of the German malaise went deeper than any warmer British welcome to the imperial table might have cured. It is true that when victory in the naval race and the revival of Russian power steadied Foreign Office nerves, an Anglo-German colonial bargain became possible, but this came too late and could not affect the fundamental dispositions of power. It was then that Grey, exaggerating Britain's freedom of manoeuvre, thought that the policy of the ententes, quite apart from their domestic necessity, would pay the dividends he had always sought. He wanted ententes and not alliances to preserve some measure of independence, some room to influence continental affairs without being left isolated. Grey misjudged his situation after 1912; Britain's freedom of action had been severely compromised. He also misjudged the situation in Berlin and felt betrayed by the Germans during the July crisis when they did not restrain Austria–Hungary. German behaviour only made sense, according to Grey, because "the men of the war party" had driven Germany and Europe into war.

Grey's policies were over-ambitious and duplicitous. He went further towards the entente powers than either the cabinet or parliament was told. But there were few, even among the radicals, who supported a return to isolation. In the final crisis, though Belgium was the fig-leaf to hide the radical defection from their principles (though essential to give popular legitimacy to British action), an altered perception of Britain's power dictated intervention. The cabinet had accepted, despite radical opposition, that Britain could not remain disinterested in the face of a major shift in the European balance. Paul Kennedy concludes that Britain in 1914 "was still *probably* [my italics] the 'number-one' world power, even if its lead was much less marked than in 1850" and then claims that this was its problem.[11] There was little unanimity in pre-war Britain about the country's global position or about the necessity to intervene in European politics in order to maintain it. Grey, himself, was pulled in different directions, confident and fearful at the same time, predicting in 1914 that the war would destroy European civilization yet arguing that it would be short and the costs for Britain acceptable. "For us, with a powerful fleet ...," he told the Commons on 3

August, "if we are engaged in war, we shall suffer but little more than we shall suffer even if we stand aside."[12] There was Grey's concern with Britain's moral position and good name (though one takes a more jaundiced view of the foreign secretary's own record than did an earlier generation of historians) and his belief, detailed in *Twenty-Five Years* (1925) that Britain had entered the war to curb Prussian militarism.

Intended to preserve the status quo, Grey's diplomacy contributed to the further undermining of the Concert of Europe and the division of Europe into two blocs. War would have come, however, even if there had been no "policy of the entente" though it would have been a different war. The roots of the conflict lay in Austria's relations with Serbia and the Austro-Russian clash in the Balkans and in Germany's dissatisfaction with the existing status quo. Britain's preoccupation with maintaining the Russian entente in order to safeguard the frontiers of India contributed to the Austrian sense of impotence but did not create it. The Anglo-German rivalry was an additional, but not the central, source of continental instability. What was at stake in 1914, for Foreign Office officials and public alike, was that Germany should not crush France.

In appeasing Britain's main imperial rivals, France and Russia, Britain had become more actively involved in the European balance of power. In this sense, imperial interests were at the heart of Britain's entrance into the Great War. At the same time, German policy fanned anxieties in a country uncertain of its own strength and fearful of changes on the continent. As argued earlier, Britain's ability to maintain the status quo in Europe was limited. Grey further narrowed her liberty of action. In 1914, British statesmen felt threatened, as they had not after 1871, by any major shift in the European balance of power. They could not, and this was the measure of their fears, choose neutrality, though without the violation of Belgium, the Liberal cabinet would have remained divided and the entrance into the war postponed. And Britain could only engage in a continental war with allies.

The experience of the Great War itself was read in a number of different ways. The extent of Britain's military contribution was unexpected but remembered particularly in France. Allies had expected her to play the part she later shared with the Americans; it was her naval, economic, and financial strength that made her "alliance worthy". Britain was more successful than any other European power in mobilizing her economy and society for an all-out war. Her "output of strategic industrial goods and their quality matched that of any other belligerent, including the United States".[13] The British Empire mobilized 9.5 million men, one-third contributed by the empire. As expected, the country became the allied banker and the main conveyer of men and goods to the continent. The white dominions and India came to the support of the mother country, fighting in Europe as well as in the Middle East and Africa. Despite this massive mobilization, the civilian population of Britain enjoyed better health and a higher standard of living than in the pre-war period.

There was a large debit side to the ledger, above all the human costs, over 730,000 dead. The shock was all the greater because most of the political elite shared Grey's beliefs about Britain's limited war-time contribution. Important, too, was the growing sense throughout the 1920s of the futility of war as a way of settling international grievances. By the end of the decade, the "peace at any price" movement had become politically significant and the numbers of those questioning the legitimacy of British intervention swelled perceptibly. The American contribution to the final victory might have raised fundamental questions about the European balance, but the war ended with unexpected speed and the British belief in the blockade weapon was rapidly revived. The war stimulated new industries but also contributed to Britain's weakened economic performance in the 1920s, when growth rates lagged behind those of almost all other industrialized countries. Britain was the country most vulnerable to the decline in Europe's share of world trade and her exports failed to return to 1913 standards. Among her new competitors, the United States and Japan challenged her at home or in parts of the empire. The new industries, directed mainly to domestic markets, failed to compensate for the loss of jobs in the export sector. Between 1921 and 1931, with the exception of one year, unemployment never fell below 1.2 million. Even more important in terms of influence, the war-time destruction of the gold standard and the new position of the United States spelled the end of Britain's domination of the world's financial structure.

From Versailles to the Great Depression

The peace and the peace process strengthened Britain's continental and imperial position and consequently her diplomatic prestige.[14] Even before the Paris negotiations began, Lloyd George had secured most of his war aims with regard to Germany; its navy was destroyed and colonies divided, with the British Empire taking the major share. Though a late British war aim, Germany was massively disarmed. Lloyd George claimed that at the peace conference, the British would be "impartial arbiters, forgetful of the passions of war". Woodrow Wilson did not dominate the peacemaking process as so many British statesmen feared. Most of the compromises found in the Versailles Treaty, for good or ill, were the work of the "little Welsh Wizard".

Both men knew that Germany would recover its great power status. Clemenceau wished to do everything possible to delay its return and to protect France from the consequences. Lloyd George, who like Clemenceau (and Wilson) wanted to see Germany punished, preferred to avoid a situation that would leave Germany thirsting for revenge. In a highly volatile and unsettled Europe, Clemenceau fought for security and Lloyd George for stability. The British premier forced Clemenceau to retreat on the Rhineland issue, and over the Saar and Danzig. The French saw the successor states as counter-weights to Germany and a barrier to Bolshevism should the White armies be defeated. Lloyd George, apart from being anti-Polish, feared the consequences of incorporating too many Germans in the new Polish state and distrusted the French patronage of the new states. The British experts at Paris, who played a major part in determining the boundaries of the successor states, modified the principles of self-determination in the interests of economic and territorial viability. They looked to some kind of economic federation which would attract British investment and trade. In contrast to the French, the British took only limited interest in the political future of the successor states and viewed the French eastern alliances with distaste bordering on alarm. Britain sought stability to avoid a continental commitment; there would be no repetiton of 1914. They also had no wish to substitute one hegemonial power for another.

It was not within but outside Europe that Britain made its most impressive gains. The immediate post-war period saw the British empire at its zenith, much expanded in territory and resources, mainly due to the division of the Arab lands of the Turkish empire. Paradoxically enough, it was in the area where the British had tried, by proxy, to extend the limits of their victories by force that stability was most lastingly restored. Mustafa Kemal's republican Turkey proved to be an important status quo power. Lloyd George informed the Imperial Conference which opened on 20 June 1921 that "The British Empire is a saving fact in a very distracted world.

It is the most hopeful experiment in human organization which the world has ever seen."[15] This enlarged empire, strategically important and rich in oil, enhanced British power. But the empire proved to be more troubled and more expensive to maintain than in the pre-war period. The dominions demanded, in return for their war-time contribution, new forms of recognition. Difficulties in India, Mesopotamia, Egypt, Palestine, and, above all, Ireland placed a heavy burden on a country returning to its pre-war military posture and trying to cut its defence expenditure.

For the most part, Ireland being the most important exception, the British succeeded in keeping what they had. There had to be concessions and new forms of power-sharing. The Statute of Westminster gave formal recognition to the new independence of the dominions. Ties were strengthened by increasing trade and investment and through the continued dependence of some dominions, especially Australia and New Zealand, on British naval strength. Concessions were made to soothe nationalist feeling in Egypt and, less successfully, to meet the rising tide of Indian dissatisfaction. Cheaper means, aircraft instead of troops, were found to police unruly natives. There were retreats, but rivals were kept at bay. In the Far East, the British came to terms with Chinese nationalism and Japanese expansion but still kept a major territorial and economic stake in the region. The Middle-Eastern spoils had to be shared with France, though Britain was left in the dominant position. The Americans made advances in traditional British markets and even in the dominions (Canada in particular), but British investment and trade with her own domains markedly increased and dwarfed the American share. The Bolshevik threat in Central Asia and China was checked without any major effort on Britain's part.

Though under pressure, above all, in India, Egypt, and Palestine, British rule outside of Ireland was not seriously threatened. There were murmurings, too, from other parts of the empire, even from the native elites enlisted to govern. The fruits of economic development were unequally distributed, producing new forms of local discontent. But the disintegrative forces were contained and with a limited use of military power. Amritsar was exceptional in its scale and public impact. In south and south-east Asia and in Africa, the inter-war period was one of considerable stability. There was an increasing concern with the problems of imperial rule. The mandate system itself underlined the responsibility of the mandatory power to protect the interests of natives and to encourage self-government. There were those in Britain who questioned the legitimacy of empire but there remained, and not just in the Conservative party, a strong sense of pride in the British record and a belief that the Pax Britannica was a force for good. There was considerable ambivalence in Liberal and Labour circles, for few dissented from the view that it was the empire that made Britain great.

In Europe, neither the hopes of the isolationists who wanted to concentrate on Britain's imperial role nor those of the Atlanticists who looked to a global partnership with the Americans could be fulfilled. Britain was compelled to play a continuing and often singular part in the political stabilization of Europe. The Committee for Imperial Defence (CID), even while developing an imperial strategy, was driven to conclude, "the country was not free to carry out our main objects which are imperial and colonial unless we are safe in Europe and it will be many years yet before we free ourselves from our responsibilities for Europe."[16] This pivotal role was undoubtedly due to the partial withdrawals of both Americans and Russians. Quite apart from their rejection of the League, the Americans would make no contribution to European security during the 1920s, and their withdrawal, financial as well as political, became even more marked under Franklin Roosevelt. In other respects, over reparations, for instance, and in other regions, the Far East, the British tried to use American strength to their own advantage.

Without American financial backing, few of the British attempts to encourage the stabilization of the European currencies would have taken place. It is important, however, not to under-estimate the British contribution, mainly through the British-dominated financial committee of the League of Nations. "Stabilization was at the centre of British economic policy," Anne Orde concludes in *British Policy and European Reconstruction after the First World War*, "and because Britain occupied a position at the centre of world trade and finance, British actions were often crucial for the reconstruction of other countries."[17] On a global scale, Britain remained the world's major investor throughout the 1920s, ahead of the United States in long-term investment, both direct and portfolio. Most of this investment went to the empire, but even the relatively small amounts directed towards central and south-eastern Europe had important if mixed effects on those countries' economies. British financial leadership on the continent remained a key source of diplomatic influence, even where it was not used for political purposes. Where the British were weak was in their unwillingness or inability to act without the Americans and their limited influence on American policy. London could have done more, through the unilateral cancellation of debts and a different attitude towards reparations, to have hastened the process of European reconstruction. More private investment might have gone to south-eastern or central Europe and a less negative view taken towards supporting trade in the Baltic and Danubian basin. Given the prevailing anti-interventionist views of the times and Britain's own restricted sources, what is surprising is how far London was able to exert its leadership.

Though Britain had lost its monopolistic position, after its return to gold, it shared with New York and later Paris the responsibility for the workings of the newly re-created gold standard. Much depended on central bank cooperation and the personal friendship of Montagu Norman and Benjamin Strong. As central bankers were not free agents, domestic preoccupations led to a divergence of views and a weakening of British influence. The burden on sterling in the reconstituted system proved too heavy to be sustained. The debacle of 1931 shook British self-confidence; the shock waves were felt throughout the world, testimony in itself to the importance of Britain's financial role. While the negative effects of the over-valued pound have been exaggerated, there is some substance to the claim that during the 1920s Britain was too internationalist in its financial and commercial policies for her own domestic good.[18] The abandonment of the gold standard to the country's great advantage, and the turn to protection, did not end Britain's global presence. Rapid recovery (the growth figures for the years 1933–37 are impressive) and the creation of a sterling bloc revived Britain's world influence in a period during which the United States was engulfed in depression.

The Washington treaties left Britain in possession of the largest number of the world's ships, with a comfortable margin of superiority over Japan and a considerable lead in the Mediterranean even in the unlikely event of a combined Franco–Italian threat. The British recognized that they could not engage in a naval race with the United States and that any war against America would be foolish and disastrous. To accept parity with the United States confirmed the country's pre-1914 retreat from world supremacy. But Britain's vulnerability with regard to the United States remained unique. What really undermined her position was the fear that with the expansion of her empire, she could be subjected to multiple and simultaneous attacks.

In the Far East, the British looked to the Americans to share the burden of maintaining regional security. In 1931, when American support was not forthcoming, the British refused to act alone. Though Professor Nish's recent study of the Manchurian crisis reveals the degree to which Japanese foreign policy was domestically determined, the cautious policy of the League was shaped by the British.[19] It was mainly the American connection that subsequently blocked a policy of further appeasement. The preference for a limited risk policy in the Far East, as in Europe, was reinforced by financial constraints. The Ten-Year rule was abandoned, but by the time the steps were taken to build up Singapore the European situation had dangerously deteriorated. The debate continues whether Britain could not have done more through independent action to stabilize the Far Eastern situation. She preferred to lean on the Americans.

Concerns about the Soviet threat began to recede after the Polish-Soviet war, and Lenin's turn, albeit as a temporary tactic, to soliciting economic assistance from the west helped to diminish the sense of crisis. The British were the first great power to negotiate a trade agreement with the Soviets (1921); Lloyd George at Genoa hoped to bring the Soviets into a wider trading circle, and in 1924, the British led the allies in concluding a treaty of diplomatic recognition. Those, like Lord Curzon, who possessed a "visceral, almost personal dislike of the Bolsheviks" and who monitored through the intelligence decrypts Russian activity in India wanted nothing to do with the Russians. In Europe, it was the Rapallo connection that was seen as the most dangerous threat to the stability of Europe. Austen Chamberlain saw in the Locarno pacts the way to neutralize this danger by attaching Germany to the western camp and isolating the Soviet Union. After 1925, Chamberlain felt confident enough to pursue a policy of "masterly inactivity".

The subsequent conservative break in relations with the Soviet Union, restored by the Labour government, was the result of exaggerated fears of Bolshevik activity in Britain and in China. During the early 1930s Stalin, preoccupied with domestic affairs, was prepared to give Litvinov a freer hand at Geneva to end Soviet isolation. There were signs even before Hitler's rise that the Soviet Union might try to join the collective security system. British distrust, however, regardless of the party in power, remained strong. No foreign secretary wanted to bring Russia into either a European or Far-Eastern security system, and French efforts in this direction were viewed with suspicion. In 1934, as the Soviets moved from a "revisionist" to an "anti-revisionist" position, Britain remained aloof. Depending on one's reading of Soviet policy in the 1930s, it can be argued that British distrust of Soviet intentions acted as a destabilizing force in Eastern Europe as the French tried to create an Eastern Locarno.

In Western Europe, the British believed they could play a more positive role. Both the French and Germans looked to London; this was the real source of British influence. Attempts at independent action or direct settlement without the British repeatedly failed. The French were considered troublesome friends, less after 1923 because of their "hegemonic" aspirations and imperial appetites than because their demands for security commitments were greater than the British were willing to give. British foreign secretaries found French fears of Germany's potential power excessive and her reparation and disarmament demands excessive. The Germans, for their part, viewed British support as essential for a modification of the treaty terms. Stresemann's policies for the recovery of Germany's great-power status depended on American financial underwriting and on British backing against France.

With the signing of the Locarno agreements, the British seemed to have achieved a position they had not enjoyed since the mid-Victorian period. This was accomplished without any accretion of material power. The accords were negotiated by three European statesmen and were concerned only with the European continent. Chamberlain did not at all regret the American absence. The British foreign secretary told the Imperial Conference in 1926 that Locarno was "in large measure a British achievement and was recognized as such by other powers. As a result British friendship is cultivated, British counsel asked, British aid sought and as in the days of Castlereagh, Great Britain stands forth again as the moderator and peacemaker of the new Europe created by the Great War."[20] The revised security system, restricted to the western frontiers, was seen as a major step towards the stabilization of the continent.

The carefully drawn guarantees, linked to but not really part of the League system, represented the limits of Britain's commitment to the European equilibrium. There was no military back-up to the guarantee and none intended. The cabinet did not intend to repeat the mistakes of Sir Edward Grey. Britain would pursue a policy of limited liability. Briand's appeasement of Germany was based on the assumption that if Locarno failed, France could count on British support. It proved to be a false assumption. At the Locarno tea-parties, the francophile Chamberlain mediated between his continental partners in the interests of European stability. The British foreign secretary was determined "to set to work to make the new position of Germany tolerable to the German people in the hope that as they regain prosperity under it they may in time become reconciled to it and to be unwilling to put their fortunes again to the desperate hazard of War...I believe the key to the solution is to be found in allaying French fears."[21] By 1928, Chamberlain, like Briand and Stresemann, began to think that the Locarno experiment might fail. In response to reviving nationalist feeling in Germany, he moved closer to Briand.

His policies were reversed by the Labour and National governments. When Britain re-emerged after the 1931 debacle, her statesmen viewed France as the major stumbling block to a new arms limitation agreement which Germany could join. Judging German rearmament to be inevitable, even those suspicious of German intentions argued for concessions to Berlin. With Hitler's rise to power, new weight was given to the argument that it was better to have Germany contained within a new security system than left outside. Without an army and unwilling to take on any new obligations beyond Locarno, the Foreign Office was relying on diplomatic skill to create an acceptable balance of power between France and Germany. Little was offered to create it and no insurance policy provided should it fail.

The financial crisis served to intensify the isolationist pressures at home. Its psychological effects persisted even after recovery began, and the country entered a period of economic growth markedly different from her weak performance in the 1920s. The popular commitment to "collective security" was based on the premise that the League system offered an alternative to military action. If the Locarno structure collapsed, however, Britain would be dependent on the same French army that they were being urged to disarm. As late as 1934, Churchill, an opponent of disarmament, trusted that the French "will look after their own safety, and that we should be permitted to live our own life in our island without being again drawn into the perils of the continent of Europe".[22] The British could have used their influence to support France. They might have joined a strengthened security system designed to keep aggressors in check. Instead, they hoped to remain free from European entanglements. Memories of the Great War were too close. The Germans were, after all, still disarmed and would not be in a military position, according to the best British military advice, to challenge the status quo until 1943.

Neville Chamberlain and the Coming of the Second World War

No inter-war British government saw the League system as a viable way of maintaining the peace and each repeatedly fought off French efforts to tighten its security provisions. Successive cabinets rode two horses, giving voice to support for collective security while defining Britain's national interests in balance-of-power terms. When public opinion forced the government to test the system in 1935, all the previously held doubts about the efficacy of sanctions were confirmed. Neville Chamberlain never took seriously any suggestion that the Geneva system might be revived in an expanded form. The British attempt to buy stability at minimal cost and at French expense proved to be a dangerous error.

"Henceforth – regardless of what tactical interludes of conciliation may be attempted with regard to us," von Ribbentrop wrote in 1938, "every day that our political calculations are not actuated by the fundamental idea that England is our most dangerous enemy *would be a gain for our enemies.*"[23] With the revival of German power, the European initiative passed into Hitler's hands, yet the creation of any new security system depended on Britain. As in the 1920s, this resulted from the absence of the other anti-revisionist powers, the United States and the Soviet Union. It was due, too, to the new weakness of France. The Führer, despite an uncertain reading of British intentions, saw Britain as the key to Germany's future in Europe. There was, in his mind, a possible agreement between the two great powers based on a delimitation of their respective continental and world-wide interests. Whatever aims Hitler had beyond Europe, their fulfilment depended upon the mastery of the continent first. The belief that a bargain with Britain was possible is a recurring theme in Hitler's writings and actions. It would be abandoned in 1938 only to be revived in the summer of 1940.

It has been, until recently, the prevailing orthodoxy to argue that the policy of appeasement, as practised from 1934 onwards but with more resolution when Neville Chamberlain became prime minister, was a realistic one for a small island kingdom with a scattered empire under threat, a fragile economy, and a citizenry wedded to disarmament and collective security. This interpretation explains the background to British appeasement but not the essence of Chamberlain's diplomacy. The international situation did deteriorate after 1934 leaving the British with the threatening possibility of fighting against Germany in Europe, Italy in the Mediterranean, and Japan in the Far East. The British had a smaller population and industrial base than Germany and began rearming later. The recovery of the economy had not erased Treasury fears about its fragility or the problems of a negative balance of payments in a future war of attrition. But Neville Chamberlain was pursuing an ambitious policy and not a weak one. He saw Britain as the peace-maker of Europe. He was not prepared to concede German domination in Europe in return for maintaining the empire. But hoping to avoid war, the prime minister thought it possible to convince Hitler by reason and diplomacy rather than "by menace and force" to join a new security system that would leave the continent more stable and prosperous than before. This was a policy not only beyond British strength but one based on a fatal misreading of Hitler's intentions.

"We are the richest country in Europe," Lord Cranborne, the under-secretary for foreign affairs told the Commons, "we are still by far the most powerful and respected nation in Europe."[24] The "rummage-bag of an empire" was not only still in existence but more united than in the 1920s. In August 1935, the Government of India Bill, while falling short of what Gandhi demanded, outlined steps towards further self-government. Only a few die-hards revolted against this attempt to guide Indian, like Egyptian, nationalism along "imperial lines" and anticipated the fall of the empire. Against this background, there was never any intention of permitting German domination of Europe. The government's first priority was to build up the country's defences; the second was to find a way to neutralize the German challenge by recognizing Hitler's legitimate grievances and, by correcting past injustices, to place the peace of Europe on a sounder and more lasting basis. In this rejection of any form of diplomatic isolation, the question of air power and the vulnerability of Britain to air attack was critical. In sharp distinction to Sir Edward Grey, Chamberlain assumed that Britain, acting alone, could contain the German challenge to the status quo without a resort to war.

Limited rearmament to correct the country's worst deficiencies began in 1934. In February 1936, the cabinet approved a programme for a possible war extending over a three to five year period. It was still a limited programme, consistent with the wish to maintain a peace-time economy and protect the rising standard of living, and in the hope that a new arms' limitation agreement could be achieved. The navy, essential for the defence of British trade and the imposition of a blockade, was to be given sufficient funds to build up a battle fleet equal to that of Japan and Germany. The air force, in accord with the Trenchard doctrine, was to concentrate on bombers, particularly important in view of the German air programme. Funding and industrial capacity for ships and aircraft was to be achieved at the expense of the army, whose continental role was down-graded. This defensive strategy was in accord with the strategic thinking of the day, and the temper of an electorate strongly opposed to continental intervention. The French army, now without its pre-1914 ally, would secure western Europe from invasion, while the British would revert to the old weapon of blockade supplemented in time by strategic bombing. When the initial 1936 programme could not be fulfilled within the limits imposed, the army role was given even a lower priority.

While pursuing this policy of rearmament, the cabinet, prodded by Chamberlain, first as chancellor of the exchequer, sought an air-limitation agreement. When Hitler speeded up the diplomatic clock on 7 March 1936, the British took up a new set of German "offers" as a way of replacing the destroyed Locarno treaties. "It is the appeasement of Europe as a whole," the foreign secretary, Anthony Eden explained on 26 March, "that we have constantly before us."[25] The main British actions during the Rhineland crisis were to prevent any damage to renewed efforts to come to terms with Germany. Proposed staff talks with France were strictly limited to the logistics of dealing with an unprovoked attack on France and Belgium. As the Germans repeatedly avoided British overtures and moved ahead with rearmament, Eden and the permanent under-secretary, Robert Vansittart, argued that nothing could be done with Berlin until Britain was militarily stronger. In the interval, they recommended that every effort should be made to discourage Hitler from moving in central Europe. Chamberlain opposed their suggestion that Germany should be 'kept guessing'. His aim, pursued with increasing vigour after 1937, was to conclude an agreement with Berlin that would avoid a damaging arms race. Believing that Hitler would be satisfied with the incorporation of German nationals living outside of the Reich and could be persuaded to achieve his objectives through peaceful means, Chamberlain sought to establish the grounds for a disarmament pact.

During 1937 and 1938, Hitler repeatedly asked for a free hand in central and eastern Europe and was refused. At the same time, the British would give no warning or promise that they would resist aggression in those regions. The prime minister, from the time of the Halifax visit in November 1937 to the German invasion of

Austria, searched for a way to deflect Hitler from central Europe. Yet neither he nor the foreign secretary were unduly alarmed by the Anschluss; it served only to convince them to act with greater haste. Some Foreign Office officials argued that Britain would have to choose between cooperating with Hitler in building a German world empire and organizing a front against Nazi expansionism. Neither Chamberlain nor Halifax believed that this was the choice they faced. Following their lead, the cabinet decided in the spring of 1938, without consulting the French, to press for a settlement of outstanding problems. At the same time, rearmament was speeded up and given top priority. It was not the warnings of the Chiefs of Staff that Britain could do nothing to save Czechoslovakia but Chamberlain's confidence that a peaceful resolution of the crisis was possible that explains his unwillingness to offer a guarantee to Prague or to France should she act in support of an ally.

Chamberlain's actions during the Czechoslovakian crisis were intended to re-assert British leadership in Europe. The French, he believed, would follow in the British wake. The Americans, he acknowledged with some relief, would take no part. He had no intention of including the Russians, who would only make his peace-building task more difficult. Britain would recognize Germany's new position in Europe but not on terms that involved the use of force or threatened Britain's future safety. "...if we can avoid another violent coup in Czechoslovakia, which ought to be feasible," Chamberlain wrote to his sister in the summer of 1938, "it may be possible for Europe to settle down again and some day for us to start peace talks with the Germans."[26] Not everyone agreed that concessions to Hitler would make the Reich peaceful. Some pressed for the creation of an anti-German coalition linked to the League of Nations while others advocated alliances and all-out rearmament. Chamberlain remained faithful to his own convictions. The prime minister had made up his mind to "solve" the Czechoslovak problem at that country's expense well before the Chiefs of Staff underlined the futility of military action on 12 September.

The cabinet agreed to the Berchtesgaden terms but drew the line when Hitler demanded at Godesberg the immediate military occupation of the disputed territories. It became a moral question, a reaction to unacceptable blackmail. "I know we and they (i.e. the French) are in no condition to fight; but I would rather be beat than dishonoured," Alexander Cadogan, the permanent under-secretary wrote in his diary. "How can we look any foreigner in the face after this?"[27] Chamberlain, it is clear from the documents, was willing to pay Hitler's price; Halifax and other colleagues refused. It was Hitler who decided, for reasons still debated, that he would not go to war. The relief in the capitals of the four participating powers was visible to all. Chamberlain felt that he had won the prize so long sought. He told Lord Hankey on 2 October that "we" had at last laid "the foundations of a stable peace, though it still remains to build the superstructure."[28] He showed open irritation with cabinet colleagues who harboured doubts about his achievement and pressed for more vigorous rearmament despite hopes for "detente".

Between Munich and Hitler's march into Prague, there was a shift in the cabinet's mood and in the country at large. The actual preparations for war taken in September left their mark. In the weeks that followed Munich there was considerable unease, publicly expressed, about the legitimacy of Britain's actions. *Kristallnacht* raised a storm of indignation. Chamberlain was warned of the change of feeling in the constituencies. False rumours intensified cabinet concerns about what Hitler intended to do next. While Chamberlain tried to quiet over-stretched nerves, Treasury restraints on rearmament were lifted, the army was prepared for a continental war, and staff talks with the French sanctioned. The air rearmament programme was re-directed from bombers to the production of Hurricanes and Spitfires and the completion of a radar network. Chamberlain, himself, worked to mollify the Americans on the economic front. The prime minister took the steps needed for the protection of Britain's position should war come. In pursuing a policy of "hope for the best and prepare for the worst", however, Chamberlain was heavier on hope than on preparation.

Hitler's march into Prague intensified the growing feeling that war could not long be postponed. The cabinet embarked, again with Chamberlain dragging his feet, on a policy of deterrence. The Polish guarantee (offered in part to prevent a Polish-German agreement) and those to Romania, Greece, and Turkey were intended to regain the initiative in Europe and to persuade Hitler that his next act of aggression would mean war. These guarantees were in Lord Chatfield's words, "militarily mad", a response to an emotional feeling that "wrong doing must stop". At the cabinet level, the need for dam building was intensified by the knowledge that neither the French nor the British would do anything to save Poland. There were curious changes in official thinking as the sense of inevitability grew which had little to do with the strategic balance of forces. The intelligence departments emphasized the difficulties faced by Germany in preparing for and winning a European war. The cabinet disregarded Treasury warnings that Britain would exhaust its reserves before war came and was in a less favourable position to fight a long war than in 1914. Halifax pointed to German difficulties that would bring a decision soon and spoke of future American financial support. In May 1939, Julian Jebb told the counsellor of the German embassy that "if such a choice had to present itself, I would infinitely prefer my country to become an American dominion than a German Gaul'".[29]

The prime minister during the spring and early summer of 1939 clung to the illusion that Hitler could be dissuaded from launching a war he could not win. The majority of the nation may have hoped that Chamberlain was right but assumed preparations for war were proceeding. The prime minister refused to bring Eden into the cabinet as Halifax suggested or as Churchill urged in an early summer press campaign. More importantly, he opposed alliance negotiations with the Soviet Union that had won the overwhelming support of the nation. At least part of his opposition stemmed from continuing hopes of future negotiations with Germany, with or without Hitler. His doubts about the utility of a Grand Alliance, shared intermittently by Halifax, and probably communicated to Stalin through a well-placed mole, contributed to the slow process of the Russian negotiations and may have been a factor in Stalin's late choice of the German option. Almost to the very end of August, privately and unofficially, Chamberlain sought from Hitler some gesture of conciliation that would open the possibility of a renewed dialogue. It never came.

From Global Power to Member of the European Community

By the time of the Nazi-Soviet pact, a majority of the British people believed war to be certain. Despite fears of air attack (a large number of people left London in September) and the belief that a long and destructive war of 1914–18 proportions would follow, the public faced the inevitable with "surprising resignation". In the final crisis, the body politic never wavered in its asumption that Hitler had to be stopped and that Britain should take the lead in stopping him. While Chamberlain and Halifax might have considered a settlement compatible with Polish independence, no cabinet member, including the prime minister, was prepared to give Hitler the freedom to seize another country. Parliament, reflecting public opinion, left no option but war open. In the end, Britain "entered the war by choice to fight for a principle and not because their country was attacked."[30] Britain was a great power and was expected to act like a great power. She entered the war not to save the empire but to stop Hitler.

How did the British think they were going to win this war if they survived, as ministers now assumed, the German air attack? The answer lay in the old Great War strategy. Britain would depend on the French army and the Maginot Line while she re-armed, mobilized the empire, and instituted a blockade. There was the additional hope of using strategic bombing to break the Germans. There were some who believed that faced with the prospects of a long war, Hitler might retreat or that the German people might rid themselves of their irresponsible leader. Even those who, like Cadogan, were uncertain of the road to victory, failed to anticipate the collapse of France. The German success in 1940 owed much to the fighting quality of the Wehrmacht and its ability to make the best use of its existing rather than superior resources, but the French also paid the price for their late rearmament and Britain's delay in raising and equipping the British Expeditionary Force (BEF). The gamble of 1914 did not succeed in 1940 and the collapse of the French shield left the British totally vulnerable. Fully mobilized and backed by the empire but without a continental ally, Britain might survive but could not win the war against Germany.

The decision to fight on alone in the summer of 1940 was based on faith and hope. Hitler was passionately interested in a negotiated peace on the old terms of a continental/global exchange. Misled by intelligence sources that Churchill would fall, he waited for the necessary first signs from London. His speech to the Reichstag on 19 July marked the turning point; thereafter, there was no possibility of an arrangement with Britain. There is no debate about the importance of Churchill's crucial cabinet intervention on 28 May, though considerable disagreement over the costs of the decision made.[31] Through strength of will and his extraordinary powers of rhetoric, Churchill was able to project his image of Britain as a great power to rally cabinet and country. The grounds for confidence were few. Churchill's belief that the German economy was near breaking point and that strategic bombing could provide the means of victory was misplaced. The widely held hope of American support and intervention in the war was hardly reflected in the realities of American policy. The prime minister's frantic wooing of the president finally produced the "bases for destroyers" deal of

August with leases on valuable bases exchanged for "fifty clapped-out ships".

At this nadir point of Britain's modern history, Churchill could invoke the legitimacy of her cause to inspire confidence in survival. Churchill's passionate obstinacy, whatever his private doubts, blocked a total German victory in 1940. The British withstood the German bombing campaign (if Hitler had not switched from airfields to London the outcome might have been different); naval strength, American assistance, and "Ultra" won the Battle of the Atlantic in 1941. British survival was critical for the continent of Europe, but it was purchased at the cost of her imperial position. This is not to argue that a negotiated peace would have saved the empire or prevented the post-war division of Europe. Churchill's intervention meant that Britain did not become Hitler's junior partner and so escaped the moral consequences of such a choice even had Hitler kept his bargain.

Britain might have repulsed a German invasion but she could not secure victory alone. With the Japanese attack on Pearl Harbour, Britain gained her all-important ally, but now the empire became vulnerable. Churchill's mistaken view of the Japanese and the string of military disasters in the Pacific meant that though the Middle East was ultimately held, Britain's Asian position was shattered. The Pacific was and remained an American show. Meanwhile, British dependence on American material assistance dramatically increased. Before the war ended, the United States was supplying almost one-third of the weapons used by British empire forces. For all its loyalty, the empire produced only one-tenth of the munitions needed. With the Americans in the war, influence was bound to shift from London to Washington. This was already happening in 1943. At Teheran, the prime minister was the odd man out, the Lepidus to Roosevelt's Mark Antony and Stalin's Octavian. At Yalta, even when the two western leaders were in agreement, it was Roosevelt who took the lead with Stalin.

The other side of the European coin was the emergence of the Soviet Union as a new "superpower", the inevitable consequence of its triumph over the Wehrmacht and advance across Europe. The failure to open a second front before 1944 left the overwhelming burden of the European fighting to the Russians. Between June 1941 and June 1944, over 93 percent of German army battle casualties were inflicted by the Red Army. Churchill's reluctance to sanction a full-scale invasion of France was based on a healthy respect for the German Wehrmacht and doubts about his own troops (a possible explanation, too, for Montgomery's caution in the battle against Rommel) and untried American forces. Whatever his concern about the Red Army's advance at the end of 1943, Churchill wavered between hope and fear when it came to dealings with Stalin. The percentages bargain concluded in October 1944, and Churchill's attempts at Teheran and Yalta to protect British interests and clients were directed at the maintenance of the three power alliance into the period of peace. There were fears of a revived Germany and the knowledge that the future stability of Europe depended on an arrangement with Stalin. Was Churchill using the same methods with Roosevelt and Stalin as his predecessor had used with Hitler? The difference lay in Churchill's recognition of British weakness, for how far Britain could save and mobilize her imperial resources to back her great power claims remained an open question.

From this low point, Britain was to recover. In the world of the superpowers, she found a part to play. As David Reynolds has powerfully argued, Britain continued to function as a global power well into the 1950s.[32] Statesmen and officials continued to speak of "managing change"; it was not until the 1960s that "decline" became fashionable. "It is part of the habit and furniture of our minds," Lord Franks commented, "that Britain should be a great power." The winning of the war restored national self-confidence and gave Britain a new moral authority in a liberated but devastated Europe. Until the mid-1950s, the British economy was the strongest in Europe, manufacturing as much as France and West Germany together. In 1952, Britain became the world's third nuclear power well in advance of France. There were expectations, reflected in Foreign Office planning, that Britain would take the lead in creating a "new Europe" or a western European bloc. By the time the Treaty of Dunkirk was signed in 1947 and Bevin's plans for a "Western Union" were taking shape, the diplomatic winds had shifted. Hopes for a peace negotiated within a Big Three framework, still discussed in late 1945, had been abandoned and the British would call again on American assistance to preserve the new status quo.

The war had shaken the weakened roots of the British empire. Given the disasters of 1941–42, it seemed possible that the whole Far Eastern empire would collapse. The fall of Singapore and the surrender of 130,000 troops had a symbolic impact throughout south-east Asia and beyond, shattering Britain's moral and racial authority to "rule". Despite the failure of the Cripps Mission, there could be only a delaying action in India. In the Middle East, the war fed regional nationalisms. Multiple factors, many indigenous to the countries concerned, undermined the basis of British over-lordship in Asia and in Africa. American anti-colonialism, however fiercely resisted, took its toll. Yet the final denouement was postponed until the 1960s. The "policy of scuttle", the granting of independence to India, Pakistan, and Burma in 1947 and 1948 and the abandonment of Palestine in May of 1948 did not lead to the empire's disappearance. An attempt was made to reshape and develop remaining "possessions" and spheres of influence so that their resources could be used to strengthen Britain's financial and strategic position *vis-à-vis* the United States as well as the Soviet Union.

If the Bevin Foreign Office thought in great-power terms, it was not because it either under-estimated the power of former allies or the financial weakness of their own country. Britain was transformed by the war from the world's largest creditor to the largest debtor. External liabilities had dramatically increased while overseas assets were considerably reduced. Export capacity had dropped so low by the war's end that even the most essential food and raw material supplies could not be covered. At the same time, the Labour party was pledged to embark on a comprehensive social reform programme, the introduction of the "New Jerusalem" that had brought the new government to power. Britain had to operate in an American-dominated economic and financial world. The Dollar Loan of December 1945, a far more generous gesture than any made in 1919, solved some immediate problems but was rapidly expended in part because of the external drains on British reserves. The costs of administering the German occupation zone, the financial involvement in Greece and Turkey, and the struggle in Palestine proved to be too expensive to be long endured. At the same time, the fear of communism in Western Europe and alarm over the perceived Soviet threat to British interests in the Mediterranean alerted the Foreign Office to the need for greater protection against the Soviet Union.

Britain, at first, took independent steps to strengthen her exposed position. Not only were the Americans giving every sign of a retreat from Europe but there were serious strains in Anglo-American relations. Peace time conscription was introduced in April 1947. It was agreed to develop an atomic bomb. Bevin revived the idea of a Western European bloc and possible customs union. There was also retrenchment. The Treasury insisted that aid to Greece must end in March 1947. The bi-zone arrangements, foreshadowed in Bevin's pronouncements before the American initiative, were an economic necessity for Britain. The abandonment of India, despite British hopes for an orderly transfer of power, and the withdrawal from Palestine formed part of this cost cutting programme. There was no plan of retreat, just a series of ad hoc decisions. Nonetheless, it was a retreat.

The Americans responded to signs of British weakness and took on, somewhat hesitantly, the major burden of containing the Soviet Union in Europe. With their re-entry, Britain's European problems were eased and its remaining power could be used to play an influential, if dependent, security role. Present research on the origins of the Cold War has emphasized the contribution made by Ernest Bevin in encouraging the American return to the continent and in negotiating the terms of the Brussels Pact.[33] In NATO, which the British helped to shape, the country achieved a far greater measure of security than the French had won during the inter-war period. Under the American umbrella, Britain could assist with the economic and military (the British made the largest European contribution to NATO) stabilization of Western Europe.

American underwriting also allowed the British a chance to revive their international financial position in an effort to offset the weakness of the pound. After the war, half the world's trade was still conducted in sterling. The crises of 1947 and 1949 suggest, however, that this policy was fundamentally flawed and that the impressive gains made during the 1950s encouraged dangerous illusions. It may be, as Corelli Barnett has argued, that the immediate post-war period would have been better spent in re-structuring Britain's economic base and attacking the long-term problems of industrial organization.[34] Whether this would have been politically or economically feasible is highly doubtful. As in the 1920s, the maintenance of the sterling area and sterling as a reserve and trading currency put additional strains on an unreformed industrial structure.

There was a parallel effort to re-fashion Britain's imperial role in order to repair her economic fortunes and strengthen her global security. Britain was still present in the Middle East, now the centre of her extra-European defence system, in South-east Asia, where the five year war in Malaya against the communist guerrillas was finally won, and in Africa, where economic investment and political guidance were intended to assist the recovery of sterling and create stable governments friendly towards the United Kingdom. By such means and others, Britain tried to free herself from American domination and to forge an independent foreign policy.

By the late 1950s, it was clear that this was an over-ambitious programme. Konrad Adenauer observed in 1958 that Britain was like "a rich man who has lost all his property but does not realize it".[35] The relativities of West-European power no longer favoured the British. American strength could not be used in Britain's interests without paying a price that was politically unacceptable. The maintenance of sterling as a major reserve and trading currency was destabilizing the economy at home. The process of decolonization speeded up in the late 1950s and early 1960s; Malaya and Singapore were given independence in 1957 and seventeen colonies, mainly in Africa, won independence between 1960 and 1964. Trade and investment in the empire had already fallen during the earlier decade. The expanded Commonwealth was but a shadow of its earlier self. The Suez crisis called into public question the very image of a "great power". It was left to the Wilson government "to abandon the old symbols of wealth and empire". The pound was devalued, troops withdrawn from Singapore and Malaysia, and the "east of Suez" defence position abandoned with the exception of the still-leased Hong Kong. Most Britons accepted the end of empire without "undue apprehension or excitement". The historians continue to debate whether the empire was a producer of wealth or a burden to Britain, a source of real strength or a temporary shield masking her decline and sheltering inefficient industries from the cold winds of global competition.

The collapse of empire, coming at a time of increasing difficulties with the United States, left only the European option if the United Kingdom was not to shrink to a small and isolated island with a glorious past and a world language. In choosing the Atlantic Community and Commonwealth cards in the Bevin era, Britain had again opted for a European policy of "limited liability". The British excluded themselves from the Schuman plan. When, contrary to Foreign Office expectations, the European Coal and Steel Community was created and the European Economic Community emerged, Britain stood aside. By the time the Macmillan government hesitantly sought entry, General de Gaulle was prepared to block it. Britain was not only excluded from the early benefits of economic integration but entered an organization shaped by others and, at least in part, on their terms. The traditional ambivalent attitude towards Europe, sharpened by the gulf created by the Second World War and even by religious prejudices, restricted Britain's contribution to the building of this alternative form of regional stability.

What role for Britain?

The present ending of the bi-polar world and the current fragmentation of continents and countries allows one to put Britain's past contribution to peace and stability in a broader perspective. The maintenance of the status quo and the pursuit of stability and peace suited British interests. Statesmen used Britain's prestige to achieve these goals even after the material and strategic bases of the home islands were eroded. The structure of the empire proved flexible enough to endure beyond its repeatedly predicted expiration date. British interest in the maintenance of sterling as an international currency, her overseas investment and involvement in world trade had meant that the empire had never become an entirely closed economic system and that Britain could exercise a global influence well into the post-1945 period. The long period of imperial rule did contribute to regional stability. This claim can be made despite the country's part in the carve-up of weak empires and in diplomatic bargaining that caused or perpetuated regional tension. The extra-European territories were never entirely peaceful but with some notable exceptions, major wars and outbreaks of violence were relatively rare. As the paramount imperial power, Britain more often opted for compromise than for confrontation.

Disengagement proved less difficult and traumatic than experienced by either the French or the Dutch. Britain did not conduct an orderly retreat either in India or Palestine; departure was followed by terrible bloodshed in the former and continuing wars in the latter. Limited war still goes on in Ulster. Nor did Britain preserve her post-war economic and defence treaties "east of Suez" without a struggle. Nonetheless, given the size and importance of the empire, the costs of dissolution were relatively low. The after-life of the empire presents a mixed picture. The Commonwealth countries which enjoyed long periods of self-government under the British defence umbrella have emerged with democratic governments and constitutional forms owing much to their British heritage. This is also true of Ireland. India, with all its tribulations, is still a functioning democracy. Elsewhere the British legacy, too often blamed for current ills, has proved surprisingly superficial. What has emerged in the African post-independence period hardly suggests that the British succeeded in leaving behind viable democratic governments. Whatever might be the virtues of independence, the "fall" of Britain has not always been a benefit to her former subjects.

As Churchill once admitted, the claim to "be left in the unmolested enjoyment of vast and splendid possessions, mainly acquired by violence, largely maintained by force, often seems less reasonable to others than to us".[36] If the empire made Britain great, it also excited the envy of rivals. The legitimacy of her global rule was questioned by the Germans before 1914, was the object of great power discontents between the wars, and was challenged by Roosevelt and Stalin during the Second World War. Britain's imperial policies did contribute, though in diminishing measure (Hitler would not have been deflected from Europe through offers of colonial or economic concessions), to the unsettling of the European status quo. The protection of British imperial interests, moreover, involved the participation of other nations. The empire and Europe did not exist in water-tight compartments. There never was a period of "splendid isolation".

It is somewhat paradoxical that, though Britain's main interest was to protect her empire, she became engaged in two great continental wars that were about the balance of power in Europe. The new weapons made the country itself more vulnerable. But a policy of isolation from Europe, however attractive, proved impossible. As has been argued throughout this paper, in European affairs, Britain has used influence as a substitute for military power and sought to secure maximum benefits at minimum costs. It was through diplomatic bargaining, ententes if necessary, and, only in the last resort, alliances, that Britain tried to create or sustain a European equilibrium. More might have been done had the British not sought continental security on the cheap, but ultimately, success or failure depended on the disposition and intervention of other states. "Limited liability" was a policy of bluff, dependent on claims to a special legitimacy (not always accepted by others) and a global presence. Once the latter finally vanished in the 1960s, Britain was stripped of that image of strength that for so long had sustained her claims to great-power status. Even had she joined the European Community earlier, it seems highly probable that her presence would have only slowed the process of integration and weakened rather than strengthened her stabilizing role. Britain could no longer exercise the "soft power" she still possessed after 1945.

The Janus-like position of Britain for so much of her history and the long "special relationship" with the United States may explain the country's inability to find its place in Europe. The present disintegration of the Community should not obscure the continuing gap, historically conditioned, between Britain and her European partners. It remains to be seen whether the country will try, in the looser international environment of the post-Cold-War world, to redefine her foreign-policy role. It seems highly doubtful. The most damaging aspect of Britain's "fall" has been its effects at home as old institutions that once united the nation are being reformed or abandoned. It is a highly disorienting experience, shaking the traditional stability and confidence of a nation that still prides itself on past escapes from the political disasters of its European neighbours. Reconstruction is taking a long time.

The psychological costs of losing the empire have been borne at home. Britain's slow fall has sapped its powers of regeneration. One doubts whether a new Churchill (and how much has depended on Britain's leaders in its period of decline?) could evoke the memories of past grandeur, though the "Iron Lady" had her moments. The old Lion still produces Nobel Prize winners, publishes more books than any other nation, and remains a major investing country. Its leaders continue to announce new peace plans and are active on the world stage. The Lion may still roar but only if it joins the chorus. For the moment, there is little enthusiasm for an increasingly ill-tuned European score.

Notes

1. George P. Gooch and Harold W. V. Temperley, *British Documents on the Origins of the War, 1898–1914.* (London: His Majesty's Stationery Office, 1926–1928.) vol. 111, Appendix A, pp. 402–3. Cited as B.D.
2. See Patrick K. O'Brien, "The Costs and Benefits of British Imperialism 1846–1914", *Past and Present*, August 1988, No. 120, and the exchange between Paul Kennedy and Patrick O'Brien in *Past and Present*, Nov. 1989, No. 125.
3. A. Ramm, "Granville", in Keith M. Wilson, ed., *British Foreign Secretaries and Foreign Policy: From Crimean War to First World War* (London: Croom Helm 1987) p. 88.
4. B.D. ii, no. 86, 29 May 1901.
5. See the extended discussion in Aaron L. Friedberg, *The Weary Titan: Britain and the Experience of Relative Decline, 1895-1905* (Princeton: Princeton University Press 1988).
6. Robert J. Scally, *The Origins of the Lloyd George Coalition* (London: Princeton University Press 1975).
7. John Gooch, *The Plans of War* (London: Routledge 1974) p. 2.
8. Quoted in Zara S. Steiner, *The Foreign Office and Foreign Policy, 1898–1914* (Cambridge: Cambridge University Press 1969) p. 69. See the statement made by the First Lord of the Admiralty in June 1934: "We are in the remarkable position of not wanting to quarrel with anybody because we have got most of the world already or the best parts of it and we only want to keep what we have got and prevent others from taking it away

from us." Quoted in David Reynolds, *The Creation of the Anglo-American Alliance, 1937–1941* (London: Europa publications 1981) p. 5.

9. Ed. Keith M. Wilson, op.cit. p. 178 (see note 3).

10. Ibid. p. 193. See Keith M. Wilson, *The Policy of the Entente* (Cambridge: Cambridge University Press 1985), Chapter VI. For a different interpretation to which I still hold, see Zara S. Steiner, *Britain and the Origins of the First World War* (London: Macmillan 1977).

11. Paul M. Kennedy, *The Rise and Fall of the Great Powers* (London: Random House 1988) p. 231.

12. Hansard, Parliamentary Debates, 5 series, 65, cols. 1809–1827 for full speech.

13. John R. Ferris, "Great Britain in the 1920s". *International History Review* vol. 13, 1991 p. 737.

14. See Erik Goldstein, *Winning the Peace* (Oxford: Clarendon Press 1991) and Alan Sharp, *The Versailles Settlement* (Basingstoke: Macmillan 1991).

15. Quoted in William Roger Louis, *British Strategy in the Far East, 1919–1939* (Oxford: Clarendon Press 1971) p. 58.

16. Cab. 4/7 10 July 1920.

17. Anne Orde, *British Policy and European Reconstruction after the First World War* (Cambridge: Cambridge University Press 1991) p. 236.

18. Ibid. p. 329 and the arguments in Robert Boyce, *British Capitalism at the Crossroads, 1919–1932* (Cambridge: Cambridge University Press 1987).

19. Ian Hill Nish, *Japan's Struggle with Internationalism* (London: Kegan Paul 1992).

20. Cab. 32/47, C1109/1/18.

21. FO 800/257, Chamberlain to Lord Stamfordham, 9 Feb. 1925.

22. Quoted in R. Alastair C. Parker, *Chamberlain and Apppeasement* (London: Macmillan 1993) p. 319.

23. *Documents on German Foreign Policy 1918–1945, series D* (London: His Majesty's Stationery Office, 1949) I, pp. 162–3.

24. Quoted in Parker, op.cit. p. 25 (see note 22).

25. Ibid. p. 65.

26. N. Chamberlain Mss. NC 18/1/1041.

27. David Dilks, ed. *The Diaries of Sir Alexander Cadogan, O. M. 1938–1945* (London: Cassell 1971) p. 104.

28. Hankey Mss. 4/30.

29. Lord Hubert Miles Gladwyn Jebb, *The Memoirs of Lord Gladwyn* (London: Weybright and Talley 1972) p. 90.

30. Donald Cameron Watt, *How War Came* (London: Pantheon 1989) p. 623.

31. See the argument in John Charmley, *Churchill: The End of Glory* (London: Hodder & Stoughton 1993) but also Maurice Cowling, *The Impact of Hitler* (Cambridge: Cambridge University Press 1975).

32. David Reynolds, *Britannia Overruled* (London: Longman 1991) Chapter 7.

33. Anne Deighton, *The Impossible Peace, Britain, the Division of Germany and the Origins of the Cold War* (Oxford: Clarendon Press 1990) and her edition of essays: *Britain and the First Cold War* (Basingstoke: Macmillan 1990). Alan S. Milward, *The Reconstruction of Western Europe, 1945–51* (London: Methuen 1984). For a different view, see, Michael J. Hogan, *The Marshall Plan: America, Britain and the Reconstruction of Western Europe, 1947–52* (Cambridge: Cambridge University Press 1987).

34. Correlli Barnett, *The Audit of War* (London: Macmillan 1986).
35. Arthur J. Marder, *From the Dreadnought to Scapa Flow: The Royal Navy in the Fisher Era, 1904–1919*, vol. 1. (London: Oxford University Press 1961) pp. 322–3. I owe this reference to an unpublished paper by David Reynolds.
36. See note 35.

4

The Fall of Austria–Hungary:
Peace, Stability, and Legitimacy

Istvan Deak

The Habsburg Monarchy demonstrated far greater vigor in the last fifty odd years of its existence than is commonly assumed. In this essay, I will undertake to support that statement. A further contention will be that the only irrefutable cause of the monarchy's fall in October–November 1918 was the wartime defeat of the Central Powers, despite a background of very serious ethnic and somewhat less that threatening social tensions. Emphasis will also be given to the fact that, despite its manifest defects, Austria–Hungary was a factor of stability in Central, East-central and South-eastern Europe, and that its collapse inaugurated an era of instability whose end is not yet in sight. Admittedly, there is a powerful argument against such a positive evaluation of Habsburg rule: if we accept the atomization or Balkanization of the region as an inescapable development, then it might have been better for all the peoples concerned if the a-national Habsburg state had not impeded these changes. One might well argue that it needed a world war to break the Habsburg stranglehold on modern nationalism.

In considering these issues, it is first worth taking a look at certain characteristic features of Austro-Hungarian history.

Perceptions of the Past

The Habsburg Monarchy has evoked a whole series of negative historical clichés: it has been asserted, for example, that in the nineteenth century, the Dual Monarchy was – after the Ottoman Empire – the "Second Sick Man of Europe"; that this anachronistic "Ramshackle Empire" was governed in a feudal and simultaneously in an absolutist manner by a dynasty notorious for stubbornness and ingratitude; that the Habsburg Monarchy was an "ethnic morass" of many nationalities, some of whom were "dominant" and others "subject" or "subjugated;" that its fall had long been in the waiting and that, though it survived until 1918, this longevity was not due to any inner strength. Survival is commonly attributed to the monarchy's having been perceived by the other great powers as a "European necessity", or to the advanced age of its "venerable Emperor," Francis Joseph, whose feelings his peoples "did not wish to hurt."

Today, only a relative handful of historical textbooks recognize that Austria–Hungary's was a remarkable economic success story; that it guaranteed ethnic peace throughout a vast region of Europe between 1849 and 1914; that the majority of its national political leaders did not desire the dissolution of the Dual Monarchy for fear of worse to come; and that, after the 1860s, politics in both Austria and Hungary were far more progressive than reactionary.

Unflattering views of Austro-Hungarian history surely reflect the predilection of the Habsburg family and its foremost servants for viewing themselves as doomed. Many pages of quotations could be produced to demonstrate that the Habsburgs and their advisers despaired of the monarchy. Suffice it here to quote Emperor-King Francis Joseph's doleful pronouncement on 28 July 1914, upon declaring war on Serbia: "If the monarchy must perish, then at least it should do so with honor."[1]

Premonitions of doom are not wanting in the history of other dynasties and states but they seem to have been particularly characteristic of the Habsburg monarchy, and this phenomenon needs to be explained. There was, to be sure, the famous Austrian penchant for despair, best expressed in a quip dating from the First World War: "In Germany the situation is serious but not hopeless, in Austria the situation is hopeless but not serious." But the chief reason must have been the multinational monarchy's anomalous position in an age of triumphant nationalism. To many, it seemed inconceivable that this vast medieval conglomerate could exist at all.

Let me stress at this point that no matter what we think of the relative strengths and weaknesses of the monarchy, or of the certainty of its ultimate doom (all very difficult matters to measure and assess), the fact is that during World War I Austria–Hungary succeeded in calling up more than eight million men to active duty, an extremely high proportion for a population of 51 million. Of these, more than a million were killed in the war, yet the army fought on until 3 November 1918, just a few days before the German Reich itself surrendered. As late as two weeks before the collapse, not a single Entente soldier stood on Austro-Hungarian soil. Hence, if one seeks an incontestable cause of the monarchy's dissolution, it is to be found solely in the fact that Germany was militarily defeated.

Yet, clearly, there had been very great difficulties for many decades before the outbreak of the war, especially with the nationalities. No less importantly, the monarchy was widely perceived to be in decline and it was this perception that inspired the monarchy's leaders to engage in war so as to prevent what they feared would be inevitable foreign aggression and a domestic crisis.

Sources of Strength and Weakness

The Habsburg dynasty derived its power and prestige from its subjects, and the latter derived their power and prestige largely from the dynasty. One was quite unthinkable without the other. As the British historian A.J.P. Taylor put it: "In other countries dynasties are episodes in the history of the people; in the Habsburg Empire peoples are a complication in the history of the dynasty. ... No family has endured so long or left so deep a mark upon Europe: the Habsburgs were the greatest dynasty of modern history, and the history of central Europe revolves round them, not they round it."[2]

The Habsburgs, whose history dates back to the tenth century, gained possession of the Duchy of Austria, hitherto a Babenberg holding, in the thirteenth century. Thanks mostly to brilliant marriage contracts, the House of Austria became, by the sixteenth century, the world's foremost ruling family.[3] In the same century, the Habsburg domains were divided between a "German" and a "Spanish" branch. The latter of these became extinct in 1700, but the German branch continued to flourish until 1918. Moreover, the German branch held an unofficial but generally recognized claim to the crown of the Holy Roman Empire, and after that institution became defunct, in 1806, the family laid claim to the presidency of the German Confederacy. The Confederacy ceased to exist after the defeat of Austria by Bismarck's Prussia in 1866.

As Holy Roman Emperors, the Habsburgs laid claim to the heritage of both the ancient Roman Empire and Holy Mother Church, thus symbolizing the universalist dreams of western Christianity. The House of Austria also derived great strength from a long tradition of relatively strict mores and a rigid family discipline that accorded absolute power to the head of the family, even in liberal times, over the hundred or so persons who made up the Habsburg family.

The Habsburgs insisted to the end that they were "German princes" (in the old, feudal sense of the term), but they were in reality very cosmopolitan. The language of communication at court was alternately and often simultaneously Spanish, French, Italian, and German, and members of the family were expected to be familiar with a number of languages spoken by their subjects, which included German, Hungarian, Polish, Ukrainian, Romanian, Czech, Slovak, Slovene, Serbo-Croatian, and Italian. One of the major reasons for the unpopularity of the heir apparent Francis Ferdinand, of Sarajevo fame, was that, unlike other Habsburgs, he had no talent for languages.

The Habsburg family, or rather their principal advisers, managed to devise over the centuries such prestigious family missions as the defence of Christianity against Ottoman imperialism and the defence of Catholic orthodoxy against Protestant heresy. The former won them occasional European-wide support, and the latter the support of the papacy. At the end of the eighteenth century, when the defence of Christianity and of Catholic orthodoxy no longer had any meaning, the Habsburg rulers Joseph II and Leopold II created a new mission for themselves: service to their peoples as enlightened monarchs. The uncommon bureaucratic diligence of these two "enlightened absolutists" established a tradition observed even by their less talented successors. Finally, in the nineteenth century, the Habsburg state was universally recognized as an all-important buffer between German and Russian imperialisms and as a factor for peace among the quarreling nationalities of East Central Europe.

Another major source of Habsburg strength lay in the monarchy's social and economic elite, made up primarily of landowning aristocrats often as cosmopolitan as the dynasty itself, who provided the state with its generals and chief administrators. Even during World War I a number of French, Danish, and Swedish aristocratic officers served in the Habsburg army.

There were also such traditional all-monarchical institutions as the army officer corps, the imperial bureaucracy, and the Catholic hierarchy, but – and here we begin to touch upon the major weaknesses of the monarchy – during the nineteenth century all these institutions fell, to various degrees, under the influence of nationalisms. The lessened loyalty of some of these groups to the House of Austria foreshadowed post-imperial developments and secured a place for many of the group members in the successor states.

The imperial bureaucracy, for instance, had been completely multinational in terms of the ethnic origin of the civil servants, particularly of the aristocrats who occupied many of the upper level positions. But even the commoners among them came from the most varied ethnic backgrounds. True, in the central Vienna offices the bureaucrats all spoke German, but this was a matter of convenience rather than persuasion.[4] In 1867, however, the Kingdom of Hungary was recognized as an equal partner with the rest of the monarchy, thereby creating a dual state: Austria–Hungary. As a consequence, the imperial bureaucracy was divided into two or, to be more precise, four parts: that of Austria, whose administrative language was German, but which included a Galician administration that officially spoke Polish, and that of Hungary, whose administrative language was Hungarian, but within which the functionaries of the subordinate kingdom of Croatia-Slavonia officially spoke Serbo-Croatian. Thus there were, after 1867, four administrative machineries with four official languages: German, Hungarian, Polish, and Serbo-Croatian. Add to this, after 1878, the administration of occupied Bosnia-Hercegovina, which was treated as a colony of both Austria and Hungary, and in which the administrative language was simultaneously German, Hungarian, and Serbo-Croatian.

Despite a reputation for indolence and sloth (the notorious Austrian *Schlamperei* or *Schlendrian*), the imperial-royal administration functioned efficiently, at least for a bureaucracy in Central and Eastern Europe. Yet gradually the administrative machinery was becoming "national", with the provincial bureaucracies adapting themselves to the local ethnic-political forces, often quite independently of the national origin of the functionaries themselves. In fact, the relatively smooth transition to new administrative machineries in the post-1918 successor states would have been inconceivable without the pre-war "nationalization" of much of the imperial and royal bureaucracy.

A certain degree of "nationalization" took place even in the central monarchical bureaucracy. In the foreign service, for instance, out of 832 civil servants, 396, or 48 percent, called themselves Germans in 1914; 229 were registered as Hungarians, and 207 said they belonged to other ethnic groups.[5] Note that as late as the 1880s, it would have been inconceivable for a census-taker to query a foreign service official about his nationality. At most, the official would have replied that he was an "Austrian," in the old, dynastic sense of the word. It is a fact that the foreign services and diplomats of the post-World War I successor states originated from the Common Foreign Ministry of Austria–Hungary.

Up to the end of the nineteenth century, the Catholic high clergy was among the most cosmopolitan in the monarchy, with a significant number of Germans, Hungarians, Czechs, Slovaks, Poles, Croats, and Slovenes in its ranks. In that century also, the social composition of the prelates changed significantly from predominantly aristocratic to a majority that was of peasant origin. Yet the Church did not escape the advances of nationalisms either, and while the prelates generally remained loyal to the Catholic House of Austria, the lower clergy provided, in the second half of the nineteenth century, much of the leadership of the Polish, Slovak, Croatian, and Slovene national movements. As for the Lutheran, Calvinist, and Eastern Christian denominations, their clerics had always been associated with particular ethnic groups, such as the Germans (Lutheran), Hungarians (Calvinist), or Ruthenes, Serbs, and Romanians (Eastern Catholic and Eastern Orthodox). The difference now was that these clergies had become politicized.

In his *Dissolution of the Habsburg Monarchy*, the Hungarian-American sociologist Oscar Jaszi added a number of newer "centripetal" groups and institutions to the above-mentioned traditional props of the monarchy: the capitalists, the Jews, and social democracy. All had a vested interest in maintaining the integrity of the monarchy: the capitalists because the monarchy constituted such a large trading and investment zone; the Jews because the Habsburg state was so amenable to their integration; and the social democrats because they perceived the monarchy to be a fertile ground for the development of an internationalist working-class movement.[6]

One has to agree with Jaszi. Without the Jews, social democrats, and capitalists (the latter two groups, in turn, often consisted largely of Jews), the late monarchy would never have achieved its spectacular economic, social, and educational successes. In 1869, for example, 67.2 percent of the Austrian population was engaged in agriculture, and in Hungary, 80 percent. By 1910, the proportion of agriculturalists had fallen to 53.1 percent and 66.7 percent respectively. Between 1864 and 1866, Hungary produced an annual average of 1,720,000 tons of wheat and 200,000 tons of sugar beets; between 1911 and 1913, the annual average was 4,910,000 tons of wheat and 4,333,000 tons of sugar beets, the latter representing a twenty-fold increase. Bosnia-Hercegovina's wheat production more than doubled between 1897 and 1913.

In 1881, Austro-Hungarian industry consumed 520,000 tons of pig iron, and in 1911, 2,150,000 tons. The index of industrial production in Austria more than tripled between 1880 and 1913; in

Hungary, the increase was even greater. In 1870, the total length of Austro-Hungarian railroads was 9,600 kilometers and in 1900, 36,300 kilometers. This meant a per capita railway mileage close to that of Germany and Great Britain, exceeding that of Belgium, and far exceeding that of Italy. In 1848, the accumulated capital of Hungarian credit institutions totalled 3.7 million Kronen, in 1867, 28.8 million Kronen, in 1890, 348.5 million Kronen, and in 1913, more than 2.5 billion Kronen. Between 1901 and 1905, the mortality rate of infants under one year of age was 21.5 percent, nearly as good as that of Prussia, which was 19 percent. In 1911/1912, there were 1705 elementary school pupils for every ten thousand inhabitants in Austria, and 1319 in Hungary. The comparative figures were 1581 in Germany, 1435 in France, 980 in Italy, and only 370 in Russia.[7]

There were repeated economic setbacks between the 1860s and 1914, but the overall trend of growth was unmistakable. In fact, the fastest expansion took place in the last few years before World War I. The main reason for all of this was the free movement of labor and goods in a free trade area that extended from the Swiss border to what is today central Romania and western Ukraine and from southern Poland to Albania. It is true, however, that in the late nineteenth century capital and labor, too, began to adjust to the requirements of a nationalistic age. Witness the division of Austrian social democracy into German–Austrian, Czech, and other ethnic parties, and the tendency of the new Jewish intelligentsia in Vienna, Budapest, and Prague to embrace German, Hungarian, and Czech secular national values. Other young Jewish intellectuals abandoned the "Old Austrian" cosmopolitanism of their elders for radical socialist internationalism. Still, the working-class movements, the Jews, and the capitalists remained the least nationalistic of all groups within Austria–Hungary. The Jews in particular were viewed by the monarch, and generally viewed themselves, as unconditionally loyal to the Emperor, their protector and benefactor. Certainly, no other groups were more adversely affected by the dissolution of the monarchy in 1918 than the socialists, the bankers, financiers, and entrepreneurs, and the Jews.[8]

Perhaps we can best explore the strength and gradual weakening of the monarchy's institutional and group base by casting a brief glance at the monarchy's most important prop: the army.

The Multinational Habsburg Army

With its massive presence in every province, the army was the most important all-monarchical institution in the realm. In 1867, when the monarchy was divided into two politically equal parts, only the person of the monarch, the foreign service, and the Common Army (so called to distinguish it from the separate and much smaller Austrian and Hungarian National Guards created in 1868) were left as permanent common institutions. But because the foreign service by its very nature was not a significant presence within the monarchy, the Common Army alone represented all-monarchical authority in every part of the dual state. Yet even within this institution one must de-emphasize the role of the enlisted men, since following the introduction of universal military service in 1868, ordinary recruits were on active duty for an average of only three years, too little time to shed an ethnic identity and acquire a supranational one.[9] We are left, therefore, with the officers and, to a lesser extent, the non-commissioned officers as the representatives of the idea of an all-monarchical military establishment.

Each of the officers had, of course, his own particular or, very often, mixed ethnic origin, but service to the monarch was his basic commitment overruling all other considerations. The officers saw themselves even more as direct subjects of Emperor-King Francis Joseph than of the monarchy if only because, by 1900, there was not a single officer in active service who had not received his commission from that ruler and sworn personal fealty to him. This ultimate connection between officer and monarch, along with Francis Joseph's own military training and predilection for military regalia, fortified the identification of each officer with the highest levels of the state. It offered a further incentive to the officer corps to act as the guardian of the multinational monarchy.

The Austro-Hungarian Joint Army used a language of convenience – German. It was the language of command and service and the mother-tongue of an absolute majority of its officers, but it was not the language of instruction or of communication with the rank and file, except in the relatively few purely German-speaking units. In other units (90 percent of the total), the "regimental languages" were those of the ordinary soldiers, and the Habsburg officer was required by law and necessity to learn to speak the languages of his men. The peoples of the monarchy, and hence its soldiers, spoke ten major and scores of minor languages. Moreover, there was a vast discrepancy between the everyday languages of the officers and those of the rank and file. The latter were recruited more or less evenly from all nationalities, but the former included a much higher proportion of those groups with a tradition of military service and loyalty to the House of Austria or of those with a relatively higher education. Like the two other great dynastic empires, Prussia/ Germany and Russia, the Habsburg was a militaristic state: its ruler viewed himself first and foremost as a soldier. He accorded army officers an exalted status in society; imperial propaganda held them up as examples for all to follow; and the officers' code of honor, putatively derived from the medieval concept of knighthood, was the accepted norm, at first among the nobles alone but later among all educated men.

Unlike German society, however, Austro-Hungarian society was distinctly unwarlike. Between the 1850s and 1914, the military budget of Austria–Hungary was proportionally the smallest of all the European great powers, far below the financial capacity of the monarchy's economy. The reason for this anomaly lay in the nationalism of the Hungarians, bitterly opposed to the Common Army. The Hungarian politicians would have preferred dividing the armed forces into two independent, although closely cooperating parts. The Hungarian national army could then have been made to serve as a major instrument for assimilating the ethnic minorities who had barely ceased, by 1910, to constitute an absolute majority of the country's population. But because Francis Joseph categorically refused to divide his army, the Hungarian parliament and government consistently sabotaged military expenditures, at least until 1912, when it was too late.[10]

In 1859 and 1866, the Habsburg army was unsuccessful in preventing the unification of Italy or of Germany. Yet while the army had lost the two major wars it had fought, it was remarkably successful in securing peace at home. This it achieved without bloodshed, at least after 1848–1849. One could argue that the peacetime successes and wartime failures of the Habsburg army between 1849 and 1914 were the result of many factors, most of them unrelated to the efficiency of the military. Domestic peace was assured by, among other things, a growing prosperity, an industrial revolution, and the conservative loyalty and political simplicity of the peasants, who provided the army with most of its recruits. Wartime defeat was brought about by the relative backwardness of the economy and society, a paucity of funds, and the superior military leadership of France in 1859 and Prussia in 1866. But the dichotomy between domestic success and wartime failure was amplified by the fact that the army was trained and equipped primarily to maintain order at home. Military education and the ideology of the officer corps were well suited to stabilizing the monarchy within; they were far less useful for imperial expansion. Francis Joseph came to recognize this clearly, but only after he had lost two wars. In fact, the emperor became so sensitive to the role of his soldiers as representatives of monarchical grandeur that he stubbornly insisted on preserving traditional splendor even when it was clearly detrimental to wartime efficiency. Contemporaries and historians have tended to ascribe this to a lack of imagination or even stupidity, but the emperor was probably correct in his sense that a cavalry squadron in gold-braided uniform, a Sunday military band concert in every town of the empire, or a magnificent military parade on a feast day could contribute powerfully to a public sense of immutable stability. Only in the early twentieth century, after the emperor had become very old, did the army undergo a drastic reorganization under new leadership. It then finally began to be trained for modern warfare and imperialist expansion. Contemporary domestic and international tensions, caused at least in part by army policy, drove the monarchy's political and military leaders to risk war as a means of diminishing the strain.

Class and Nationality

So far, I have said much more about nationality than about social class, and this despite the fact that, during the nineteenth century, social classes gradually replaced the old feudal estates, or more precisely, that more and more people identified themselves as belonging not to an estate, such as that of the burghers, but to a social class. It is true, however, that the majority of industrial workers, a modern social class, still betrayed their peasant origin by often commuting from the land, or cultivating small plots after work, or maintaining close ties with their rural families. Similarly, the new urban middle class, especially those within it who were of landed noble origin (which was the case for the majority in Hungary, Transylvania, Croatia, and Galicia), tended to preserve in the city what they perceived as superior rural and feudal values. They viewed with contempt the very lifestyle and culture of which they were inevitably becoming a part. Urban intellectuals professed a desire to return to the land, and developed a cult of the peasantry and of the sacred soil that actually often served as an excuse for anti-Semitism and xenophobia.

The main reason, however, why I have said so little about class is that in the Habsburg monarchy class was inextricably intertwined with confessional grouping and nationality. The so-called historical nationalities, such as the Germans, Hungarians, and Poles, who belonged to Western Christianity, and whose historical tradition included the presence of a large and powerful estate of native noble landowners, were very different from the Czechs, for instance, whose Protestant nobility had been more or less eliminated in the seventeenth century, to be replaced by an alien, "Habsburg" and Catholic aristocracy. In the nineteenth century, there arose among the Czechs a new social and political elite composed of industrialists, businessmen, professionals, and politicians, all mostly of peasant origin. Yet the class composition of the Czech nation also fundamentally differed from that of such an "a-historical" nation as, for instance, the Ruthenes (or Ukrainians), who consisted mainly of Eastern Christian peasants. Their newly formed professional elites had just begun to challenge the rule of their Polish and Hungarian noble masters when the monarchy came to an end.

What must be ultimately underscored is that class by itself played a minor role in the fall of the Habsburg monarchy, which is our subject here. As we have said, the working class movement was, as a whole, favorably inclined toward the preservation of Austria–Hungary, although this does not necessarily mean that the workers themselves were of the same opinion. As for the middle class (a vague term at best), the politically active among its members constituted the leadership of the nationalist movements. In 1918, it was almost exclusively middle-class professionals and creative intellectuals who set up the new governments and established the successor states in the name of national self-determination and bourgeois democracy or, in a few cases, international socialism.

The Habsburg Monarchy in the First World War

It is no exaggeration to say that, with the outbreak of the Great War, the Habsburg Monarchy lost much of its legitimacy. Following the decline of such legitimating religious concepts as the fight against the Infidel and the defence of Catholic orthodoxy, the secularized empire's main appeal in the nineteenth century was its ability to preserve domestic peace, to improve economic and social conditions, and to accord equal treatment to its many ethnic groups.

The first great breach in the system came with the Compromise Agreement of 1867, which incorporated into law the supremacy of Hungarian-speakers in the Hungarian half of the monarchy and created a pseudo-nation state where there had been a simple multi-national state. From that time on, the Hungarian government's goal was to translate the principle of national uniformity into political reality. This it tried to achieve through forced or voluntary assimilation, economic growth, urbanization, modernization, and the vigorous cultivation of a Magyar national ideology. Inevitably, all the other ethnic groups followed the Hungarian example, demanding special rights for themselves in territories whose boundaries inevitably overlapped with the boundaries claimed by others.

Until 1914, these claims could be contained by the refusal of the German Reich government to support the nationalist claims of the German-speaking Austrians; the weakness and divisions among the Slavic politicians; the remarkably liberal ethnic policies prevailing in the Austrian half of the monarchy; and the spectacular economic and social progress achieved since the 1860s. All these props began to fall away, however, following the outbreak of the war. German military successes and Austro-Hungarian military setbacks strengthened the move on both sides of the border toward an Anschluss of the German-Austrian lands with the German Reich. The same military successes and setbacks led many Slavic national politicians to believe that they had little reason to tie their fate to that of the Habsburg dynasty, for the Habsburgs would no longer be able to defend them against Germanic imperialism. Furthermore, very early in the war the Austro-Hungarian High Command put an end to the liberal ethnic policies of the Austrian civilian administration. Instead, the generals neatly discriminated against such "unreliable" nationalities as the Czechs, Ukrainians, and Serbs, a process that inevitably became a self-fulfilling prophecy. Finally, prosperity ended in 1914, to be replaced first by an economy of shortages and later by starvation.

It is nearly impossible to decide whether the population of Austria–Hungary applauded or opposed the war at its outbreak in 1914.[11] In all likelihood, in the vast multi-national monarchy, no generalization is entirely valid. The order for mobilization was surprisingly well obeyed, but there was even more disorganization in the barracks than usual in such circumstances; moreover, the army was poorly led from the beginning and there were grave shortages in ammunition and guns. Armament production increased, at first slowly and then rapidly, but only until the third year of the war;

thereafter, production of artillery shells, rifles, and machine guns actually declined. At the front, the Austro-Hungarian armies were seen by the enemy as an easier target, which led to a concentration of enemy forces against them in all the major offensives. The subsequent near catastrophes were averted only by the rushing of German reinforcements to bolster the Austro-Hungarians.

Despite everything, the overall results of Austria–Hungary's war effort were most satisfying, at least outwardly. Serbia was occupied in 1915 and most of Romania in 1916; the Italians were driven back in 1917, and late in the same year, Russia quit the war. All this helped to create the dangerous impression among many at home that the war had been won. In reality, Austria–Hungary had been unprepared – economically, militarily, psychologically, or politically – for fighting a total war. What had functioned quite satisfactorily in peacetime now became fatal flaws: the feudal mentality of the ruler,• the multi-ethnic composition of the state, its dualistic political structure, the non-functioning parliament in Vienna, and the Magyar-dominated parliament in Budapest.

A particularly sore issue was the uneven social and ethnic distribution of battle casualties. It became well known that the peasants, who made up the bulk of the infantry, paid a particularly heavy price in blood. Likewise, the German–Austrians, Magyars, Slovenes, and Croats lost more men than the others. This was because the army high command had greater faith in these ethnic groups and tended to send their units to the more dangerous sectors. Criticism of this understandable policy was unduly heightened by the newspapers and politicians (especially in Hungary, where censorship was lax and the parliament remained in session), contributing in no small measure to growing hostility among classes and nationalities.[12]

Because the bulk of the monarchy's trained soldiery had become casualties by the end of 1914, the rest of the war had to be fought mainly by over-aged or under-aged men, or by previously untrained civilians. In fact, by 1915 the traditional Habsburg army had been transformed into a militia. It was led, moreover, by an inadequate number of civilians in uniform. What this meant in practice was that the non-Germans among the newly commissioned non-professional officers had had no time to learn good German, let alone the language or languages spoken by their men.

The war vastly increased ethnic tensions, which now also affected the army. There had been a few ominous signs in the military even before 1914, but only during the war did ethnic disaffection become a serious problem. Both in 1914, and again in 1916 (during the great Brusilov offensive of the Russian army), entire Czech divisions as well as some smaller units made up of Slavs or Romanians went over to the Russians. However, it is impossible to tell how many of these had come over voluntarily and if so, why. The front in the east was fluid and intermittent, enabling soldiers to surrender *en masse*, as the Russians did, too, well before the collapse of the Russian war effort.[13]

Developments in the Austro-Hungarian prisoner of war (POW) camps of Russia, Serbia, and Italy nevertheless helped to exacerbate national and class conflict within the monarchy. Soon the population at home learned through POW letters and rumors that the Russian and Italian commands treated the German–Austrian and Hungarian prisoners far worse than the rest. Also, Slavic, Romanian, and Italian prisoners were recruited into volunteer legions to fight against the monarchy. The military importance of these legions was very small, but their psychological importance was very great indeed.

On the home front, there was at first a period of national or, rather, this being Austria–Hungary, dynastic unity. All political parties, including the Social Democrats, supported the war effort, and the Hungarian parliament vied with the Slavic politicians in declarations of loyalty to the House of Austria. The Hungarian National Guard divisions proved to be among the most reliable units in the army.

Food rationing began in the hinterland in 1915, and it soon became clear that Hungary, the breadbasket of the monarchy, was much better off than the Austrian provinces. This led to grave antagonisms between the two parts. In addition, the Budapest government began to behave as if it were independent of Austria; it concluded separate trade agreements with Germany and began to formulate its own war aims. In Austria, meanwhile, left-wing socialists gradually turned against their authoritarian government.

Francis Joseph died on 21 November, 1916. The efforts of his young successor, Charles, to reform the monarchy failed no less than his attempt to negotiate a separate peace with the Entente.[14] Early in 1918 the monarchy's leaders and the nationalist politicians realized that, win or lose, the post-war situation would be critical for all. Victory would cause Austria–Hungary to lose her independence to an all-powerful Germany.[15] Defeat would inevitably lead to a Slavic preponderance in Austria and, most probably, civil war in Hungary. The longer the war lasted, the more the Austro-German and Hungarian elites clung to the German alliance, and the less the Slavic politicians became interested in the preservation of the monarchy. The failure of the Ludendorff offensive on the Western front in 1918 marked the end of the "German course" of the Austro-Hungarian leadership. The food crisis and the impact of Russian revolutions caused a wave of industrial strikes to roll over Austria and Hungary in January 1918. The surrender of Bolshevik Russia resulted in the return of hundreds of thousands of POWs, few of whom were willing to fight again. In the west, self-exiled Slavic politicians persuaded enemy politicians, including President Wilson, to recognize Czechoslovak and South Slav independence. Thus, by the fall of 1918, a still non-existent Czechoslovakia and Yugoslavia had become Entente co-belligerents. The immediate consequences of this action were very limited, for the Czech, Slovak, Serbian, Croatian, and Slovene soldiers of the Austro-Hungarian army did not desert *en masse* to the enemy, but the long-range psychological consequences were momentous. The German–Austrian and Hungarian soldiers were to remember for a long time that their defeat in the fall of 1918 marked the "victory" of their fellow-combatants from the other nationalities.

War was finally brought to an end by major Entente offensives in Italy and the Balkans. It was also hastened by the mutiny of starved and discouraged soldiers – first among the non-combatant elements of the army and later at the front.[16] The last minute efforts of Emperor-King Charles to achieve the federal reorganization of the monarchy met with general indifference; by the end of October 1918, power was everywhere in the hands of newly constituted national councils. Sooner or later, each of them declared for complete national independence. When, on 3 November, the Habsburg high command signed an armistice with the Italians, there had been no Habsburg monarchy for several days.

After the Fall

The dissolution of the Habsburg Monarchy was both a very slow and a very rapid process. Some argue that it began in the late eighteenth century with the national cultural awakening of the Germans, Hungarians, and others. Others say that it started with the clash of nationalities in 1848–1849. As I have tried to show earlier, one can well see the beginning of the end in the Compromise Agreement of 1867 when multi-ethnic Hungary proclaimed itself a sovereign nation-state, thereby violating the a-national premises on which the

Habsburg Empire had been built. One can also point to 1914, of course, when the monarchy went to war, no longer over a dynastic or territorial issue, but over questions of nationality. Finally, the beginning of the end can be placed early in 1918 when the peasantry turned against the state and when mutinies started in the navy and the army. The actual collapse was, however, a very quick process. Between mid-October and mid-November 1918, five new states sprang up on the territory of the former monarchy, each with a practically ready-made government, administration, police, and army.[17]

But while it was easy to win over to the new state bureaucrats who wanted nothing more than to be allowed to remain at their desks, or to make returning soldiers swear loyalty to the new state which promised them their pay, it was much more difficult to define the new form of government, to write a constitution, or to determine the boundaries of the new country. These efforts prompted a stultifying number of internal conflicts and border clashes. Overall, the violent conflicts endured from late 1918 to 1920, only to flare up again during World War II and then after 1990.

There was, however, a fundamental difference between developments in the defeated and in the so-called victorious nations.[18] While the countries that had been accepted by the Entente Powers as "co-belligerents" embraced Wilsonian democratic principles, defeated and dismembered Hungary tried to substitute Bolshevik internationalism for the false Wilsonian promise of national self-determination. In the new Republic of Austria, too, Marxist socialism proved a much stronger and more radical current than in the other new states, except of course Hungary.

Later, both Hungary and Austria moved from the far left to the right; all this in the hope of in one way or another reversing the *faits accomplis* created after the war. In Hungary, especially, territorial revisionism became the alpha and omega of national policy, not surprisingly considering that the country had lost two-thirds of its territory and sixty percent of its inhabitants. Hungarian revisionism ultimately drove that country into the arms of Nazi Germany, followed by all the other countries that were dissatisfied with the results of World War I. Paradoxically, this was also true of some of those countries, such as Romania, who felt insecure because they had gained too much at the end of the war.

The boundary issues of 1918–1919 led to so many border clashes and minor wars as to defy listing here. Suffice it to say that every single successor state was engaged in such a conflict on practically every one of its borders, and that even though the number of troops involved was usually quite small, the results were decisive. On the whole, the various Paris peace treaties in 1919– 1920 merely confirmed the results of earlier military conquests. Finally, the greatest international problem ensuing from the fall of the Habsburg Monarchy was the power vacuum created in Central Europe. Admittedly, Francis Joseph had given up Austria's role as a buffer between Russian and German imperialism when he permanently tied Austrian foreign policy to that of Bismarck's Germany in 1879. But things could have changed later, and in any case what the area was left with after 1918 was a number of mutually hostile small states, waging continual real or customs wars against each other. The so-called Little Entente concluded in 1921 between Czechoslovakia, Yugoslavia, and Romania aimed uniquely at containing Hungarian revisionism. But Hungary was totally powerless, and the anti-Habsburg and anti-Hungarian prejudices of the Little Entente politicians blinded them to the growing danger of Germany. The worst features of international politics in the interwar period were the inadequacy of French power and interest in the region and British jealousy at even this limited French intervention.

Conclusion

Immediately following the Napoleonic wars, four conglomerate states – Prussia, Russia, Austria, and the Ottoman Empire (plus tiny independent Montenegro) – occupied the whole of what we customarily identify as Central, East-central, and South-eastern Europe. By 1914, the newly independent states of Greece, Bulgaria, Albania, Serbia, Romania, and Hungary (the latter in partnership with the Austrian Empire) had been added to the list. At the end of World War I, came the turn of newly independent Poland, Czechoslovakia, the Austrian republic, Yugoslavia, and the three Baltic states. This still left such dissatisfied nationalities as the Ukrainians, Slovaks, Croats, Bosnians, and Macedonians. Their turn came, however, during World War II, when some achieved at least nominal independence under the protection of Nazi Germany. The defeat of the Axis powers marked the temporary defeat of these ambitions; the peoples in question were returned to the pseudo-national states that had been created after World War I.

This, in my opinion, is the essence of the changes wrought by the decline and fall of the Habsburg Monarchy. The weakening of

Habsburg power in the nineteenth century inaugurated – and the collapse of the monarchy in 1918 accelerated – a process in which the proto-national or a-national Habsburg empire has been gradually replaced by new, smaller multinational states. The new states have successfully used the modern language of ethnic self-determination to hide their multinational composition. The Kingdom of Hungary had opened the way, in 1867, when it proclaimed itself a multi-lingual but mono-national Magyar state. After 1918, the new Polish nation-state harbored a minority population of nearly one-third; in the Czechoslovak nation-state more than 35 percent of the population was neither Czech nor Slovak; and in Yugoslavia there was a considerable minority of peoples who were neither Serbs, nor Croats, nor Slovenes.

In order to achieve a statistical majority for their own people in the country, the Czechoslovak and Yugoslav regimes created the fiction of a "Czechoslovak" and, respectively, a "Yugoslav" (Serbian, Croatian, and Slovene) nation. As recent events have shown, there have never been such nations. Interwar Czechoslovakia was dominated by the Czech intelligentsia and interwar Yugoslavia by the Serbian military and bureaucratic establishments. The post-World War II Communist regimes strove to alleviate the situation by refusing to distinguish among nationalities in making their appointments to state and Party positions, but the Communists' shying away from an open discussion of ethnic – or any other – problem, negated what was otherwise a valuable effort. The legitimacy of Habsburg rule rested on highly complex feudal and dynastic arrangements as well as on military conquest. The Habsburg claim to the most important Hungarian and Bohemian crowns, for instance, was based on a marriage contract concluded in 1515 between themselves and the Jagiellonian dynasty. The original contract was subsequently reinforced by the election in 1526 of a Habsburg archduke to the thrones of Bohemia and Hungary; the military defeat by the Catholic Habsburgs of the Protestant Bohemian estates at the White Mountain in 1620; the Habsburg reconquest of Hungary from the Turks between 1683 and 1699; and the defeat of the Hungarian Rakoczi Rebellion in 1711. To cite another example: the Habsburg claim to Galicia was based on this province having been appropriated, for a short time in the Middle Ages, by the Kings of Hungary, and on a diplomatic agreement concluded between Prussia, Russia, and Austria in 1772 for the partition of the Polish kingdom. Considering that Francis Joseph's "Great Title" contained the names of at least one hundred kingdoms, principalities, duchies, counties, down to simple manors (plus two "etc.'s" at the end of the list), it is clear that the listing of such complex claims to legitimacy could be continued *ad infinitum*.

The legitimacy of the successor states was simpler in appearance only, for even though all claims were theoretically based on the Wilsonian principle of national self-determination, in reality other types of claims often played a much more important role. Thus, the Western boundaries of Czechoslovakia were made conterminous with the historic boundaries of Bohemia and Moravia, irrespective of the presence of more than three million ethnic Germans in those lands. The boundaries of Slovakia and Ruthenia, on the other hand, were officially approved in Paris on the basis of a skilful mixing of ethnic, economic, political, and even strategic arguments. What, however, ultimately gave a certain legitimacy to Czechoslovakia was its democratic constitution and its relatively tolerant practices toward the ethnic minorities. The same kind of claim to legitimacy could not have been made so easily by other successor states.

After 1918, and even more after 1945, the new multinational "nation-states," including democratic Czechoslovakia, made great efforts to translate into reality the promise contained in their nationalist ideology. In other words, they set out to transform themselves into genuine nation-states. This they strove to achieve through such methods as forced assimilation, expulsion, population transfer, deportation, and, ultimately, genocide. The results have been quite spectacular: today every Habsburg successor state is much closer to being mono-national than it was in 1918. The recent "ethnic cleansing" in former Yugoslavia represents one of the final, if again awful, steps in this process.

Notes

1. Cited in Franz Conrad von Hotzendorf, *Aus meiner Dienstzeit 1906–1918*, 5 vols. (Wien: Rikola Verlag 1921–1925), vol. IV, p. 162.
2. A.J.P. Taylor, *The Habsburg Monarchy, 1809–1918: A History of the Austrian Empire and Austria–Hungary* (New York: Harper 1965), p. 10.
3. On the Habsburg dynasty, see Adam Wandruszka, *The House of Habsburg: Six Hundred Years of a European Dynasty*, trans. by Cathleen and Hans Epstein (New York: Doubleday 1964). Some of the major histories of the Habsburg monarchy in English are Robert A. Kann, *A History of the Habsburg Empire, 1526–1918* (Berkeley: University of California Press 1974); C.A. Macartney, *The Habsburg Empire, 1790–1918* (London: Weidenfeld 1968); Arthur J. May, *The Hapsburg Monarchy, 1867–1914* (Cambridge, Mass.: Harvard University Press 1951); Alan Sked, *The Decline and Fall of the Habsburg Empire, 1815–1918* (London and New

York: Longman 1989); and Victor L. Tapie, *The Rise and Fall of the Habsburg Monarchy*, trans. by Stephen Hardman (New York: Praeger 1971).

4. The best source on the pre-modern Habsburg civil service is Waltraud Heindl, *Gehorsame Rebellen: Burokratie und Beamte in Osterreich 1780–1848* (Wien: Böhlau 1991).

5. Statistical data on the ethnic distribution of foreign service officials are given in Adam Wandruszka and Peter Urbanitsch, eds., *Die Habsburger-monarchie im System der internationalen Beziehungen* ("Die Habsburger-monarchie 1848–1918," vol. VI/I; Vienna: Verlag der Österreichischen Akademie der Wissenschaften 1989), p. 106.

6. Oscar Jaszi, *The Dissolution of the Habsburg Monarchy* (Chicago: University of Chicago Press 1929).

7. The statistical data were culled from Alois Brusatti, ed., *Die wirtschaftliche Entwicklung* (Adam Wandruszka and Peter Urbanitsch, eds., "Die Habsburgermonarchie 1848–1918," vol. I Vienna, Verlag der Österreichischen Akademie der Wissenschaften 1973), pp. 16, 18, 22, 26, 237, 318, 476, 496, 563; T. Ivan Berend and Gyorgy Ranki, *Economic Development in East-Central Europe in the 19th and 20th Centuries* (New York, Columbia University Press 1974), pp. 65, 78., and Alexander Sixtus von Reden, *Österreich–Ungarn. Die Donaumonarchie ·in historischen Dokumenten* (Salzburg: Nonntal Bücherdienst 1984), p. 106.

8. On the history of Austro-Hungarian Jewry, see Steven Beller, *Vienna and the Jews, 1867–1938: A Cultural History* (Cambridge and New York: Cambridge University Press 1989); William O. McCagg, *A History of Habsburg Jews, 1670–1918* (Bloomington, Ind.: Indiana University Press 1989), and Robert S. Wistrich, *The Jews of Vienna in the Age of Franz Joseph* (Oxford–New York: Oxford University Press 1990).

9. On the Habsburg army in modern times, see Istvan Deak, *Beyond Nationalism: A Social and Political History of the Habsburg Officer Corps, 1848–1918* (New York and Oxford: Oxford University Press 1990); Gunther E. Rothenberg, *The Army of Francis Joseph* (West Lafayette, Ind.: Purdue University Press 1976), and Adam Wandruszka and Peter Urbanitsch, eds., *Die bewaffnete Macht* ("Die Habsburgermonarchie, 1848–1918," vol. V; Vienna: Verlag, der Österreichischen Akademie der Wissenschaften 1973).

10. On the history of modern Hungary, see Peter F. Sugar, ed., *A History of Hungary* (Blooomington, Ind.: Indiana University Press 1990); Jorg K. Hoensch, *A History of Modern Hungary, 1867–1986*, trans. by Kim Traynor (London: Longman 1989), and Andrew C. Janos, *The Politics of Backwardness in Hungary, 1825–1945*, (Princeton, N.J.: Princeton University press 1982).

11. Of the voluminous literature on Austria–Hungary's role in World War I, see the following military histories in particular: Rothenberg, *The Army of Francis Joseph*, chapters 12–14; Deak, *Beyond Nationalism*, chapter 11; Norman Stone, *The Eastern Front, 1914–1917* (London: Hodder and Stoughton 1975); Robert A. Kann, Bela K. Kiraly, and Paula S. Fichtner, eds., *The Habsburg Empire in World War I: Essays in Intellectual, Military, Political and Economic Aspects of the War Effort* ("East European Monographs," No. XXIII; New York: Columbia University Press 1977), and "Conrad", *Aus meiner Dienstzeit 1906–1918*, (Wien, Rikola, 1921– 1925).

The political history of the Dual Monarchy between 1914 and 1918 is ably discussed by, among others, Z.A.B. Zeman, *The Break-Up of the Habsburg Empire* (London: Oxford University Press 1961); Arthur J. May, *The Passing of the Hapsburg Monarchy, 1914–1918*, 2 vols. (Philadelphia: University of Pennsylvania Press 1966), and Leo Valiani, *The End of Austria–Hungary* (London: Secker & Warburg 1973). See also Istvan Deak, "The Decline and Fall of Habsburg Hungary 1914–18", in Ivan Volgyes, ed., *Hungary in Revolution, 1918–19* (Lincoln, Nebr.: University of Nebraska Press 1971), pp. 10–30; and Gabor Vermes, *Istvan Tisza: The Liberal Vision and Conservative Statecraft of a Magyar Nationalist* ("East European Monographs," No. CLXXXIV; New York: Columbia University Press 1985), chapters 10–18.

12. On the uneven social and ethnic distribution of the war dead, see the pamphlets of the Austrian statistician Wilhelm Winkler: *Die Totenverluste der ost.-ung. Monarchie nach Nationalitaten* (Vienna: L.W. Seidel und Sohn 1919), and *Berufsstatistik der Kriegstoten der öst.-ung. Monarchie* (Vienna: L.W. Seidel und Sohn 1919).

13. There are a number of fine studies of the Austro-Hungarian POWs in Samuel R. Williamson, Jr. and Peter Pastor, eds., *Essays on World War I: Origin and Prisoners of War* ("East European Monographs", No. CXXVI; New York: Columbia University Press 1983), pp. 105–264.

14. The most recent biography of Francis Joseph is by Jean-Paul Bled, *François-Joseph*, (Paris: Fayard 1987). On Emperor-King Charles, see Robert A. Kann, *Die Sixtus-Affäre und die geheimen Friedensverhandlungen Osterreich–Ungarns im Ersten Weltkrieg* (Vienna: Verlag für Geschichte und Politik 1966); Arthur Graf Polzer-Hoditz, *Kaiser Karl* (Zurich–Vienna: Amalthea-Verlag 1928); Reinhold Lorenz, *Kaiser Karl und der Untergang der Donau-Monarchie* (Graz: Verlag Styria 1959); Ottokar Czernin, *Im Weltkriege* (Berlin: Ullstein 1919), and Gordon Brook-Shepherd, *The Last Habsburg* (London: Weidenfeld and Nicolson 1968).

15. See, Garry W. Shanafelt, *The Secret Enemy: Austria–Hungary and the German Alliance, 1914–1918* ("East European Monographs", No. CLXXXVII; New York: Columbia University Press 1985).

16. On mutinies in the Austro-Hungarian army and navy, see Richard G. Plaschka, *Cattaro-Prag. Revolte und Revolution* (Köln: Böhlau 1963). On the last days of the Habsburg armed forces, see Edmund Glaise von Horstenau and Rudolf Kiszling, eds., *Österreich-Ungarns letzter Krieg 1914–1918*, 7 vols., with 10 supplements (Vienna: Verlag d. Militärwissenschaftd. Mitteilungen 1930–1938), vol. VII, Appendix 3., and "Letzte Kriegsgliederung der öst.-ung. und der dem k.u.k. AOK unterstellten deutschen Streitkrafte am 15. Oktober 1918," ibid., vol. VII, Supplement 32; and Oskar Regele, *Gericht uber Habsburgs Wehrmacht. Letzte Siege und Untergang unter dem Armee-Oberkommando Kaiser Karls – Generaloberst Arz von Straussenburg* (Vienna-Munich: Herold 1968), pp. 93–109, and Bogdan Krizman, "Der militarische Zusammenbruch auf dem Balkan," in Richard Georg Plaschka and Karlheinz Mack, eds., *Die Auflosung des Habsburgerreiches. Zusammenbruch und Neuorientierung im Donauraum* (Wien: Verlag für Geschichte und Politik 1970), pp. 270–292.

17. Here are some titles, in English, on the Central and East Central European

revolutions and the successor states: Francis L. Carsten, *Revolution in Central Europe, 1918–1919* (Berkeley: University of California Press 1972); Arno Mayer, *Wilson vs. Lenin* (New York: Meridian Books 1964); Joseph Rothschild, *East Central Europe Between the Two World Wars* (Seattle: University of Washington Press 1974); Charles Gulick, *Austria from Habsburg to Hitler*, 2 vols. (Berkeley: University of California Press 1948); Barbara Jelavich, *Modern Austria. Empire and Republic, 1800–1986* (Cambridge: Cambridge University Press 1987), chapters 3–4; Volgyes, *Hungary in Revolution, 1918–19* (Lincoln, Nebr.: University of Nebraska Press 1971); Janos, *The Politics of Backwardness in Hungary, 1825–1945* (Princeton: Princeton University Press, 1982); Hoensch, *A History of Modern Hungary, 1867–1986* (London and New York: Longman 1988); Rudolf Tökés, *Béla Kun and the Hungarian Soviet Republic* (New York: Praeger 1967); Victor J. Mamatey and Radomir Luza, eds., *A History of the Czechoslovak Republic, 1918–1948* (Princeton, Princeton University Press 1973); Ivo Banac, *The National Question in Yugoslavia* (New York: Cornell University Press 1984); Fred Singleton, *A Short History of the Yugoslav People* (Cambridge: Cambridge University Press 1985); Henry L. Roberts, *Romania* (New Haven, CT: Yale University Press 1951); Norman Davies, *God's Playground. A History of Poland*, 2 vols. (New York: Columbia University Press 1982), vol. II, and Hans Roos, *A History of Modern Poland from the Foundation of the State in the First World War to the Present Day* (New York: Knopf 1966).

18 I use the term "so-called" because it would be ludicrous to pretend that such countries as Czechoslovakia had genuinely won the war, even though it was recognized as one of the victors at the Paris peace conference in 1919. After all, over ninety percent of the new country's soldiers had fought against rather than for the Entente Powers, and except for those in exile, all Czech and Slovak politicians had consistently proclaimed their loyalty to the monarch during the war.

5

The Fall of Germany: Peace, Stability, and Legitimacy

Wolfgang J. Mommsen

In a general analysis of the decline of great powers the case of Imperial Germany occupies perhaps a special place. For unlike the majority of other cases in question its eventual downfall involved the world in two disastrous world wars. And, not surprisingly, in the 1950s many experts, among them also quite a few Germans, had come to the conclusion that the existence of a strong German nation state in the centre of Europe was not in line with the legitimate interests of its neighbours, and, hence, of Europe as a whole. The collapse of the Soviet empire, however, made the unlikely possible again, namely the re-emergence of a new German nation state in the centre of Europe. This makes it all the more necessary to inquire into the German case, notably with regard to the chances for the permanent maintenance of peace and stability in the centre of Europe. The process of decomposition of traditional authority which we observe further east, especially in the states of the former Soviet empire, makes this all the more important.

Legitimacy in European Political Thought

In the German case, at any rate, it is somewhat difficult to use the notions of legitimacy, stability, and peace as interpretative guidelines. For the decline of Imperial Germany, as a major power within the European system of states, and its eventual downfall culminating in the devastation of the Second World War and the dismemberment of Germany, cannot be accounted for simply in terms of a progressive loss of legitimacy. In a historical perspective, legitimacy is anything but a clear-cut concept; rather, in the course of time, the invocation of the principle of legitimacy occurred for very different objectives, and the world views informing it often stood in stark contrast, if not in conflict, with one another. Indeed, German history may be described as the battleground of different notions of legitimacy, associated with patterns of political stability and peace greatly at variance with one another. Today we have

grown accustomed to the idea that the legitimacy of a political
system depends above all upon the consent of the citizens, and
government by consent necessitates the existence of a constitutional
order which guarantees individual freedom, freedom of speech, of
assembly and of the press, and provides an orderly legal framework
for transferring the consensus of the citizens, or at any rate, its
majority, into political action. Besides, constitutional democracy, to
use the term introduced by Finer, is supposed to provide internal
stability and to guarantee a peaceful conduct of the relations of the
polity with other powers. This notion of a stable and peaceful world
governed by the principle of the national self-determination of all
peoples goes back to the ideas of the Enlightenment. It was first
voiced emphatically by Guiseppe Mazzini one and a half centuries
ago, but it represents an ideal notion which, however respectable it
may be, is largely utopian. Even so, it may serve as a guideline for a
policy aiming at creating a more humane and more peaceful world,
and likewise as a principle of orientation for the study of the past.

Yet it may be doubted whether legitimacy, couched in these
terms, is a useful yardstick for an assessment of past history. As
already indicated, historical reality was determined by the constant
struggle of different patterns of legitimacy. The concept of legitimacy was introduced into international law by Talleyrand during
the Congress of Vienna, which had brought together the statesmen
of Europe in order to design a new, more stable, and possibly
peaceful order in Europe after the upheavals of the Napoleonic
wars which had broken out in the wake of the French Revolution.
Talleyrand thereby sought to justify the restoration of the Bourbon
monarchy in France and the defence of the territorial integrity of
France; only a reconstruction of Europe according to the principle
of monarchical legitimacy, so he argued, could guarantee a return
of stability and peace, and put a definite end to the revolutionary
upheavals of the past decades. This principle, then, was universally
accepted; the Austrian Chancellor Count Metternich embraced it as
an ideological justification for the return to semi-authoritarian rule
in the German territories. Legitimacy thus became a catchword of a
policy directed against constitutional liberalism and revolutionary
democracy alike.

In actual fact, the principle of monarchical legitimacy, though
not the term as such, had already a long tradition in European political thought, long before it was introduced into international
politics by Talleyrand. Though the authority of princes and kings
had usually been established in the first place by the right of con-

quest (considered in international law a source of legitimacy until very recent times) and usurpation of power thanks to charismatic qualities, it had received, as time went on, support by the invocation of religious arguments, notably the claim of rightful rule by the grace of God ("Gottesgnadentum"), by reference to rightful hered- ity and, in a more general sense, by reliance upon tradition, or more specifically, the principle of prescription. Indeed, Edmund Burke had defended the principle that there could be no legitimate gov- ernment unless based upon prescription, that is to say on the faith- ful observation of traditional, time-honoured principles of obedi- ence and rule. Neither stability nor peace, in domestic affairs just as well as in the international arena, was possible otherwise. Certainly this conservative notion of a legitimate order of things had been effectively challenged by the new message of natural law. The philosophers of the Enlightenment had argued that governmental authority has its limits in the inalienable rights of the individual, and that all government depended upon the consent of the ruled. Yet for the time being the conservative versions of the principle of legitimacy could count upon a much larger following, at any rate in Europe. Besides, remnants of older communal forms of legitimacy had survived; here the justification of the exercise of political power depended upon the fair participation of the lower estates, notably the aristocracy and the clergy, in the process of policy-making, and, in the case of the so-called Holy Roman Em- pire of the German Nation, the "election" of the emperors by the German princes and notables, although this election process had little in common with modern democratic electionary practice.

From the Holy Roman Empire of the German Nation to the German Nation-State

In medieval times the German peoples enjoyed a sort of informal hegemony over Europe, at any rate as long as the rule of the medie- val emperors was not in dispute. In this system the ethnic German element, which in fact developed into a distinct unit only during the tenth century, never exercised more than a predominant influence; nationality, though not altogether absent, did not play a major role in the medieval world. The Holy Roman Empire of the German Nation, which emerged since the fifteenth century, was restricted by and large to the territories predominantly inhabited by Germans. Ethnic factors did not matter in any substantial degree, although the German element etablished a loose dominion over other ethnic groupings, notably wide stretches of Slav territories in Eastern Europe. The hegemony of the Germans, or rather the aristocratic elites of the various German tribes, over ethnically non-German peoples in large parts of Central Europa was possible precisely because national factors were considered as being of secondary importance. Instead a cluster of traditional forms of legitimacy dominated in the political arena, or to put it more precisely, a combination of communal legitimacy and monarchical legitimacy symbolized by the well-known slogan "Kaiser und Reich". The emperor's main duty was to guarantee the rights and the freedom of the various princes and feudal lords participating in the conduct of public affairs, and to provide security against external foes.

With the rise of the territorial state since the seventeenth century the loose power structure of the Holy Roman Empire was increasingly fragmented, and in the end it retained only a shadowy existence. Given its complicated political structure, which was due not least to the mixture of legitimacy patterns to which it was supposed to pay respect, Samuel von Pufendorff called it a legal "monstrum". Originally it had been designed to guarantee peace and stability in the German lands and in Central Europe, but this was no longer the case. Instead Germany became a helpless victim of repeated interventions by foreign powers, notably France. Eventually the Holy Roman Empire just faded noiselessly away in 1806. The upheaval of European politics which had been caused by the Napoleonic invasion into Central Europe fundamentally changed the conditions of German politics. Its legacy was a Germany divided into a multitude of states and territories; up to 1867 it seemed to many that Germany was not likely ever to be united in one nation state; rather it appeared that it would be organized for the forseeable future in a plurality of states, with Austria and Prussia, which both contained substantial non-German ethnic groups, as the most important ones. Indeed, in many cases a sort of territorial patriotism developed which took the place of what elsewhere was considered national consciousness.

However, the French Revolution and its repercussions in the rest of Europe changed all this. The cluster of traditional notions of legitimacy hitherto in operation was effectively challenged by the new message of popular sovereignty. It questioned the legitimacy of traditional princely rule and raised the banner of national self-determination. The invocation of popular sovereignty seemed to undermine the order of things throughout Europe, and notably in Germany, even though it was far from clear who could be safely entrusted with the right to vote or the right to be appointed to political office, and who ought to be excluded from it, since the assumption was widespread that only those who owned substantial property were suitable to participate in the conduct of political affairs. The belief in the principle of democratic legitimacy was still in its infancy, but even so its influence was substantial.

Far more powerful proved the impact of the idea of nationality associated with the idea of popular sovereignty, though in a more indirect and supple manner, which was proclaimed by the French revolutionaries as the new guiding principle for a reconstruction of European affairs. In a way the idea of national self-determination gained far wider recognition among the educated classes than the democratic ideas of the French revolutionaries. The new national movements which emerged throughout Europe soon became a powerful agent of change, and were seen as an immediate threat to the traditional monarchical order. It is in this veiled and distorted form that the new principle of democratic legitimacy was introduced into European politics. Ideally the fulfilment of the national aspirations and the implementation of the principle of individual self-determination were collateral, as Guiseppe Mazzini argued in his great vision of a future Europe constituted by a plurality of free, constitutionally governed nation states which by definition would be a stable and peaceful one. In reality things turned out otherwise. National aspirations and respect for the rights of other nations collided more often than not, and the implementation of the principle of self-determination often left much to be desired.

This proved to be the case already during the German Revolution of 1848/49, the first bid of the Germans for a united nation state governed according to constitutional principles. The nationalist aspirations of the delegates in the Frankfurt Constitutional Assembly extended far beyond the boundaries of what could be called ethnic German territories; they by and large followed the pattern of the former Holy Roman Empire of the German Nation. The German nation-state which the revolutionaries envisaged was supposed to encompass large tracts of Slav territories in which the Germans had traditionally played a dominant role, though numerically in a minority. Neither could the delegates agree on the principles of the new constitution; the democrats found themselves in a minority, and the initial support by the masses for their radical programme soon faded away. Eventually the great attempt to reconstruct Germany against the princes and monarchical governments failed. The liberal version of national self-determination foundered on the rocks of the existing German states, which regained control of events, in part thanks to Czarist help, already late in 1848. In the following period of reaction great efforts were made to eliminate the revolutionary achievements in constitutional respects, however limited they had been, and to firmly establish once again the principle of monarchical legitimacy.

Two Sets of Legitimacy

In the event, German national unity was brought about by Otto von Bismarck in a "revolution from above" on a "kleindeutsche" base, in recognition of the separate status of the Austrian Germans within the boundaries of the multinational empire of Austria–Hungary. Imperial Germany was created in the course of three European wars, and it never wholly got rid of the vestiges of its martial origin. Under Bismarck's aegis it speedily became the dominant power on the European continent, superseding, as it were, France which had enjoyed the role of the dominant power in Europe for almost two centuries. It may be said that Imperial Germany during Bismarck's rule became a force of peace and stability in Europe, though perhaps not on liberal lines. This was the case, in the first place, because by the foundation of the "Reich" the dynamic, and potentially destructive forces of nationalism had been defused, if only to some degree. The German bourgeois classes now made their peace with the Bismarckian system, although in a constitutional respect it left much to be desired.

Indeed, the compromise between the liberal and the conservative strands in German society which was represented by the constitutional system of Imperial Germany with its mixture of different principles of legitimacy – monarchical, nationalist and, to some degree at least, democratic – worked for the time being in favour of stability. Bismarck would argue at the time that this had been possible only because the forces of popular democracy and nationalism were held in check by a conservative order of things (which essentially was based upon the principle of monarchical legitimacy). Indeed, in theoretical terms, Imperial Germany was built upon a compromise between two sets of legitimacies, the traditional monarchical legitimacy, on the one hand, whereby all power emanated from the rightful monarchical authority (in this case, as Bismarck often argued, the Princes and Monarchs of the various German states who had in 1871 jointly agreed to founding the "Reich"), and democratic legitimacy, on the other hand, as represented in the institution of the Imperial Diet and, to some degree, the parliaments of the various federal states. Although in strict democratic terms the German Empire was a semi-constitutional system which deprived the parliamentary institutions of the right of effective control of government while retaining considerable powers in the hands of the Emperor, respectively the various regional governments, notably Prussia, it enjoyed a high degree of legitimacy in the eyes of the public.

Admittedly, it was initially only an "unvollendeter National-staat", an incomplete nation state, but, as time went on, it certainly became a more complete one. Indeed, the institution of the Emperor, regardless of the personal quality of its individual holders, became the centre piece around which the loyalty of the public crystallized. There operated a mixture of loyalties; traditional respect for the monarchical institutions, the impact of the personal charisma of Bismarck, the identification with the new, powerful nation state with its glittering splendour and its strong economic performance; all these factors were part of the legitimation which the system enjoyed in the eyes of the public, although it fell far short of a genuine constitutional, let alone a democratic, monarchy.

This state of affairs in fact provided a political base for a policy of stability and consolidation in foreign affairs. Indeed, from its very beginnings the Imperial government had officially declared that after the process of unification had been completed Imperial Germany did not harbour any further territorial claims in Europe, and that it was ready to conduct a policy of peace and stability in Europe, in cooperation with its European neighbours. Bismarck's role as "honest broker" at the Congress of Berlin in 1878 could be seen in this light; he was working hard to mediate between Czarist Russia and Austria–Hungary regarding the controversial issue of the future of the Balkans, and he earned considerable recognition for that in the West, notably in Downing Street though not, regrettably, in St. Petersburg.

However, it ought to be recognized that Bismarck's foreign policy rested upon decidedly conservative premises, both because Bismarck preferred an alliance of the three conservative powers Imperial Germany, Czarist Russia, and Austria–Hungary to any other combinations, and because it by and large tended to rigidly subordinate the national aspirations of the peoples in the Balkans and elsewhere to the power interests of Imperial Germany. On the whole, Bismarck acted upon the assumption that nationalist movements were politically dangerous and had to be contained as far as possible (though at times he had not hesitated to join forces with some of them, if necessary). The limitations of Bismarck's policy of stability and peace in Europe are therefore obvious; it was a political strategy which reckoned in the first place with the legitimate monarchical rulers of Europe, and with the conservative elites, whereas it was reluctant to pay attention to public opinion. Therefore it gradually got out of touch with the trends of public opinion, both at home and abroad. It was a classic case of cabinet diplomacy which conducted foreign relations as a rational game between a limited number of responsible players; it acted upon the premises that foreign policy ought to be conducted entirely independently of public opinion, and upon the assumption that public opinion could be manipulated by the governments *ad libitum*. This policy was eventually bound to lose touch with public opinion, and this was the case since the late 1880s. Bismarck's successor Caprivi was undoubtedly right in arguing that foreign policy could not be conducted indefinitely without regard to public opinion, and that therefore a break with Bismarck's diplomatic practice had become unavoidable.

Besides, Bismarck's policy of maintaining peace and stability in Europe had one drawback which in the long run proved detrimental to the German position within the international system and eventually also to the maintenance of peace, namely the tendency to divert the tensions within the European system of states to the periphery, or, to put it somewhat less amicably, to exploit the differences between third powers on the Balkans, in Africa, in Egypt and elsewhere in order to strengthen the German position in the centre of Europe. This eventually backfired, all the more so, as by 1889 Imperial Germany abandoned the policy of near abstention from imperialist acquisitions overseas and in particular in the Middle East, which, by and large, had been Bismarck's line of approach, though with a sudden deviation in the mid-1880s when Imperial Germany had half unwillingly acquired a couple of colonial territories overseas.

Factors of Destabilization in the Political Fabric

It may be argued that the very factors which initially made Bismarck's policy of saturation and peace in the centre of Europe possible began in the longer term to undermine its very foundations. Three factors will have to be mentioned, above all,

a) militarism
b) bourgeois nationalism
c) the belated, but extremely rapid industrialization of German
    society.

Indeed the belated, but for that matter all the more rapid industrial
revolution in Imperial Germany resulted in far-reaching shifts in the
social structure which altered the social composition of the polity to
the disadvantage of the traditional aristocratic elites. However, the
Imperial constitution, which had been so designed as to make any
major constitutional change impossible, was not adjusted to these
new conditions. This resulted in gradual, almost unrecognizable,
changes in the prevailing pattern of legitimacy of the political
system. The rifts between different sections of German society
widened, and new patterns of loyalty emerged which were no
longer reconcilable with one another in the same way as had been
the case in the 1870s and 1880s.

Undoubtedly the tradition of Prussian militarism, that is to say of
giving preference to the military element in society, was continued
under Bismarck's rule. In fact, in some ways Bismarck supported
this trend in as much as he tended to shield the military establishment as far as possible against all effective control by the Imperial
Diet, or, for that matter, by public opinion, with the involuntary
consequence that the range of affairs considered to be subject to the
personal decision of the monarch and his entourage was extended
considerably, a process that accelerated during the years of William
II's rule. Undoubtedly the militarist mentality, which had been part
and parcel of the Prussian tradition, was taken up, and at times even
intensified, by the upper middle classes, in particular the academic
elites, as can be gathered from the fact that the status of being a
reserve officer was universally considered an important distinction
which justified social elevation, and certainly was seen as a positive
factor in one's own business career. Eventually these leanings
toward militarism gave rise to a mental disposition in favour of war
among important sections of the middle and upper classes. In the
last decade before 1914 a major European war was considered by
many no longer a distant possibility, but rather, if needs be, a
means, however unwelcome, to solve the problems of German
world politics by force.

Perhaps more important was the rise of the New Nationalism.
Initially the German national movement had been essentially
emancipatory in its goals; the ideal of the nation state and of consti-

tutional government in line with the principle of national self-determination for all "mündige" citizens alike had been altogether dominant, even though from the start imperialist expectations had been associated with it. After 1871, however, nationalism gradually and silently changed its meaning. It identified with the German power state rather than with the fortunes of the Germans as an ethnic or cultural group, although the older cultural nationalism was not abandoned altogether. Now, an integralist version of the national idea became dominant, a version which demanded that all cultural or ethnic minorities, including German Jewry, must assimilate themselves to the dominant national culture. It was Heinrich von Treitschke, above all, who acted as prophet and mouthpiece of this New Nationalism, which stressed at the same time that the nation state ought to be a strong, imperialist power state, and that the people be united under the scepter of a coherent national culture, which, not surprisingly, was to be Protestant, mildly authoritarian, and idealizing the classic bourgeois values of the New Humanism of the late eighteenth and early nineteenth centuries.

This bourgeois nationalism hardened in parts of the public mind into an imperialist creed which directed its efforts both against the ethnic minorities inside the boundaries of Imperial Germany, notably the Poles and the French minority in Lorraine, and against rival nations in Europe. To some degree this was an ideology that contained an emancipatory element of sorts; the middle and upper-middle classes discovered a strong nationalist attachment to the Imperial system as a means of securing a higher degree of political influence, instead of by and large accepting the predominance of the established power elites. Furthermore, the nationalist affiliation was seen as an effective antidote against the allegedly internationalist Social Democrats.

In a way, the intensified nationalism during the Wilhelmine period was correlated with deep tensions within society. The internal conflicts and troubles caused by rapid and uneven economic growth were transferred onto the periphery: a forceful foreign policy seemed to offer a way to overcome internal strife and stabilize the given order of things. The new nationalist agitation associations, in particular the Pan-German League, became the mouthpiece of a radical, aggressive and at times even "völkisch" nationalism which, as time went on, evolved into a major disrupting force in German politics in the last decade before 1914.

The real basis of the strength of Imperial Germany as the hegemonial power in pre-1914 Europe was to be found, however, in the astounding success of the German economy, which in part had been helped along by momentous advances in the natural sciences and in technology. Karl Helfferich (then one of the Directors of the German Bank) wrote in 1913, on the occasion of the twenty-fifth anniversary of William II's accession to the throne, that the German economy had grown three and a half times during this period. Indeed, Imperial Germany's economic success in the last three decades before the First World War amounted to the first "economic miracle" in its history. By 1900 it had definitely surpassed Great Britain in industrial production, it controlled nearly four fifths of the pharmaceutical production throughout the world, and it had become, next to Great Britain, the leading trading nation in the world. Only in terms of capital investments overseas did it lag behind Great Britain and France, though perhaps not to the degree which for a long time had been assumed by economic historians. In terms of its industrial power it had reached the zenith of its long history, and only the United States was likely to surpass it in the near future. It filled the German bourgeois classes with legitimate pride as to their achievements, and instilled in them an exuberant mood which made them prone to overestimate their economic and political potentials in the pre-World-War-I world.

Discrepancies between Expectations and Reality

In the opinion of large sections of the German population, Germany's economic success had not found an adequate expression in the political arena; here, so contemporaries believed, Germany was lagging behind other powers, notably her foremost rival Great Britain. They came to believe that the distribution of power within the international system ought to be adjusted to economic reality. Admittedly, in the contemporary race for the acquisition of territories overseas Imperial Germany had been a latecomer, and the attempts to further expand German colonial possessions, in particular in Africa, had so far brought only meagre results, even though in 1911 considerable pressure had been exercised upon France, almost urging on a major European war. In economic terms Imperial Germany could well do without large tracts of colonies; her own colonial possessions were, with the exception of German Samoa, highly deficitary affairs, whereas her informal economic position overseas, notably in Latin America and in the Middle East, somewhat less so in China, was, if not splendid, at any rate rather good. Her export trade, often assisted by subsidiary companies in the respective territories, and more often than that by special overseas banks, did exceedingly well.

Yet actual economic needs and expections in the field of imperialism are two different things. Besides, important non-economic motives played a significant role, which may be summarized under the heading of "social imperialism", in the meaning of this term coined by Hans-Ullrich Wehler, that is to say expansionism as a means of diversion from internal political and social problems. The imperialist message impeded a further rise of the Social Democrats, at least according to contemporary opinion. Another aspect was the powerful effect of the cultural-imperialist message propagated most effectively by Friedrich von Bernhardi in a famous book bearing the title "Germany and the Next War". Bernhardi preached to the German educated classes that German culture would be in mortal danger of falling into oblivion if Imperial Germany did not become a world power overseas as well, and rise to an equal status with the British Empire, the United States, the French Communauté, and the Czarist empire, which were going to determine the future of the globe among themselves, whereas all the other powers were destined to fall into a secondary position which eventually would no longer allow them to maintain their own national culture effectively. This message was heeded all the more as it argued its case with reference to the great tradition of New Humanism and Idealism symbolized by the spirit of Weimar.

These were the ingredients that eventually made up a particular "neudeutsch" Nationalism, which increasingly lost sight of reality, in particular the limitations of Imperial Germany's power position in the pre-World-War-I world. The governments were exposed to mounting pressure that they ought to come forward with concrete successes in the field of foreign policy, even at the risk of conducting a strategy of "dry war", as it was put at the time by Hans Delbrück, that is to say by a policy of threatening that Imperial Germany would not shrink from going to war if the essential objects of German policy could not be secured by peaceful means. It was this mentality that gradually penetrated all sections of the public and, in particular, the political elites, even though the latter by no means believed that Imperial Germany actually needed grand territorial acquisitions overseas. It could be shown that, measured by the standards of the time, German imperialist expansion, both informal and formal, was doing not too badly before 1914. The predominant position of Imperial Germany in the Ottoman Empire had become unassailable, even though it had to be consolidated by compromises

with Great Britan and France in 1912 and 1913, and the great goal
of establishing a German "Mittelafrika" was by no means beyond
reach.

But this was to little avail. For the public was engulfed in a
nationalist mentality which would not be satisfied by vague hints
about the allegedly splendid prospects of German world politics,
nor by the fact that Germany's position in the world's markets was
excellent and not likely to be seriously endangered by its rivals,
provided that this constellation were not interrupted by a general
war. Hugo Stinnes, one of Germany's leading industrialists, in 1913
pointed out to the chairman of the Pan-German League, Heinrich
Claß, that if Germany was given another couple of peaceful years
her economy would be the strongest in the world. This was perhaps
overdoing things a little, but there can be little doubt that neither the
German banking nor the German business communities welcomed
the outbreak of war in the least when it eventually came in July
1914.

The reasons why there developed a growing discrepancy
between expectations and reality, between economic requirements
and political activity, will have to be sought in the fact that the
political system of Imperial Germany had not been adapted to the
changing needs of a society which by 1900 had become one of the
world's leading industrial nations. To put it otherwise, its political
fabric was still dominated by a traditional elite which, though no
longer exclusively recruited from the aristocracy, still depended
upon it. There can be little doubt that the pseudo-constitutional
system of government which Bismarck had given Imperial Germany no longer sufficed to canalize the political energies of the
country into useful directions. The rifts within German society,
notably between the working classes and the business elites, were
transferred to the political arena, and thereby a constellation of
distrust and restlessness emerged which otherwise might have been
overcome without serious political repercussions. In the event,
internal unrest and crisis spilled over into international politics. The
public demanded a strong policy overseas, partly, because it was
assumed that thereby Germany's domestic problems might be
solved, partly, because it believed that its "legitimate" overseas
interests had not been taken care of in an appropriate manner. In
part, this may be explained in terms of a crisis of the traditional
patterns of legitimacy in Imperial Germany. The ruling elites were
confronted with the demand that Imperial Germany ought to pursue
a vigorous world policy and that the parties and the public be given

a larger say in foreign affairs; under given conditions this request for a foreign policy in line with popular demands could only result in an intensification of nationalism and aggressiveness in as much as there were no sufficient counterweights against an extremist agitation which a fully developed parliamentary system might have provided.

It is important, in this respect, to realize that the expectations of the public, and to some degree of the bourgeois parties, as to Imperial Germany's future role in world politics had largely lost sight of the real conditions within which German foreign policy had to operate. Theirs was an imperialism without definite limitations, "ein Imperialismus ohne angebbare Grenze" (Schumpeter), which in principle could not be satisfied by whatever concrete successes the government might achieve in its encounters with rival powers. The worsening international constellation which the Germans believed to be the result of a systematic policy of encirclement by Britain and France made this all the more difficult. The military establishment began to press for a preventive war, as the military chances of Imperial Germany were in their view deteriorating rapidly. And in the public there developed a fatalist expectation that war would come anyway sooner or later, which eventually hardened into a self-fulfilling prophecy. When on 28 June, 1914 the assassination of the Archduke Francis Ferdinand all of a sudden created an international crisis, the government of Bethmann Hollweg took recourse to a "Flucht nach vorn" much against its own better wisdom, largely under the diffuse pressure of the nationalist forces among the public and the bourgeois parties, on the one hand, and by the military establishment, on the other, and embarked upon a forward policy rather than let the constellation, which initially presented a unique opportunity to Imperial Germany, enforce a realignment in the European alliance system.

The First World War as an Attempt to Stem the Tide

The First World War was on the part of Imperial Germany a gigantic attempt to stem the tide, and to establish hegemonial control over the European continent. An intense public debate raged over a wide range of war aims involving acquisitions both in the West, notably the direct or indirect annexation of Belgium, as well as in the East. Furthermore, a grand scheme of a Central European Economic Union was propagated, which, if realized, would have given Imperial Germany nearly complete economic control over Central and South-east Europe. It is a matter of dispute to what degree the government of Bethmann Hollweg actually shared these extreme views, or whether it was pushed by public opinion into a strong showing regardless of the chances of these plans eventually being realized. There can be no doubt that the dynamics of the debate on war aims increasingly lost touch with the realities. The very fact that a favourable peace on negotiable lines was not in sight, made more and more people believe that everything must be put on one card: either Imperial Germany would win and establish unrestricted hegemonial control over Europe, or it would go under anyway. The collapse of the Czarist Empire and the rise of Lenin to power, which made the Treaty of Brest-Litovsk possible, were indeed momentous events, and the extremely onerous conditions imposed upon the new Soviet government, which in due course were hardened even more, show what would have been the destiny of the rest of Europe had the Central Powers won the war. It is, by the way, quite wrong to assume that this was actually impossible; by the spring of 1917 the internal collapse of both Italy and France was, in fact, not all that far away!

In the spring of 1917 Imperial Germany was undoubtedly at the peak of its power. But internally things were pointing in the opposite direction. Among the masses unrest mounted, and the desire for peace at any price was now spreading among the population. Offical war propaganda did its best to suppress these tendencies, but it now became clear that the propagation of extremist war aims effected the contrary of what had been assumed, and even the "Vaterlandspartei" tended to modify its tone rather than to blow the trumpet louder.

The military situation, with German troops deep inside France and with large tracts of Russia and the Ukraine occupied, still appeared fairly good. But with the entry of the United States into the war the scales had been turned. In domestic affairs the division between those who still insisted upon a full-scale victory associated with large-scale annexations, and those who hoped for a negotiated peace of sorts, and, last but not least, the still fairly small groups among the working class that now opted for peace at any price, possibly associated with a socialist revolution, became more marked. The rest of the story is well-known. The hubris of the pre-War years, which had risen to unprecedented heights, now collapsed, at the front and at home. The Revolution of 1918/19 was primarily a rebellion against the military authorities in order to deprive them of control and to prevent any further continuation of the war; it marked the near complete collapse of the legitimacy of the Imperial system. Now only recourse to parliamentary rule could stabilize the social order again. This was done, by and large, successfully; the attempts by the political Left to turn the Revolution into a socialist one failed.

Now the democratic notion of legitimacy triumphed. The new German state took over the Western model of parliamentary democracy, although certain remnants of the former imperial system survived in its constitution; this is the case in particular with regard to the strong position assigned to the popularly elected president of the Republic, who, in some ways, was supposed to operate as an "Ersatzkaiser". There was considerable hope, both inside and outside Germany, that the Democratic Republic of Weimar would henceforth enter upon a path of stability and peace which was outlined in the Paris peace treaties with the foundation of the League of Nations.

However, the Democratic Republic of Weimar, which was born out of the violent convulsions at the end of the war, rested from the start on most fragile foundations. In actual fact it was only a minority of the people who were sincere adherents of the democratic ideals on which it was based. The democratic legitimacy to which it adhered in constitutional terms appeared to many people merely an imposition by the Western powers which was not in line with the traditions of German history. Although the Wilhelmine tradition was for the moment discredited, in particular the middle and upper classes, perhaps with the exception of the Catholic population, were inclined to take the allegedly glorious past of Imperial Germany as their point of orientation, not the apparently miserable present. Given this mentality among large sections of the German people, in particular the intelligentsia and the academics, the establishment of the parliamentary system of Weimar was not a new departure, as some politicians assumed at the time. In fact the comparatively short period of twelve years during which the Weimar Republic existed, marked merely the final decomposition of Imperial Germany, with Adolf Hitler picking up the fallen fruits. The Germans, with but a few exceptions, refused to accept defeat, and those who were prepared to face realities and to reconstruct the German polity accordingly, like Matthias Erzberger and Walther Rathenau, were soon branded traitors, as were the Social Democrats.

Weimar Germany: A Polity Sort of Legitimacy

Weimar democracy never enjoyed a sufficient degree of legitimacy in the opinion of the public. In fact the legitimacy patterns of the past lingered on in the minds of the people, though usually only in veiled, clandestine ways. Few people really believed in parliamentary democracy, nor were they prepared to accept the new system of international politics symbolized by the League of Nations as a genuine innovation designed to guarantee peace and stability. Admittedly, there was a brief period of consolidation between 1923 and 1928 during which it appeared that the Germans had finally settled down. But the divisions between the rival political camps were far too deep. Under the tutelage of the Comintern the Socialist Left made repeated attempts to re-ignite the socialist revolution, with the sole consequence of discrediting socialism in all its varieties. The Right rallied behind von Hindenburg, who during the First World War had, without seeking to do so, risen to the role of a symbolic leader. It sought an opportunity to overthrow the hated republic and to return to Wilhelmine conditions.

In the end it was the massive popular support that the National Socialists had been able to mobilize during the Great Depression which created the chance for the Right to overthrow the democratic order of Weimar Germany. Undoubtedly, the traditional elites had not intended an uncontrolled take-over by Hitler; rather they had intended to use him as a tool in order to install a conservative government which was expected to restore authoritarian political rule and possibly might introduce the monarchy again. But, as is well-known, things soon got out of control; the avalanche of National Socialism could no longer be stopped by manipulation and tactical tricks on the part of the old Wilhelmine elites.

Charismatic Leadership and Social Darwinism: a Legitimacy of Sorts

The National Socialist regime very soon broke through all remaining constitutional barriers and pushed aside all political rivals by force. Even so, it would be misleading to argue that the National Socialist take-over was merely an illegitimate usurpation of power. Things were more complicated than that. For one thing, Hitler had been appointed to the chancellorship in a formally legal manner. Second, it cannot be denied that Hitler enjoyed considerable public support, though it initially fell short of the majority of voters, and that he masterfully played the cards of a sort of legitimacy which was the very opposite of democratic legitimacy. Nonetheless, he mastered a good deal of support, notably among his followers, but also among the population in general. The charismatic appeal of his personality to the masses was also a prime factor, even though in hindsight it is difficult to understand why his rhetoric had so much success at the time. Besides, the social-Darwinist argument that those who prove themselves strongest in the continuous contest of life have a natural right to rule, and not those who are elected in a cumbersome electoral process, had at the time a considerable following, all the more so, as it appeared to be supported by the Nietzschean doctrine of the "Herrenmenschen" who have a natural right to be the masters of the "Far-too-Many". It may be mentioned in this context that Nietzsche's book "Der Wille zur Macht" had been largely a concoction by Elisabeth Förster-Nietzsche! In any case, at the time this Social-Darwinian version of legitimacy was rather attractive, all the more so, as it was assisted by a massive campaign against the hated "system of Versailles" and an extreme Anti-communism which did not refrain from using terror and sheer brute force against its adversaries, notably the Communists.

This social-Darwinian variety of legitimacy to which the National Socialists adhered was, of necessity, closely associated with struggle and warfare, rather than with stability and peace. Its very essence was that all conflicts must, in principle at least, be fought out violently rather than settled peacefully by negotiation or by legal means. Hence it is not surprising that Hitler was bent on going to war from the start. In fact, he wanted to turn back the pages of history, and fight the First World War over again. Its results should be redressed by force whatever the costs might be. The links beween the First and the Second World Wars are obvious; they do not require to be accounted for here in detail. This time the war was to be conducted as a genuine "total war". It was to be ensured that those factors which allegedly had caused defeat, especially the "treachery" on the so-called "home front", would be cut out ruthlessly this time. Nor should Germany once again suffer from insufficient weaponry and war material. This required not only a systematic policy of rearmament, and of restructuring industry in regard to potential war production, but also a regimentation of the work force.

Although in the first years of his rule Hitler publicly paraded as a peace-loving statesman who wanted a reform of the "Versailles system" by peaceful means, he in fact acted upon the assumption that his essential objectives could only be obtained by means of a world war, and a war of gigantic proportions for that matter. In hindsight it is frightening to see how Germany was systematically brought into gear in order to be able to conduct such a war. The traditional elites undoubtedly welcomed Hitler's plans to overthrow the Versailles system; but many among them, notably in the military establishment, were soon frightened by the pace and radicality with which Hitler pursued his war plans without much regard for the limitations of German power. But it is typical that they were no longer capable, let alone willing, to step in his way; all internal opposition was soon silenced.

It would certainly be misleading to interpret the aggressive nature of National Socialism only as a continuation of Wilhelmine power politics. Rather, one could argue that as a consequence of the developments during the First World War and its aftermath German politics went off the rails altogether. The potential forces of resistance to the extremist policies of National Socialism had been weakened to such a degree, morally and ideologically, that it proved impossible to put up effective resistance to Hitler's plans. The class-ridden policies of the 1920s had also resulted in a fatal political weakening of the working classes and their political representation. The bitter rivalry between the Social Democratic and the Communist parties during the 1920s had in effect immobilized them politically; in 1933 they were unable to combat National Socialism effectively. Soon they were brutally suppressed and their illegal organizations smashed by the Gestapo.

The consequences were far-reaching. The National Socialist attempts at mobilizing a maximum of political, social, and economic resources for the great encounter with the West which Hitler planned for 1942 or 1943 but which then came about unexpectedly already in September 1939, resulted in massive distortions in all sectors of German society. In a way, the whole fabric of German society was restructured in the service of the nascent war economy in order to bring about a maximum of readiness for war, regardless of the negative long-term consequences for the economy. This trend of affairs was obviously intensified after the outbreak of war. On the other hand, the strains to which German society were exposed by the exigencies of the war economy were somewhat softened by the systematic exploitation of the occupied countries and territories· which had to supply not only goods and raw materials of all sorts, in particular agricultural products, but also a large work force in order to keep the depleted war industries inside Germany going.

It can be shown that the attempts to conduct the war in an ever more total form were self-defeating in the end, as they eventually led to a far-reaching decomposition of the social fabric and resulted in chaotic conditions. By 1944 the National Socialist command economy was on the verge of collapse, and Speer now allowed the industrial managers to organize things on a market-oriented base once again. More important was it that the political order itself was geared to bring about its eventual self-destruction. The gradual undermining of the remnants of all traditional state authority and of a rational legal system by a plurality of competing agencies respectively a "Sonderführer" was bound to end in utter confusion and the waste of scarce resources. In fact, Darwinian legitimacy ended in permanent internecine strife and increasing public disorder. Besides, it further accelerated the radicalization of the political system without regard to the availability of manpower or of material resources, let alone the steadily worsening military situation.

The eventual military defeat and the collapse of the National Socialist regime in May 1945 left Germany and vast tracts of Europe in ruins. Likewise, the intellectual and moral traditions of German society had been compromised severely. It was difficult to imagine how the Germans could ever recover from this catastrophe again. The loss of the territories in the East, the expatriation of about 11 million Germans from East-Central and South-east Europe, the occupation of the country by the victorious powers followed by the loss of national unity were the logical, and seemingly irreversible consequences of the momentous attempts of National Socialism to reverse the results of the First World War by a gigantic war effort and to establish themselves as the masters of continental Europe for the foreseeable future.

It is perhaps worthwhile to contras the far-reaching plans of the National Socialist regime with the idea of a Europe of democratic nation states associated in the European Union which we are about to establish. Hitler's idea of Europe would have meant establishing a firm system of domination by the Teutonic master race throughout the continent; this would indeed have provided a peace of sorts, and stability in internal and international affairs alike, thanks to force and suppression of all elements of resistance throughout Europe, with the cooperation of the Fascist movements in other countries. These policies were geared to violence on a scale hitherto unknown in history, notably the physical destruction of vast numbers of peoples, Jewish or otherwise, which were believed to stand in the way of National Socialist domination over Central

Europe. The new European order by which the National Socialists wanted to supplant the bourgeois-democratic order all over Europe might have brought peace, but this would have been a peace achieved over the graves of millions of peoples, and it would have been devoid of any legitimacy whatsoever.

After the Catastrophe: The Emergence of a Democratic Polity in Germany after 1945

It is difficult to imagine that this National Socialist imperium could have survived for long, even given the unlikely possibility that Germany and her allies might have won the war. In the end, the military defeat of National Socialist Germany left behind a devastated country and many millions of dead and mutilated people throughout Europe. The attempt to reverse the course of history since 1914 had ended in a catastrophe of gigantic proportions. This time the Germans were prepared to accept defeat, and they realized that they would have a political future only if they broke radically with their past. The authoritarian and Social-Darwinist notions of legitimacy which had played such a substantial role in past decades had now been discredited once and for all. Likewise the dream of German great-power politics was over. Now for the first time the Germans were prepared to accept voluntarily the principles of democratic legitimacy without reservations as a guideline for their future political orientation.

The story of the two successor states of Imperial Germany which emerged from the ashes that National Socialism had left behind is strictly speaking not a subject of this essay. There cannot be any doubt whatsoever that the period of German great-power policies lies behind us for good. The reunited Germany that has become the strongest economic system in Europe is not likely ever to harbour any such grand designs as those which fascinated their fathers and grandfathers. Rather the contrary is the case, namely the willing acceptance of the basic fact that the Federal Republic of Germany is, at the most, a medium power ("eine Mittelmacht"), which is determined to act in international affairs always in conjunction with her allies. The linkages with the past have not been broken altogether. But it would appear that Germany now stands firmly in the Western camp. She has accepted the value principles of constitutional democracy and is an active member of the CSCE. There is no reason to believe that this will change in any way in the foreseeable future. Democratic legitimacy has visibly brought stability and

peace to the Germans, and they are not likely to throw it ligh-heart-
edly away again.

References

Hirschfeld, Gerhard and Lothar Kettenacker, eds. *Der "Führerstaat": Mythos und Realität*, with an introduction by Wolfgang J. Mommsen (Stuttgart: Klett-Cotta 1981).

Kershaw, Ian. *The Nazi Dictatorship. Problems and Perspectives of Interpretation* (London: Edward Arnold 1985).

Kielmannsegg, Peter Graf, ed. *Legitimitätsprobleme politischer Systeme, Politische Vierteiljahrsschrift*, Special volume 1976.

Kielmannsegg, Peter Graf and Ulrich Matz, eds. *Die Rechtfertigung politischer Herrschaft* (München: Alber 1978).

Lepsius, Rainer M. "Das Modell der charismatischen Herrschaft und seine Anwendbarkeit auf den "Führerstaat" Adolf Hitlers", in Rainer M. Lepsius, *Demokratie in Deutschland. Soziologisch-historische Konstellationsanalysen. Ausgewählte Aufsätze*, (Göttingen: Vandenhoeck & Ruprecht 1993), p. 95ff.

Mommsen, Wolfgang J. *Das Ringen um den nationalen Staat. Die Gründung und der innere Ausbau des Deutschen Reiches unter Otto von Bismarck* (Berlin: Propylen 1993).

von Rotteck, Karl. "Legitimität", in Rotteck/Welcker, *Staatslexikon*, 2. edition, Vol. 8, 1847.

von Srbik, Heinrich Ritter. *Metternich. Der Staatsmann und der Mensch*, Vol. 1 (München: F.Bruckmann 1925).

Weber, Max. "Die drei reinen Typen legitimer Herrschaft", in Weber, *Wirtschaft und Gesellschaft*, 5th edition (Tübingen: Mohr 1972), pp. 122–176.

Winkler, Heinrich August. *Weimar 1918–1933. Die Geschichte der ersten deutschen Demokratie* (München: Beck 1993).

Württemberger, Thomas. *Die Legitimität staatlicher Herrschaft. Eine staatsrechtlich-politische Begriffsgeschichte* (Berlin: Dunker und Humbolt 1973).

6

The Fall of Empires –
Russia and the Soviet Union

Alec Nove

We can say that the empire fell twice: in 1917, and again in 1991. So it seems appropriate to devote some space to the rise and fall of the tsarist as well as of the Soviet state. The Bolshevik revolution had as its avowed object the destruction of the empire, yet already under Lenin it was in the process of being resurrected under another name and with a very different ideology: Stalin could be seen as a successor of modernizing tsar-autocrats. So one has to go back in time, to place the collapse of 1991 in a much older historical context. Did both "falls" have similar causes? What was the contribution, in each instance, of nationalist centrifugal forces? Or were other forces predominant?

Veliki Petr byl pervy bol'shevik, "Peter the Great was the first Bolshevik", wrote the poet Voloshin. "Peter's methods were purely Bolshevik", wrote the eminent philosopher, Nikolay Berdyaev. The economic historian, Alexander Gerschenkron, expressed a similar view. Furthermore, Stalin himself would have agreed, since he instructed his court historians to consign the theories of the marxist Polrovsky to the dustbin and to treat Peter as one of his great predecessors.

So what collapsed in 1991 could be regarded as the empire founded by Peter, the first Emperor. It is a paradox that his city has again been called St. Petersburg, at the very time that the empire he had founded fell to pieces. Peter, it will be recalled, occupied what are now Estonia and Latvia, and defeated Charles XII at Poltava, now in independent Ukraine.

The Rise and Fall of the Russian Empire

The map at the back of Platonov's history of Russia, a standard textbook in 1917, shows in colour the territorial acquisitions of various tsars, illustrating how the Grand Duchy of Muscovy expanded from small beginnings in the period of the Tartar conquest. Under Ivan the Terrible, Kazan and Astrakhan were added; the conquest of (largely empty) Siberia was begun. But to the West, what are now Ukraine and Belarus formed part of a powerful Polish–Lithuanian kingdom, which threw back Ivan's forces. Constant wars in the seventeenth century led to the gradual incorporation of the eastern half of today's Ukraine. More was acquired under Catherine, in the partitions of Poland, while wars with Turkey resulted in the occupation of the Crimea. Georgia and Armenia accepted rule from St. Petersburg as a protection from Islamic neighbours, while the northern half of Azerbaijan was acquired after a war with Persia (1829). Finland was taken from Sweden in 1809. The mountaineers of the Caucasus proved a hard nut to crack, and military campaigns against the Chechen, Cherkess, and other warlike tribes paralleled British operations on the North-West frontier of India. To Britain's alarm, the second half of the nineteenth century saw Russia's expansion into Turkestan, to the borders of Afghanistan. The 1913 Baedeker tells us that any foreign visitors to Turkestan had to give six months' notice to the Russian embassy, and, on arrival, had to present themselves to the Russian resident ("dress clothes obligatory"). Finally, pressure on China resulted in the acquisition of the Maritime province, whose chief city is Vladivostok.

The great land-based empire, covering a sixth of the world's land surface, contained, by 1900, a mass of nationalities, whose level of development, degree of national consciousness, and attitudes to the imperial power differed widely, as could be seen by what happened when the tsarist empire collapsed, and, indeed, after 1991, too. A full analysis would require a book, not an essay. But the following can and should be distinguished (the distinctions still matter today).

1. *Small nations in the Eurasian land-mass*, some partly assimilated, with Russians often a majority in their ethnic territories. Examples: Maryi, Karelians, Udmurt, Volga-Tartars, Malmucks, Buryats, Bashkirs, Yakuts. Fully incorporated in the tsarist imperial system, these and other nationalities were given special status (as autonomous republics) in the Soviet Union.

2. *The Central Asians ('Turkestan')*, (Uzbeks, Tajiks, Turkmen, Kirghiz). Each had a sizable population of Russian settlers, but retained strong national and religious traditions. In 1916, an attempt to conscript native men led to open rebellion. The Soviets had to use troops to reimpose order in and after the civil war. They replaced native Khans by selected native first-secretaries of the party, though the second secretary was almost always Russian.

3. *Transcaucasia*. Georgia, Armenia, and Azerbaijan declared their independence in 1918, as soon as the centre seemed to have broken down. Moscow imposed its authority by stages, the last act being the invasion of Georgia in 1921. An attempt to create a Transcaucasian federation of the three republics proved unsuccessful. They were and are deeply distrustful of one another. Georgia contains other nationalities, one of which (the Abkhaz) is now rebelling against Tbilisi. Armenia and Azerbaijan are at war with each other.

4. *The Balts*. Estonia and Latvia had been dominated by German descendants of the Teutonic knights. Successive emperors used the services of these Baltic Germans in high military and civilian posts, but also played them off against the "natives" in a classic *divide et impera* procedure. Lithuania's rulers had become Polonized; the towns were largely Jewish. (Today's capital, Vilnius, was under Poland from 1921 to 1939.) All three were independent states between the wars but were re-annexed under the Molotov-Ribbentrop pact. The Germans departed, and the Jews were massacred in 1941–42. Many Russians moved in after the war.

5. *Ukraine and Belarus*, fellow Slavs, were a special case. Russian history and legend locate the foundation of Russian statehood in the Grand Duchy of Kiev, which was destroyed by the Tartars in the thirteenth century. Russians regarded Kiev as "the mother of Russian cities", and Ukrainians as "Little Russians" (*Malorossy*). Before 1914, the cities were predominantly Russian and Jewish. Ukrainian culture and language were suppressed; the native poet, Shevchenko, was jailed. Nationalism grew in the western Ukraine, especially in Galicia, which was then part of the Austrian empire. Ukraine declared independence amid the confusion of civil war, but was finally retaken by the Soviets in 1920. Between the wars, western Ukraine and western Belorussia were part of Poland.

What is now *Kazakhstan* did not then exist under that name. Its northern half was part of Siberia; its south was labelled "Kirgiz" on maps. Half of the population of today's Kazakhstan is Russian.

Finland was given special status within the empire as a "Grand Duchy", with its own currency and constitution (with an elected legislature). Russian Poland (1815–1914) saw major rebellions in 1830 and 1863, but that is a separate story.

On what foundations did the tsars base their imperial ideas?

Every tsar sought, with varying degrees of success, to expand the empire, stopping only when encountering superior force, as Nicholas II found when the Japanese gave his armies a bloody nose in Manchuria and sank his fleet at Tsushima. Perhaps aggrandisement, the imperial equivalent of profit maximization for a business firm? It used to be said that the cossack will acquire anything carelessly put away. However, the British empire, too, expanded through the nineteenth century. If Russia's seizure of adjoining territories such as the Crimea or Turkestan needed explaining, what of Britain's acquisition of Burma or Guyana? However, it would seem the Russian empire's successor, the USSR, retained the old habits. Red cossacks still tried to acquire whatever was carelessly put away – but in the name of a very different ideology.

It is noteworthy that men rose in the tsar's service almost regardless of their ethnicity if they spoke Russian and were loyal servants. In this there was a resemblance both to the Habsburg empire and to the Soviet *nomenklatura*. There was an important linguistic distinction, which still exists, between *Russki* and *Rossyiski*, which (almost) parallels the distinction between English and British. It was not *Russkaya imperiya* but *Rossiyskaya imperiya*; the emperor was *Vserossiyski*, usually mistranslated as "of all the Russias". Today, too, since Russia, despite territorial losses, still contains many dozens of nationalities, one finds Yeltsin speaking of the citizens not as *Russkiye* but *Rossiyane*. Just as the British (not "English") army was frequently commanded by Scottish or Irish generals, so, in 1812, one Russian army was commanded by Bagration, a Georgian, the other by a man of Scottish descent, Barclay. Ukrainian names abounded, as did Baltic German. The one exception, treated as aliens (*inorodtsy*), were the Jews. Anyone, ethnic Russian or not, who was promoted above a given rank in the civil or military service became a hereditary gentleman or service-noble (*drovyanin*). (Lenin was one because of his father's rank.) However, in contrast to subsequent Soviet policy, the empire established no national administrative sub-units, except for Finland and Turkestan (and Poland before 1863), and repressed local nationalists. The attitude to Ukraine was similar to that of Franco to Catalonia.

Genuine or forced allegiance to the Tsar-Emperor held the structure together. And as Theodore von Laue pointed out, the structure was at all times threatened by internal weakness: imperial ambitions and economic backwardness were in contradiction. Enormous spaces supported a sparse and poor population. Catherine II's Russia in the second half of the eighteenth century had a population similar to that of France. Open frontiers provided both opportunity and danger. Thus, in 1571, Tartar slave raiders reached Moscow, which in 1610–11 was occupied by the Poles. Serfdom came late, when it was already obsolete in the West: otherwise peasants would flee to the empty eastern borderlands and escape taxes and service obligations which sustained the tsar's army and the civil service. Peter used serf labour on a large scale. As V. Grossman pointed out, "Europeanization" coexisted with slavery, with mass mobilization imposed from above.

However, especially in the long reign of Nicholas I, the Russian aristocratic system found itself unable to create the preconditions for the industrial revolution. Serfdom remained. Nicholas's ministers were suspicious of railways – they permitted people to move around of their own volition. The officers who had seen the West in 1815 became bearers of new and subversive ideas, and the "Decembrist" conspiracy of 1825 showed the autocrat the consequences of allowing these subversive ideas to circulate. Even the gentry were strictly policed: the great poet, Pushkin, was never allowed to travel to "Europe". (A parallel has been noted with Stalin's repressive measures in 1946–48, since many Russian officers and soldiers had seen what life in the West was like as a result of victory in war.) The imperial reactionaries faced a contradiction: if Russia was to be a great military power Western technology and education was essential, but this could create an alienated educated stratum, which could present a political danger. However, Stalin both needed Western technology and feared the impact of Western ideas. The shock of defeat in the Crimean War (1853–55), when Russia had no steam warships and no railway south of Moscow, contributed to the death of Nicholas I and to an era of reform, which some observers likened to Gorbachev's *perestroika*. Even the term *glasnost* was used. And Cheryshovsky, a rebellious intellectual, remarked: "*Glasnost*, gentlemen, is a bureaucratic term, a substitute for freedom of speech". But, unlike under Gorbachev, censorship was maintained, as was the autocratic principle. And when Alexander II was blown up by a terrorist bomb, his successor took some steps backwards, resisting all calls for a constitution, as did *his* successor, Nicholas II, on his accession.

What caused the empire to collapse? And how was it resurrected in a new guise? I disagree with Richard Pipes, who writes: "Nothing in the early twentieth century pushed the country towards revolution except the presence of an unusually large and fanatical body of professional revolutionaries".[1] Of course, there *was* such a body, but it would have been crying in the wilderness in the absence of other elements making for the disintegration of the imperial system. These elements were much written about *before* the event.

First, *the peasants*. Freed from serfdom, granted a part of the land but anxious to seize the rest, restricted until the Stolypin reforms of 1906–11 to communal forms of land tenure, they were revolutionary material which was proved in the riots and land seizures in 1905–06 and 1917–18. Stolypin had the imagination to see that a strong landowning peasantry could become a conservative force and save tsardom, but his reforms came late, were interrupted by World War I, and were largely undone in 1917–18 by the peasants themselves. It is worth recalling that peasant revolts in the seventeenth century and the Pugachev rebellion in the eighteenth, showed them to be capable of extremes of violence.

Second, many *workers*, mostly of recent peasant origin, who were concentrated in the big industrial centres, poorly paid, and housed and rootless, were ready, as in 1905, for highly politicized strike action. The boom in industrialization begun in the 1890s, and facilitated by the policies of Witte, had many positive features, but inevitably caused social strains. The growth of Western-style capitalism produces a backlash, which can be both revolutionary and conservative at the same time: one thinks of the Ayatollah in Iran.

Third, even those *intellectuals* who were not Pipes' professional revolutionaries were, by and large, against Western mercantile values. Herzen, usually considered a "Westerner", saw much to disgust him in western bourgeois society. The slavophils' aversion to these values is well known. Such great and influential writers as Tolstoy and Dostoevsky were also out of sympathy with West European notions of legal order and free markets.

Fourth, the *autocracy* and its methods conflicted with the needs of a modern industrial power. It is interesting to compare the Russian empire after 1861 with the Japanese empire after 1867. While both gave priority to military power, the Japanese were far more radical in changing the class and educational systems, and when the two empires collided in 1904–05, the blow to tsardom, its reputation among its own people and its confidence in itself, contributed to the spread of revolutionary sentiments. One must add that, in an autocracy, much depends on the autocrat, and Nicholas II, in obstructing constitutional change, was not suited to the role. The contrast with Japan was noted at that time. Thus, in the preface to a book published in London in 1904, one finds this sentence: "Whereas Japan has incontestably proved that she is emerging from the darkness of centuries, Russia is content to remain in a state of semi-barbarism ...". And the author, writing even before the 1905 cataclysm, makes dire prophesies about an imminent breakdown.[2]

Finally, the rising *middle class*, or bourgeoisie, kept by the tsarist bureaucracy from power and responsibility, and understandably fearful of revolution from below, provided no alternative basis for political power. To cite Hugh Seton-Watson: "The demand for a free society, based on civil liberties, representative institutions and due process of law was ineffective because the social forces which supported it were too weak".[3]

All this was an explosive mixture. Already in 1884, according to the memoirs of the future German chancellor, von Bülow, the then tsarist minister of education told him: "Attempts to introduce western parliamentarianism in Russia will fail. If tsarism is overthrown, in its place will come communism, the fully fledged communism of Herr Marx, who died in London last year".[4]

And in the symposium, *Yekhi* ("Milestones"), published in 1909, M. Gerschenzon expressed the despair of would-be liberals caught between autocracy and the dark "masses": "Such as we are, we cannot dare to hope to join with the people – we must fear them more than any state power, and we must bless that power, which with its bayonets and prisons still protects us from the people's wrath".[5] (*Pace* Pipes – no such "wrath", no revolution!) There was also a vast gap separating the radical intelligentsia from the "dark masses", but that is another and tragic story.

The professional revolutionaries operated in a fertile soil. Then came World War I, which showed up the weaknesses of the Russian government, the military, and the economy. No one doubts that the war was the immediate cause of collapse of the empire, but there were clearly other and more long-term causes at work. It is not enough to attribute the end of the empire to defeats at the front and hardships at the rear, though they were a reality. In 1941–42 the defects were greater, and the hardships of civilians far greater than in 1917, but Stalin's Soviet Union did not come to an end. The tsar's government fell a victim to its own paralysis.

Missing from the above list of "actors" are the nationalities. They are missing because, though there were certainly nationalist movements growing in many parts of the empire, they did not, in fact, play any decisive role in the disintegration of the empire. Except in Poland, the 1905 revolution was *not* notable for nationalistic uprisings, or else they were sidetracked, as in the Ukraine, into anti-Jewish pogroms. Nationalisms took advantage of the collapse, filled the power vacuum, but cannot be seen as a major cause of the fall of tsarism.

But once the Tsar abdicated, authority dissolved. The Duma, elected on a highly restricted franchise, faded rapidly from the scene. The provisional government coexisted uneasily with the Soviets, in a situation reminiscent of Yeltsin's stand-off with the legislature today. "Dual power" meant no power. The government lacked legitimacy *vis-à-vis* the Russian people as well as in relation to increasingly restive nationalities. It is most instructive to compare the increasingly strident claims from the Ukrainians in 1917, first for autonomy, then for independence, with what happened in 1991. There are many parallels. Kerensky faced demands from Kiev very similar to those faced seventy-four years later by Gorbachev.

With the war still raging, and with a disaffected peasantry eager to seize land, the provisional government was plainly unable to govern. Could a military dictator, such as General Kornilov, have done better? We shall never know. Plainly, while traditional allegiance to *Tsar-batyushka* was no longer capable of commanding the obedience even of Russians, where was the alternative source of authority? A constitutional assembly? But when the Bolsheviks, soon after they seized power, sent it packing, the masses remained indifferent. There was no basis of legitimacy.

The Soviet Union and the Nationality Question

Breakdown led, as we have noted, to the creation of many independent republics. Finland and the Baltic states held on to their independent status after 1919, though in many instances with the help of foreign troops, such as the German *Freikorps*. (Latvian riflemen were among the more reliable elements in the Red Army.) The rest of the empire was back under Bolshevik control by 1921. The history of the civil war is not our subject. But a few words are necessary about the way in which the empire was restored in a new guise, with a very different nationalities' theory to underpin it. It should be recalled that Stalin wrote his first major work on this very question, that he was the first commissar for nationalities, *and* that he was a Georgian.

For Lenin, the empire had been a "prison of the peoples". He could see local nationalisms as a weapon of disruption, just as he believed in "workers' control" and in loosening military discipline so long as he was not in power. But as soon as power had been won, he soon converted to one-man management and strict obedience to military commanders, and to the subordination of the nationalities to the general 'Soviet' interest, as seen by the party leadership in Moscow. While eloquent in his denunciation of "Great-Russian chauvinism", he was committed to what he saw as proletarian internationalism, in the pursuit (then sincerely believed in) of world revolution. In each segment of the former empire, the aim was to set up a regime run by the local communist party, but this party would be a subordinate part of the communist movement, whose headquarters were Moscow. It was all lengthily discussed in the run-up to the creation of the USSR in 1922. Russia (itself a federal republic) and the other republics were nominally sovereign members of the new Union. This Union had no national element in its name, so that, as and when revolution spread, other countries could join.

In practice, given the principle of so-called democratic centralism, Moscow dominated the whole, and as early as 1923 Stalin earned the disapproval of the dying Lenin for the crudity of his actions in Georgia. But that same Lenin had ordered the Red Army into Georgia in 1921.

It would, however, be wrong simply to regard the USSR as a unitary state in disguise, though in some essential respects this is what it was. The creation of union and autonomous republics stimulated national consciousness. Internal passports labelled everyone by "nationality" (the tsarist document mentioned only the estate – *sosloviye* – and religion). The leadership, though communist, could be said to have a dual role: to represent Moscow in their republics, but also the republics' interests in Moscow. Perhaps it was the suspicion that the latter was primary that led Stalin into a drastic and bloody purge. During the 1930s, almost *all* communist party secretaries and heads of the Soviet in *every* union and autonomous republic were shot. And after the war, the suspicion that a power centre was to be based in the Russian republic led to the so-called Leningrad affair and the last of Stalin's political massacres. After the Baltic republics and what had been Eastern Poland were taken over in 1939, hundreds of thousands were deported to Siberia. Also during, and just after, the war came the episode with the so-called "punished peoples": several autonomous republics (Crimean–Tartar, Kalmuck, Volga–German, Chechen, Balkar, etc.) were abolished and their inhabitants deported, including the party officials, supposedly because of wartime disloyalty. And Khrushchev subsequently expressed the view that Stalin would have ordered the deportation of Ukrainians, too, if there had not been so many of them.

So, at the end of the Stalin era, the nationalities were, so to speak, both self-conscious and conscious of the dangers of so being. To cite Tamara Dragadze, one had both "ethnicization of territory" and "the territorialization of ethnicity".[6] The union republics had sovereignty with the right to secession inscribed in their constitutions (the tsars would never have tolerated this!), but everyone knew that to take these rights seriously would lead to an involuntary journey north-eastwards, or worse. However, when Gorbachev's *glasnost* came, so did the demand that this right be made a reality. What seemed empty formalism took its revenge, and helped to destroy the Union.

Under Stalin, a gradual transformation of the real content of Soviet ideology had taken place. In its first years, it was militantly internationalist. In the 1930s, however, came a change. Stalin, himself Georgian, chose to present himself as a great *national* leader, and Russians emerged as more equal than others. History was rewritten. Ivan and Peter became great rulers of a mighty Russian state, while fighters for national freedom against the Russians, such as Shamyl in the Caucasus, once seen as positive figures, were turned into traitorous agents of foreign imperialists. Bolshevism, as Vasili Grossman noted in his great novel, *Life and Fate*, turned into national Bolshevism. While it was all supposed to be *Soviet* patriotism, in fact it was the Russian idea, and Russian officers and officials who dominated. Non-Russians in the top leadership (Stalin himself, Beria, Mikoyan, Kaganovich) acted as if they were Russian nationalists.

Every effort was made to prevent "infection" from fellow-nationals or co-religionists abroad. Two examples: The first relates to the alphabet used in Central Asia. Initially, it was switched from Arabic to Latin but when the Turks converted from Arabic to Latin, orders went out to switch to Cyrillic. The second example is the anti-semitic campaign, which intensified with the creation of the state of Israel.

The war brought to the fore patriotic symbols, with Stalin quoting Alexander Nevsky, Suvorov, Kutuzov, and reintroducing tsarist uniforms and ranks. Victory in war not only strengthened the regime, but also brought into the Soviet orbit a number of formerly independent countries. By the time of Stalin's death, the empire could be said to include Poland, Hungary, East Germany, Czechoslovakia, Romania, Bulgaria (but no longer Yugoslavia), all ruled by communists appointed by Moscow. (China was a special case). In 1952, Czechoslovakia could be said to be no more "sovereign" than Ukraine or Latvia. Stalin's rejection of Tito's Yugoslavia, his successor's rejection of Mao's China, proved that subordination to Moscow, rather than commitment to socialism-communism, was the determining factor in its acceptance or non-acceptance.

Success in war provided opportunities for expansion. The motives, clothed in communist phrases as they were, could well have been appreciated by a tsarist foreign minister. Control over Poland was an aim of Russian policy already in Catherine's time, and, before the partitions, she saw to it that one of her lovers be "elected" king. Stalin could not do that, but he sent one of his marshals, Rokossovsky, to command the Polish army.

So, what held the Soviet empire together? Force, certainly, but, as Talleyrand said long ago, one cannot indefinitely sit on bayonets. Thus, the Czech and Romanian party comrades obeyed not just because they feared the consequences of not doing so, but because at that time they believed in Moscow and in Stalin, in the ultimate triumph of communism, or in the linking of their careers with those who seemed to them most likely to win. In the Soviet Union itself there was surely not only fear, but also enthusiasm and commitment, even a belief in the necessity of fear. ("How can one tolerate a situation when the government is more frightened of the people than the people are of the government?" remarked a puzzled citizen at the beginning of *perestroika*.)

Organizationally, the role once played by the tsarist bureaucracy, *Okhrana* and the army, was played by the party, whose full-time functionaries ruled, although under Stalin they had reason to fear for their lives. There was, it is true, a vast gap between what doctrine asserted and what actually existed. Who actually believed in the formal ideology which everyone had to profess? Any regime requires at the very least the loyalty of its officialdom, the *nomenklatura*, and the acceptance (maybe with mixed feelings, but acceptance nonetheless) of the legitimacy of the regime by a sizable fragment of its citizenry. The rulers must feel that they have the right to rule. Under Stalin, many trembled and obeyed. But, after the execution of Beria and his associates, physical terror was no more. In the outlying parts of the empire, in Hungary in 1956, blood did flow. But by 1968, when Czechoslovakia was invaded, there were no executions, and the "normalization" that followed was, by past standards, a velvet repression, followed, as we know, by a velvet revolution.

The Fall of the Soviet Empire

So we finally come to the stages by which the Soviet empire dissolved. It was, as this chapter emphasizes, a second dissolution. An empire existed, an empire collapsed; a new empire was created with new slogans and an allegedly totally new ideology. It has collapsed in its turn.

There is a phrase of Lenin's which even his worst enemies accept as valid. Collapse, revolution, occur when the rulers can no longer rule in the old way, and the people no longer obey in the old way. Just as many of the Tsars' officials had lost confidence in their own functions by 1917, a similar process can be traced in Russia and its empire after the 1950s. It cannot be "documented"; these things are of their nature based on circumstantial evidence. One element in the process can be blamed on Stalin: he not only destroyed anyone with original ideas near the seats of power, he also killed most of the genuine believers. To be a Bolshevik intellectual in the 1930s was a most dangerous occupation. Most of them perished. They were replaced by upwardly mobile men of the people, the *Vydvizhentsy*, the promoted ones, among whom many soon became time-servers and careerists. Khrushchev seems to have retained genuine beliefs, but the long reign of Brezhnev was a period that must be seen as one of petrification, or decay. Brezhnev himself surely had no interest in, or commitment, to marxism-leninism other than as a convenient catechism, or as a card-index of appropriate quotations.

Expansionism was now rendered dangerous by the existence of nuclear weapons. The so-called "Brezhnev doctrine" was: what we have, we hold. One could say that there was also an "internal" Brezhnev doctrine: high officialdom shall hold on to power and the privileges that go with *nomenklatura* status. As for the people, many observers imagined the existence of a species of social contract: job security and low prices of necessities with no longer any serious fear of arrest unless one acted to challenge the monopoly of the power-apparatus, and toleration of modest work effort. Until the mid-1970s, living standards did show an upward trend. Life was intellectually dreary, but normal and calm. Asked at this very time what he thought about it, Molotov replied: *Esli spokoino zhivetsa, bolsheviki ne nuzhny*. "If life is calm and normal, Bolsheviks are not needed".[7] The formal ideology seems unchanged, but gradually such life as it had, was extinguished. Cynicism spread, so did corruption. The empire outside the Soviet Union's borders was also affected, though in different ways. The Ceausescu-despotism in Romania consciously ignored Moscow. Few indeed in Czechoslovakia after 1968, or in Poland after 1956, believed in Moscow any more, although they retained a healthy respect for the Soviet army. The same was true in Hungary, even among those who remained party members.

To this mixture was added a sense of economic failure. Not only was the USSR not "catching up and overtaking", as Khrushchev had hoped and forecast, it was falling further behind. The scientific-technical and informational revolutions provided challenges which the centralized and bureaucratized planning system was incapable of meeting. It was appreciated that change had to come. Even Brezhnev himself declared, to the Twenty-fourth Party Congress, that "in an age of scientific-technical revolution a fundamental change in our methods of management is essential" – but reforms all proved to be timid and the "basis" of the system remained unaltered. Growth slowed. Expectations were disappointed. In Hungary, the early promise of the 1968 reforms, which enacted a species of market socialism, turned into stagnation and even decline after the mid-1970s. In Poland, an unsound boom under Gierek in 1971–75 was followed by crisis, which gave birth to *Solidarność* and a series of political shocks. In the USSR, the chronic troubles of agriculture led, in the 1970s, to a very large increase in investments and in subsidies, but, as the disappointing production statistics bear witness, these large sums were largely wasted on grandiose and unsound projects.

Superimposed on all this was the arms race. At the time of the Cuban missile crisis, the USSR was plainly very far behind the United States, both in numbers of nuclear weapons and in the means of delivery. Under Brezhnev, efforts were made to catch up, efforts the cost of which were hidden by statistical juggling (the defence budget as published covered at most a quarter, perhaps a sixth, of real expenditures). When Reagan speeded up the American arms programme the strain on the much weaker Soviet economy correspondingly increased. I do not subscribe to the simple view that Reagan "won" the cold war by doubling US arms spending. But it was a factor, among others, in explaining the stagnation of the Soviet economy after the mid-1970s.

Interestingly, Robin Matthews, of Oxford, in a recent lecture noted that the Western economies, too, suffered a marked slow-down after the mid-1970s, and wondered if there were not some common causes.[8] I doubt whether there were, but it is as well to be reminded of the fact that we have had problems too, and still have. Also, it is worth noting that, after 1989–90, production fell steeply in the "East", and that many Russians and Ukrainians look back upon Brezhnev's time as a comparative golden age. Then they (or most of them) could afford to purchase many goods and services, if they could find them (the bottleneck was supply), whereas now choice is far wider but few can afford to buy. There is no known way to compare the two situations. Price and wage indices can be misleading if there is a major change in availability and accessibility. But most do feel poorer.

There was enough evidence, by 1985, to justify a number of observers, including this one, speaking of "a crisis of system", a crisis of confidence, deeply affecting the ruling stratum itself.

We know this from subsequent declarations by Gorbachev, from the fact that it was he who was elected General Secretary, and from plenty of other evidence which appeared when *glasnost* allowed full freedom of expression. Perhaps typical of the time was N. Shmelev's statement, which Gorbachev accepted as a true picture:

> It is essential to realize that the cause of our difficulties is not only and not solely due to the heavy burden of military expenditures and the very expensive global responsibilities of our country. If we expended them correctly, even the remaining resources would be sufficient for maintaining a balanced and technically progressive economy and for satisfying the traditionally modest needs of our population. However, prolonged attempts to break up the objective laws of economic life, to suppress the age-long natural stimuli for human labour, brought about results quite different from what was intended. Today we have an economy characterized by shortage, imbalances, in many respects unmanageable, and, if we were to be honest, an economy almost unplannable... We have one of the lowest levels of labour productivity of any industrial nation, especially in agriculture and in construction, since through the years of stagnation the working masses have reached a state of almost total disinterestedness in freely-committed and honest labour...
>
> Apathy, indifference, thieving... have become mass phenomena, with, at the same time, aggressive envy towards high earners. There have appeared signs of a sort of physical degradation of a sizable part of our population, through drunkenness and idleness. Finally, there is a lack of belief in the officially announced objectives and purposes, in the very possibility of a more rational economic and social organization of life... Clearly all this cannot be swiftly overcome – years, maybe generations, will be needed.[9]

In *Novyi mir*, there also appeared an article by Khanin and Selyunin entitled *"Lukavaya tsifra"* ("Cunning Figures"). It was a species of time-bomb. The authors pointed out that the official indices, if chained, would show that Soviet national income grew 90-fold from 1928 to 1986. In their considered view, the real figure was between six- and seven-fold. This was surely the largest downward amendment in growth rates known in recorded history![10]

Some devastating criticisms of official statistics were published in *EKO* by the Leningrad economist, A. Illarionov. The official long-term growth rates were nonsensical: were they correct, the USSR's per capita GNP would now be 2.8 times higher than that of the United States. If the annual statistics are to be believed, the USSR reached 67 percent of the US national income in every year from 1975 to 1984, but this "fell" to 66 percent in 1985–86 and to 64 percent in 1987 – despite allegedly higher growth rates – so that "Achilles, though running faster than the tortoise, falls ever further behind". The national income growth figures in current and "un-changed" prices are in blatant contradiction – even to the official price index – and so "by publishing mythical growth tempos, the central statistical department continues to conceal the truth about economic stagnation". The USSR is falling further behind.

"Of the five largest economic centres of the world – USA, EEC, USSR, Japan, and China – our country has the lowest growth rates, in fact, close to zero. We are in a dramatic situation, which can have catastrophic consequences. Yet, because of prolonged, systematic statistical falsfication, our society is still not fully aware of the seriousness of the situation".

Housing space per capita is one third of US levels. In the number of cars per thousand inhabitants, the USSR is far behind Hungary and even Mexico. Grain harvest yields are among the lowest in the world, behind even Turkey, Pakistan, Brazil, and Mexico. "... Our agriculture has reached a state of total paralysis". Consumption of paper per capita is a small fraction of the countries of Western Europe, less even than Mexico and Chile. There are far fewer telephones per head than in Portugal and Yugoslavia. Per capita consumption of goods and services the author puts at 30 percent of US levels, because of a lower share of consumption and a higher share of military expenditures. So "we are at least a semi-developed country", in the same category as "Spain, Ireland, Venezuela, Greece, Uruguay, Argentina, Portugal, Chile, and Brazil".[11]

It was claimed that most Western recomputations had been over-favourable, and that, in fact, the USSR in 1985 was as far behind

America as the Russian empire had been in 1913! Meanwhile the denunciation of Stalin's crimes, begun partially under Khrushchev and silenced under Brezhnev, went further and further: numbers of victims, including peasant victims of the great famine, the scale of war losses (at least six times higher than those suffered by Russia in World War I), and so on. Travel to and from the West was eased, and more and more of the citizens could see how backward Russia was in many respects. Were all their sacrifices then in vain? How far were Lenin and Marx responsible? By 1989, it became possible publicly to question and even to denounce Lenin and Leninism, to stress the connection between Leninism and Stalinism, and Lenin's own ruthlessness. Solzhenitsyn's *Gulag Archipelago*, Koestler's *Darkness at Noon*, and the works of other long-banned critics and memoirists, appeared in profusion. The net effect was to undermine the legitimacy of the Soviet regime.

Glasnost meant real freedom also for the nationalities. They reacted to opportunities variously, depending on the intensity of national feeling. Thus, not surprisingly, the three Baltic republics were in the lead, pressing claims for real sovereignty, which turned into demands for independence. Then came the Georgians (whose real feelings I witnessed in 1956 when I was in Tbilisi in the aftermath of nationalism-inspired riots). Ukraine followed. The conflict between Armenia and Azerbaijan further weakened the Union. Attempts to impose order in the Baltic republics and in Georgia were half-hearted and had the effect of further strengthening nationalist opposition. So did the growth of economic difficulties, with growing shortages undermining the rouble and leading to the spread of inter-regional barter.

In retrospect, it is interesting to note that Gorbachev's reform programme was inhibited not only by the (very considerable) practical problems involved in fundamentally changing the principles upon which the economy functioned and by the fact that powerful interest groups resisted change, but also by a side-effect of the very democratization which was a key element in Gorbachev's strategy.

He hoped to rely on support from below in his struggle with the enemies of reform, for whom the word "market" was like a red rag to a bull. However, even a gradual move towards a real market economy was necessarily associated with higher prices and with a threat to job security, and neither was popular. Citizens wished to have plenty to buy in the shops, but at existing prices, and without too much work-discipline. The government did not feel able to challenge this implied social contract. This led to timidity: price rises for highly subsidized necessities kept being postponed, with disastrous effects on the state budget and in exacerbating shortages. In retrospect, it may seem paradoxical that, in 1990–91, Gorbachev did not dare to multiply three-fold the price of meat for fear of the consequences, since after his fall the price increased literally a hundredfold in the course of a year. But, by then, it was not the government that fixed the price. Anyhow, increasing economic difficulties were beyond doubt a major cause of political disintegration: why continue an association with failure?

Legitimacy, Peace, and Stability

However, a key element in the process of disintegration has yet to be given sufficient stress. This was the weakening of the communist party machine which, in practice, had run the Soviet Union for many decades. The Soviets had been little more than a facade. The party, centralized, ran the show and ensured that most orders were obeyed. Gorbachev faced a dilemma. He desired to convert the USSR into a democratic state with a large element of marketization, though he was admittedly confused and inconsistent about what steps to take and how far to go. (I have written elsewhere at length about the confusion and errors of his policy.) But one thing became clear: the domination of party functionaries was a major obstacle in the path of his reform programme. To give an example: in 1986–87, a campaign was launched against "unearned incomes", which local party officials interpreted as a signal to stop even legitimate forms of private enterprise, such as peasants growing tomatoes under glass. The legalization of even small-scale private firms, employing labour, was not achieved until as late as March 1991.

So Gorbachev sought to downgrade the role of party functionaries, bring life to the Soviets, and, in March 1989, actually held real elections with a genuine choice of candidates in the constituencies. Nationalists in the republics were now free to have their say. But all this gravely weakened the political structures on which the Soviet rule rested. Who would obey orders if the party functionaries no longer functioned? And, as we have seen, a number of them in the republics donned nationalist colours: thus Brazauskas in Lithuania already in 1989 began to claim that the party in that country was no longer subordinate to the central committee in Moscow.

As for the empire outside the USSR, once Gorbachev let it be known that the Soviets would no longer interfere, each went its own way at its own pace, away from Sovietism. Clearly, while the

Soviet regime grew on Soviet soil and had roots and antecedents in Russian history, it was (and was felt to be) an alien imposition in such countries as Poland, Hungary, Czechoslovakia, and East Germany. What was imposed by Soviet arms could not long subsist without them. Khrushchev in 1956 could see the necessity of armed intervention in Hungary; Brezhnev in 1968 in Czechoslovakia. But the ageing Brezhnev was less ready to act in Poland, where the situation was, from his point of view, far worse than it had been in Czechoslovakia (though Jaruzelski did find it necessary to declare martial law, albeit of a velvet kind). Gorbachev surely realized that his policy of non-intervention would be tantamount to withdrawal from these countries. *Why* did Gorbachev let them go? Surely, much like the British faced with demands from India, Nigeria and the rest, there was no longer any sense of having the right to dictate their form of government. In the name of what? Again, the gradual loss of the sense of legitimacy worked its way through, in Russia itself and on the periphery.

The words "legitimacy" and "ideology" give rise to confusion and misunderstanding. Thus, for Marx the word "ideology" had a pejorative meaning, as a kind of false consciousness, but in the Soviet Union the one "correct" and compulsory world-view, supposedly derived from Marx, was THE official ideology, and there was even an "ideological secretary" in the Party's central committee. (How much even the ideologists believed in it may be suggested by the fact that the man who was ideological secretary of the Ukrainian communist party, Leonid Kravchuk, found no great difficulty in 1991 in painting himself in the yellow-and-blue national colours and becoming president of the independent Ukraine.) The Party rested its claim to rule on being the heir to the October Revolution and on the task of "building Communism", guided by the "sure compass" of Marxism-Leninism. But it was no simple matter to define the role and nature of the ideology in the late Soviet period.

Some critics sought to deduce the "real" ideology of the regime from its actions. It repressed dissidents (and under Stalin killed them), it imposed strict censorship, suppressed free trade unions, and forced the peasants into pseudo-collectives: therefore THIS was their ideology. But this is a species of circular tautology: ideology is what they do, and what they do is due to the ideology. But Marx and, before he took power, Lenin, repeatedly said they were opposed to the death penalty, to censorship, and favoured freedom for workers and peasants. So, once the terror was over, the first challenges to legitimacy came from those who pointed to the gap between what was and what, according to the ideas of the founding fathers, should have been.

In practice, many, if not most, of the regime's policies can be explained by the interest of the ruling group in maintaining itself in power, and many problems arose from the contradiction between this and the needs of minimal economic efficiency: excesses of inefficiency also threatened loss of power. As for foreign policy, in many, if not most, instances it was the logic of great-power politics that counted, and these policies would have been understood by Tsar Alexander II's foreign minister, Gorchakov. Whether, during Brezhnev's long reign, he and his comrades believed in communism or in Marx, is open to grave doubt. But no doubt they believed in their right to rule, and were convinced that the alternative to a one-party state plus repression (mild by Stalinist standards) was disintegration.

Did the mass of the citizenry regard Soviet rule as legitimate? Plainly, in what used to be the "satellites" this was very dubious: there was acceptance, there being no alternative. There was more than that in Russia itself: even after Stalinist terror was just a memory, open dissidents were remarkably few. There was the traditional Russian fear of disorder, *bezporyadok*, fear of anarchy, the need felt for a strong state, and also some pride in the great-power status of the USSR (in reality of Russia). But Brezhnev remained at the top too long. The country came to be ruled by doddering geriatrics. When Gorbachev became leader, someone asked: "Has he support?" The reply came: "He does not need support, he can walk unaided".

Gorbachev was, of course, a younger and more energetic man. But *glasnost, demokratizatsiva* and economic reform constituted a revolution, maybe as great as Peter the Great's. Peter was an autocrat and a most severe taskmaster who could cut off heads with his own hands. Gorbachevian freedom opened the door to centrifugal forces.

Within the USSR, there were a variety of opinions concerning the scale and acceptability of disintegration. A few hard-liners believed in preserving the Union in its then existing boundaries. Some believed that the Balts had to be allowed to go, but the rest could continue in a looser federation. There were good grounds for supposing that Belarus, Kazakhstan (where ethnic Kazakhs are a minority), and Central Asia would wish to keep together, and the republics in the Caucasus may have been persuaded to go along, if only to avoid conflict with each other. But it was not to be. An important contributory factor in the collapse of the Union was the role chosen by Yeltsin, in his capacity as head of the *Russian* federal republic. In his battle against Gorbachev, he chose to stress republican and local sovereignties, and, following the failure of the putsch in August 1991 and Gorbachev's ouster, the so-called Commonwealth of Independent States has (so far) proved to have no political or economic meaning – other than to provide a team for the Olympic Games. There is neither a mechanism nor an ideology to hold it together.

It was noted earlier that the fall of the tsarist empire could not be attributed to centrifugal nationalisms. These came to the fore as a consequence, not as the cause, of the collapse of the central power. In the collapse of 1991, the nationality issue played a larger role than in 1917, but it was, in my view, only one factor among many. The collapse of the legitimacy of communist rule and of the party as ruler was primary. Since the nominally sovereign republics were in fact subordinated to Moscow through the centralized nature of the all-union communist party organs and their republican out-stations, the decline of party rule, even before the formal abolition of the party after the failed coup, has to be given pride of place among immediate causes. No tsar, no emperor, no empire. No party, no Union.

Sir William Hayter, former British ambassador to Moscow, wrote twenty years ago: "The Soviet rulers believe, and history provides little evidence to contradict this belief, that Russia can only be governed as an isolated autocracy". Plainly, applied to the USSR, this was also the belief of Stalin, and of Brezhnev, too. As they survey the wreck from wherever they are now, they would be saying: "We told you so". A similar view is held by T. von Laue: "Was there any chance of success for Gorbachev's reforms? Could the Soviet Union have been saved? Not according to the analysis here sketched. Gorbachev himself had repudiated the essentials of government in a united Eurasia: centralized control, protection of cultural sovereignty and the use of force as the ultimate guarantee of unity. Once the lid was taken off, even if slightly, the underlying traditional anarchic diversity reasserted itself, especially as economic conditions worsened".[12] It is hard to find reasons to quarrel with this verdict.

What consequences for peace and stability follow from the break-up of the Soviet empire? Russia's withdrawal from East-Central Europe seems final: there is no serious force in Russia with pretensions to intervene in Prague, Warsaw, or Budapest. There is, however, a pro-Serbian view among the nationalists, which could be a relevant factor if the Balkan tragedy continues. The same nationalists are inclined to support Iraq, and to criticize today's Russian foreign policy as being excessively pro-American.

More immediate and more serious is the strife on the periphery of the former Union: the war between Armenia and Azerbaijan, bitter fighting in Tadzhikistan, in Abkhazia, simmering problems in Moldova. There is the potentially dangerous dispute with Ukraine over the Crimea, Sevastopol, and the Black Sea fleet, which has already been made into political issue by Russian nationalists even of moderate hues, and this is doubtless a factor in Ukraine's unwillingness to relinquish nuclear weapons.

Is Russia trying to keep the peace in what was its empire, or is she fishing in troubled waters (and troubling them further) in the hope of reuniting much of that empire? Western observers are divided. By a remarkable coincidence, on the very same day two major British newspapers printed articles expressing totally opposed viewpoints: Geoffrey Hosking argued that "The West must let Yeltsin police the East" (*The Times*), and Jonathan Eyal that "Moscow's imperial memories linger" and that consequently the West should do no such thing (*The Independent*), both on 6 July 1993. My own view is that Russian policy is still in flux, pursuing both policies at once even though they are contradictory.

One of the unknowns is the treatment to be accorded to the (at least) 25 million Russians living outside the Russian federation. There is marked contrast between Ukraine, which emphasizes equal rights for all citizens regardless of ethnic origin, and Latvia and Estonia, which discriminate against Russians; while in some of the Islamic republics the considerable Russian minority feels in physical danger (thousands have fled). A harder-line Russian government may find in such circumstances a reason to intervene, with unpredictable consequences.

But there are also centrifugal forces within the Russian federation itself, and not just the national republics such as Tatarstan, claiming sovereignty (and the retention of oil revenues). Some purely Russian regions, such as the Far East, or Cossack areas, are claiming sovereignty too, and failure to cope with economic chaos can provide motives for a break-up, or for a new "Time of Troubles", paralleling that which followed the death of Boris Godunov. (Except that this time, unlike in 1610, Polish troops will not occupy the Kremlin.)

I do not know what will happen next: I have no crystal ball. The Archbishop of York has recently suggested that even God does not know the future. So what claim have I?

Notes

1. Richard Pipes, *The Russian Revolution* (London: Collins Harvill 1990) p. 122.
2. Hugo Ganz, *The Downfall of Russia* (London: Hodder and Stoughton 1904) p. 5.
3. Hugh Seton-Watson, *The Russian Empire, 1801–1917* (Oxford: Clarendon Press 1967) p.733.
4. As quoted by F. Dan, "Proiskhozhdenie bol'shevizma", *Novaya demokratiya* (New York: 1946) p.444. From Fürst von Bülow, *Denkwurdigkeiten, Vierter Band* (Berlin: Ullstein, 1930–1931) p. 573.
5. M. Gershenzon, "Tvorcheskoe samosoznanie", *Vekhi*, Moscow: 1909 p. 89.
6. Tamara Dragadze, "Soviet economics and nationalism", *Annali della Fondazione Feltrinelli*, 1992 pp. 77, 78.
7. Sto sorok besed s Molotovym, *Terra* Moscow: 1991 p. 312.
8. Robin C.O. Matthews, "Political and economic causes of the economic slowdown", *Scottish Journal of Political Economy*, May 1993 pp. 129 ff.
9. "Avansy i dolgi", *Novyi mir*, No. 6, 1987.
10. "Lukavaya tsifra", *Novyi mir*, No. 3, 1987.
11. A. Illarionov, "Ode my nakhodimsya?" *EKO*, No. 12, 1988, pp. 39–55.
12. Theodore von Laue, "Gorbachev's Place in History", *The Soviet and Post-Soviet Review*, Nos. 1–3, 1992, p. 273.

7

The Fall of the Soviet Union:
Peace, Stability, and Legitimacy

Alexandr O. Chubarian

The fall of the Soviet Union became the most important event of the second half of the twentieth century. The Soviet state collapsed so quickly and unexpectedly that its demise was a shock both for its own citizens and for the rest of the world. However, little time has expired since that event, and the processes created by the fall of the Soviet Union are still both contradictory and incomplete. For both these reasons it is difficult to present a general analysis of why and how the Soviet monolith – outwardly so stable and invulnerable – in the end collapsed.

A number of Western analysts have now started to use the term "the Soviet Empire" both for the form and for the period of Soviet rule. I believe it would be more appropriate to use the term Pax Sovietica. In this concept I include the striving of Soviet leaders to spread their model of political, economic, and ideological development to other parts of the world. In the post-war period this became a global strategy, envisaging the projection of a Soviet type of socialism not only in Europe, but also in Asia, Africa, and America. The heads of the Communist Party of the Soviet Union (CPSU) rejected any attempt by the leaders of other Communist parties and national liberation movements to come up with their own versions of socialism ("socialism with a human face," "Eurocommunism," etc.). In this global context the fall of the Pax Sovietica meant the fall of the Soviet economic, political, and ideological model, the final disappearance of the socialist idea as a globally attractive model for development and political action.

Pax Sovietica also referred to a certain territory. First, it referred to "the Socialist Commonwealth" in Eastern and South-eastern Europe, the areas which through the revolutions of 1989 broke away from Moscow's rule. Second, it described the far-flung territories of the Soviet state itself, a global region which now contains 15 independent and self-governing countries. For all these areas, the sudden fall of the Soviet Union meant the collapse of an historical epoch and the need to sort out domestic and external conflicts *outside* the framework of a Pax Sovietica.

To explain the forces which led to the break-up of the Soviet Union and the Pax Sovietica, one needs to ask the right kind of questions. These are some of them:

1. What was the impact of the international political system of the Cold War on the fall of the Soviet Union? To what extent does the process of ending the Cold War correlate with the break-up of the Pax Sovietica? (Here, it is also of importance to define the retroactive impact of this break-up on the processes of today's international economic and political system).
2. What was the correlation between the break-up of the USSR and the issue of international stability viewed both in a global context and at the regional level?
3. How did the twentieth century ideological conflicts between liberalism and socialism influence the Soviet collapse?
4. How did the issue of legitimacy and the dissemination of democratic principles influence the break-up of the Soviet Union?

I will deal with these main issues two by two, first with the latter two, ideology and legitimacy, and then with the external factors of Cold War conflict and regional and global stability.

Ideology, Legitimacy, and the Soviet Collapse

Viewed in a wider context, the fall of the Soviet Union and the dissolution of the Pax Sovietica was the result of the destruction of socialist totalitarianism as an ideology. The Stalinist and the post-Stalin epochs were characterized by an extreme centralization of the economy, predominance of bureaucratic administrative methods of management, and the failure of all attempts at reforming the economy. This resulted in ever-growing pressure on the economy, military expenses becoming too much of a burden, agriculture declining, and the country – outwardly stable – approaching the critical point.

Perestroika and the course towards the setting-up of a market economy (though it was imperfectly thought out) destroyed the economic ties created by socialist totalitarianism, leading to the tangible decentralization of the economy. The market, which was to become, in principle, a new way of establishing ties within the union and in the framework of the "Socialist Community", began to emerge. And this situation in the economy stimulated the sentiment that the independent development of Eastern Europe and the Soviet republics was possible and, indeed, necessary. Many republics, rich in natural resources (oil, gas, diamonds, coal, grain, etc.) tended to believe that their independent development would enable them to enjoy a rich life, trading profitably on the world market.

In the political and the ideological spheres the Soviet state lost the binding and unifying factor – the ideology of Marxism–Leninism and the dominance of the Communist Party. The party and the political system which seemed unshakeable and which enabled the Soviet elite to exercise a high degree of control, started eroding in the course of perestroika. In addition, the ideology of Marxism–Leninism was discredited in the countries of the "Socialist Community," on the world arena, and even within the Soviet Union.

Thus both ideologically and politically the country was becoming more disunited, losing its former binding factors, which were being replaced by a nascent multi-party system and democratic forms of organization of public life. Democratic forces had no time to develop, and therefore failed to unite the emerging elements of a new economy and society on a national level.

In the late 1980s, there was nothing with which to fill the post-communist vacuum, formed after the destruction of the Communist and socialist ideology. Values of democratic liberalism were but declared, never becoming a political factor which could bind the nation together. The democratic space was too undeveloped and fragile and the diverse peoples living under the Pax Sovietica had practically no experience of pluralist societies. Meanwhile, nationalism, chauvinism, and conservative thinking still had deep roots in the minds of all the Soviet nations. These traditional ideological elements enhanced the conflicts between republics and regions within the Soviet state.

One of the most significant reasons for the Soviet collapse was the emergence during the 1980s of an understanding that the totalitarian one-party one-policy model of a multinational state was wrong. The very concept of development which existed in the Soviet Union, which was built on an extremely high degree of centralization, gave rise to nationalist ideas and created nationalist movements.

In the years of Soviet rule, and especially in the 1960s–1970s ethnocratic elites were formed in the republics, which sensed that after the break-up of the Soviet system their ruling role could in the long run be endangered. They tried to snatch the initiative from the hands of various democratic and nationalistic movements, to appropriate their slogans and to use them to strengthen their own positions in the republics.

In Russia the resistance of the conservative forces, which united old nomenclature and the newly emerging nationalist forces, tried to slow down reforms and revive the old order. But by doing so, they were in reality eroding the former system, and assisting in the demise of the Soviet Union. On the other hand, Gorbachev's half-baked reforms did not allow for the filling of the vacuum that formed after the Communist structures lost their grip on society, and the diminishing of the role of ideology of Marxism–Leninism. Under pressure, the legitimacy of the former regime and the former federal state was gradually losing its strength and significance. But Gorbachev never managed to create a new nation-wide legitimacy, a new legal system and a new order which could have kept the country together.

In the view of many a reformer who came to power and who was engaged in creating new parties and movements, legitimacy was a priori associated with capitalism and democracy. And if democracy in the true sense of the word was not legitimate in the former Communist countries, the new leaders of the Soviet Union also could not or did not manage to legalize in due time the democratic process that was under way in the country in the broadest scope possible.

The new elite believed that it was enough to proclaim the values of democratic liberalism and capitalism to bring about change in the Soviet Union. But the road to a market economy is long and hard. And in the political sector Gorbachev did not dare to institute real democratic processes, the only method that could have prevented a break-up of the Soviet state. Instead of democracy there was the continuous inter-party struggle, with relentless rivalry among the CPSU leaders. These battles did much to enhance the existing centrifugal tendencies.

The issue of legitimacy plays an important role in the Soviet collapse. There was in the late 1980s a slow destruction of the very legitimacy of the Soviet state, a legitimacy which had a rationale of its own.

The Stalinist and post-Stalinist system in the Soviet Union and in the countries of the Eastern bloc had created their own framework of legitimacy, determined by political and ideological factors and perpetuated by a ramified system of legal documents. This legitimacy included various legal norms, established traditions, and the observation of a certain political order and even a certain life-style.

The Soviet legitimacy was symbolized by its legal order, legalizing the leading role of the Communist Party in all spheres of life in the country, its various republics and regions, and by other legislative acts, complete with a system of federal administrative bodies. The seventy years of Soviet power had created ideological cliches and stereotypes, and particular legal norms, which as often as not were counterposed against the norms and humanitarian values of the rest of mankind. As the ideology behind the formal framework for Soviet legitimacy began to crumble, the legal body could not be upheld and the ensuing revision of legal norms and laws, all the way down to the revision or abolition of articles of the Constitution, prepared the final collapse of the Soviet state.

The Fall of the Soviet Union and the End of the Cold War

In the conditions after the end of the Cold War and the fall of the Pax Sovietica the full collapse of Soviet global power was unavoidable and predestined. The loss of Soviet positions in Asia, Africa, and Latin America was connected with the processes under way in the Soviet Union itself, with its revision of its international policies, and its relinquishment of its imperial ambitions.

I think it is important to underline that the fall of Soviet power abroad was connected with a general weakening during the 1980s of the ideas of socialism and communism and, as a consequence, the defeat of Communist parties and movements, especially in Western Europe. At the same time there was an invigoration of ideas of liberal democracy and a further strengthening of conservative parties and movements. This process is more complicated than as depicted, for example, by the US political analyst Francis Fukuyama. What seems to be happening is the formation, at the end of the twentieth century, of a new global ideological synthesis, marrying values of liberal democracy, conservatism, and some notions of collective values.

These overall tendencies first became visible in Eastern Europe. The developments in Hungary, Poland, and Czechoslovakia were a clear indication not only of the weakness of the Communist regimes in these countries, but also of the decline of the socialist idea. That these processes started here is due to both the Eastern and South-eastern European nations having some experience in developing the framework of a market economy and a multi-party system, and the stronger influence of Western Europe. In addition, the

Soviet Union's own activities in Poland, Czechoslovakia, Hungary, and Romania did much to enhance non-socialist sentiments there, thereby assisting in the transformation process.

Perestroika in the USSR and the refusal of the Soviet leaders to stick to their former policies of Socialism, the end of the Cold War, a public denunciation in the USSR of the invasions of Hungary in 1956 and of Czechoslovakia in 1968 brought about and accelerated new developments. As a result, the 1989 revolutions were practically bloodless and ended rather swiftly in the fall of the communist regimes. All these nations witnessed a rapid dismantling of former structures, restoration of pre-war parties, and the emergence of new parties, movements and organizations.

A similar situation was found in East Germany. But apart from the above factors, a trend toward German unification was influential there. It was also important that the policies pursued by the Soviet leadership gave the green light to the unification of Germany, and so did its pledge of non-interference and the statement that Soviet troops in the territory of the GDR would not be used to interfere in the internal affairs of the two German states.

There has, since the break-up of the Soviet Union, been an intense debate in Russian historiography on the effects of the East–West confrontation – the Cold War – on the Soviet collapse. The traditional viewpoint, both in the Soviet Union and in the West, was that the Cold War was a destabilizing factor in Soviet domestic policies and its international affairs. In the Soviet Union, it was also regarded as axiomatic that the Cold War was unleashed by the United States and their allies, while the policies of the USSR were a factor of global stability and an answer to the aggressive activities of the West.

The historiographers have now changed their views, at least in Moscow. Newly discovered archival documents indicate that far from being destabilizing, the Cold War did much to hold the Soviet Union together. The Cold War, in this perspective, was a period in the development of international relations which led both to the threshold of war and to times of evident relaxation of tensions, but which gradually brought about an externally stable bi-polar world.

It should be admitted, however, that the period of the Cold War created a special type of international stability, which was accompanied by an arms race and a grave confrontation along the perimeter of East–West relations. This did contribute, at least peripherally, to the Soviet collapse. Even so, throughout this period the leaders of the confronting blocs and nations avoided a military conflict.

The Cold War, however, was based on principles which were a far cry from the principles of democracy and human rights. On the one hand, the United States pursued the doctrine formulated by the Yalta agreements, assuming that the world should be divided into spheres of influence and of special interests. On the other hand, the Soviet Union was also guided by the Yalta documents, with the later addition of the Brezhnev doctrine of "a limited sovereignty", which enabled the USSR to interfere in the affairs of its allies in the "Socialist Community".

Perestroika dramatically altered the character of the Soviet Union's development and its role on the international arena. A different approach to international stability appeared. The late 1980s became the time of a gradual destruction of the Yalta-type of international system and the end of the Cold War.

In the global policies of the USSR in the late 1980s, humanitarian values became a top priority, alongside the issue of the Soviet Union's integration in the world community.

With instability growing inside the USSR, Gorbachev realized that his survival depended on the international situation and on international stability. And in the first years of perestroika the Soviet leadership did manage to dramatically change Soviet foreign policy to contribute to these aims, and thereby to their own survival in power.

By the early 1990s the world had become a much safer and a more stable place. At international meetings diplomats and scholars started to foresee the establishment of a new world order, the transition to a new system and a new epoch in international relations. In this new structure the Soviet Union was to play a new role – that of a state which was about to switch over to democracy, to deep-going disarmament, and ready to give up its former imperial ambitions.

But instead, within just a few years, the Soviet state was no more. In its place, there are now fifteen independent countries, members of the United Nations and other international organizations. The Commonwealth of Independent States, created in Minsk in December 1991, seems to be a rather ephemeral entity.

Instead of being a partner in international stability, the territory of the former Soviet Union has become a hotbed of tension and bloodshed. There is warfare going on today in the Caucasus, and the situation in Moldova and Tajikistan is extremely unstable.

Russia itself is quite unsteady and unstable, and the uncertain character of the development of democratization in Russia is creating instability in Eastern Europe. Such instability is inevitable in the wake of the break-up of a country as big as the Soviet Union, but it is also connected with the domestic difficulties in Russia and its slow moving toward a civil society, which is one precondition for greater stability in the Eastern European region and in all of Europe.

Before 1992, many thought that the break-up of the Organization of the Warsaw Treaty, the Socialist Community, and the Soviet Union would remove tensions and bring greater stability. But, as we have seen, developments went in a different direction. The course of these developments has once again proved that the break-up of a great state, not to speak about a modern superpower, causes wide and unpredictable repercussions, which, in most cases, will temporarily destabilize international affairs.

After the break-up of Austria–Hungary and the revolution in Russia at the beginning of the twentieth century many new independent states were formed, riding the wave of the nascent nationalist sentiment. After World War II the unification trend helped to create new multinational states. But after the breakdown of the Pax Sovietica the momentum of decentralization resulted in a sudden explosion of nationalism. It caused the formation of independent states in Eastern Europe and in the Balkans, only some of which had a former history as autonomous states. In some cases, but far from all, these transformations are accompanied by open military conflicts.

Likewise, those who believed that the end of the Cold War would mean an end to regional conflict in the third world have been mistaken. There are still harsh confrontations in the Middle East and in Arab countries, in Angola and in South Africa. In these areas, more than anywhere else, the pattern of international development shows that the world was ill-prepared to face a new situation, and to respond to a worldwide challenge of nationalism at the end of the twentieth century. In the Yugoslav case, attempts to put the UN mechanisms, the Conference of Security and Cooperation in Europe, and the European Community to use as preventers of conflict have so far failed to produce tangible results.

As a result, there is more which demands mending in today's international society than there ever was during the Cold War. A new international political regime and new concepts of security must be worked out. Much will depend on Russia's place and role in the working out of such a new world order. But today the instability in Russia and in the republics of the former USSR makes it impossible to clearly define or imagine their future development and their role in tomorrow's world.

The domestic economic crisis continues to pervert Russia's international role, and reforms drag on in the face of tremendous difficulties in overcoming powerful resistance. As of today, the population is disappointed, leaving behind the democratic visions of 1990–1991 and any potential for constructive initiatives internationally. In addition, the severing of economic and political ties between republics in the wake of the break-up of the Soviet Union had a negative effect not only on the economies of the former member-states of the Soviet Union, but also on their will to engage in international affairs.

Primarily, Russia's international role will necessarily be concerned with restoring the ties within the former union. This certainly does not mean the restoration of the old union based on the dictates of the central authorities and command methods in the economy. It is rather a new type of an economic association, based on the principles of the market economy and the common integration of these states in the world economy.

Russia must play a key role in this process. The retention of Russia's status as a great power will depend on the role it plays in its region. Today this role is made more difficult by a revival of a chauvinist mentality, which is widespread in various spheres of life in Russia. Its government must steer Russia toward a society based on the principles of democracy and pluralism, on the priority of common humanitarian principles and values, on the norms and provisions of international law. Russia, which geographically connects Europe and Asia, could bridge the gap between two great traditions, basing its new concept of foreign policy on this bridging role.

In addition, it will be extremely important for Russia to identify its new role in Eastern Europe. If it could get rid of all of its former policies of hegemonism and dictates, Russia could be a constructive force in a new regional stability encompassing Poland, Czechia and Slovakia, Romania, Hungary, Bulgaria, Latvia, Lithuania, and Estonia. By tradition as well as by present-day analysis, these states know that their relationship with Russia is a decisive element in their economic and political development.

But the initial steps in these processes and the strengthening of international stability resulting from them depend primarily on the domestic developments in Russia. The continuation of the course of reforms, the course of the implementation of democratic principles and norms, the change from a Communist legitimacy to a democratic one, the change from a Pax Sovietica to a peoples' peace – all these processes must continue if the region and the world is to overcome its present difficulties and move toward a new and better stability. The task that Russia as a society and a state faces today is to minimize the turbulence created by the break-up of the Soviet state and by the end of East–West confrontation. It is, in this sense, both a return and a new beginning.

8

The Collapse of the Soviet Union: Leadership, Elites, and Legitimacy

Vladislav M. Zubok

The disappearance of the Soviet Union from the map of the world left historians with a number of questions. Why was the collapse so sudden and complete? Why did the communist regime, renowned for its bloody past, die peacefully? Did the death of communism as a system and ideology have to produce the disintegration of the Soviet empire and the state?

The Soviet implosion took most observers by surprise,[1] but there are at least two schools of thought that emphasized the possibility of a fall the Soviet empire. One assumed that the Soviet Union was "the last empire," a direct descendant from the empires of the Tsars, whose life had only been prolonged by communist deception and terror, but that it would eventually perish under pressure from different nationalities.[2] Another claimed that the Soviet Union would fall as a result of "imperial overstretch," including the costs of the arms race, the aid to foreign regimes, and interventions like that in Afghanistan.[3]

These approaches, however, do not explain the strange death of Soviet communism.[4] Many knew that the Soviet Union was sick, but few could imagine that her leadership, secret police, and military machine would surrender without a major battle.[5] Some even predicted that "the Soviet Union would risk nuclear war if her leaders believed the integrity of the empire to be at stake."[6] Even the analysts who predicted the "fragmentation" of the Soviet Union, indicated it would be "highly unlikely" and stressed instead the likelihood of "decay" and "communist authoritarianism."[7] The costs of empire and economic decline, the nationalities' pressure, the dismal quality of life, all taken together, put the Soviet regime in great danger. But it would take something else to cause its end in a way that reminded one of a suicide.

This "something else," in my opinion, was not a revolt of nationalities or social pressures from below. The cause was at the top, in the Soviet leadership, particularly Mikhail Gorbachev, and in the behavior of the Soviet elites.[8] To borrow from the military vocabulary, the Soviet command became engaged by their own will in a serious offensive, then turned to defence, and finally surrendered without serious fighting. The foremost leader, namely Gorbachev, chose to preside over the dissolution of the empire and the state, rather than to use force to preserve it, and the key power elites, unlike their predecessors in the tsarist Russia, failed to resist.

The issue of political legitimacy might help to find a clue to this mystery. Unwrapped from various historic forms (monarchist, republican, populist, etc.), political legitimacy means largely the right to rule. It usually comprises three meanings or components. The first of them can be called "self-legitimacy," and is a set of beliefs that justify to rulers themselves their power and actions. The second can be named "popular legitimacy," which is the acceptance of the ruling groups and their methods by the broad masses. The third should be defined as "external legitimacy," which is the acceptance of the regime and its ruling groups by other states and (especially in the modern world) by influential segments of public opinion. I will focus on "self-legitimacy" and will show how its decades-long erosion and rapid transformation in the Gorbachev years had much to do with the fall of the communist regime of the Soviet Union.[9]

Revolutionary and Stalinist "Legitimacy"

Since ancient times empires created and sustained a legitimacy of their own in the form of the universally accepted "natural right" of conquest and coercion. First religious beliefs, then secular ideologies – from nationalism to Nazism – helped to forge powerful alliances between the rulers and the ruled. The communist creed, which preached economic egalitarianism and world revolution by the working people and oppressed colonies, was the source from which the Bolsheviks from 1917 drew their legitimacy. And it remained, despite major revisions, the basis for the self-legitimacy of the rulers of the Soviet Union from Stalin to Gorbachev.

The first generation of Bolsheviks were the true believers who hoped, with all the power levers of the modern state at their disposal, to carry out their grandiose mission: the elimination of all traditional empires and states, equality for all ethnic groups and races, the expropriation of the rich and the fair distribution of goods, and, last but not least, the "science-proven" leap into the realm of material abundance and happiness. In their eyes this mission justified the organization of a conspiratorial, tightly disciplined party and the use of mass terror to overhaul the whole fabric of the society. The Bolsheviks never bothered about their lack of popular and external legitimacy. They had an unshakeable confidence in their right to act and speak in the name of the working classes, both domestically and internationally.

This exclusive sense of self-legitimacy gave Lenin, Trotsky and other Bolsheviks a huge advantage over other parties and power manipulators. It allowed them to overcome the fierce resistance of the old ruling groups, and, in fact, of the majority of Russian workers and peasants and also of the other nationalities that by 1921 turned *en masse* against the communist regime. They successfully suppressed non-Russian nationalists and restored most of the old boundaries of tsarist Russia in the form of the Soviet Union.

The consolidation of the regime in the 1920s gave rise to hopes that the radicalism would pass away: the policies of economic liberalization (NEP) and "nativization" brought about peace with the peasantry and the nationalists. In a few years most of the world's powers (with the exception of the isolationist United States) granted diplomatic recognition to the new regime. But these achievements, much as they enhanced the popular and external legitimacy of the regime, ran counter to the party's self-legitimacy, which was supposed to stem from implacable opposition to the "*petit bourgeois*" majority inside the country, and from the "hostile imperialist encirclement."

By unleashing genocide against the peasantry, the national provinces, and, finally, against the Bolshevik elites, Joseph Stalin repeated the trick of the revolution: he recruited new elites whose enormous will for power was justified by the vision of radical social transformation.[10] Stalinist "legitimacy" borrowed most of the trappings of its revolutionary predecessor (dubbed "Leninism", together they became the basis of official state ideology). The Stalinists spurned representative liberal democracies as a sham designed to protect the rights of a few rich. Stalin's regime, they argued, was a historically inevitable bridge from the crumbling capitalist order to the realm of justice and happiness. They viewed the state as the only possible catapult from backwardness to industrial society. The party was regarded as the only means to prevent the state from degenerating into a bureaucratic monster. And the leader, Stalin, was seen as the only factor that could prevent the party from falling into a paralysis of warring factions.

Stalinist "legitimacy" emphasized "socialism in one country" and was regarded by many as "national-Bolshevism," a revolutionary promise frozen into a statist ideology.[11] For a while it was a huge success. Millions in the Soviet Union, squeezed between indoctrination and terror, began to believe that the horrors of Stalin's regime was an acceptable price for rapid industrialization ('*Les rubiat, schepki letiat,*' they used to say, "Chips have to fly when you cut wood"). Quite a few intellectuals abroad bought this logic, too, refusing to notice the signs of terror.

Under Stalin the grandeur of the state replaced the egalitarian promise of the revolution as the regime's legitimization basis. The heroic Soviet resistance to, and final defeat of, Nazi Germany in 1941–1945 catapulted the Soviet Union to the status of superpower, even before it acquired nuclear weapons. Stalin became the senior among "the three" who decided the world's future at international conferences at Yalta and Potsdam. The victory and ("Russian") patriotism became the main staples of self-legitimacy for the war-decorated Soviet elites and very much the basis of popular legitimacy (the propaganda machine droned that "Stalin means victory;" some objected, but the majority believed it).[12] Even when Stalin's shameless imperialism became one of the sources of the cold war and the Soviet Union lost much of her external legitimacy, this hardly bothered the Stalinists in the satellite states and "fellow-travellers" elsewhere, who continued to believe that the Soviet Union was "the main bulwark of peace and democracy."

There were, however, severe problems with Stalinist "legitimacy." First, it justified the right of Stalin and his secret police to purge and kill any "enemies of the people," including the rulers themselves. Stalin's purges replaced politically vigorous elites with bureaucratic eunuchs at the tyrant's court; instead of lawyers and economists with middle-class backgrounds Stalin recruited people from the lowest classes who had no idea of what intellectual or political life was. Second, Soviet "legitimacy" became totally personalized: Stalin alone spanned the chasm between the revolution and the empire, the power and the people.[13] None of Stalin's successors could fill this role. For these reasons only, Stalin's death was bound to cause a crisis of legitimacy in all its three dimensions.

For the post-Stalin leadership and elites it was impossible, nor was it desirable, to restore Stalinist "legitimacy." They had to reform it, according to their new nature as guardians, not builders of power. The majority of rulers supported de-Stalinization – the end of indiscriminate terror and the restoration of a modicum of "legality". To increase the popular acceptance of their rule, they took some measures to alleviate the appalling misery of the majority and tolerated the cultural "thaw" for educated groups of the society. They also sought accommodation between the Soviet Union and the outside world.

De-Stalinization, however, came at a price for the Soviet regime. Mao Zedong once remarked that Stalin was a powerful weapon either in the hands of the friends or of the enemies of socialism. Official denunciation of Stalin's crimes by Khrushchev (February 1956) left a deep and open wound in the very heart of Soviet legitimacy. It immediately triggered uprisings against the communist rule in Eastern Europe, mass defections of intellectuals from Western communist parties, and, as KGB documents now reveal, a smattering of protests against the regime even in the Soviet Union itself. There were two ways, short of total dismantlement of the official ideology, to deal with this problem. One was to revive the initial egalitarian impulse of communism and make at least some attempt to match it with performance. That is what Khrushchev, with halts and checks, attempted to do in his best moments. The second way led to xenophobic nationalism (some Eastern European regimes preferred it). But this could only destabilize the multi-ethnic Soviet Union and furthermore undermine the image of the "big brother" among the satellites. The Brezhnev administration stumbled into a third way: it covered up the crimes, exalted Victory and patriotism to the skies, and made everybody follow the rules of the game.

The Decline of Soviet Legitimacy: Domestic and External Factors

"The fish starts rotting from the head", so went a popular Soviet saying. And it was the "head", the Soviet rulers and elites, who became the prime grave-diggers of the regime's legitimacy. The elite consolidation after Stalin's death accounted for this paradox. The officials who filled the ranks of the party *nomenklatura* and security structures were children of Stalin's purges, not fathers of the revolution. Unlike the first generation of Soviet rulers, they no longer saw themselves as a vanguard of the working majority with a special mission. On the contrary, they despised, feared, and cynically manipulated the Soviet people. Socially, the top rulers of the generation of Brezhnev were mostly of the poorest peasant origins and through the system of *nomenklatura* they selected their own kind, keeping intellectuals, especially lawyers, out of power structures.[14] In their motivations they were quickly turning into a "leisure class, which put the amenities of a good life much above the goals chartered by official ideology. They lived in a secluded, privileged world that made a mockery out of the egalitarian promise of the revolution. In various parts of the Soviet Union, especially in the Transcaucasus and Central Asia, but also in Ukraine and some regions of the Russian Federation, including Moscow and Leningrad, local cliques emerged who combined the privileges of status with the benefits of corruption and illegal entrepreneurship.

The consequences of this elite evolution can be simplified into the following formula: the more the Soviet elites prospered, the shakier was their self-legitimacy whose basis was still presumably the communist creed. This pushed many of them towards the acquisition of more solid status symbols like higher education, scholarly degrees, closeness to literary and artistic bohemia, etc. The status-seeking became a hall-mark of the next generation of the Soviet elites, which included such diverse individuals as Mikhail Gorbachev, Yegor Ligachev, and Boris Yeltsin. The whole phenomenon of "the next generation" is tightly related to the rise of continuity, education, and middle-class values in Soviet society. Most urbanized and educated persons among the younger elites, according to a Russian analyst, believed in the official ideology "no more than dissidents". But they did not come up with any ideological alternative either; the ideological fervor of the Bolsheviks and the Stalinists ceased to be *comme il faut* and was replaced with "negativism with regard to the dogmas of the official Marxist-Leninist ideology, orientation to the national pre-communist past, in part, to the West – the trips there were becoming a crucial status symbol."[15]

True, in the eyes of many of the Soviet elites, the image of the prosperous, comfortable "West" took the place of the world revolution of the proletariat and the oppressed peoples of the colonies. But when and how did this happen, and how was it related to the expansion of the Soviet empire and the temperature swings of the cold war?

It would be tempting to conclude that Cold-War tensions prolonged the life of the Soviet empire. From 1947 on, Stalin successfully "proved" to a majority among the elites and the masses that the United States was bent on denying to the Soviet Union her very existence. The US nuclear armadas posed an immediate threat to the Soviet regime, but this boosted both the regime's self-legitimacy and its acceptance by the Soviet masses. The building of superpower status was still justified by the rhetoric of world revolution, resurrected in the form of the doctrine of "two camps." But more pervasive and lasting were *realpolitik* arguments of security: if we pull out (or stay out), the Americans will surely move in. As late as 1986 Mikhail Gorbachev was still saying that about Afghanistan.[16]

The magnitude of the US challenge made Soviet elites and the masses all the more united in their determination to spare no economic resources in fending off the war threat; all attempts to reform the Stalinist economy were defeated by the "defence" priorities of the military-industrial complex. When in July 1962 the Soviet regime doubled the prices on food staples, the workers in Novocherkassk rebelled and had to be put down by military force. But in other places the majority agreed to have less butter so that the state could have more guns to safeguard peace.[17] The phrase *'lish bi nie bylo voini'* (Anything but war!) became a household litany for at least the two generations of Russians who had experienced the Nazi invasion.

A closer look, however, reveals that even the most dangerous, early phases of the Cold-War had an ambiguous impact on the legitimacy of the Soviet regime: the Soviet expansion into new domains in 1945–47 and in 1955–61 provided tens, perhaps hundreds of thousands of Soviet functionaries, both elite and rank-and-file, with the opportunity to visit the outside world. Exposure to it was often a shocking experience that revealed to the Soviets the misery of the Stalinist "paradise" and transformed them into unbridled consumerists. However, at that time the Soviet rulers still managed to keep the Soviet Union away from "pernicious influences" and persuaded themselves that Western societies were rotten and capitalist economies on the brink of major crisis.

The 1970s changed it all. The systemic crisis occurred not in capitalist economies, which marched forward apace, but in the Soviet economy. The moral decay, revealed by the receding glacier of Stalinism, ate up the top echelons of the Soviet Union. The precursors, "the first birds" of the change were, not coincidentally, the most privileged Soviet officials of the next elite generation (among them Oleg Penkovsky and Yuri Nosenko), for whom admiration for "the West" became the new article of faith and the reason for betrayal and defection. Many others still posed as staunch defenders of the Soviet empire, but preferred to do it in Geneva, Paris or New York, rather than in the Urals or Kazakhstan.

It is obvious that the causes of this turn lay hidden in the Soviet elites' evolution and perceptions (affected by the growing ability to compare Soviet and Western living standards), rather than in the ups and downs of the US–Soviet confrontation. Yet, the ebb of tension by the end of the 1960s and the "detente" of the 1970s significantly accelerated the decline of Soviet legitimacy. The fear of war and the foreign threat, tangible for so long, began to melt away. As the Soviet Union was reaching for strategic parity and started arms negotiations with the United States, the feeling spread among the elites and people alike that peace, even with the Cold War lurking behind, could be stable and long. The propaganda cries about the imperialist wolf ceased to be credible, as had many years earlier the propaganda about the communist "bright future." *The Voice of America* and *Radio Liberty* began to compete with Soviet media as sources of information, natural for any educated urbanite professional. Simultaneously, as the Soviet Union became the maritime empire where the sun never set, and the big exporter of oil, the trickle of Western trips and goods for the Soviet elites turned into a veritable shower. The very success of the empire brought about the relaxation of tensions inside it. In as much as the early confrontation helped Stalin to mobilize the empire against the external challenge, so "detente" contributed to the empire's flabbiness, to the regime's growing preference for accommodation with the United States and other Western countries, and to the feeling of "long peace" among the Soviet elites and masses.[18]

Most importantly, external legitimacy, spurned by Stalin in 1947, became thirty years later increasingly important for the Soviet rulers, although, as the invasion into Afghanistan demonstrated, they were still prepared to sacrifice it in the name of the empire's security.[19] The Soviet elites' attitude to their "enemy number one" changed perceptibly. The running for their lives that motivated their arms race with the United States in the 1950s was over; now they searched for geopolitical equality with Washington. "America" became a symbolic plank ("to catch up and surpass"), the object of emulation, obsession, and eventually of envious *Hassliebe*. When Soviet officials in the 1970s advocated "fraternal aid" to various regimes overseas, they did so without much ideological drive and did not mean it to hurt "the detente" with Washington.[20] The Brezhnev administration had a big stake in good US–Soviet relations and decided to invade Afghanistan only because it assumed the Americans had already rejected "detente."

What about the last phase of the Cold War under the Reagan Administration? Many on the American Right claim that the Reagan military build-up and the support for the anti-Soviet guerillas in Afghanistan helped speed up the Soviet decline and even brought about the collapse of the empire. True, these factors did put the Soviet leadership before tough budgetary and policy choices, filled them with dire forebodings and even dismay. However, this was not enough in itself to force the regime to throw in the towel.[21] The same developments could have evoked a fiendish reponse from the Soviets, had they had *the will* for that and had they been *the same Soviets* as forty years earlier. Many in Washington, as we have seen, feared that reaction and it finally trickled up to Reagan himself.[22]

But the Soviets and their perceptions had changed. The older generation of Soviet rulers no longer wanted to consolidate their regime with the help of the cold war. They just wanted to restore the superpower's prestige and to normalize Soviet–US relations; and this willingness stemmed from reasons other than the Reagan challenge, no matter what the importance of the Strategic Defence Initiative (SDI) or "Stingers."[23] Most Soviet foreign policy experts began to discuss the possiblity of ditching the puppet-regime in Kabul and of retreating even before the CIA brought "Stingers" into Afghanistan, because the Afghan bloodshed undermined Soviet legitimacy world-wide, and, most importantly, hurt Soviet relations "with the West".[24]

Again, the internal dynamics were crucial: the Soviet economy and society were in crisis. This is not the place to dwell on the reasons for the Soviet decline, evident in economic stagnation, demographic down curve, the rise of national sentiments, the over-bloated military industries, etc. All these trends were crucial for the decline of the elites' self-confidence; they were present as a grim and menacing background for the empire's march to the no longer certain future.[25] Among both the old and the next elite generation, these trends produced deep pessimism and unwillingness to pre-serve the empire as it was. Younger educated nomenklaturchiks cared even more than the Brezhnev gerontocrats about normaliza-tion of relations with the West, and saw the Afghan war, and the cold war, for that matter, as an obstacle to this normalization which should be removed.

The nomination of Mikhail Gorbachev as general secretary of the CPSU in March 1985 was a long-overdue change of political generations in the Soviet Union. The young leader gropingly started a campaign for reforms and immediately got support from the majority of key power elites, including the KGB, the military, and the military-industrial complex. But there was little will or energy in them for involvement in reform politics (if one takes *politics* in its real, power-charged meaning), i.e. their old self-legitimacy, largely Stalinist, had almost evaporated, without any replacement, be it the imperial honor of the tsarist ruling class, or the nationalist patriotism of the ruling groups in other contemporary great powers. As the Gorbachev *perestroika* took on a more radical character and began to threaten the empire's integrity, the elites' reaction turned out to be ridiculously weak.

The Gorbachev Enigma and the Fall of the Soviet Union

The transformation of the Soviet elites from the formidable Stalinist "Teutonic order" into an enormous, corrupt and sloppy bureaucracy, full of cynicism and status-seeking, was only one side of the coin. The same transformation led to the emergence of Mikhail Sergevich Gorbachev and his circle of reformers. The role of the elites as a vanguard of the Soviet decay, their unwillingness to fight for the preservation of the empire were crucial factors. But it was Gorbachev and his close comrades who put the empire on the skids, down to self-destruction.

Why, instead of the expected "intensely chauvinistic" leadership, predicted by some pundits in the West, did there come this version: idealistic, evolving (as has become very clear) towards the vision of reformed socialism, a peculiar blend of Marxism–Leninism, the humanistic ideas of the Enlightenment, and some tenets of modern liberal democracy?[26]

Mikhail Gorbachev was often portrayed in the West as a unique hero, but he was not; he represented the educted, Westernized part of the next generation of Soviet political elites. He belonged to the last cohort of reformers that the moribund Soviet elites could marshal at this fateful moment. A comparison was made between Gorbachev and the Russian Tsar Alexander I who had started the Great Reforms in 1860s with a group of "enlightened bureaucrats."[27] Gorbachev was an "enlightened bureacrat" himself. There were specific moments in the socialization of the Gorbachev generation that produced not only cynical operators of power, but also reformers and communist idealists.

A change of political generations was by itself bound to bring change: the younger Soviets who waited until the Brezhnevites vacated their seats, were vastly better educated and often had strong pro-Western cultural and intellectual orientations. But that could

not turn them automatically into opponents of the empire. Hugh
Trevor-Roper once reflected on a generational pattern in the history
of empires: the tremendous effort of the builders, the pause in the
next generation, who relax and enjoy their gains, then, with the
grandsons in power, the imperial drive is resumed. "After the
second defeat," in Trevor-Roper's words, "imperialism expires."[28]

Mikhail Gorbachev, Aleksandr Yakovlev, Eduard Shevardnadze,
and scores of other "enlightened bureaucrats" of the 1980s were not
simply disillusioned apparatchiks; they were *the grandsons*,
sometimes literally, of the revolutionaries and the heroes of the
Civil War who had been killed by Stalin. They sympathized with
the ideas of the sophisticated Bolsheviks like Nikolay Bukharin and
believed that Stalinism was a terrible deviation from the original
promise and potential of the revolution.[29] In one apt quotation,
Gorbachev's view was that "the system has gotten off the tracks, not
that the tracks were laid wrong".[30] But still they rejected the empire
instead of resuming the imperial drive. Why?

Gorbachev and the Gorbachevites had been brought up in the
communist tradition, but the denunciation of Stalin's crimes in 1956
made them think about human lives, justice, and the dangers of
state violence – highly subversive substances for Stalinist self-
legitimacy. Then they waited too long for power and for fifteen
years watched how the reforms in the "socialist camps" were
smothered and how the country slid into Brezhnevite "stagnation."
As a result most of that generation escaped into cynicism, some
secretly dreamed about the West, but the third group attempted to
revive and reform the communist self-legitimacy, this time "with a
human face."

This attempt led Gorbachev himself to a contradictory blend:
communist in form and humanist in content. The communist form
was seen in the proclamations about a return to revolutionary
basics, which created the illusion that the basis for Gorbachev's
self-legitimacy, as the party head, was still robust and intact. But
the search for substance carried Gorbachev away in directions most
unlikely for an orthodox Leninist. He found his soul-brothers
among revisionists of the communist creed, Eurocommunists,
Social Democrats, and among the apostles of "social Christianity,"
including, most surprisingly, Pope John Paul II.

This search brought Gorbachev to a fundamental choice:
between violent and non-violent ways of changing the system.
Remarkably, in 1985–91 Gorbachev systematically avoided the use
of naked force. Of course, he no longer possessed the ruthless

determination of the Bolsheviks (not to mention the Stalinists) to kill "in the name of" Utopia or national security. And luckily, the crumbling of the dogma about the "historic inevitability" of communism opened to Gorbachev, a graduate of Moscow State University, the door to intellectual inner freedom. But it was his search for a new self-legitimacy, his planetary mission "to humanize" communism, that led him to renounce violence and force – the very fundamentals of his power. More so, he drove one wedge after another into cracks and chinks in the Soviet regime and empire. He embraced the principle of national self-determination (December 1988, the UN speech), this time without Lenin's incendiary rhetoric. He supported the program of nuclear abolitionism. He spoke approvingly, without any knowledge about the matter, on the introduction of "elements" of a market economy into the Soviet system. First he let *glasnost* spin out of control, then he had to outlaw Stalinism (we "became hostages of *Stalinshchina*," he admitted to A.Ochetto),[31] and eventually the official myth about Lenin's revolution was torn to smithereens by shattering revelations. Thereby Gorbachev, still omnipotent ruler of the Soviet Union, undercut the remnants of his own legitimacy as the chief of the communist party.

Behind the sweeping randomness of Gorbachev's experimentation was his amazing self-confidence and determination, whose source was his belief in the potency of rediscovered "human communism." As often happens, confidence of this kind was coupled with ignorance of the power realities in the Soviet Union. Like the first Bolsheviks, perhaps, Gorbachev believed that the creation of the new system could to a large extent be an act of will, given propitious "historical circumstances". By the latter he meant largely detente with the West and disarmament.

Gorbachev's non-Moscow background explained, too, his confidence and optimism, in contrast to the pessimism of his colleagues in the epicenter of power. Gorbachev was the darling of Brezhnev's political cohort, not a desperate Moscow pyramid-climber. He inherited his position without a major struggle, never grasped the major lessons (even Khrushchev learnt them, instinctively) that Machiavelli and Tocqueville formulated for authoritarian rulers. Some blood-thirsty hardliners in the Kremlin believed Gorbachev was a wimp. But the abstention from violence and blood was not a personal weakness of the last Soviet leader (as Andrey Gromyko informed the Politburo in 1985, he had teeth of steel). It, was, ironically, the result of his extreme self-confidence and the exaggeration of his abilities to manage the cauldron of change.

His power immaturity was visible in the way the Soviet economy was mishandled and the Soviet empire was lost. Gorbachev, as if he believed that politics were rational, completely misread the forces of nationalism that were brewing in Eastern Europe and in Soviet republics thanks to his liberalization policies. The Gorbachev –Shevardnadze team was so obsessed with the idea of ending the cold war and of reaching "partnership" with the United States that they ignored the fire in their own backyard until it was too late. Gorbachev's belief that economic interests would temper the forces of nationalism inside the Soviet Union bordered on naivety; the confiscatory nature of the centrally-planned Soviet economy created a feeling in every region of the Soviet Union that it would be better off economically if it became independent from Moscow. And in the Russian Federation, too, nationalists claimed that Russia would live better without the other republics.

But the Soviet elites still remained firmly in control of the formidable state machine and could have stopped the disintegration of the Soviet Union, with the possible exception of the Baltics. One could imagine that emphasis on economic, rather than on political liberalization (as in communist China), could have given the Soviet regime and state better chances for survival. Instead, Gorbachev's political experiments undermined both. It would be wrong to portray Gorbachev as an apostate (or sly Delilah) who deftly cut the power of the party *nomenklatura*. Behind Gorbachev's choice of political liberalization was his belief that the CPSU could again become a political agent of change that would profit from the ideas of all sorts of "democratic movements." As a result, however, the party apparatchiks were trounced in elections, and the party itself came off looking like a scarecrow; soon it became crippled by defections and splits.

Gorbachev's choice to remain "a good Tsar," to avoid force, proved to be decisive in a political system where the will of the leader since Stalin's times was the imperative. The unintentional destruction by Gorbachev of the formal basis for self-legitimacy of the Soviet ruling elites, along with his tolerance of "democratic movements", opened the dams for centrifugal dynamics in the Soviet Union. The increasing number of outsiders threatened to dislodge the old elites, and a growing number among these elites could see no other choice but to paint themselves in nationalist colours, to become "ethnocracies." In other words, they began to rethink their legitimacy in nationalist and populist terms.

Gorbachev's policies brought to the Soviet Union the external legitimacy that the Brezhnev leadership with all their missiles and navy could not achieve; the USSR, only recently a world pariah and aggressor, was accepted as a major world player, equal to the United States. "Gorbomania" among the broad segments of public opinion in Western Europe and the United States made other world leaders pale in comparison. But at the very same time Gorbachev was quickly losing his right to rule in the eyes of the Soviet masses, and even among the power elites.

The end came with the ascendancy of Boris Yeltsin, Gorbachev's Nemesis, on the platform of anti-communism and the "national resurrection of Russia." Yeltsin's popular election to the presidency of the Russian Federation in June 1991 was a *coup de grace* to the Soviet "legitimacy." From now on only a ruler elected by popular majority could become a recognized authority both in the eyes of the people and the majority of bureaucrats within the Federation's boundaries. This development made the disappearance of the Soviet state in its old Stalinist form inevitable. Gorbachev belatedly recognized that and opened negotiations with the key segments of Soviet elites who already began to act as ethnocracies representing their republics. But the replacement of Gorbachev became a foregone conclusion: increasingly his legitimacy did not go beyond the Kremlin walls. The inept attempt of the hardliners in the Gorbachev administration (19-22 August 1991) to prevent the reform of the state structures towards a loose federation, only short-circuited the collapse of the Soviet Union. The coup ended in a whimper and catapulted Yeltsin to power as the first leader of *new Russia*.

Conclusion

I am far from seeing the fall of the Soviet Union and her empire as the direct result of the idealism, perceptions, and mistakes of Gorbachev and Soviet political elites. Without the multi-faceted crisis of the Soviet system this fall would not have been possible. The reader can find plenty of data on the scope and dimensions of this crisis in other publications. What I am arguing is that the complete and peaceful nature of the Soviet collapse cannot be understood without the analysis of internal changes in the Soviet power elites' beliefs and in the leader's perceptions – defined here as "self-legitimacy". Gorbachev and his reformist friends were the products of the empire's successes: stability and security, progress of education, the rise of middle-class standards. But their attempts at reforms revealed the enormous contradictions of this empire, and they proved unable to cope with the challenge. Their search for a new self-legitimacy led them to the renunciation of force and, eventually, they lost ground to nationalist and populist-oriented rivals.

The definition of the real agents and wellsprings behind the fall of the biggest empire of the twentieth century can satisfy more important needs than a historian's curiosity. Various explanations cast different slants on the past, but, more importantly, they become starting points for looking at the present and the future of the Commonwealth of Independent States (CIS). The focus on the transformation of the self-legitimacy of the Soviet elites gives a different picture from what one could get had one assumed the decisive role of nationalties or imperial overstreach, useful as these perspectives may be.

One difference is that the flare-up of nationalism in the former Soviet Union was not the cause, but the consequence of the empire's collapse. In most cases the Soviet elites did not develop a deep nationalist mentality, rather they only used national colors to mend their tattered legitimacy. That does not mean at all that nationalism, especially in the future, cannot present a threat to peace and stability in the post-Soviet successor states. But it helps explain the relative weakness of nationalist and fundamentalist forces today among the elites and even in the masses in the Russian Federation, Kazakhstan, Belarus and even Ukraine.

Another difference is that the return of some groups of the last generation of the Soviet elites to power should not be overdramatized since their "communist" self-legitimacy has long evaporated and been replaced by fuzzy sets of beliefs, some of them quite compatible with a market economy and even representative democracy. The fact that the Soviet elites themselves, not outsiders (dissidents, nationalists) were instrumental in the regime's dismantling, accounts for the absence of any counter-elite. On the one hand, it leaves us with an almost non-existent civil society, the lack of a viable multiparty system and with the same crowd of rulers, interspersed with a few new faces, in the Kremlin and especially in local state branches. On the other hand, so far there are no political groups on the horizon who could challenge the ex-Soviet elites' current combination of Western liberalism and moderate nationalism in the CIS – in the way the Bolsheviks, the Fascists or the Nazis had challenged the transitional ruling groups in the past in Russia, Italy, and Germany. This underlines an overall stability behind the continuing power struggle in Russia and the other CIS countries.

The analysis presented here does not help much to build over-arching generalizations about the fall of empires. The Soviet case, however, can be put in a broader historical perspective. Traditional forms of legitimacy in China, Persia, the Arab world, the Roman empire, and Russia could withstand centuries of societal pressures. By contrast, the new type of "legitimacy", created by the Bolsheviks and Stalin to replace the traditional forms, lasted only for a few decades and planted the seeds for self-destruction. It could mean that national democracies remain today the only modern form of viable and lasting political legitimacy. But it could also mean that new groups, whose self-legitimacy is based on radical belief systems (be it Muslim fundamentalism or Nazism), may still accomplish brief, but extremely destructive, feats in the art of empire-building. It would not be wise to take a Western form of legitimacy for granted as the basis of a future world order. At the same time, as the cold war demonstrated, it is possible to contain radical elites within their imperial boundaries and then wait until their dangerous creed fades away.

Notes

1. The same thing happened in the field of international relations: John L. Gaddis, "International Relations Theory and the End of the Cold War", *International Security*, Vol. 17, No. 3 Winter 1992/93, pp. 5–58, especially pp. 34–38.
2. Andrei Amalrik, *Prosushchestvuet li Sovetskii Soiuz do 1984 g.?* Amsterdam 1969; English translation: *Will the Soviet Union Survive until 1984?* (New York: Chalidze Press 1970); Alexander J. Motyl, ed., *The Post-Soviet Nations. Perspectives on the Demise of the USSR* (New York: Columbia University Press 1992).
3. Paul Kennedy, *The Rise and Fall of the Great Powers: Economic Change and Military Conflict from 1500 to 2000* (New York: Random House 1987); Anthony Arnold, *The Fateful Pebble: Afghanistan's Role in the Fall of the Soviet Empire* (Novato, CA: Presidio, 1993).
4. In a most recent attempt to dissect the corpse of the Soviet Union, a historian found many causes for sickness, but none of them lethal in itself, see Walter Laqueur, "Gorbachev and Epimetheus: The Origins of the Russian Crisis", *Journal of Contemporary History*, Vol. 28, No. 3 July 1993, pp. 387–419.
5. Seweryn Bialer, *The Soviet Paradox: External Expansion, Internal Decline*, (London: Tauris 1986).
6. Colyn S. Gray, "The Most Dangerous Decade: Historic Mission, Legitimacy, and Dynamics of the Soviet Empire in the 1980s," *Orbis*, Vol. 25, No. 1, Spring 1981, pp. 16, 18, 24, 25.
7. See, Zbigniew Brzezinski, *The Grand Failure. The Birth and Death of*

Communism in the Twentieth Century (London: Macdonald Book 1989), pp. 99, 100, 254–255.

8. By Soviet elites I mean largely key power elites: party apparatchiks, the KGB, the army, the military-industrial complex – but also "surrounding" groups, particularly in Moscow.

9. In this paper, "self-legitimacy" is meant to include not only systematic, overt beliefs of the elites, formalized in ideology, but "group belief systems" that include informal, but often more real perceptions and images. For various theoretical interpretations of this phenomenon see Richard Little and Steve Smith eds., *Belief Systems and International Relations* (Oxford: Basil Blackwell 1988), in particular the chapter by Margot Light, "Belief Systems and Soviet Foreign Policy", pp. 109–126.

10. John Archibald Getty, *Origins of the Great Purges: the Soviet Communist Party Reconsidered, 1933–1938* (Cambridge: Cambridge University Press 1985).

11. See Robert C.Tucker, *Political Culture and Leadership in Soviet Russia from Lenin to Gorbachev* (New York: Norton 1987).

12. Elena Zubkova, "Obchestvennaiia atmosphera posle voiny (1945–1946) (The mood in the post-war society), *Svobodnaia mysl*, #6, 1992, pp. 8–9.

13. Konstanatin V.Pleshakov, "Joseph Stalin's World View" in Thomas G. Paterson, Robert J. McMahon, eds., *The Origins of the Cold War*, Third Edition (Lexington, MA: D.C. Heath and Co. 1991), pp. 60–73.

14. Among the top *nomenklatura* officials in 1981 80.4 percent came from families of peasants and unskilled labor, 3.6 percent from skilled labor; 5.4 percent from "white collar" families (nizkokvalifitsirovannie rabotniki umstvennogo truda) and zero from the families of professionals! T.P. Korzhikhina, Yu. Figatner, "Sovetskaia nomenlkatura: stanovleniie, mekhanizmi deisviia" (Soviet nomeklatura: formation and mechanisms), *Voprosi istorii*, No. 7, 1993, p. 32.

15. Dmitry Furman, "Nasha strannaia revolutsiia"(Our strange revolution), *Svobodnaia mysl*, No. 1, 1993, pp. 13, 14, 15.

16. See "The secret documents from special dossiers: Afghanistan," *Voprosy Istorii*, No. 3, 1993, especially p. 26.

17. "The Novocherkassk tragedy, 1962" (Publication of the reports of the KGB to the Soviet leadership from the Storage Center of Contemporary Documentation, Moscow), *Istoricheskii arkhiv*, No.1, 1993, pp. 110–136.

18. On the lulling stability of the Cold War see John L. Gaddis, "The Long Peace: Elements of Stability in the Postwar International System," *International Security*, Vol. 10., No. 4, Spring 1986, pp. 99–142.

19. See the most recent findings from the Soviet archives in Odd Arne Westad, "The Road to Kabul: The Soviet Union and the Afghan Communists, 1978–1979," *International History Review*, Vol. 16, No. 1, February 1994.

20. There was, on the other hand, the process that Jack Snyder called "log-rolling" behind this expansionism. See Jack L. Snyder, *Myths of Empire: Domestic Politics and International Ambition* (Ithaca: Cornell University Press 1991).

21. The opposite opinion is expressed by many, including Arnold, *The Fateful Pebble*.

22. Don Oberdorfer, *The Turn: From the Cold War to a New Era. The United States and the Soviet Union 1983–1990* (New York: Poseidon Press 1991),

pp. 66–67.

23. For a different opinion, see "SDI, Chernobyl helped to end the Cold War," *Washington Post*, 27 February 1993. I attended the conference at Princeton University where the former Soviet foreign minister Aleksander Bessmertnik confirmed the impact of the SDI, but, according to my records, he was in the minority among the Russian participants. What Anatoly Chernyaev, Gorbachev's principal national security adviser, stressed was the great impact of the Chernobyl hernobyl disaster.

24. This motive was mentioned by Yuri Andropov in 28 March 1983 in the discussion with Peres de Cuellar. The other five were Soviet prestige in the other "socialist countries," relations with the Islam world, with the "third world" in general, and, finally, the negative effect on the domestic situation of the USSR, her economy and society – G.M. Kornienko. "How the decision was taken to intervene into Afghanistan and to withdraw," *Novaia i noveishaia istoria*, No. 3 (May–June 1993), pp. 108, 112–113; Also: S.F. Akhromeiev, G.M. Kornienko, *Glazami marshala i Diplomata* ("With the Eyes of a Marshal and a Diplomat: a Critical Look at the Foreign Policy of the USSR Before and After 1985") (Moscow: Mezhdunarodniie otnosheniia, 1992).

25. On this, see Paul Kennedy, *The Rise and Fall of the Great Powers,* chapter 11.

26. The erroneous prediction was in Colin Gray, "The Most Dangerous Decade" (see note 6).

27. Valerie Bunce, "Domestic reform and international change: the Gorbachev reforms in historical perspective," *International Organization*, Vol. 47, No. 1, winter 1993, p. 117.

28. *End of Empire. The Demise of the Soviet Union. G.R. Urban in conversation with leading thinkers of our time.* (Washington, D.C.: The American University Press 1993), p. 80.

29. See Steven F. Cohen, *Rethinking the Soviet Experience. Politics and History Since 1917* (Oxford: Oxford University Press 1985), pp. 79–92.

30. Judy Shelton, *The Coming Soviet Crash,* (New York, 1989). I found this quotation in Wlodzimierz Brus, "'Perestroika': Retreat of a Revolution?" in E.E. Rice, ed., *Revolution and Counter-Revolution* (Oxford: Wolfson College Press 1991), p. 185.

31. M.S. Gorbachev – A. Oketto, 28 February 1989, the transcript of the meeting, *Svobodnaya mysl*, 4, March, 1993, pp. 37, 38.

9

The End of the Cold War and the Future of American Power

Aaron L. Friedberg

Over the course of the past half century the United States has declined but, unlike its former Soviet rival, it has not fallen. From the point of view of the United States, the relevant questions now are, first, how the end of the Cold War will affect the subsequent trajectory of its power, and second, how changes in American power (and, more broadly, in the distribution of power in the international system as a whole) will affect the legitimacy and stability of the post-Cold-War order. In this essay I will concentrate primarily on the first set of issues, examining in turn how the events of the late 1980s and early 1990s will combine with longer term trends to shape the further evolution of American economic, military, structural, "soft," and political power before turning briefly to a consideration of the larger significance of these trends. Because so much is contingent, both aspects of this discussion are necessarily speculative, with the projections of the second portion building on those of the first. Although there are a number of contrary trends, I conclude that, on balance, the end of the Cold War will accelerate the *relative* decline in American national power. Changes in the distribution of power will lead to mounting disputes over the legitimacy of existing rules and institutions and, as a result, to a protracted period of international instability. This turmoil is likely to give rise, not to a new, unified, world order, but to a set of separate, competing sub-systems.

American Power and the End of the Cold War

Economic power

Between the late 1940s and the early 1980s, America's shares of total global output, worldwide production of manufactured goods, world trade, and exports of high technology products all diminished, along with its former wide lead in national economic productivity and its once unquestionable position as the leading source of innovations in virtually every category of technology.[1] With these facts generally agreed to, the decline debate of the late 1980s centered on three issues: First, whether the erosion of the post-war period had run its course or would continue. Second, whether it was inevitable (the product both of the world-wide recovery that followed the devastation of World War Two and of an ineluctable global diffusion of technological competence and productive capacities) or at least partly the result of mistakes and misguided policies. And, finally, if it was not completely unavoidable, to what extent the relative economic decline of the United States had been caused by the excessive exertions of forty years of competition with the USSR.

The end of the Cold War should shed considerable light on each of these controversies, especially the last. We are about to witness that rare event: a "natural experiment" in which the unfolding of history may actually help to resolve an ongoing scholarly dispute. With the collapse of the Soviet Union, US defence spending (which had been declining since the mid-1980s) began to diminish rapidly, and it is likely to continue to do so for at least the remainder of this decade. The United States is already spending a smaller fraction of its gross national product on defence than at any time since before the Korean War (around 4.1 percent in fiscal year 1994) and, barring some unforeseen international disaster, the figure will fall still further in the years ahead. In all, the share of GNP devoted to defence is likely to shrink to below 50 percent of its Reagan Administration peak, from 6.3 percent in 1985 to no more than 3 percent (and perhaps less) by the beginning of the twenty-first century.[2] If, in the past, the United States was held back in competition with other industrial nations by the comparatively heavy weight of its military expenditures, in the future those burdens will diminish and American economic performance should improve. The end of the Cold War may therefore provide an opportunity for an enhancement, not only of absolute American domestic *welfare*, but of relative American international economic *power*.[3] How realistic are these expectations?

In the short term, the economic effects of the Cold War's conclusion have been almost entirely negative. Cutbacks in defence spending have reduced the level of aggregate demand in the American economy and thus slowed its growth. In this way the collapse of Communism has already contributed to the protracted recession of the late 1980s and early 1990s and thus, ironically, to the electoral difficulties of the Republican party. Aside from their overall effects, defence reductions have hit hardest at certain industries (notably aerospace, electronics, and shipbuilding) and at the regions of the country in which they happen to be concentrated (especially the "gunbelt" that extends from the far Northeast, down through the South and across the South-west to the West coast). In all, by the end of the 1990s, the post-Cold-War builddown will have resulted in the loss of well over one million defence sector jobs, including those of more than 100,000 highly trained scientists and engineers.[4]

As these figures suggest, the end of the Cold War will free substantial resources, human as well as financial, from their previous allocation to the manufacture of military power. The issue now and for the future is where those resources will go and, specifically, whether they will be applied effectively to the production of national *economic* power. One simplified and stylized way of approaching this problem is to ask the following question: Suppose that defence spending *does* fall from 6 to 3 percent of GNP. What will happen to the 3 percent of GNP that is freed up as a result? If this fraction of national income is invested (whether by government or private business), the impact on future American economic performance could be positive and substantial. To the extent that it goes to boost present consumption, on the other hand, the long-term benefits will be diminished.[5]

Private investment could be increased most effectively by devoting every dollar saved on defence to reducing the federal budget deficit (in other words, by allowing defence to fall without cutting taxes or increasing non-defence programs). As the deficit shrinks, the government will have to borrow less money and it will therefore compete less vigorously with private business for scarce capital. The result will be falling interest rates, more investment by industry in new plant, equipment, and research and, in the long run, higher rates of growth in productivity and national income. Similar benefits might be derived if some of the savings from defence were used to finance selected public investments, such as improvements in the roads, bridges, ports, and communications networks that make up the nation's "infrastructure," or more spending for education and scientific research.

At the other end of the spectrum of possibilities, the "peace dividend" could wind up being consumed by either the private or the public sectors. If every dollar saved from defence were given back in the form of tax reductions, private consumption would rise, but the deficit and the level of private investment would remain substantially unchanged. A short-term increase in welfare would be purchased at the expense of slower growth and less substantial increases in future welfare (and power) than would otherwise have been possible. Reductions in military expenditures could also be offset by increases in other forms of public spending that would resemble consumption more closely than anything that might reasonably be labeled investment. Federal dollars devoted to huge pork barrel highway construction projects, for example, or expanded health care and retirement benefits for middle and upper income citizens would make some people better off, but their contribution to the long-term economic well-being of the nation would be dubious, at best. The problem is that, precisely because of their size and the broad dispersal of their benefits, such spending programs have proven enormously popular with large and influential blocks of voters. Cutting them back or even reducing their rate of growth will not be easy. By comparison, some of the more worthwhile forms of public investment (spending to support basic scientific research or improvements in the health and education of the nation's poorest citizens) have never been nearly as popular.

A perfect allocative process would channel the resources freed by defence cutbacks into an optimum mix of public and private investments. In the real world of American domestic politics, however, such an ideal outcome is inconceivable and, indeed, it is unlikely even to be approached. To the extent that it is not, however, the benefits that could conceivably have been derived from the end of the Cold War will go unrealized.

But the difficulty may lie deeper than the allocative inefficiencies of the American political system. It is possible and, indeed, likely that a number of the nation's problems will not prove readily susceptible to repair through the simple expenditure of money, whether public or private, and it is even conceivable that some could actually be made *worse* by well-intentioned but ill-conceived government policies. Drug abuse, violent crime, teenage pregnancy, and declining levels of literacy all represent a drag on national economic performance, both directly, through their effects on individuals who might otherwise have become more productive members of society, and indirectly, through their diversion of resources to policing, emergency medical care, and unemployment support which, in a better world, would have been put to more productive uses.

As important as they are, however, it is not obvious that any of these ills could be cured even by massive new government programs, let alone by those that are likely actually to be initiated. For all of their economic implications, most of these problems are not purely or even primarily economic, but rather social or cultural in origin. Their solutions cannot come entirely "from above," nor can they take the form simply of a transfer of material resources. If, as some critics now claim, economic rejuvenation depends on "cultural renewal," on the rebuilding of the social and civic institutions that inculcate the values of "self-control, compassion, tolerance, civility, honesty, and respect for authority," then the United States is likely to be saddled with serious (and, compared to most of its competitors, disproportionate) liabilities for many years to come.[6]

To sum up: the end of the Cold War will result in some improvement in the performance of the American economy, but positive changes are unlikely to be large or to come quickly. As compared to a number of other nations (especially those on the eastern edge of the Pacific Rim), the United States will probably continue to grow less rapidly, and its relative economic power will therefore continue to decline as the twentieth century draws to a close.

Military power

The collapse of the Soviet Union and the fragmentation of its armed forces has left the United States in a position of unquestioned global military preponderance. In terms of the sheer quantity of firepower at its disposal, the United States is and will remain for the foreseeable future the world's first-ranked military power. That said, it is nevertheless also true that the end of the Cold War is hastening a world-wide diffusion of military capabilities that has already been under way for some time. This diffusion, when coupled with the ongoing reduction and retraction of American forces, will lead in some areas to a greater equalization in the balance of effective military power.

American military planners have already identified the most meaningful measure of post-Cold War capability as the capacity of their forces to engage and defeat those of hostile regional powers.[7] While *total* US resources will continue to be greater than those of any local opponent, the results of an actual military engagement would, of course, be determined by the forces that the two sides were willing and able to bring to bear against one another. Here, for a variety of reasons, the margin of American advantage over some potential enemies is likely to diminish in the years ahead.

Among the forces now being demobilized are some, like aircraft carriers, that would be necessary for purposes of "power projection." Moreover, as the total size of the US military shrinks, the fraction of remaining forces that would have to be committed to any future regional conflict will grow, and the willingness of the nation's political and military leaders to risk their engagement may diminish. In 1991, with its capabilities still at close to Cold War levels, the United States was able to deploy overwhelming power against Iraq without serious concern for its continuing responsibilities in other parts of the world (such as the Korean peninsula). By the turn of the century, a serious conflict with a powerful regional opponent will require something more nearly approaching a complete commitment of American capabilities. In the late 1960s the issue was whether to prepare for "one and a half" or "two and a half" wars (i.e. a major war with either China or Russia, or both together, along with a lesser conflict somewhere in the Third World). In the early 1990s US planners, eager to make still deeper cuts in defence spending, debated the virtues of a "one half" versus a "two half" war force.

The ability of the United States to deploy and sustain large forces at great distances in its 1991 war with Iraq also depended critically on access to bases, communications facilities, and supply stockpiles in and around the Persian Gulf. Most of these were acquired as a direct result of the Cold War. With its conclusion, changing alliance relationships and mounting domestic budgetary pressures are likely to result in the dismantlement of much, if not all, of this far-flung infrastructure. Even with substantial advances in communications and transportation technology, distance still matters in military affairs. The loss of facilities outside its home territory will steepen the "power gradient" facing the United States and make it that much more difficult for it to bring overwhelming force to bear in every corner of the globe.

As the absolute capacity of the United States to project power dwindles, the military capabilities of a number of states in the Middle East, South-west and North-east Asia will continue to grow. This is a process that has been going on for some time, with countries like Libya, Israel, Saudi Arabia, Iran, Iraq, India, Pakistan, Taiwan, China, South and North Korea seeking over the past several decades both to import sophisticated weapons from their Cold-War allies and, in many cases, to acquire a greater indigenous capacity for their design and manufacture. The end of the Cold War will serve to accelerate this long-term trend toward the diffusion of military capabilities. With their traditional enemies still in place but their former superpower patrons either gone or no longer as reliable ıs they once were, many countries will seek to enhance their capacity for self-defence. In this way, the retraction of both Soviet and American power is likely to stimulate rather than dampen local arms races.

The collapse of Communism in the East and the corresponding contraction of domestic arms markets in the West is also changing the character of the stream of military exports flowing from North to South. With military enterprises struggling to survive and governments desperate for hard currency, the variety and quality of the items available for sale from the former Soviet empire has already increased considerably (although, as the export business has moved to a cash-only basis, the total volume of arms transfers has, for the moment, gone down). Many Western arms manufacturers and governments, meanwhile, are looking to exports to keep assembly lines open and production costs down. In the resulting buyer's market, countries with the ability to pay cash for their purchases will have a better chance of obtaining the most sophisticated weapons, and also the kinds of technology transfers and joint production agreements that will enable them eventually to build their own advanced armaments.[8]

Weapons aside, the relaxation of the US-led Cold-War export control system, the general diffusion of scientific and engineering competence beyond the United States and its allies, and the increasing blurriness of the line separating military from civilian technologies will also combine to ease access worldwide to what might best be labeled "strategically significant technologies." The ability of regional powers to scramble their communcations with low cost encryption devices or to receive extremely precise navigational signals or reconnaissance imagery from overhead commercial satellites will further narrow the gap that presently separates the capabilities of their armed forces from those of the most advanced nations, including the United States.

Even if they cannot hope to match their American opponents missile for missile, plane for plane, and tank for tank, it is likely that an increasing number of states will soon have access to weapons of mass destruction, the "Great Equalizers" of the late twentieth century. A nation armed with a small arsenal of deliverable nuclear weapons could not hope to survive, still less to win, an all-out war with the United States. But, by threatening to use such weapons against American power projection forces, regional allies, or home territory, even a lesser nuclear power might be able to deter the US from acting against it. Certainly, had Saddam Hussein been possessed of a working nuclear arsenal, the United States would have been far less willing to station half a million troops, a sizeable fraction of its air forces, and a large naval armada within easy reach of his frontiers. In the near future, the southern and eastern edges of Eurasia may be dotted with "nuclear porcupines," nations that may not be capable of projecting their own power at great distances, but which outsiders will find it difficult and dangerous to approach.

Structural power

Even if the American share of various power *resources* (total global product, world nuclear stockpile etc.) continues to decline, it does not follow that the American ability to control important events and processes will necessarily erode proportionately, or even that it need deteriorate at all. Throughout the Cold War the United States derived great influence from the fact that it was able largely to set the rules and organize the institutions through which so much of the world's economic and political business was transacted. In the 1980s Susan Strange argued persuasively that what she called America's "structural power" had persisted, indeed increased in some respects, even as its share of the world's stock of various traditional power resources diminished.[9] With the collapse of Communism and the pending absorption of much of the East into the political and economic order of the West, the scope of American structural power seems set to grow, perhaps dramatically.

There can be no question that the United States played a decisive role in shaping the most important international institutions (defined broadly to include everything from formal organizations to less tangible regimes) put in place at the end of the Second World War. It is also true that, to a very considerable degree, the construction of these institutions reflected American values, American interests, and, most important, American power. The United States was able to get others to accept the structures that it had devised largely, although by no means exclusively, because of its preponderance in economic and military resources. Once in place, these structures continued to operate in ways that benefited the United States, as well as its allies and trading partners.

American structural power is critically important in explaining the workings of the post-war world. But if the years immediately following 1945 marked the creation of a distinct new order, then it seems likely that the world is on the threshold of another founding, one in which different structures will be assembled that will then go on to shape the pattern of relations in the post-Cold-War world. Like their predecessors, these institutions will mirror the distribution of power resources existing at the moment of their creation. For this reason, the new pattern of structural power will be far less fully a manifestation of American values and concerns, and it is likely, therefore, to operate in ways less favorable to American interests than the one first established some forty-five years ago.

Looking first at institutions in the sense of formal organizations, many of the mechanisms through which the United States exerted influence during the Cold War will wither in importance now that it is over, and some may cease to exist altogether. It is not obvious, for example, that the North Atlantic Treaty Organization can long outlive the enemy it was built to oppose. Continuous rhetoric and occasional symbolic gestures to the contrary notwithstanding, NATO was, from first to last, an American-built and led organization. If it is involved at all, the United States will play a far less dominant role in any new arrangements for the maintenance of European security.

While they may maintain their outward appearance, some of the international organizations built up after the Second World War will undergo significant changes in their internal workings and hence in the pattern of their outward operations. These changes too will follow shifts in the distribution of power away from the earlier era of American preponderance. The granting of permanent membership on the United Nations Security Council to Japan and Germany would both reflect their increased capabilities in relation to the United States and, by adding an important new structural dimension to their power, further enhance their comparative ability to exert influence. The enormous growth in the Japanese contribution to various international financial institutions certainly entitles them to a greater say in their management; but, here too, as the extent of Japan's structural power increases, the former dominance of the United States is bound to diminish.[10]

Finally, the end of the Cold War seems likely to accelerate the construction and consolidation of new, regionally focused economic, political, and military organizations in which the American role will be, at best, limited. The movement toward greater European integration and the elevated importance of the governing mechanisms of the European Community is the prime example of this tendency. The United States is presently encouraging the formation of multilateral organizations designed to enhance trans-Pacific economic cooperation and to promote East Asian security.

But it cannot be said to be controlling either process; nor will it dominate the institutions that emerge as fully as those it planned, paid for, and built at the end of World War Two.

Turning now to the less formal manifestations of its structural power, Susan Strange has argued that, well into the 1980s, the United States continued to have an extraordinary capacity "to choose and to shape the structures of the global political economy within which other states, their political institutions, their economic enterprises, and (not least) their professional people have to operate." This influence had its basis in, among other things, the ongoing American dominance of the systems through which production is organized and knowledge diffused.[11] Although these less tangible forms of structural power may prove more persistent than their more concrete counterparts, here too there is evidence of considerable, ongoing erosion.

Strange maintains that the true measure of American economic preponderance is not the share of goods and services produced within its borders, but the proportion produced "a) in the United States, and b) by enterprises ultimately headquartered in the United States and responsible to the government in Washington."[12] Because of their extensive investments in plants and facilities in foreign countries, US firms and, by extension presumably, the US government are able to exert a far greater influence over the world economy than might at first appear to be the case.

While they have sometimes been willing to do Washington's bidding, American multinational corporations have certainly not always been the faithful overseas executors of offical policy. Indeed, as one recent study demonstrates, the ability of the US government to impose its will on the overseas subsidiaries of American corporations has declined considerably since the 1960s.[13] With the disintegration of Soviet communism, government officials have largely lost the national security rationale that provided them with a powerful source of leverage over the offshore activities of self-interested corporations. Indeed, compared to some of its more dirigiste competitors, the post-Cold-War American state, with its free market ideology and porous political structure, is likely to be particularly ill-equipped to control the behavior of "its" businesses overseas.

Corporate power does not necessarily translate smoothly and easily into national political power. In any case, the degree of one-sided American dominance of the world's productive structure has diminished in recent years. Beginning in the mid-1980s the flow of foreign direct investment into the United States increased dramatically. If the foreign-based affiliates of American corporations are ultimately responsible to the US government, then it seems only reasonable to assume that the American-based affiliates of foreign firms owe similar allegiance to *their* home countries. A greater equality in investment flows should therefore offset some of the previous structural advantages enjoyed by the United States.[14] Where the firms of one particular country invest more in the US than American companies invest in it, that country may actually hold something of a bilateral edge in this particular form of structural power.[15]

In addition to being itself penetrated by foreign investment, the United States is now also no longer so clearly the dominant external investor either globally or in many important regions of the world. Between the mid-1970s and the early 1990s the United States went from supplying almost half of the total foreign direct investment flowing out from the most industrialized countries, to accounting for only around one sixth.[16] Whereas in 1970 fully half of the world's 7,000 multinationals were American or British, twenty years later the United States, Japan, Germany, and Switzerland together provided a base of operations for half of an expanded total of 35,000 multinational firms.[17] In East Asia, Japanese foreign direct investment flows are now considerably larger than those of their US competitors.[18] Within Western Europe, an increasing fraction of "inward investment" comes from other European countries.[19] Japanese companies are rapidly expanding their investments in parts of Central and Latin America,[20] and it is European, rather than American firms that are leading the way in investing in many parts of the former Soviet empire.

US dominance of what Strange calls the "knowledge structure" is also no longer what it once was. Over the past thirty years, other advanced countries have been increasing their expenditures on scientific research and development at almost twice the pace of the United States.[21] The cumulative impact of this trend (arguably heightened by the fact that a sizeable portion of American R&D has been devoted to military rather than commercial ends) has come to be reflected in a variety of quantitative and qualitiative measures. In 1981, of the top 15 corporate patent recipients in the United States, 8 were American-owned firms and only two were Japanese; ten years laters those figures stood at 5 and 6 respectively.[22] In 1991, of 15 companies with the fastest "technology cycle times" (a measure of the speed with which firms introduce innovations), all but one were Japanese. In the same year, Japanese companies were the leading recipients of US patents in 4 of 13 high technology sectors.[23] Since the early 1970s, the US share of world high-technology exports has decreased somewhat,[24] and the trend in a variety of specific sectors appears to be even more marked. Commerce Department experts have estimated that US firms are presently losing ground to their Japanese competitors in five of twelve important "emerging technologies" (advanced materials, biotechnology, digital imaging, sensors, and superconductors) and to the Europeans in one more (flexible manufacturing). In terms of the introduction of new products (as compared to new ideas) the situation looks even less promising. Even in four other areas where US companies may continue for a time to hold their own in research (advanced semi-conductors, data storage, high speed computing, and optoelectronics), Japanese firms are likely to do better in commercializing new technologies.[25]

This last point is important both for what it portends for the future shape of the global knowledge structure, and for what it reveals about the essential character of the American system. Because commercial success means more money for research, an edge in production can lead eventually to advantages in innovation. It is unlikely that the United States will be able to continue indefinitely as the world's leading source of new ideas if it does not also increase its capacity for turning a number of them to its economic benefit.[26] In the long run, Nobel prizes may be less important than high-tech trade statistics or, rather, trade statistics may be a leading indicator of Nobel prizes. Ironically, America's very creativity and openness is one factor that has contributed to the speed of its relative economic decline. By making it so easy for others to study and invest within its frontiers, the United States has eased the outward flow of innovations first developed in American universities and laboratories. A country less committed to the unrestricted movement of people and ideas would be less free and less appealing, but also (and partly as a result) better equipped to husband its lead over rising competitors. The next technological hegemon may well try to pursue more restrictive policies.

"Soft" power

It has been suggested that the ultimate source of America's influence in the world is not the size of its economy, the might of its military, or its control of important international institutions, but rather the appeal of what it represents, the seemingly universal attraction exerted by its culture and ideology. Advances in communications technology are speeding the spread of America's message to every corner of the globe. And each country that adopts capitalism and democracy as a result will further amplify the power of the American example. It is at the level of ideas, finally, that the United States most decisively won the Cold War, and it is here too that some observers believe it will win the peace that follows.[27]

The reach and resonance of American popular culture are undeniable, even if its precise political significance is often difficult to discern. Iranian militants may drink soft drinks and wear track suits first made popular in America, but this hardly means that they love the United States, still less that they embrace the policies of its government. The rapid growth of a global market for American cultural products made possible by rising incomes and improved technologies seems also to be exerting a homogenizing feedback effect on the creative process. With a sizeable portion of potential profits to be made overseas, American movies are now produced with an eye on the foreign audience and often with the help of foreign investors. Such films, as one critic puts it, "might as well come from the moon or the Cayman Islands" as from Hollywood.[28] Increased foreign investment in US movie and recording studios seems likely to accelerate this tendency and to render their products less uniquely "American." In both Europe and Asia there is also evidence that growing economic and technological integration is being accompanied by an intensified interest in creating a modern popular culture with a more distinctly regional flavor. In all, globalization appears to be leading, not to a strengthening of America's importance as a producer of popular culture, but to a dilution of its prior dominance.[29]

It is worth recalling finally that as the volume of images of American life transmitted around the world grows, so too does the number that are mixed or negative. The same satellites that beam each breathlessly awaited episode of "Dallas" or "Beverly Hills 90210" into untold millions of households also carry live, uncensored coverage of urban riots and self-immolating religious cults. The American penchant for national self-absorption and self-congratulation goes hand-in-hand with a remarkable taste for self-exposure and self-criticism. The pictures that linger longest in the minds of external observers will not always be those that are the most flattering.

Certainly the most important trend of the late twentieth century is the apparent convergence in many parts of the world on the norms of political democratization and economic liberalization. These are principles for which the United States has long been the most out-spoken advocate. It does not seem unreasonable therefore to expect that their growing acceptance should result in a substantial enhancement of American power. The fact that an increasing portion of the world's leaders and people are now on the same wavelength as their counterparts in the United States may mean that they will be more receptive to its guidance. Indeed, writes one political scientist, because its "purposes are more widely shared in the world today . . . America does not need as much power as it did 20 or 40 years ago. It can maintain its leadership by being more of a global pope than a global power."[30]

As appealing as this vision of low-cost leadership of a like-minded world undoubtedly is to many Americans, there are several reasons to regard it with skepticism. There is, first of all, the question whether democracy and capitalism will ultimately flourish in all of the places where they have recently set down roots. The history of past waves of democratization suggests that there will eventually be some measure of recession, leaving a net gain in the number of democratic states, but one not as large as appeared possible at the moment when the tide was running at its fullest.[31] The failure of democracy and capitalism quickly to solve the prob-lems of ordinary people will inevitably lead in some places to an upsurge of anti-Western and specifically anti-American feeling. Having finally tasted the forbidden fruit of freedom, and finding it less sweet than advertised, residents of some parts of the former Soviet empire may soon be much less impressed by the American example than they were during the Cold War.[32]

The extent to which democracy and capitalism will eventually spread has yet to be determined. In some parts of the less developed world (and especially those dominated by Islam) the recent defeat of the Soviet Union may actually increase the feeling that Western values and institutions represent the greatest threat to local auton-omy. During the Cold War it may have been necessary to resist the depredations of both godless communism *and* secular capitalism, but there were also opportunities to play one off against the other. If there was previously any doubt, the United States has now emerged as the single, unchallenged "Great Satan" against whom all ideo-logical energies must be mobilized.

Even those societies that do turn increasingly towards democracy and capitalism will not necessarily embrace the American variants of those general forms. Indeed, given its long-standing social prob-lems and its more recent difficulties in international economic competition, some observers are likely to see the United States, not as a role model, but as an illustration of how *not* to organize important aspects of societal life. In Asia and in other parts of the developing world there is growing interest in a Japanese, Korean or even a Chinese model for economic and political development, one that places more emphasis on stability than freedom, stresses group responsibilities over individual rights, and assigns a substantial role to the state in "governing the market."[33] Systems built on such principles may be capitalist democracies by some definition of those words, but they will be very different from the United States and they are unlikely to look to it as their "pope."

Political power

In one sense, American power can be thought of as being merely the product of all of the various elements discussed thus far. But national political power is more than just the sum of these disparate parts; it involves also an intangible, dual-edged element of will. Whatever the objective capabilities of the United States, it may lack the willingness to apply them towards any coherent purpose. Even if it attempts to do so it may find that others are unwilling to follow its lead and that they can be compelled to do so, if at all, only at considerable cost.[34] In either case, the real political power of the United States would be significantly less than it might appear.

Some observers have argued that, even if its relative power *has* declined in certain ways, the United States nevertheless remains the most powerful state in the international system and that it is therefore "bound to lead."[35] Needless to say, such assertions represent expressions of a particular set of preferences rather than any iron-clad prediction about the future. What may arguably be necessary will not always be possible. Especially in a democracy, the gap between the policies that some members of the elite believe to be essential to the promotion of the nation's interests and those that the public is willing to support can, if sufficiently wide, be decisive.

In the aftermath of the Cold War, America's willingness to lead has declined sharply. The inward-turning impulse that determined the outcome of the 1992 Presidential campaign was in part the product of short-term considerations, a certain psychological exhaustion following the triumphant end of the Cold War and the somewhat less stirring termination of hostilities in the Persian Gulf, coupled with the effects of a lingering economic recession. But that inclination also feeds from deeper sources, and there are reasons to believe that it is more likely to intensify than to dissipate. The growing awareness of problems at home and the desire for domestic rejuvenation reflect a recurring pattern in American politics that is driven and sustained in part by generational change.[36] Although the election of an unusually young President has accelerated the process, the chances are good that the next twenty years or so of American politics will be dominated by figures whose views were shaped by the events of the 1960s and 1970s (the civil rights movement and Vietnam) rather than the 1940s and 1950s (World War Two and the opening phase of the Cold War). Such people are likely to be more skeptical of foreign entanglements and more concerned with (and optimistic about) the prospects for domestic reform than those who went before them, or those who come after.

Some measure of disengagement would also be in keeping with the larger pattern of American involvement in world affairs. This does not mean that the United States is necessarily on the verge of a new era of isolationism. The received image of total American withdrawal in the 1920s and 1930s is, in any case, exaggerated. But it is worth recalling that, for most of the past century, an active, extensive, and continuous US role has been motivated and justified by the existence of a perceived threat to the nation's survival. It is not yet clear what, if anything, can take the place of resistance to such a menace as the organizing principle around which to build the nation's foreign and defence policies. Appeals to bloodless abstractions such as the inevitability of interdependence, or the importance of supporting international institutions may not hold the attention of the many, however much they excite the imaginations of the few.

The US post-war posture was built on global economic preponderance and, through the 1960s, vigorous domestic growth. Taken together these allowed Americans both to feel generous towards (and superior to) their less well-to-do allies and to bear the burdens of their world role without any undue strain. Growing anxiety about relative economic decline has already eroded the sense that the United States has a unique capacity and responsibility for global leadership. If the previous discussion of the prospects for American economic power is accurate, such feelings will not diminish substantially in the years ahead. On a more practical level, the present budgetary bind is tight enough to continue to constrict spending for external purposes (including defence and foreign assistance) until the end of this century, if not beyond. While the current mood of introversion could change, in the absence of some catastrophe it seems likely that the American recession is closer to its beginning than to its end.

Ironically, as the willingness of the United States to supply leadership diminishes, the demand from others that it do so may increase, at least in the short run. This is a result, not only of the crises of the moment, but of a generalized uncertainty about what the future will hold, coupled with a growing realization that, at long last, the Americans may finally be going home. The old Cold-War debates over diplomacy, burden-sharing, alliance military strategy, and export controls quickly developed a stylized quality, like the recurrent squabbles of an essentially stable family. Americans felt free to complain about allied irresponsibility and shiftlessness (and the allies, for their part, did not hesitate to criticize the United States for being overbearing and reckless) but both sides knew that, in the end, they were stuck with one another. Now the future of their mutual relationship is much less certain and the balance of bargaining power between the parties has begun to shift. A radical change in existing arrangements would impose heavier burdens on America's allies, even as it promised to lighten the load borne by the United States. It is because they would prefer not to assume these burdens, at least for the moment, that others may be especially attentive to American concerns and receptive to American leadership.

This situation is unlikely to last. On the one hand, American foot-dragging and buck-passing will push its former allies to assume more responsibility for themselves. On the other, an effort on the part of the United States to maintain its dominance by driving hard new bargains and passing off to others a far greater percentage of the cost of existing arrangements will eventually have the same effect. Over time, both in Europe and in Asia, the US and its old allies will increasingly go their separate ways. In the absence of a unifying common threat, more independent diplomatic and military policies seem inevitable and divergent economic policies far more likely. This does not mean that the United States and its former allies will not continue to consult and to cooperate on many issues, still less that they will become enemies. But the coalition of which they were a part is rapidly dissolving, and with it will go much of the influence that the United States once derived from its position as coalition leader.

Implications and Conclusions

What has been described thus far is a more plural world, one in which the United States will continue to be *primus inter pares*, but in which, in many important respects, its relative power will decline at an accelerated pace. In terms of its raw economic capabilities, the position of the United States in relation to Japan (and eventually China) is likely to erode still further. In the military realm, the balance of effective capabilities between the US and a number of growing regional powers (including, perhaps, Iran, India, and China) will shift from the center toward the periphery. Some of America's structural power will flow to other nations, some (and some of its "soft" power as well) will find its way into the hands of non-state actors like multinational corporations. And, assuming that no other country takes on an equivalent leadership role, much of what the United States gives up in the way of political power will simply be dissipated.

What will be the implications of these changes in the distribution of power for the legitimacy and stability of the international system? Legitimate orders, whether domestic or international, are stable because most of the participants, most of the time, accept the principles on which they are based and the rules, procedures, and institutions through which they operate. Systems in which power is distributed in very different ways can enjoy equivalent measures of legitimacy and stability. Equality among members and a say for all in the creation of the system's norms and institutions can promote their acceptance and enhance stability, but hierarchical systems in which some are willing to accept subordinate roles can also be both legitimate and stable. *Changes* in the distribution of power, on the other hand, are almost certain to give rise to disputes over the legitimacy of existing arrangements and hence to at least a temporary reduction in stability. This is most dramatically the case when a formerly hegemonic power is challenged for pre-eminence by a single rising state. Then, writes Robert Gilpin, "the legitimacy of the system may be said to be challenged" and an unrestrained struggle for dominance will typically result.[37]

The trends described here are less stark and their consequences will almost certainly be less cataclysmic. America's decline in most categories of capability is relative rather than absolute and, perhaps even more important, the United States is not being challenged in all areas simultaneously by a single rising competitor. The diffusion of power throughout the international system is therefore likely to result, not in a single, epic convulsion, followed by the rapid consolidation of a new order, but rather in a period of many, simultaneous, lower-level disputes over existing institutions and practices. This interval of declining legitimacy and increasing instability is already well under way and, given the nature of the changes that underlie it, there is reason to expect that it will persist for some time. The United States no longer has the capacity single-handedly to create a "new world order," but neither does anyone else.

If it is to emerge at all, a new global order will have to grow out of a process of inter-state bargaining and enlightened compromise. Optimists believe that this process will be eased by a global convergence on liberal, democratic, capitalist norms. It is possible to imagine a new international system, made up of similarly organized states, that would enjoy a far greater degree of legitimacy and a higher measure of stability than the old order. But, for reasons that have already been suggested, this is not the only, nor necessarily the most plausible scenario. Convergence remains a projection and a hypothesis rather than an accomplished fact, and cooperation in the post-Cold-War world is turning out to be an illusive goal, even among states that appear already to have a great deal in common.

There is no law of nature that requires the pieces of the old system to resolve themselves into a single, all-encompassing whole. Indeed, given the fragmented foundation of power on which a new order will have to be built, what seems more likely is the gradual emergence of several sub-systems. These might be organized regionally (Asia, Europe, America), on the basis of wealth (North vs South) or perhaps along "civilizational" lines (Western, Confucian, Japanese, Hindu, Slavic-Orthodox, Islamic).[38] Each sub-system might enjoy a degree of internal legitimacy and stability, but the relations between them could well be fraught with conflict. The liberal dream of "one world" seems as distant at the close of the Cold War as it did at the beginning.

Notes

1. A variety of these indicators are discussed in Aaron L. Friedberg, "The Strategic Implications of Relative Economic Decline", *Political Science Quarterly*, 104 (Fall 1989), pp. 401–409. See also Paul Kennedy, *The Rise and Fall of the Great Powers* (New York: Random House 1987), pp. 413–540; Joseph S. Nye, *Bound to Lead* (New York: Basic Books 1990), pp. 69–78; Robert O. Keohane, *After Hegemony* (Princeton: Princeton University Press 1984), p. 36.
2. The Clinton Administration now projects that defence outlays will be 3 percent of GNP in FY 1998. Deeper cuts are a distinct possibility. See Secretary of Defense Les Aspin, "Statement Before the House Armed Services

Committee in Connection with the Clinton Defense Plan," (mimeo, 30 March 1993), p. 19.

3. In the disscussion that follows I will use size of GNP as a very rough indicator of national economic power. For a concise discussion of the concept of economic power see Samuel P. Huntington, "The Economic Renewal of America", *The National Interest,* 27 (Spring 1992), p. 15. Also Klaus Knorr, *Power and Wealth: The Political Economy of International Power* (New York: Basic Books 1973), pp. 75–104.

4. For useful overviews see Office of Technology Assessment, *After the Cold War: Living With Lower Defense Spending* OTA-ITE-524 (Washington: U.S. GPO, 1992). Conrad Peter Schmidt and Steven Kosiak, *Potential Impact of Defense Spending Reductions on the Defense Industrial Labor Force by State* (Washington: Defense Budget Project, March 1992). On the "gunbelt" see Ann Markusen, Peter Hall, Scott Campbell and Sabina Deitrick, *The Rise of the Gunbelt: The Military Remapping of Industrial America* (New York: Oxford University Press 1991).

5. For a brief overview see Congressional Budget Office, *The Economic Effects of Reduced Defense Spending* (Washington: CBO, February 1992), pp. 5–20.

6. See, for example, William J. Bennett, "Quantifying America's Decline", *The Wall Street Journal* (15 March 1993), p. A12.

7. See, for example, the statement by General Colin Powell, Chairman of the Joint Chiefs of Staff before the Subcommittee on Defense of the Senate Appropriations Committee (mimeo, 21 April 1993), p. 2.

8. For overviews see Office of Technology Assessment, *Global Arms Trade: Commerce in Advanced Military Technology and Weapons* OTA-ISC-460 (Washington: U.S. Government Printing Office 1991); Congressional Budget Office, *Limiting Conventional Arms Exports to the Middle East* (Washington: CBO, September 1992); Keith Krause, *Arms and the State: Patterns of Military Production and Trade* (New York: Cambridge University Press 1992).

9. This argument is advanced in Susan Strange, "The Persistent Myth of Lost Hegemony," *International Organization,* 41 (Autumn 1987), pp. 551–74, and, at greater length, in Strange, *States and Markets* (London: Pinter, 1988). Strange defines structural power as "the power to shape and determine the structures of the global political economy" (p. 24), but the concept may also be applied more broadly to include the political as well as the economic arena. For a similar usage see Bruce Russett, "The Mysterious Case of Vanishing Hegemony; or, Is Mark Twain Really Dead?", *International Organization,* 39 (Spring 1985), pp. 207–31.

10. For a discussion of the possible implications of these changes see Jeffrey E. Garten, *A Cold Peace: America, Japan, Germany, and the Struggle for Supremacy* (New York: Times Books 1992), pp. 184–189. Among other things, increased Japanese influence in international lending institutions is likely to mean a departure from American standards for appropriate economic and human rights policies on the part of potential aid recipients. See Paul Blustein, Steven Mufson, et al., "Japan Seeks to Redefine Aid Policy", *The Washington Post* (27 April 1992), p. 12.

11. Strange, "The Persistent Myth of Lost Hegemony," pp. 565–571. The two other interrelated elements of structural power to which Strange refers are

"power in the security structure" and in "the ability to control the supply and availability of credit."

12. Ibid., pp. 566–567.
13. Steven Kobrin, "Enforcing Export Embargoes Through Multinational Corporations: Why Doesn't It Work Anymore?", *Business in the Contemporary World*, 1 (Winter 1989), pp. 31–42.
14. For data through the late 1980s see Edward M. Graham and Paul R. Krugman, *Foreign Direct Investment in the United States* (Washington: Institute for International Economics 1989), pp. 1–44.
15. Certainly, since the early 1980s, the flow of Japanese foreign direct investment into the United States has far exceeded that of American firms in Japan. For figures see Dennis Encarnation, *Rivals Beyond Trade: America Versus Japan in Global Competition* (Ithaca: Cornell University Press 1992), p. 150.
16. See the table in "Another World," *The Economist* (19 September 1992), p. 14.
17. Bill Emmott, "Multinationals: Back in Fashion", *The Economist* (27 March 1993).
18. Encarnation, op.cit., p. 150 (see note 15).
19. "The Non-Global Firm", *The Economist* (27 March, 1993).
20. See, for example, Nathaniel Nash, "Chile: Japan's Backdoor to the West", *The New York Times* (15 April 1993), p. D1.
21. For an overview of the trends see John Alic, et al., *Beyond Spinoff* (Cambridge: Harvard Business School Press 1992), pp. 87–132.
22. Jeff Nesmith and Elliot Jaspin, "Ingenuity Becoming Japanese Buzzword: Americans Out-Invented for High-Tech Patents", *The Plain Dealer* (21 February 1993), p. 1E.
23. "Global Innovation: Who's In the Lead?," *Business Week* (3 August 1992), p. 68–73.
24. From just under 30 percent in 1970–73 to just over 20 percent in 1988–89. Laura D'Andrea Tyson, *Whose Bashing Whom?: Trade Conflict in High-Technology Industries* (Washington: Institute for International Economics 1992), p. 22.
25. See Department of Commerce, *Emerging Technologies: A Survey of Technical and Economic Opportunities* (Washington: National Technical Information Service 1990), p. 13.
26. On this point see Harvey Brooks, "Technology as a Factor in U.S. Competitiveness", in Bruce R. Scott and George C. Lodge, eds., *U.S. Competitiveness in the World Economy* (Boston: Harvard Business School Press 1985), p. 32. Also Office of Technology Assessment, *Making Things Better: Competing in Manufacturing* OTA-ITE-443 (Washington: U.S. GPO 1990).
27. For variations on these themes see Russett, "*Vanishing Hegemony*", pp. 228–30; Francis Fukuyama, "The End of History?", *National Interest* 16 (Summer 1989), pp. 3–18; Nye, *Bound to Lead*, pp. 193–5; Henry R. Nau, *The Myth of America's Decline: Leading the World Economy into the 1990s* (New York: Oxford University Press 1990).
28. Todd Gitlin, "World Leaders: Mickey, et al.", *The New York Times* (3 May 1992), p. F1.
29. In the television industry, for example, where at one time "all roads led

straight to Hollywood . . . now those routes veer off to London, Paris, Milan, Madrid and Munich." See Mark Shaprio, "Lust-Greed-Sex-Power. Translatable Anywhere", *The New York Times* (2 June 1991), p. 29. Something similar seems to be happening in the extraordinarily lucrative popular music business. See William E. Schmidt, "In Europe, America's Grip on Pop Culture is Fading", *The New York Times* (23 March 1993), p. 3. Also Teresa Watanabe, "Toward a New Asian Order. Culture: In the East, Pop Audience Gets Icons of Its Own", *Los Angeles Times* (19 May 1992), p. H2.

30. Nau, op.cit., p. 11 (see note 27).
31. On this process see Samuel P. Huntington, *The Third Wave: Democratization in the Late Twentieth Century* (Norman, Oklahoma: University of Oklahoma Press 1992).
32. On this possibility see Zbigniew Brzezinski, *Out of Control: Global Turmoil on the Eve of the 21st Century* (New York: Scribners 1993), pp. 167–81.
33. See Clayton Jones, "Japan Seems Pleased With Signs of Activist U.S. Economic Policy", *The Christian Science Monitor* (10 March, 1993), p. 1. Also Robert Wade, *Governing the Market: Economic Theory and the Role of Government in East Asian Industrialization* (Princeton: Princeton University Press 1990).
34. On the importance of "followership", see Andrew Fenton Cooper, Richard A. Higgott, and Kim Richard Nossal, "Bound to Follow? Leadership and Followership in the Gulf Conflict", *Political Science Quarterly*, 106 (Fall 1991), pp. 391–410.
35. This, of course, is both the title and the essential argument of Joseph Nye's book.
36. See Arthur Schlesinger, Jr., *The Cycles of American History* (Boston: Houghton Mifflin 1986).
37. Robert Gilpin, *War and Change in World Politics* (New York: Cambridge University Press 1981), p. 199.
38. See Samuel P. Huntington, "The Clash of Civilizations?" *Foreign Affairs*, 72 (Summer 1993), pp. 22–49.

10

The "Fall" of the United States: Peace, Stability, and Legitimacy

Susan Strange

In this key discussion of the alleged decline of US power, and of the consequences for the world system, I speak first for the toads beneath the harrow, the grass that is bruised by the elephantine superpowers whether they make love or war. For I think it important for Americans to realize the extent to which their perceptions of American hegemonic decline were never widely shared outside the United States. For us the "Fall" should indeed be put in inverted commas.

Secondly, I want to argue not in terms of international relations, but in terms of international political economy. That means, for me, attempting an analysis that goes beyond the relations between governments – states and nations – and that puts international relations in the context of structural changes that are technological, economic and financial, and – not least – social and psychological. In my view, inter-state relations exist within a larger context of global political economy, of certain basic structures of security, production, finance, and knowledge which may have been created or shaped as a result, in part, of decisions taken by governments but which then, in turn, constrain the decision-making of those governments and of others.

(This larger context produces a different perspective on the problems posed in this book – different, that is, from the answers coming from much conventional (comparative) political science and conventional international relations. Some contributions have answered the question about the connection between peace, stability, and legitimacy against the background of the fall of various empires in state-centric terms. A minority, it seems to me, (notably McNeill, Kennedy, Gaddis) have attempted answers in global or system-centric terms. I shall try to do the same.)

Thirdly, I want to argue that, interesting as historical analogies always are, they can, and often do, mislead. Ruskin's idea that nineteenth-century Britain was a modern version of Rome was never very convincing. The Europeans – the French especially –

who saw themselves in the post-war world of the 1950s as the cultured, intellectual Greeks to the crass and clumsy American Romans were equally deluded. Thus, a great deal of American discussion of the nature and consequences of hegemony has been mistakenly based on a false analogy of US power and influence over the twentieth-century world with British power and influence in the nineteenth-century world. I shall argue, on the contrary, that the United States experience – and that of the toads beneath the harrow – was a special case. It was a special case because of structural changes that took place between Britain's heyday and America's. These were changes not in the international political system *tout court*, but in the world of finance, industry, trade, and information, in short, in the structures of the global political economy. Lighting can distort and create illusions as well as illuminate ; and the light thrown by historical comparisons may sometimes distort rather than illuminate our understanding of current problems and predicaments.

For this reason, the substance of this essay will be a historical interpretation of American power based on the above assumptions. In the course of that interpretation I shall also challenge two prevailing conventional assumptions: first, that hegemonic influence is necessarily benign; and, second, that the incidence of conflict and insecurity in the world at large – and indeed, of justice and legitimacy – is the product solely (or even primarily) of policies adopted by the great powers.

Fifty Years' Retrospective

Fifty years back from today takes us to the year 1943. By that time, there could be little doubt about the predominance of US power over that of Britain, Canada, and the exiled governments of France, Belgium, the Netherlands, Belgium, Norway, Poland, Denmark, and Czechoslovakia. Arguments then about the future management of finance and exchange rates were resolved in favour of US ideas about what was possible and desirable; Keynes had only limited influence, the record shows, over Harry White and the US Treasury. The participation of America's major rival among the allied powers, the Soviet Union, in the final discussions at Bretton Woods was perfunctory and irrelevant. France and Canada both had rival plans that were totally ignored. The two innovative international organizations in monetary matters, the Bank and the Fund, were so designed with weighted voting as to give the US exceptional powers over both the source of credit to be dispensed and the conditions of access to it.

Over the next two years, the international team of nuclear physicists assembled by the US government in New Mexico had succeeded in designing and making an atomic bomb, a weapon that not only ended the war in the Pacific but thereafter gave the United States leverage over any country that looked for protection against the Soviet Union. It was also enough to create a balance of power with the latter, a counterweight to the superiority of the Red Army in conventional weapons and manpower.

By the end of the war, too, its economic consequences in America and Europe had established the dollar as the dominant currency in the non-socialist world market economy. It was not just that the US now commanded the lion's share of gold reserves. More important was it that the US economy had prospered and grown as a result of the war while Europe's had suffered destruction and disruption. The dollar alone gave access to the wherewithal for post-war reconstruction. With demand outrunning supply, the post-war years were years of "dollar shortage".

American power rested on these two pillars of military and monetary predominance. Because of them, in the world economy outside the Soviet bloc and Communist China, the US had the power to take decisions about how the western alliance was to be managed, about who was to have the credit necessary to rebuild damaged economies, about the principles on which trade between countries was to be carried on, about a whole list of matters on which opinions differed and destinies depended.

About this, there is not much dispute either among historians or teachers of international relations. Alan Milward is perhaps one historian who has always argued that American power and influence over Western Europe in the post-war period was much exaggerated, that the Europeans, despite their dependence on the largesse of American Marshall Aid, had actually been cunning enough to defeat American plans for a United State of Europe – or something like it – and to preserve intact the nation-state. But in my opinion, Milward himself exaggerates. While it is true that the Economic Cooperation Administration did not achieve all its objectives for a reconstructed, market-oriented western Europe, it did achieve quite a lot. And those objectives were not in fact shared by all other parts of the US government. Nor were the Europeans the last-ditch defenders of the nation-state as he sometimes suggests. The discussions at Dumbarton Oaks and at San Francisco showed that

most governments rejected an international organization with powers to intervene in matters of domestic jurisdiction. The discussions
in the UN's Military Staff Committee in the late 1940s also showed
there was no support for a truly international police force – any
more than there is today. In short, Milward overstates his case, just
as much perhaps as some American historians overstated the extent
to which the US in the heyday of hegemony wanted to remake the
whole world.

Where the US did use its hegemonic power in the first two
decades after the end of World War II, I would argue, it did so with
mainly benign intentions and with constructive consequences. The
record for those 20 years from 1945 to about 1965 was, on balance,
beneficent. It contrasted quite strongly, in my judgment, with the
record of the subsequent 20 years. In Western Europe particularly,
the achievements of the European Recovery Programme (ERP)
have to be credited to American enlightenment and diplomatic
skills. The contrast with the failure of the European Community in
the past three years to emulate the ERP in its treatment of Central
Europe is striking. In the first place, the credit extended was very
large by the standards of the time. But it was conditional on the
recipients achieving consensus on the share-out year by year. Every
year, they bickered and whined, but every year at the eleventh hour
they reached agreement simply because the Americans would not
otherwise release the dollars. And in the second place, in contrast to
the way the EC member states are behaving today towards central
Europe, the US was self-denying in that, while insisting on the
liberalization and privatization of trade between the Europeans, it
allowed them to discriminate strongly against its own exports. This
not only let them husband their scarce dollars; it created openings
that might otherwise never have existed for intra-European export
trade. The fostering of the local market was further assisted by the
US initiative of the European Payments Union – another initiative
which the EC should have copied in the 1990s but failed to do. The
EPU's multilateral payments scheme was the major means by which
the constraints of barter and bilateralism in trade were swept away;
the lack of a similar liberalizing mechanism to replace the cumbersome (and hated) Comecon system in Central Europe again shows
up the blindness and supine inaction of the Europeans after the
Cold War compared with the vision and enlightenment of the
Americans in the earlier post-war years. Nor do I think it can
entirely be explained by the exigencies of the perceived threat of
communist revolution within and Soviet threat without. Obviously,

that galvanized both Americans and Europeans into policies that they might otherwise never have contemplated. But, in addition, credit must also go to a generation of officials endowed with the conviction that change was desirable and possible.

That same generation achieved comparably radical but different results in American-occupied Japan. Without the star-spangled Mikado and his staff as reforming imperialists, the social and economic foundations for Japanese political stability and economic growth would not have been laid. The reform of agricultural land tenure and the break-up of the *zaibatsu* which gave an opening to new manufacturing enterprise were American achievements which served no direct US interests. Indeed, as in Europe, the US promoted policies like the Japanese laws on foreign investment which were actively self-denying. The protection from foreign competition which these laws gave to Japanese firms in many sectors of manufacturing may have been contrary to free-market ideology but were a necessary condition for the Japanese economic miracle.

To reiterate, the beneficence of US hegemony in the two postwar decades is not to deny that there were some other items on the debit side of the balance. Two are worth recalling. The hopes raised in Latin America – the only "southern" (i.e. developing) continent then seriously represented at the UN – by Truman's Point Four promise of economic aid were soon disappointed and US–Latin-American relations continued to decline through the 1950s and 1960s. Promising US aid as the "missing component" for development was, in retrospect, rash. It sowed dragon's teeth in the form of unfulfilled expectations in the developing countries. Only those on the front line in the Cold War got to benefit substantially from US assistance.

The second weakness in US policy was the tendency to make sudden and unforeseen U-turns. The first of these was the cancelling of Lend-Lease in 1945. The second was the denial of funds to UNRRA in 1947. Both were the consequences of constitutional constraints on US Administrations – constraints which would continue to affect policy-makers in subsequent years.

There was, too, a price to be paid by the Europeans and the Japanese for American beneficence and enlightened policies for their reconstruction. The implicit Cold War bargain with both was that they would enjoy nuclear protection and US indulgence toward their economic interests; but in return they were to leave the US virtually free to conduct security matters and major issues of international finance as it thought best. The North Atlantic Treaty put nc restrictions on the use of US forces out of area. The 1960 agreement to set up the OECD put no restrictions on US policy-making in matters of trade, exchange rate management or financial regulation. In all three, the US was left free to act unilaterally and, if it chose, irresponsibly. And it continued to exercise through the Bank and the Fund an effective veto on any changes proposed by others. Perhaps inevitably, the US started around the mid-1960s to take advantage of its unconstrained freedom of action. In the subsequent decades, power has, as always, proved corrupting.

Opposed Interpretations

For the second phase of American power in the last half-century, there are, broadly speaking two opposed interpretations. The prevailing one in America is what might be called the Paul Kennedy version – that economic pre-eminence tempted policy-makers into an overstretched defence programme which in turn put too great burdens on the economy and handicapped it in competition with the very rivals it had helped to resuscitate after World War II. The alternative view, now at last finding voices inside the US (Nye, 1991; Hendrickson and Tucker, 1992; Veseth, 1990; Nau,1990) as well as amongst those of us outside (Strange, 1987), is that US policies shifted from the positive, beneficent, constructive use of hegemonic power to negative misuse, not intentionally but nevertheless effectively, maleficent toward the world market economy. It was not, in short, the management of the system that was the problem, but its mismanagement in the short-term interests of the United States.

In this latter interpretation, there were a number of wrong turnings taken unilaterally by the United States, beginning in the mid-1960s. Of these, perhaps the most serious was the escalation of the Vietnam War, initiated by President Kennedy but executed in the Johnson Administration. It was not just that this was risky and ended by revealing, as it did, the limitations of American military power. It was that the deficit financing of the war, the decision to resort to inflation rather than raising taxes, imposed an indirect kind of taxation without representation on the rest of the world market economy.

Also in the mid-1960s there was the associated American refusal to contemplate any reform of the gold exchange standard system which had emerged from the Bretton Woods agreement. That agreement to maintain fixed exchange rates among the major currencies could not be sustained, as Robert Triffin justly argued, so long as one country alone enjoyed the "exorbitant privilege" in de Gaulle's words, of settling its debts with IOUs. The Vietnam War, it was true, was only one factor contributing to persistent US balance-of-payments deficits, but it was an important one, since it expressed the claim to legitimacy in making unilateral decisions in defence and foreign policy.

The result was not – as it is often described – the "collapse" of the Bretton Woods system, but its deliberate destruction. Its rules were consciously rejected by President Nixon when he first closed the gold window (by which the dollar IOUs held by other countries could until then be changed for gold) and then allowed the dollar to float, leaving the exchange rate to be determined by market forces.

Other major turning-points in the 1970s in this interpretation would be the US response to the first OPEC oil price rise in 1973; the open adoption of unilateralist trade policies in the 1974 Act; and the delay by the Carter Administration in checking inflation not just in the US but in the whole world market economy.

A better, more enlightened, less confrontational response to OPEC would have been to initiate discussions on ways to stabilize or index-link oil revenues. This was the French idea when they initiated the fruitless Conference in International Economic Cooperation (CIEC) meetings in the mid-1970s. Instead, the US chose to oppose OPEC with the IEA, although any teeth it might have had fell out when the Congress denied funding for an adequate oil stocking operation. The confrontation was compounded by the US response to the fall of the Shah, to his succession by the ayatollahs, and to their holding of American hostages.

The 1974 Trade Act opened new doors to protectionist lobbies in the United States. It did to the GATT what Nixon had done to the IMF by devaluing the dollar; it substituted unilateral national policy for a set of agreed international rules and practices. Subsequent trade laws and their administration by the US Trade Representative's office and the US Treasury only took the US further down the road to unilateralism and protection.

Carter's delay in first acknowledging and then tackling the matter of accelerating inflation, which by the late 1970s was not only undermining US national security but was imposing real costs on all holders of dollar assets, was perhaps more to blame for some of the miseries of the 1980s than Reagan's violent U-turn in monetary policy after his 1980 election. As monetary historians have always observed, the longer inflation is allowed to go on, the more drastic the deflation necessary to check it. That deflation took the form of high real interest rates suddenly imposed on all who had borrowed bank credit at floating interest rates. The pains of adjustment to this U-turn in US monetary management hit both indebted governments in developing countries and the banks who had imprudently lent to them. But the general policy response was to take steps to protect the banks from the consequences of their folly, but not to do the same for the debtors. Only Mexico, close neighbour of the US, was given a helping hand to get out of the mess.

At the risk of making the interpretation wearisome I would only add the increasing tendency of US policy in the 1980s to put the blame for its self-inflicted problems on the Japanese. Whether the problem was the surplus capacity of the aircraft manufacturers or the indebtedness of US rice growers, the instant response was to find fault with Japan for failing to do what the US demanded. Second to Japan, of course, came the European Community and especially its Common Agricultural Policy. But for the CAP, US trade diplomats argued, the US farmers would not be troubled by over-production, costly debt and falling prices, nor would the US government – paying out far more than the EC to its farmers – be saddled with the high cost of deficiency payments. Far easier to blame the Japanese and the CAP than the agricultural technology which in both continents was producing surplus crops that the market could not absorb at prices that would keep farmers in business. Far easier too to blame foreign exporters of manufactures for "dumping" than to recognize that technological change – in industry as in farming – was substituting machines for men, and that unemployment was neither a cyclical nor a commercial problem but a structural one.

The Structural Context

The structural aspect just mentioned leads to the obvious question, Why? Why did the US use its hegemonic power in a beneficent, positive way until the mid-1960s but thereafter become increasingly tempted to use it negatively, at the expense of the system rather than in favour of it ?

The answer, I think, is not particularly original: the role became more difficult, more demanding. Managing interdependence asked for greater change than ever before in policy-making and in national habits of mind and of action. As the integration of the world economy increased, so did the need to act collectively, for the whole world economy, in matters that hitherto had been confined within national borders. Structural change had the US having to run faster just to stay in the same place, just to fulfil the basic responsibilities of the hegemonic authority in the system.

The explanation of why and how the role became more demanding lies not in international relations but in structural changes chiefly in the world economy, changes affecting investment, production, trade, payments, and the consequent perceptions of the legitimacy of the system. The most important of these changes, in certain basic sciences and technology, seems to lie outside the bounds of social science. This is probably why it is given too little attention either by economists or by political scientists. Yet it lies at the root of the problems faced by all governments, and especially by the US as the leader of the affluent industrialized countries in the world market economy. Briefly, the accelerating pace of technological change – in agriculture, in industry, in transport and communication, and in banking and finance – means that enterprises of all kinds are forced to try and sell on a world market. National, local markets will not absorb enough of the products of services of the enterprise to give it a return on the capital it has invested sufficient to amortise the debts it has incurred to finance the last big technological innovation. That innovation was costlier than the one it replaced, and will become obsolete more quickly. It will be replaced, so long as technological change continues to accelerate, by a new technology even costlier in capital and destined to become obsolete even more quickly than the last.

This is a better explanation for the process known as the internationalization of production (or, more popularly, as the rise of the multinationals) than the advantages of internalizing transaction costs. True, there are such advantages, but they alone would not explain the sense of urgency experienced by managers of all sorts of enterprises who, in recent decades, have decided that they must break into foreign markets and, if need be, locate their production, or a part of it, in other countries in order to make themselves welcome. Cheap labour is seldom a decisive factor. Nor is the fear of trade barriers to exports, though obviously both play some part in the decision to produce "offshore".

That decision, multiplied millions of times over, has been made much easier by structural change in finance as well as in technology. The old ways of raising money to put into offshore production were cumbersome and risky. Foreign direct investment conventionally meant issuing bonds or transferring funds from one currency into another. Change in the way the financial markets work – aided, it must be added, by falling costs and greater efficiency in transport and communications – have made it unnecessary to cross the exchanges. Funds can be raised locally or in the relatively unregulated, untaxed Euro-currency markets. Finance can be swiftly organized. New forms of investment – joint ventures, licensing agreements, build-operate-transfer deals, buy-back arrangements – are efficient and invisible.

In the post-war world, the first to respond massively to the new opportunities for international production – and therefore gain competitive advantage over their rivals – were American firms. Indeed, for a time, the phenomenon of the "multinational" was often thought to be a peculiarly American phenomenon, whereas now there are multinationals from most countries, most recently, Taiwan and South Korea. Robert Gilpin and Andrew Shonfield were two writers who foresaw the difficulties which international production by American and British firms would pose for their respective governments (Gilpin, 1975; Shonfield, 1959). Both were right – and both were helpless to stop a move of production offshore in response to the structural changes I have mentioned.

That shift has made a big hole in the power of all states, even including the United States. Firms are no longer solely beholden to one national government. Governments no longer have the control over their balance of payments, the levels of employment, and the trade account that they used to have. An early example was the failure of the Johnson Administration to stop US multinationals going abroad to the detriment of the US balance of payments in the 1960s. As the country with still by far the largest stock of (visible) foreign direct investment, the US has been most vulnerable for the longest. Both its own national problems of economic management and the problems of global management have become far more complex and far more intractable – as the sparse results of successive G7 summits have abundantly demonstrated.

Three additional factors have added both to the difficulties for the United States in behaving as a positive hegemon, and to the temptations leading it to act as a negative one. One was the importance attached to getting ahead and keeping ahead of its great rival, the Soviet Union, especially in military capability. The second was – and is – the American perception of the United States as the ideal country, the model for others, the *primus inter pares* whose moral pre-eminence in the family of nations should never be challenged. And the third is the very US Constitution which was designed as a safeguard against overbearing, centralized power but which also sometimes acts as a drag on global leadership. The first should be getting less important with the end of the Cold War, but the other two remain.

The first factor, the obsession with keeping ahead of the USSR, forms a strong part of the Kennedy school argument. Too many financial resources, too much human capital pre-empted by the defence programme, including NASA; too little room for balancing the budget and cutting the deficit; too few resources for civilian research and civilian manufacturing. (Kennedy, 1987; Cohen and Zysman, 1987; Tyson, 1992; Thurow, 1993; Calleo, 1992.) The interesting question remains, why, now that the race is over, is the US still running so hard in defence spending? Why is there not more pressure to cut back on military research and the armed forces?

The second factor, the resentment of opposition, of challenges to US authority from whatever quarter it comes – de Gaulle, Fidel Castro, OPEC, the Ayatollahs, Saddam Hussein, Colonel Qaddafi – has always been a common feature of imperial powers. And as with others, it has been a powerful distorting influence on policy-makers, causing them to act impulsively and irrationally. It would be less influential if the declinist school of American opinion were to lose their persistent hold on academic opinion. A return of American self-confidence would be the best defence against self-destructive paranoia.

As to the US Constitution, enshrining the separation of powers and the principles of the Declaration of Independence, it was well suited to a peripheral agricultural country in the eighteenth century. Whether and how change could be affected without damage to its basic ideas but with benefit to the hegemonic role of the US in the twenty-first century are questions deserving of much more attention than they have so far received.

Conclusions

The most important of these in my opinion is the role of structural change, making the US as a great power or hegemon a rather special case. It is a special case not only because the legitimacy of the American state depends hardly at all on blood and ethnicity but on nationality voluntarily acquired by multi-ethnic immigrants. Much more, it is a special case because the world system demands so much more of the United States than of any earlier dominant power.

Because of structural changes in technology, production, and finance, the prosperity, stability, and even legitimacy of other states depend much more on the ability and willingness of the United States to act as stabilizer, arbiter and regulatory hegemon to the world system than it ever depended on any other imperial power. If the US fails in this difficult task, the world market economy also will fail to grow and prosper; irreparable harm may be done to the whole planet.

The fundamental point about structural change is that it is creating ever-increasing tension between the legitimacy of the international political system and the legitimacy of the world market economy. Liberalism in political terms – self-determination and national sovereignty – is in constant and increasing conflict with liberalism – an open world market – in economic terms. The United States is asked to resolve this inherent conflict of ideas. The almost irreversible integration of the world economy, the visible homogenization of world society at the upper and middle levels of civil society, create ever-increasing tension between world economy and society on the one hand and the traditional inter-national system of territorial states on the other. Economic necessity and political capability do not match, and the mismatch will continue to put strains on both. Between the two, the US is in the hot seat, afflicted like others by the limitations on national government but still possessing pre-eminence in the two things that matter – military power and financial influence.

The second conclusion is obvious perhaps, but worth stressing because so much emphasis has always been laid in the literature on the beneficial aspects of hegemony. It is simply that systems can have good and bad hegemons, just as employees can have good or bad managers and children good or bad parents. It may be that what the world economy needs is not just that the US should behave better, but that the Europeans and Japanese, abetted hopefully by others, should combine forces to *make* the US behave better. Together they could certainly make an effective "loyal opposition". But as long as the Europeans fail so signally to agree among themselves, and as long as so many French people regard Japan as a bigger threat than America, it may be too much to hope for. In the meanwhile, anything that can persuade the US of the rewards to be had from pursuing enlightened long-term interests instead of ephemeral short-term ones will be to the benefit of the United States no less than to that of the rest of the world.

The third and last conclusion addresses the general question of whether the fall of great powers tends to result in opening Pandora's box, releasing conflicts hitherto suppressed but not resolved by the dominant authority, increasing instability and putting legitimacy into question. My point about the US being a special case is relevant here. It is caught up by structural changes, especially in finance, that it has itself helped to bring about. It is overtaken by accelerating technological and economic changes that make the governance of the global economy more difficult and more demanding. John Gaddis's observation in his essay that there may be more danger from anarchy than from tyranny applies particularly to the world economy no less than to politics. His other observation that you cannot dis-invent the stirrup, or indeed satellite communication technology, is also to the point. It is technological change and the mobility of that technology, and of finance, that have complicated the hegemonic role of the United States and tempted successive administrations into policies that have had negative instead of positive consequences for others.

This is why I would warn against taking historical examples too seriously. It is almost impossible to draw firm conclusions about the prospects for stability, non-violence, and legitimacy from the experience of earlier empires. Nor is it possible entirely to separate the consequences of technological and economic change engineered by science and by firms from the consequences of state policy. Sometimes aided, sometimes hindered by state policies (or the lack of them), the structural changes I have been able to sketch only briefly are having contradictory consequences. Some appear to be altering the international behaviour of some states to other states, and of states to foreign firms. In the former case, it is the dogs that have not barked, nor bitten each other, that strike me, the wars over territory and minorities that have not broken out – between India and Pakistan, for example, or North and South Korea, between Taiwan and mainland China, even between Hungary and Rumania over Transylvania. In some of these cases, peace has been kept despite old grudges and much mutual provocation. Perhaps this betokens a "sea change" in international relations, a political change resulting from economic change. I do not mean to say that growing world trade brings mutual understanding and pacific feelings towards trade partners as the old liberals like Comte and Cobden hoped. I mean that national self-interest, and notably the interest of ruling elites whose credibility and prestige is fast being eroded in many countries, requires that energies should be more and more directed to a different kind of bloodless competition – the competition not for more territory or for domination over others but for shares of the world market and shares of production for the world market. Only by pursuing policies that lead to success in that competition can governments survive. Barring foreign firms from national territory comes to make much less sense than in the 1970s. Conflict and war increasingly become too expensive luxuries to indulge in. Such wealth-seeking policies do not consist only in doing away with monopolies, public or private; having good schools and universities to produce skilled, intelligent workers; having clear and efficient legal systems to define and protect property rights, and all the rest of it. There is a social dimension that cannot be ignored. Political stability rests on social consensus and some satisfaction of minimal notions of justice in civil society. Thus, structural change rather than great power intervention may give the best hope for both more peace between states, and more justice, at least for some, in the distribution of income. Unfortunately, it may also increase the chances of violent conflict within states. The arms and money made available through the open world economy make rebellion and civil conflict easier, not more difficult. And, for reasons already given, the legitimacy of the liberal world economy may be simultaneously reduced by the unchecked increase in uncertainty, volatility, economic crime and disorder. The balance sheet, both for the system, for international relations, and for national societies is consequently mixed.

References

Calleo, David. *The Bankrupting of America; How the Federal Budget is Impoverishing the Nation* (New York: Morrow 1992).

Cohen, Stephen S. and John Zysman. *Manufacturing Matters* (New York: Basic Books 1987).

Gilpin, Robert, *U.S. Power and the Multinational Corporation; the Political Economy of Foreign Direct Investment* (New York: Basic Books 1975).

Hendrickson, David and Robert Tucker. *The Imperial Temptation; the New World Order and America's Purpose* (New York: Council on Foreign Relations 1992).

Kennedy, Paul. *The Rise and Fall of the Great Powers* (New York: Random House 1987).

Nau, Henry. *The Myth of America's Decline; Leading the World into the 1990s* (Oxford: Oxford University Press 1990).

Nye, Joseph. *Bound to Lead; the Changing Nature of American Power* (New York: Basic Books 1991).

Shonfield, Andrew. *British Economic Policy since the War* (London: Penguin 1959).

Strange, Susan. "The myth of lost American hegemony", *International Organization*, Autumn 1987.

Thurow, Lester. *Head to Head; the Coming Economic Battle among Japan, Europe and America* (London: Brealey 1993).

Tyson, Laura D'Andrea. *Who's Bashing Whom? Trade Conflict in High Technology Industries* (Washington: Institute for International Economics 1993).

Veseth, Michael. *Mountains of Debt; Crisis and Change in Renaissance Florence, Victorian Britain and Postwar America* (Oxford: Oxford University Press 1990).

Part III

Peace, Stability, and Legitimacy in Africa, Asia, and the Middle East

11

Peace, Stability, and Legitimacy in Africa: The Factor of Colonialism and Neocolonialism

J.F. Ade Ajayi

Establishing imperial rule, or influence amounting almost to imperial rule, over other peoples is one of the attributes of a Great Power. To the extent that such an empire centralizes the management of international relations, particularly decisions on issues of war and peace, controls competition and conflict among the subject peoples, and thus reduces the incidence of war, it may contribute to peace. The quality and durability of such peace is, however, dependent on the extent to which the regime of the Great Power acquires legitimacy, and therefore comes to rely more on the willing compliance of the subject peoples than on coercion. The "fall" of the Great Power in such circumstances is therefore likely to lead to a fragmentation of decision-making on peace and war, resumption of conflict among the subject peoples, and competition among would-be successors to the power and influence of the Great Power.

The aim of this chapter is to examine the factors of colonialism and neocolonialism in the African situation against the background of this general hypothesis. Imperial rule in Africa seemed to have promoted relative peace and stability among the subject peoples. However, because of the multiplicity of imperial powers, and even more because imperial rule failed to acquire legitimacy, some resistance and protests continued throughout the colonial period. The end of imperial rule did not restore independence or the freedom of action of pre-colonial states. The end of empire, as such, had no noticeable effects on stability on the continent. The former imperial powers remained in control of the economies of supposedly independent African countries in a neocolonial situation, and they in turn were within the sphere of influence of the USA. However, competition between the USA and the USSR during the Cold War produced more disastrous wars among African peoples than the competition among imperial powers had during the heyday of colonial rule. The hope that the restructuring of the world system after the Cold War will bring Africa some stability and legitimacy remains a hope.

Before Colonialism

There were far-reaching changes going on in Africa in the nineteenth century before the imposition of imperial rule which did not make for peace or stability either at the local or regional levels. These included:

(i) The overseas slave trade, which was at its height at the beginning of the century. It fed on wars and, in turn, bred wars and insecurity. The instability and wars that accompanied the slave trade are particularly well documented by the eye-witness accounts of missionaries and other travellers in East and Central Africa as Europeans and Indians in South-east Asia financed the ivory trade and the Arabs of Zanzibar established clove plantations.

(ii) The abolitionist movement, which was expected eventually to end the slave trade, also promoted wars and instability, not so much from resistance to abolition as from encouraging increased domestic slavery and internal slave trade as source for the labour required to produce and transport palm oil, ground nuts, ivory, and other items of "legitimate" trade.

(iii) The instability resulting from both the slave trade and the abolitionist movement encouraged the growth of centralized states with rulers becoming less ritual and more executive, with warlords building up small states at the expense of their neighbours, and large federations and regional alliances breaking up into smaller, more militarized states. Wars became "total" in the sense that they aimed at the total obliteration of the corporate existence of peoples, and their integration into the victorious states. The most notable, but by no means the only, examples were the widespread migrations and upheavals, and new Nguni states, associated with the rise of Shaka. The impact of the Mfecane was felt all the way from Natal to Swaziland, Lesotho and the Eastern Cape, to Matabele and Mozambique, to Western Tanzania and the southern shores of Lake Victoria.

(iv) The break-up of the Ottoman empire in North Africa and the rise of national states in Egypt, Tunisia, Morocco, and even Algeria to some extent, produced a series of conflicts in the short run, especially as European powers sought opportunities to intervene in the wars by way of enforcing treaty rights secured from the Ottoman rulers. The Egyptian wars spread down the Nile Valley and affected the efforts to re-establish imperial authority in Ethiopia.

(v) Partly to redress a feeling of injustice built up from the era of the slave trade, partly in reaction to increasing European influence, a number of Muslim leaders proclaimed reform and holy wars, and established theocratic states and caliphates. They acted under the auspices of different Brotherhoods: the Quadriyya in Northern Nigeria and Massina, the Tijaniyya in the Western Sudan, the Sanusiyya in Lybia and the Sahara, and the Mahdi in the Eastern Sudan.

(vi) European missionaries and traders tried to take advantage of the wars and the abolitionist movement to penetrate into the interior of Africa and secure footholds. European intervention, especially in Southern Africa and Algeria, fuelled wars of resistance as Europeans tried to expropriate Africans from their land.

These different movements involved profound changes in the daily life of most communities. On the social, religious, economic and political planes, the traditional order was challenged. There can be no doubt, therefore, that whether they were reluctant or enthusiastic, or even acting against their innate desires, people accepted and absorbed much change and innovation. This belies the anthropological myth that developed in the 1920s and 1930s that pre-colonial Africa was a static and unchanging society. And yet the picture drawn in the 1880s of a Hobbesian state of nature waiting to be "pacified" by the European rulers was equally a myth. People were able to absorb all the changes, innovations, and instability of the nineteenth century as long as they retained a sense of continuity with the past. It was this that produced what the anthropologists later mistook for an unchanging traditional order. Life in traditional societies was certainly not idyllic, least of all during a period of wars, instability, and rapid changes. But the people coped because they identified continuity with the past as the essential basis of legitimacy.

In spite of many challenges to the traditional order, the most widespread concept of legitimacy predicated the authority to govern in conformity with ancient custom, that is to say, in continuity with the past, with what the ancestors had established. Continuity was maintained even in the face of revolution. Revolution may appear to have disrupted continuity, for example in the Hausa states in the early nineteenth century; but as soon as the new regime could establish new "customary procedures", continuity was deemed to have been restored and the sense of legitimacy was re-established. This was possible only where the people were able to perceive change as making for development, for improvement in their lives in accordance with the "wishes and designs of the ancestors". By linking up legitimacy with a notion of development, they were able to reconcile change with continuity.

Thus, generally, the acceptance of custom and continuity with the past also implied respect for what may be called the ideology or the basic principles of traditional legitimacy:

(i) *Humanism*, that is, accepting all human beings as creatures of God, each with some dignity and moral worth that needs to be respected; extended not only to friends and relations, but also to strangers and even enemies. This principle spread across whatever divisions existed in society: rulers and ruled, urban and rural dwellers, farmers and cattle rearers, rich and poor, masters and slaves, elders and youth, men and women. Hence the "classlessness" in most of the societies whether power was decentralized and egalitarian, or centralized and hierarchical.

(ii) *Community*: Society was organized not round the rights of individuals, but round the interests of the community, the small, affective, homogeneous community, worshipping at the same shrine, speaking the same language. They might be descendants of a common ancestor, but they might also have a complex history of migrations, conquest, and assimilation within a common territory. The community remained autonomous even when absorbed into a larger political system. Power was decentralized. The community managed its land and other vital economic resources, educated and organized its youth, and to a large extent managed its own religious and judicial life with due regard for the basic security of the individual.

(iii) *Participation* in the life of the community was both a right and a civic duty. Social, economic, religious, and political interaction was intense, either through the lineage or age-grade associations or both. Participation was not the Western democratic right to be consulted periodically in the choice of leaders, but participation in lineage meetings, age-grade associations, and village assemblies conducted on the basis of consensus. Participation was an essential feature of social justice, linked to the right to protest and, if not satisfied, the right to secede and seek fresh land or a new home elsewhere.

(iv) *Right to land* as a basic guarantee of the economic security of the individual. Land was granted by the community to households or family units and access to it was an aspect of the participation of the individual in the life of the community. Dispute within the lineage over entitlement to land or office was the most likely cause of secession. Access to land was extended even to slaves in recognition of their humanity and as a way of socializing them into membership of the household.

In a sense, these principles derived from traditional African religions, but generally they had become part of the culture of African peoples so that they could survive conversion to Islam. These were in turn sustained by other factors such as the abundance and non-commercialization of land. Outside the oases in the desert, the urge to commercialize land was limited and resistible. Relative ease of access to land as the most vital economic source was crucial to a willing compliance with the right of government to govern. There were also limits to accumulation: technological limitation to the accumulation of agricultural produce and of available pasture to the size of herds of cattle. Even for office-holders, wealth invested in gold, ivory, slaves, etc., was discouraged by the imposition of death duties and the practice of distributing wealth on succession. Hence, there was limited scope for differentiation in society in types of dress, houses, types of food, etc. Finally, there was the right of protest, including the right to secede. A good ruler was the one who extended the size of the community even by welcoming strangers, not the one who caused its fragmentation.

The Impact of Colonialism

Thus, on the eve of the European conquest, in spite of the conflicts and divisions, the spate of wars and relative instability in Africa, there was an underlying consensus on continuity with the past as a basis of legitimacy. By contrast, the initial impact of imperial rule in Africa, the so-called period of "pacification" – 1885–1920 –

brought more wars and upheavals and a greater feeling of instability than ever before because of the fundamental challenge to the traditional concept of legitimacy.

Europeans intervened in intra-African wars, usually taking sides and ending such wars to their own advantage. By 1900, the majority of the wars had ceased to be intra-African as such and had become wars of resistance to and conquest by the imperial powers, punitive expeditions, and generally forcing Africans to accept the imposition of European rule and show respect for European authority. There were wars to break up and undermine the authority of the larger and more powerful African polities. The warriors were disarmed, fined, humiliated. The manufacture of guns and other offensive weapons was outlawed. Taxation, forced labour by free men, recruitment into European armies, incomprehensible European laws, and other unpopular measures were imposed by force.

These were largely Europeans fighting Africans, but in a sense the wars remained intra-African because only the officers and the armaments were European: the soldiers were predominantly African recruits fighting Africans. The core of the armies were freed slaves incited with animosity against former masters. To this was added the racism of the European officers, reinforced by confidence in their ultimate technological superiority. The intensity of the wars and wanton destruction of lives and property were thus on a scale unusual in intra-African wars.

If there had been a single Great Power instead of a multiplicity of imperial powers, the history of the scramble, partition, and pacification would have been different. In the absence of rivalry and competition, the single Great Power would have taken time in acquiring African land and in choosing how and when to compel obedience. This factor should, however, not be exaggerated. Following the accord at the Congress of Berlin and the Brussels Agreement on limitation of arms and liquour, the European powers contained their rivalries and managed the installation of imperial rule with admirable consensus. The best evidence of this was the control of armaments, such that none of the African rulers who considered themselves experienced in playing one European power against another – not even Emperor Menelik II of Ethiopia, the most successful of them – managed to obtain even one maxim gun. When, however, the suppressed European rivalries and unresolved conflicts broke out into a World War in 1914, Africa felt the added instability of being subject to a multiplicity of imperial powers. Africans were fully involved in the massive recruitment to fight in the deadly trenches of France, and in British and French armies to conquer German territories of the Cameroons, Togo, Tanganyika, and Namibia where the opposing armies similarly relied upon African soldiers.

By the end of World War I and the Peace of Versailles, where the German colonies were shared out and the principle of trusteeship established, the period of "pacification" was over, and relative peace and stability was established in most of Africa. European aggression and African resistance continued only in a few places like the mountainous parts of Morocco. The most notorious case was that of Libya and Cyrenaica where the Italians were still trying to enforce their rule while refusing to observe agreements made with African rulers. Italian aggression continued almost without interruption until their invasion of Ethiopia in 1935, with war planes and poison gas. In spite of this, and occasional localized resistance by recalcitrant groups or protests against gross official injustice and abuse of power, which were easily suppressed, the period 1920–39 was the most peaceful in Africa under colonial rule.

Intra-African wars had been outlawed and, saving occasional violent border clashes between rival communities, had been brought under strict control. The maintenance of law and order and the provision of necessary infrastructure and facilities for economic exploitation were the primary aims of the colonial administrations set up in the different territories. It was incumbent on the different administrations to do this at minimum expense to the imperial powers and with very few European officials on the ground. The provision of infrastructure in terms of education, railways, harbours, roads, and telegraphs was thus kept to the minimum, and it was necessary to recruit allies and collaborators locally to assist in the quest for low cost administration. Broadly, three different situations emerged:

(i) Initially, Britain licensed groups of private investors to acquire territories and concessions and run the administrations. King Leopold's International African Association may also be regarded as a chartered company granted the powers of government. The iniquity of granting private investors powers of government, allowing them to control Africans solely for the purpose of maximizing their own profits, was soon made obvious, the most notorious example being the mutilation of thousands of Congolese who failed to supply prescribed quantities of rubber. But even after the charters were withdrawn and officials of the imperial power were granted rights of supervision, the concessionaire companies could not be adequately supervised or controlled. In the Portuguese territories, for example, official agents were close allies and often dependants of the powerful multinational companies. Concessionaire companies remained the preferred mode of exploitation in the mining areas such as the gold and diamond fields of South Africa and the copperfields of Katanga and Zambia. It was incumbent on the official agents to expropriate large numbers of Africans from their land so that they could be the source of cheap labour for the insatiable appetite of the companies. This did not promote peace or legitimacy.

(ii) On the Mediterranean coast, particularly Algeria, in South Africa and the high plateaux of Kenya, Southern Rhodesia, and parts of Angola and Mozambique with equable climatic conditions and rich agricultural land, the imperial powers encouraged the settlement of European nationals, usually on farms of large acreage. Like the concessionaire companies, they too had an insatiable demand for cheap labour with the consequent continuous expropriation of Africans from their land, gross racial discrimination, unjust pass laws, and other forms of abuse. The settlers tried, usually with a great measure of success, to control the local administration and undermine any resolve it might have to protect whatever rights were left to the African population. This too produced a situation of constant European aggression and sullen African resentment which did not make for real peace or legitimacy.

(iii) In other areas, the colonial administrations sought to exploit the labour of Africans on their own farms. They co-opted cadres of traditional rulers to assist with the collection of taxes and, through courts administering modified versions of traditional laws under the supervision of the colonial officers, to assist in the maintenance of law and order. This was the British Indirect Rule. The French, in their policy of association, and even the British also to some extent, preferred to elevate to the rank of chiefs any collaborators they could rely on, without regard to previous claims to traditional rights of rulership. By the introduction of European currency and taxation payable only in money, Africans were forced to produce for the European market. Sometimes there were regulations as to what each family household must produce or express demands for forced labour for building roads, railways, harbours, and other public utilities. Sometimes, the production of cash crops for export brought the

African people some degree of prosperity and consequent acquiescence in the unpopular measures of government. Thus there was
relative peace and stability, but acquiescence rather than legitimacy.

It needs to be emphasized that in all the three different situations,
what obtained in Africa was not imperial rule so much as colonial
rule. In spite of the French and Portuguese rhetoric about treating
colonies as overseas departments of the metropolitan provinces,
there was no real intention to integrate Africans into European
empires, or seeking to get Africans to confer any degree of legitimacy on European rule. Colonial rule in Africa was the sequel to
centuries of the Atlantic Slave Trade, which was characterized by
racism and ruthless exploitation of labour. These same characteristics, albeit in more subtle forms, were also the main features of
colonialism in Africa.

This is not to deny that some Africans who had welcomed Europeans as allies tried to legitimize European rule by pointing to
oracles and diviners who predicted the coming of the Europeans
and in other ways attempted to find a basis of continuity between
colonial rule and the traditional order. But such efforts were hardly
appreciated or reciprocated. The colonial rulers preferred to justify
the right of Europeans to rule Africans without their consent, or
even consultation, explicitly by reference to the racial superiority of
Europeans, manifested not only in technological, but also moral,
cultural, and intellectual superiority. Colonial rule was thus bolstered up, not by searching for a basis of legitimacy, but by forcing
Africans to accept and respect that superiority. Codes of behaviour
of Europeans were meant to uphold this superiority at all times.
Policies for the education of Africans were similarly geared to
maintaining the cultural superiority of Europeans. Education under
the control of missionaries was regarded as suspect because of its
tendency to lead Africans to question the basis for the claims to
superiority. In the end, it was the agitation of the Western educated
elite for a more meaningful role that led to policies of decolonization during and immediately after World War II.

"Decolonization"

The Second World War ended the period of relative peace and
stability. The conflict between Vichy France and Free France was
transferred to Africa since the Governor-General of French West
Africa (AOF) based in Dakar accepted the authority of Vichy

France while the Governor-General of French Equatorial Africa (AEF) based in Brazzaville decided to support Free France. The ports of West Africa thus became strategic centres for the early part of the war and staging posts later for the Desert War in North Africa. The Italians were, in consequence, driven out, not only from Libya but also from Ethiopia, and Emperor Haile Selassie was restored to his throne. African troops played prominent roles in all those theatres of the war, as they did also in Burma and Indochina. With such massive involvement in the war, African demands for reform of the colonial systems could not be ignored. Hence the introduction of the notion of "colonial development and welfare", an attempt to reform the colonial system and substitute acquiescence with some degree of legitimacy.

These reforms have generally been described as decolonization, that is, a termination of colonial rule, control, and dependence. A closer look will show that in fact what the constitutional reforms of 1945–60 achieved was the deepening of dependence and replacing of formal political control by Europeans with tighter economic subservience. Decolonization thus marked the beginning of the transition from colonialism to neocolonialism. A number of factors leading to this eventuality may be highlighted:

(i) In both the British and the French colonies, the post-war constitutional reforms were framed around the territories created by the partition, not the pre-colonial polities. As such, it was the Western educated elite, not the traditional elite through whom "native" administration had hitherto been carried out, that became collaborators in the reforms. As enunciated by Senghor in 1957, the educated elite wanted not independence as such, but "the abolition of prejudice, of all superiority complex in the mind of the colonizer, and also of all inferiority complex in the mind of the colonized". To this end, they clamoured for more, not less, of the institutions of the imperial powers because of their belief that those were the institutions that guaranteed and promoted for Europeans the very freedoms and development that they sought. It was largely in this period, therefore, that colonial models of the legislative, judicial, and even executive branches of the metropolitan constitutions began to be established in Africa. The Western educated elite saw themselves as the natural successors to the colonial powers, and not as restorers of pre-colonial independence.

(ii) Instead of the principles of traditional legitimacy – humanism, community rights, participation, and access to land – the new constitutions sought to erect and reinforce new values. Instead of community rights, the new legal systems and constitutions stressed individualism and the principle that all men are created equal and endowed with equal rights, equality before the law, one man one vote, representative democracy or equal access to office. Instead of active participation in decision-making, the values of the new age were unlimited accumulation, commercialization of land, the law of the winner takes all in place of the traditional judicial system that seeks to redress injuries and to reconcile litigants rather than to identify who is right as such. The state in the new countries sought not continuity with the past, but acceptance in the world community of nations, ostensibly as sovereign entities, but in reality largely as appendages of the former metropolitan powers.

(iii) The imperial powers were not prepared to weaken the economic ties. The surplus balance of payment accounts held by the imperial powers in the metropolitan countries were important factors in rebuilding the value of the pound sterling and the French franc impoverished by the war. Rather than weaken the ties, the imperial powers conceived of "colonial welfare and development" before independence, and "technical aid" after independence, as calling for fresh investment from the metropolitan powers to reinvigorate the economic ties. They considered replacing formal political control by new forms of association, the British within the Commonwealth, the French within an emergent French Community. In the process of "decolonization", they established economic aid, technical assistance, and military agreements to facilitate continued domination. The French went beyond decolonizing within the boundaries created at the partition. With the active connivance of many of the African leaders, the two federations of AOF and AEF were decolonized as 11 separate countries. There were thus created several landlocked countries of the Sahel under pressure from the creeping desert, and with frontier constraints against free movement of pastoralists. All of them, excepting Guinea, were tied to the franc zone by special arrangements which seriously limited their fiscal autonomy. The Belgians were unwilling to go along even with this limited form of "decolonization". Suddenly, they agreed to political independence in 1960 provided they could retain control over the copper and diamond mines through a secessionist regime in their pay. The Portuguese remained adamant until they were forced to negotiate political independence in 1974–75.

(iv) "Decolonization" may also be illustrated in the field of education where pre-World War II policies had stressed adaptation to local conditions in elementary education, limited secondary education, and discouraged higher education. After the war, education began to be liberalized. University institutions were encouraged locally, granting the degrees of London and the Sorbonne, but with curriculum and recruitment of staff controlled from London and Paris. Colonial universities thus became instruments of "decolonization" in the sense of deepening dependence. Scholarship programmes were also initiated to train cadres of Africans largely in the metropolitan countries, to man the new administrative positions.

The western educated elite rallied support from urban workers, market women, farmers, and the bulk of the traditional elite, enough to give the new collaboration between the imperial powers and the African Western educated elite some degree of legitimacy. Peace and stability were thus ensured except in the areas of European settlement, especially Algeria, Kenya, Southern Rhodesia, and Namibia, and the Portuguese territories where decolonization was achieved through armed struggle and under the shadow of the Cold War. The struggle is still proceeding in South Africa.

Thus "decolonization" failed to advance the cause of African freedom and development. Instead of promoting independence, it deepened dependence. Instead of terminating colonialism, it initiated neocolonialism. The illusion of legitimacy in the new states soon paled. There remained among the populace an inherent disbelief in the equality of all citizens and the virtues of individualism on which the new states were based. The ballot box has regularly failed to reflect the will of the people at elections, and is, by no means evidence of popular participation. Hence the continued crisis of the state.

Decolonization in Africa might therefore signify the rolling back of some aspects of empire but not the "fall" of any Great Power. What has been evident is that the boundaries established by the imperial powers at the time of partition became the title deeds of the states they created by the process of colonization and "decolonization". Ironically, the Organization of African Unity (OAU) has been more attached to the boundaries and has been obliged to defend them even more vigorously than the imperial powers needed to do. There has therefore been no scramble to redraw the political map of Africa. The struggle to complete the process of "decolonization" has been strictly within the context of the partition boundaries. This is probably the clearest evidence of the reality of neocolonialism.

The Cold War and Neocolonialism

It is often argued that the Cold War was a major factor in the "fall" of Britain and France as Great Powers. The argument is that the United States emerged from World War II as the leader of the Western alliance against the Soviet bloc; that the United States upheld a pronounced anti-colonial policy, urging termination of colonial rule wherever a stable political order could be found to which power could be devolved, provided it was willing and able to resist communism; and, as such, demanded the rolling back of empire as a condition necessary for sustaining the ideology and solidarity of the Western alliance. For Africa, the most notable example usually cited in support of this argument is the Suez crisis of 1956 when the US refused to support the British–French–Israeli conspiracy against Egyptian nationalization of the Suez Company, and the failure of the conspirators to restore Britain to the control of the strategic naval base. That debacle was something of a watershed, which led to the prime ministership of Harold Macmillan and his "Winds of Change" in Britain and prepared the way for the recall of de Gaulle in 1958. On the other hand, it can also be argued that the Suez conspiracy failed because it was an aberration, a recourse to nineteenth-century gunboat diplomacy, inconsistent with the overall policy of decolonization in the middle of the twentieth century; that it demonstrated the wisdom of the policy of decolonization by showing up the follies of the doubters who were slow to see the light; and it thus strengthened the hands of those advocating and pursuing policies of decolonization.

The argument can therefore be sustained that it was the Cold War and the intrusion of the US which provided the opportunity for the imperial powers to proclaim mid-twentieth-century anti-colonialism while exploiting US bellicosity to continue the practice of nineteenth century gunboat diplomacy behind the facade of the war against communism. The imperial powers were thus enabled to "decolonize", to devolve political responsibility and international recognition on African leaders while keeping in their own hands the essential elements of economic power in Africa needed to ensure continued political subservience. No doubt the dominance of the US in the Western alliance meant a dimunition in the international status of France and Britain – a dimunition that France most of the time, and Britain occasionally resented. But the Western alliance enabled the imperial powers to save on the military expense of keeping unwilling peoples within the empire, while retaining the economic advantages, and without easing the colonial yoke on the back of the Africans or in any way diminishing the reality of neocolonialism as the end product of "decolonization".

In the light of this, the impact of the Cold War on peace, stability and legitimacy in Africa can best be examined in three parts:

(i) Countries where only some nudging from the international community was necessary to achieve "decolonization". This includes most of Africa under British and French domination, except Southern Rhodesia, Namibia, and South Africa. De Gaulle made peace with the FLN liberation fighters in 1961, and in 1962 Britain agreed to the release of Jomo Kenyatta and the dissolution of the Central African Federation. The rest was left to the politics of ethnicity and the ability of African leaders to put together credible coalitions to which power could be devolved. What needs to be emphasized is that decolonization was within the context of the partition boundaries. Attempts, such as by the Central African Federation, to modify these were seen by Africans as, and probably were intended to be, obstacles to decolonization. The secessionist movement in Biafra should be seen in this context as part of the struggle for power within the partition boundaries of Nigeria, and not as a serious threat to modify those boundaries. The Cold War as such had no direct bearing on the actual sequence of events, though it remained a factor in the international context within which problems such as the Nigerian civil war were handled.

(ii) Countries where, because there was no commitment to peaceful decolonization, the Cold War had a direct and usually disastrous impact on the process of decolonization:

(a) Although the Belgians had agreed to the "decolonization" of the Congo in 1960, no credible coalition was put in place. The overthrow and subsequent murder of Lumumba, secessionist movements in Katanga and South Kasai, and other local insurrections, brought in the intervention of the United Nations at the height of the Cold War. Eventually, after five years of some of the most gruesome in-fighting in Africa, the Western alliance, led by the US, assisted the Congolese army under Mobutu Sese Seko to assume control, establish peace and stability, but with little and rapidly diminishing legitimacy.

(b) Portugal, protected and armed within the North Atlantic Treaty Organization (NATO), refused to decolonize. Various resistance movements emerged, resorted to guerilla warfare, and sought assistance from international enemies of Portugal and NATO, notably the USSR and China. PAIGC, FRELIMO, and MPLA had some measure of success. More importantly, they ensured that the strain of maintaining the over 150,000 troops that Portugal had to deploy in its three colonies was more than its economy could bear, even with US support. The freedom fighters thus helped to liberate Portugal, opened the way for its modernization, and forced it to decolonize. But the US and South Africa refused to recognize the regimes of FRELIMO in Mozambique and MPLA in Angola, arming RENAMO and Savimbi's UNITA to continue the civil war, sabotaging efforts to achieve peace, stability, and legitimacy. Yet the socialist ideology of MPLA and FRELIMO did not make their regimes outstations of Soviet or Chinese communist power. Their economies were already integrated into those of Portugal and the Western alliance, and Soviet help availed little beyond military supplies and personnel. The Cold War therefore constituted a formidable obstacle to peace, stability, and legitimacy in both Mozambique and Angola.

(c) In Southern Rhodesia, the European settlers demanded independence as a reaction to the dissolution of the Central African Federation, and proceeded to seize control of the country through the Unilateral Declaration of Independence. When it was obvious that the British imperial power was unwilling to take necessary steps to suppress the rebellion, African resistance groups took up arms and sought outside help. Eventually the settlers' army accepted defeat; the British intervened and made peace. The successful transformation of Southern Rhodesia to Zimbabwe made possible the similar decolonization of Namibia. Because of the intervention of Britain as the imperial power, it was possible to keep the Cold War factor to the minimum in the final settlement of both Zimbabwe and Namibia. But it was under the influence of the Cold War that the racist white minority regime of South Africa tried to link up the crude racism of apartheid with the anti-communist crusade, thus gaining the support of the United States for its inhuman policies. The ANC, PAC, and other resistance movements resorted to armed struggle. Since the end of the Cold War, the international community has been more willing to assess the apartheid regime on its demerits rather than according to the rhetoric of the Cold War.

(iii) Countries where war and upheaval have been more directly the products of the Cold War, and therefore the principal actors have been willing to challenge the Partition boundaries if necessary. The extent to which internal struggles for power have been internationalized have varied with the perceived importance of mineral and other vital economic and strategic factors. The ongoing imbroglio in Chad has been contained largely within the OAU and Franco-Libyan relations because the economic factor is relatively minor. The Western Sahara/Saharawi issue, however, has attracted more international attention, but the Soviet Union has shown no major interest and the Cold War factor within the international dimension of the dispute has consequently been limited.

It is the Horn Country that has exemplified the direct impact of the Cold War, partly because, in decolonizing the area, the western alliance took advantage of the defeat of Italy to revise the rather arbitrary boundaries of the partition: British and Italian Somaliland were merged into Somalia; Italian Eritrea was incorporated into Ethiopia as an autonomous region, to give Ethiopia access to the sea. Various groups in Eritrea, however, claimed independence from Ethiopia, while Somalia yearned for a Greater Somalia to include Somali-speaking Ogaden in Ethiopia and the northern part of Kenya. With the support of the Western alliance, the Emperor's Ethiopia was able to resist both Eritrea and Somalia. In pursuit of internal reform, students and elements within the army overthrew the emperor and sought Soviet assistance to prevent a restoration of the monarchy. The United States, hitherto a major factor in the emperor's Ethiopia, then intervened in Somalia with military support to protect strategic interests against the Communist presence in Ethiopia. It was the primacy of strategic interests of the Cold War over the interests of the peoples of Ethiopia and Somalia that has been so disastrous. In the process, the communist regime of Mengistu was eventually overthrown; the state of Somalia dissolved into anarchy, and Eritrea has become the only state that has so far successfully challenged the boundaries agreed to on decolonization. However, this is only because the Eritrean freedom fighters have claimed all along that they were the ones defending the partition boundaries.

Conclusion

Imperial rule, as rule by Great Powers, was capable of increasing peace, stability, and legitimacy in Africa, because the act of partition greatly reduced the number of independent polities capable of deciding on issues of peace and war. In fact, colonial rule in Africa did not achieve much peace and stability, partly because of the pronounced militarism of the imperial powers themselves, and partly because of the military and racial superiority which they made the foundation of their administrations. They destroyed existing bases of legitimacy and did little to establish any viable alternatives. The rhetoric of empire apart, the colonial regimes took too little interest in the development of Africa for them to approach the issue of legitimacy in any meaningful way.

Consequently, in the peculiar situation in Africa, the rolling back of empire has produced not the end of colonialism, but the beginning of neocolonialism. This is largely because of the nature of colonialism in Africa which should be seen not as imperial rule as such, but as a continuation of the Slave Trade for the exploitation of African labour and other resources for the benefit of Western Europe. The aims and the manner of the processes of decolonization were to deepen dependence, and not to promote independence. Decolonization thus did not much affect the balance of interest groups in any significant ways except in the areas where the imperial powers resisted decolonization. There, the Africans were forced to resort to armed struggle and to seek support from the Soviet bloc and communist China. The Western powers usually reacted by exploiting ethnic divisions to foment civil war and ideological conflicts unrelated to the interests of Africans, and unrelated to the rolling back of empire. At all events, the result either of negotiated "decolonization" or "armed struggle" has been similar – increased dependence and neocolonialism.

Decolonization produced 53 African states, each in theory capable of taking decisions on issues of war and peace in place of the five or six imperial powers. In practice, few of them are likely to embark on war outside their partition boundaries without the connivance or active encouragement of external powers, usually the former imperial power. The greatest threats to peace and stability in Africa have, therefore, been internal – civil wars fomented from outside, failure of the state to provide the minimum of basic essentials of food, shelter, security, and social justice. The partition boundaries have produced several land-locked states in difficult ecological zones. Some states have collapsed – Uganda, Liberia, Somalia; others do not exist for substantial parts of their people – southern Sudan, Zaïre and, increasingly, Togo.

The crisis of the state is also a crisis of legitimacy. The internationalization of African problems during the Cold War produced increased militarization, but lack of any genuine concern for the human interests of African peoples. For the United States, there were some areas of Africa that held vital strategic mineral resources, notably South Africa, Zaïre, and Nigeria, from which it was imperative to exclude any major Soviet influence. For the Soviet Union, Africa remained of marginal interest, largely as an irritant to the policies of the United States. During the Cold War, therefore, their military objectives took clear precedence over the interests of the African peoples. Usually, their interest was not to win any war they initiated among African peoples, but to prolong it so as to keep the other side busy. Hence the cynical manner in which they changed sides in the Horn country, and the nonchalant way they watched Somalia disintegrate, and prolonged indefinitely the agonies of Angola and Mozambique. During the Cold War, there was little concern for the legitimacy, human rights record, efficiency and capability of the regimes that were propped up to serve these strategic or economic interests of external powers and multinational corporations.

Africa has thus been constrained to try to develop within the parameters of its partition boundaries, with so many states that cannot be regarded as viable entities. It is not surprising to note that, for the majority of the population, the quality of life in most of Africa today, in terms of basic needs of food, shelter, clothing, health, education, security, and social justice, is worse than in the pre-colonial period. So also the concern of rulers and their capacity to do anything about these basic needs. Above all, there is a complete breakdown of all notions of legitimacy. The atrocities that were committed during the in-fighting of the Congo crisis, in Burundi, the Central African Empire, Idi Amin's Uganda or Liberia testify to the gross deterioration not only of the quality of life but also of basic human values. The traditional principles of legitimacy have been grossly undermined and we have not been able to put anything in their place. We thus seem to lack even the values for reconstructing peace, stability, and legitimacy.

The collapse of the Soviet Union has, at least, removed the necessity to foment wars which hurt Africans so badly merely to keep an ideological opponent occupied. The Soviet Union had been cutting its losses in Africa: hence the fall of Mengistu, hence the withdrawal of Cuban troops from Angola, which has made it possible for the US to review its support for the racist apartheid regime of South Africa. Hence also the recent recognition of the MPLA government of Angola. In this way, the fall of the Soviet Union should at least reduce the bellicosity of the United States. It would, however, not reduce the reality of neocolonialism. And it remains to be seen whether the neocolonial powers in Africa, relieved of the necessity for an arms race, might be willing to commit some of the funds thus saved to a serious effort at developing and truly decolonizing Africa.

The rolling back of empire has thus not improved the chances for peace, stability, and legitimacy in Africa. That much seems to be common knowledge. The fact of dependence and continued exploitation is not denied, but it is sometimes said that dependence and exploitation are to be preferred to economic neglect. That is a measure of the dependence and the extent to which the centuries of slave trade, colonialism, and neocolonialism have impaired the capacity of African leaders to take initiatives in the development of Africa. Already some commentators are discussing re-colonization as a way out. The analysis above would tend to show that the contrary should be the case. The way out, consistent with the goal of peace and stability in the world, is to promote legitimacy in Africa. This is tied in with the question of development, and it needs to be tackled at the continental level. The question is how to transform the OAU into an effective organ of development and decolonization.

Development will come, not from continued neocolonialism or re-colonization, but from genuine decolonization: a review of Africa's partition boundaries through regional security pacts and economic communities, massive injection of capital and technical skills into providing education, railways, roads, telecommunication, and other basic infrastructure. The world that has taken so much out of Africa through the slave trade, colonialism, and neocolonialism owes Africa that injection of capital. That is the case being made by the Movement for Reparations or Restitution.

References

Ade Ajayi, J.F. "The Search for a New World Order: an African Perspective" in Geir Lundestad and Odd Arne Westad, eds., *Beyond the Cold War: New Dimensions in International Relations* (90th Anniversary Nobel Jubilee Symposium Oslo: Scandinavian University Press 1992).

Ade Ajayi, J.F. "Africa on the Eve of the European Conquest" in *Africa in the Nineteenth Century until the 1980s* Vol. VI of the Unesco *General History of Africa*, ed. J.F. Ade Ajayi (London: Heinemann 1989).

Hargreaves, John D. *The End of Colonial Rule in West Africa: Essays in Contemporary History* (London and New York: Harper & Row 1979); *Decolonization in Africa* (London: Longman 1988).

Gifford, Prosser, and W. Roger Louis. *The Transfer of Power in Africa: Decolonization 1940–1960* (New Haven: Yale University Press 1982); *Decolonization and African Independence: The Transfers of Power 1960–1980* (New Haven: Yale University Press 1988).

Louis, W. Roger. *Imperialism at Bay, 1941–1945: the United States and the Decolonization of the British Empire* (Oxford: Oxford University Press 1977).

Nzongola-Ntalaja. *Revolution and Counter Revolution in Africa: Essays in Contemporary Politics* (London: Zed Books and Institute for African Alternatives 1987).

Twaddle, Michael. "Decolonization in Africa, A New British Historiographical Debate" in B. Jewsiewicki and D. Newbury, eds., *African Historiographies: What History for which Africa?* (Beverly Hills: Sage 1986).

12

Empires and Anti-empires: Asia in World Politics

Wang Gungwu

This book uses the term "Great Powers", a designation that is drawn from European history. It describes the power rivalries in Europe that evolved into the modern international system of war and diplomacy. "Great Powers" has become the subject of a vast literature of politics, law, and history that came eventually to include the continent of Asia. This happened partly because the Ottoman Empire spread westwards into Central Europe and the Russian Empire extend in the other direction across Central and Northern Asia to the Pacific Ocean. Both were accepted as great power protagonists and both included large parts of Asia. Another reason, equally important, was that the great powers of Western Europe had brought their rivalries by sea into the Indian Ocean and then to the China Seas. As a result, for most of the nineteenth and the first part of the twentieth century, the term "Great Powers" in Asia referred mainly to the metropolitan countries of Europe which ruled over largely multilingual and multicultural empires overseas.

In short, the term "Great Powers" does not fit in well with Asian perceptions of the past. In Asian history, the terms closest to the idea of "Great Powers" would be variations of words more readily translated as "Empires".[1] The word, "Empires", of course, is no more precise or accurate than the term "Great Powers". Empires were not necessarily great, and if great, not for very long. Nor did they have clearly defined boundaries; nor could they ensure strong and stable regimes for any length of time. The word has been used to describe large territorial expanses which had been conquered and ruled by a central government. It has also been used to cover areas in which a variety of kings, princes, and chieftains from time to time acknowledged the suzerainty of one emperor or another while retaining varying degrees of autonomy. In some cases, the word has been used for small kingdoms which had acquired neighbouring lands and elevated their kings to emperor status.

What was common to them was that their societies could usually be described by at least one (but usually more than one) of the following words: multilingual, multiethnic, multicultural, even multiracial. In addition, more explicitly than the term 'Great Powers', the word "Empires" excludes the modern phenomenon of nation states. That is to say, the intense quest by newly emerging states of Asia for identity and commonality was clearly the antithesis of what empires stood for. These states were structured to eliminate the minority and non-conformist interests they inherited from Western empires. They saw empires as anathema, certainly unacceptable to nation-building peoples. But their reaction was not limited to nationalism. A much deeper bond among them was the anti-empire beginnings that led each of them to independence and freedom.

Thus, I have used the word "Empires" here because it captures the continuities in Asian history and also relates directly to the experience of all emerging nations in Asia. It is the word through which most Asians see their ancient and immediate past as well as the shape of future threats in their respective regions. Consequently it is the word for which its opposite, which I shall call "Anti-empires", would highlight the way in which groupings of territories, countries, or nation states have reacted against past and future empires. Although more positive concepts like nationalism, regionalism, internationalism, even globalism, governed the rhetorical framework of diplomacy and strategic thinking, the underlying dynamics of political action was driven by anti-empire concerns. "Anti-empire" is also distinguished from the more familiar "anti-imperial" in the following way: "anti-imperial" is backward-looking in that it marks the opposition to past imperial theory and practice; "anti-empire" stresses the unwillingness of the new nations to permit future empires to arise again.[2] Thus, in the context of new Asian states in search of peace, stability, and legitimacy after the fall of empires, the word "Empires" would better reflect reality than the term "Great Powers". I shall therefore use "Empires" and its contemporary opposite throughout the paper and hope to show that, by redrawing the outlines of modern history in Asia in terms of empires and anti-empires, the two words could also give us new perspectives on Asian responses to the post-Cold War world.

There is probably not much anyone can teach Asians about empires and the territories inside or outside which have to deal with imperial systems. If they did not actually invent the idea and the practice, most Asian emperors ruled as if they did. H.J. MacKinder has described how the first Persian empire was brought into the heartland of world politics. The Hellenistic empire left its mark on

Asoka's empire in India as did Asoka's empire in the western parts of South-east Asia. Both left military, commercial, and cultural vestiges in a string of Central Asian oases where they eventually met the westward advances of a newly unified Chin-Han empire. This, and the dynastic empires that followed, had also expanded southwards to meet the cluster of Indianized states in South-east Asia, thus completing the circle.

Thereafter, Asian history can be depicted as a succession of greater or lesser empires bordered and interspersed by polities, or fragments of polities, with or without kings, princes, and tribal chiefs of one kind or another. Such polities were rarely more stable or more legitimate than the empires they succeeded. As for the peoples of Asia, whether or not they saw empires as blessings which protected or liberated minorities from the harsh oppressions of majorities in various princely states is hard to determine. But there were certainly examples of empires which did provide a great peace for varying periods under strong administrations and laws which tried to give fair treatment to peoples of different origins. The notable ones that endured long enough to leave records of imperial success were those in China and Central Asia, in parts of India and the Middle East.

This is the Asia into which the Portuguese, English, Dutch, and French navies, traders, and missionaries entered after 1500 and in which each of them began to build a new kind of maritime empire.[3] The ease with which the Europeans erected their long-distance trading and military structures was closely related to the fact that the older Asian empires were either already feeble or about to undergo turmoil and decline and to the fact that, for most peoples in Asia, being ruled by foreign warriors or mercantile groups was nothing new. Indeed, the two remaining significant empires of the seventeenth and eighteenth centuries in India and China were both ruled by relatively small numbers of foreigners, the Moghuls who had conquered most of the subcontinent from the northwest and the Manchus who had done the same in China from the northeast. The new "red-haired" and "white-faced" foreigners from Europe who began to carve out little bits of coastal districts to be included in what was to be their versions of empire would have appeared normal and within the Asian experience. The ships and guns might have been different, the Christian cross and administrative laws a little strange, but the claim to provide fair trading conditions and some form of justice was very much in the tradition of all previous imperial claimants.

Thus the grand British and French empires, the modest Dutch and Spanish empires in South-east Asia, and the negligible bits of the Portuguese empire, could all be slotted into Asian history without much difficulty until the middle of the nineteenth century. It was not until the industrial revolution had given the Europeans total military superiority over all Asian states, and the Westerners sought to establish permanent global empires, that the nature of imperial rule in Asia began to change radically.[4] In addition, the rise of modern republics and the kind of citizens' nationalism in Europe and the Americas projected a universalist world-view that fundamentally changed the nature of Asian attitudes towards empires. Some of the rhetoric might have been cast in terms of the European concept of "Great Powers", but it was the newly extended meaning of "Empires" and the modern reaction against empires, or "Anti-empires", that left the greatest impact on the Asian consciousness.

It was this consciousness that has determined the major strands of Asian thinking about post-imperial peace, stability, and legitimacy during the twentieth century. I believe that this remained the main thrust of Asian strategic thinking during the Cold War years and, following the fall of the Soviet "empire" in Eastern Europe, it also colours that thinking about the future place of the United States in their region. The essay is chronologically divided into two parts: the first briefly examines the last century of the era of the empires and the second considers the role of anti-empires during the period of the Cold War and beyond.

During and after the Empires

In Asian terms, it would be more appropriate to talk of the nineteenth and early twentieth centuries in terms of the periods during and after the empires rather than of colonial rule. For the hundred years after the middle of the nineteenth century, only the Chinese, the Russian, the British, and the Japanese empires may be described as imperial powers in Asia. The fall of the Chinese and Russian empires was disguised by their respective transformations into "revolutionary" regimes in 1911 and 1917. In their new forms, they would play crucial parts during the Cold War years. The Japanese expansion was a late development, something of an aberration, which was quickly stopped by the end of the Pacific War. Although brief, the empire left its mark on the post-war world. For most of Asia, however, the British empire was the greatest among all the "blue-water" European empires. For the purposes of this essay, it will represent all the others, which were but subordinate versions of it. In any case, the British empire alone survived as a significant force beyond 1945, although not for very long.

Let me begin with the residual glow of the Chinese empire at the turn of the nineteenth century. At that time, this could still be described as the last great example of the traditional Asian tributary empire, with many parts of it sending personal tributes from their kings, princes, and tribal chiefs to the emperor. The Chinese tributary system had been formally institutionalized during the Ming dynasty, partly in reaction against the Mongol urge to conquer vast areas of territory, acts of expansion that could only lead to eventual defeat, withdrawal, and exhaustion. The Ming system was also confirmed as sound imperial policy when they themselves experienced the disastrous cycle of invasion, conquest, over-extension, defeat, and withdrawal in Vietnam during the early fifteenth century. The Manchus and their Mongol allies, who destroyed the Ming in 1644, had restored the expansionist mode during the first century of the Ching dynasty (mid-seventeenth to mid-eighteenth centuries) and had spread their empire northwards and further westwards, but they eventually returned to the Ming tributary system and recognized that it was more realistic than one which over-stretched imperial resources into alien parts. The system, in any case, did not preclude military interventions to score political points from time to time, but shied away from any conquest and rule that could not be supported by the economic resources available to the imperial government. The focus was on political influence through the right to legitimize tributary rulers, on affirming the goals of peace and stability in the neighbourhood, and on manipulating a series of controlled trading networks.[5]

Whether or not this essentially non-expansionist system contributed to the stagnation and ultimate decline of Ching China as a "Great Power" is not relevant here. The fact is that the tributary empire was confronted in the nineteenth century by the expansionist forces of the Western international system released by the scientific and industrial revolution. This had been spearheaded by British maritime power in Asia, but the new system also reinforced the earlier overland expansion of the Russian empire into Central and northern Asia. That expansion brought Russian power to the borders of British India and Ching China. As one of the Great Powers, the British understood the Russian empire in their own terms. The Chinese, however, were slow to recognize that the Russians had changed dramatically between the seventeenth and the mid-nineteenth centuries and continued to view them as traditional overland enemies until it was too late. The ramifications of that failure to understand the change which led to the Russian revolution will be taken up later in the context of the Cold War after 1945.

Similarly, all other regimes in India, South-east Asia, and East Asia had failed to see that a different system of empire-building representing new technologies and political forces had come by sea. This was one that had grown out of long-distance maritime trade, but was now supported by a strong manufacturing base with access to global resources. The new system was also backed by vastly superior naval power and by a growing sense that the West had a civilizing mission, and had even earned the right to world dominance. That overseas system was led by Britain. Unlike the system within Europe itself, it was the maritime muscle of the Great Powers that mattered outside, and the British separation from continental Europe had given them great advantages in the Indian Ocean and the Far East. Eventually, the United States also became an Asian power and, belatedly, and somewhat reluctantly but inevitably, linked up with the others in the new global system of Great Powers.[6]

The nominal Chinese tributary system was no match for such a global network and disintegrated in the face of British maritime expansionism. It did not take long before the European rivalries were brought to the shores of Asia and the fall of the Chinese empire as a Great Power became inevitable. This led to divisions within China, to warlordism and civil war and, ultimately, to the Japanese invasion. For the region as a whole, the China vacuum contributed directly to the re-drawing of the map of East and Southeast Asia.

For a century until the end of the Second World War, however, the British empire, especially British India, remained the classic model of the Great Power empires in Asia.[7] This empire was a complex creature. It had at least three main parts: the conquest empire, the colonial empire, and the trading empire. The conquest empire was largely located in Asia and Africa while the more widespread colonial empire sank deep roots in North America and Australasia. The trading empire became global very early and was supported by the colonial and conquest empires while they lasted. It adapted quickly, however, to changing circumstances after the formal imperial institutions had disappeared and can be said to survive today, in a highly diluted form, through various multinationals. Its greatest legacy lies in the spread of English as the lingua franca of international trade. The colonial and trading empires, therefore, were distinct from the conquest empire in that, in the long run, they did not depend on conquests. On the contrary, they both evolved, especially in North America and Australasia, to lend support to anti-empire strategies and ideologies, and also alternative trading models, that helped to discredit the empires of Global Powers in Asia and Africa.

The British conquest empire in India as well as in South-east Asia was unique. Never before had a maritime empire thousands of miles from its home base ruled over so large a territory with so many historic and mature kingdoms. Never before had such an empire faced two massive land empires, China, still strong albeit weakening, and the Russians, both powerful and still expanding. For such an empire to hold sway over so large an area under such challenging circumstances for a hundred years was a remarkable feat. Predictably, it could not last as an Asian empire.

Nevertheless, for most Asian peoples, such an empire was of great historical significance. The Chinese had stopped conquering territory by the middle of the eighteenth century. No other Asian empires were active by that time. The arrival of the British at the end of that century as a power ready to acquire territory, in defence of trade or for whatever reason regarded as justifiable at the time, was a major transformation for Asian politics. The British were cautious for a long while, conscious of the dangers of over-extension of their limited resources and suspicious of the value of territorial assets against costs and administrative burdens. But once the decision was made to enter the Indian hinterland, there was no turning back. And when India proved invaluable in the growing China trade, and especially after the Opium Wars, further territorial advances into Burma and the Malay States and elsewhere were only a matter of time. These were matched by the Dutch in their East Indies archipelago and the French in Indochina and, surprisingly, by the Americans seizing the Philippines from the Spanish. Thus, for all Asians the century had soon become one of conquest empires.

As conquest empires went in Asian history, none of them lasted very long. Clearly the British model had the greatest impact, not only because it was a new phenomenon, a maritime empire that penetrated deeply into the continent, but also because it brought modern technology and new financial, legal, and administrative structures to Asia to an extent unknown in the past. Where the British installed technologies and governing structures, theirs was really more than an empire. It was also the strongest representative of the modern Great Powers that brought their intense rivalry to Asia and, at the same time, also led the way in introducing modern economic and political ideas to new generations of Asian elites.[8]

Was the British empire simply too ambitious? Did it fail because it began to over-extend itself by the end of the nineteenth century? Or was its failure really inevitable because of challenges in the West itself, ultimately because of the far superior economic and human resources of continental powers like Russia and the United States? Or was something within Asia equally important – the reactions against Western dominance, the readiness to learn from the West in order to throw back the West, the movements led by the Japanese and supported by increasingly large numbers of national-ists and anti-imperialists?

The Japanese certainly saw it as their venture to become a modern conquest empire as an integral part of that reaction to the West. Together with some Indians, a few Chinese and South-east Asians, the Japanese were the first to respond to the broader chal-lenge of the West. The Japanese ambition to expand was inspired, in particular, by their admiration of what the island peoples of Britain were able to achieve at sea, coupled with their fascination with the overland conquest dynasties of China in the past (the Khitan, the Jurchen, the Mongol, and the Manchu) and the Russian advances in the Siberian Far East. They persuaded themselves that they wanted to be a Great Power and, in Asia, that meant they would have to become a modern empire. Their justification for doing so was that they shared the desire to throw the Western empires out of Asia.[9] Ironically, this first thrust of anti-empire propaganda spurred the Japanese to launch the first and last imperial adventure in Asia modelled on the West.

This was an enterprise doomed from the start. It could not disguise the fact that it was an attempt to gain a place in the white man's Great Power club. Yet it could not avoid being trapped in its own dubious rhetoric by claiming to be leading an Asian defence against the West and eventually, on the eve of the Pacific War, found itself having to take on the four main Western empires in Asia all at once. It would have been difficult anyway to square their claim to save Asia for the Asians with the fact that they had spent 50 years trying to conquer much of the East and North-east Asian mainland (Korea, Manchuria, North China, and finally the rest of China), something even the strongest Great Powers had never tried to do. In the end, the Japanese drive to empire exhibited a degree of desperation and irrationality that may be compared to the ambitions of the Third Reich. It simply did not have the economic preconditions for success in the context of the global Great Power system.

No less important is the fact that the abortive Japanese attempt to replicate Western expansionism in Asia contributed to the growth of anti-empire thought and emotions among most Asian leaders. To that extent, the rapid rise and even speedier fall of the Japanese empire helped to deepen the role of anti-empire sentiments in Asia. The most remarkable feature of the Japanese failure was that it may have created more long-term suspicion against themselves than against the Westerners whom they thought their Asian neighbours really hated.

This brings me to the themes of peace, stability, and legitimacy. Did the era of empires ensure peace with neighbouring regimes? Among the western European powers, despite the traditional rivalries which were translated into competitive trade, there was a broad understanding about carving up territories and spheres of influence to guarantee peace among themselves. The balance of power they failed to establish in Europe would be produced in Asia by endorsing the status quo wherever possible. But it did not work in East Asia, where the German latecomers lost out because China and Japan were drawn into the Anglo-French side during the First World War. That loss was the trigger for other wars. It gave encouragement to the Japanese, who took over from the Germans in Shandong to make further advances into China. It endorsed the Japanese aggrandisement that had begun with their victories against China in 1895, Russia in 1904, and Korea in 1910. It led ultimately to the war in Manchuria, in North China, and the Sino-Japanese War of 1937–45.

The broad understanding among the European empires fared better in South and South-east Asia. Apart from the eccentric American war in the Philippines, which really was outside the system of Great Power rivalry, the powers did not fight one another in the region for over a hundred years. Careful efforts were made to enable Thailand to survive between the British and French advances towards the underbelly of China. A minor Pax Europa was sustained. If we could be sure that the native states in the region would have been at war if the Great Powers had not been there, such an achievement would certainly have been remarkable.

The external stability that accompanied relative peace between the powers is one thing. Stability within each of the empires is another matter.[10] Indian nationalism had encountered difficulties in the face of older and deeper Hindu–Muslim tensions and the concerns of other minority groups like the Sikhs and the Scheduled castes. Divisions among the major Burmese "nationalities" were exacerbated by British policies, not least by administering Burma as part of British India. The French in Indochina appeared to keep the peace, but laid the foundations of future wars by the way they separated the three parts of Vietnam. Both the British and the Dutch succeeded in dampening down the rivalries between various kings and chieftains in the Malay archipelago but their importation of Chinese and Indian labour produced areas of potential instability. As for China, Great Power rivalries over a period of nearly forty years, encouraged the economic, and ultimately the military, fragmentation of the provinces and made the period one of the most unstable in Chinese history. In Taiwan and Korea under Japanese rule, resistance was met with fierce suppression and a degree of enforced stability did follow, but whether this was the kind of stability expected of empires is very doubtful.

Undoubtedly, there was enough stability in British India and in the British, Dutch, French, Japanese, and American territories for local officials and traders, and their families who identified with the respective regimes, to prosper. To some extent, each fulfilled the imperial role of acting as protector of the various cultural and linguistic minorities. Also, economic development was significantly advanced in some parts of the empires. Health, transportation, and education did noticeably improve everywhere. Modern laws and bureaucracies were provided for all subjects of whatever origins. Even sections of the peasantry and a new proletariat could point to benefits in standards of living. But there is little doubt that, despite all these, anti-imperial feelings grew apace. Indeed, the greater the stability and the identifiable benefits, the sooner more people were prepared to demand the end of imperial rule.

This leads me to the larger issue of legitimacy. The age of modern empires opened the subject to new dimensions of thought and practice. This was not simply an abstract question of sovereignty or of mandate to rule. That was quite familiar. Different elite groups in various parts of Asia have encountered such questions again and again in the past, with special reference to rulers of foreign origin. Nor was the issue one of democracy and human rights. Those matters would come later, in most cases after the people had obtained their independence. What was foremost was the wish to put an end to empires whose only legitimacy was based on power and conquest, to the whole idea of Western dominance in Asia and, by extension, to any kind of dominance of one country by another, including any one group of people by another.

The sources of this strong feeling were many. At one level, the inspiration came from the anti-empire nationalist movements in modern Europe, ranging from the Dutch, the Greeks, the Italians, and the Germans to the Czechs, the Poles, and the Irish. At another level, the reaction followed the Social Darwinist racial claims of the White Supremacists, who saw their empires in Asia and Africa as conclusive evidence of their superiority. At yet another level, the theories of imperialism introduced by Hobson and Lenin provided great encouragement to those who sought ways of mobilizing opposition not only to the empires that oppressed them but also to all forms of social and economic dominance.[11]

But there were also many kinds of indigenous sources which added strength to the anti-empire sentiments that stemmed from modern political attitudes. Notable examples were the fierce emotions felt by Hindus and Sikhs against Muslim rule and by southern Chinese against the Manchus. Other examples were Vietnamese feelings against Chinese domination, Cambodian resistance to both Vietnamese and Thai encroachments on their territory, Malay defensiveness towards Javanese power, and the bitterness underlying Tamil and Singhalese relations.

It would be simplistic to think that anti-empire sentiments challenging the legitimacy of empires could put an end to imperial rule. By themselves, they might unite disparate peoples, prick the consciences of some imperialists, and undermine loyalties to imperial institutions. Unfortunately, empires did not end that easily, especially Great Power empires that relied on regular victories against all kinds of opponents and enemies to ensure their Great Power status. This might be even more true of those empires that won adherents by skilfully depicting themselves as ensuring peace and stability, raising standards of living, and offering good laws and civilized values.

For Great Power imperialists to fold back their empires and return home, many other factors would have to be present at the same time. It helped greatly if they proved to have over-stretched themselves (as the British had in India and the French had in Indochina), if they had weakened relative to other empires (as many of them had in Asia relative to Japan by 1941), if their home countries were threatened (as were all the European states by 1939), and if their own people had lost faith in, or lost the will to support, the imperial cause (as in Britain and France).[12] But a universal reaction against the legitimacy of empires and against empires themselves as active agents of war and instability would turn the tables on future aspirants. That reaction emerged during the early twentieth century and assisted the development of anti-empire institutions as well as groups of peoples and nations. This development was further strengthened through the years of the Cold War.

During and after the Cold War

The dismantling of Great Power empires after 1945 took several decades, but the end of the maritime empires was never in doubt by the end of the first decade. This did not mean, however, that an age of "anti-empires" had dawned for Asia. What had replaced the European empires were emerging nation states of varying sizes which inherited the often artificial boundaries drawn up by the colonial powers. Their sovereign identities were bolstered by their membership of the newly formed United Nations Organization and by the idealistic and untried principle of the equality of nations old and new. These nation-states soon found that imperial power in other forms, both actual and potential, was still alive. The main difference seemed to have been that the threat of empire came under the shadow of the Cold War between two superpowers that had come out of the Second World War stronger than when they went in.

In short, the world was still no less a dangerous place. None of the new relationships was straightforward, and no peace could be guaranteed. Only the outlines of an international framework of world order had been sketched, and a great deal of work would be needed before reality could be made to fit that framework. At least three large shadows hung over such efforts for the next forty years, all with consequences for Asia's place in world politics. The first was that of the extensive power of the Eurasian land empire that the Soviet Union had inherited from Tsarist Russia. The second was more pervasive. It came from the destabilizing features of super-power attempts to find global equilibrium through the Cold War. The third took the shape of external and internal challenges to the legitimacy of post-colonial nations, but was also influenced by the Cold War. The shadow could be darkened or lightened by super-power decisions whether or not to intervene in the affairs of these new nations.

Within Asia itself, there was a fourth shadow that showed new features, but derived its significance from relationships deeply rooted in the pre-modern past. This was a shadow cast by the great unevenness in the size of nations, for example, China and India in their new guise as nation states, stable Japan and unstable Pakistan and Indonesia, a divided Arab world and a fiercely united Israel, Iran and Afghanistan neighbouring the Soviet Union. All these relationships were reminders that traditional imperial dominance could easily re-emerge, the dominance by rich nations over the poor, and large nations over the small, whether they were called empires or not. It thus appeared that the immediate past Asian experience of empires and anti-empires was still highly relevant.

During the four decades of the Cold War, all four shadows played a part in Asia's response to world politics, but the fourth was not prominent. The uneven size of Asian states remained largely a dormant factor while the two superpowers wielded overwhelming power. This factor is returning to the foreground after the end of the Cold War and will become significant in speculations about the future. The three large shadows of the Cold War period, however, deserve more attention here.

The first of them had predated the collapse of Great Power empires. The Russian Revolution of 1917 had made an impact on various parts of Asia, not only because it espoused an anti-imperial rhetoric and supported a number of anti-empire alliances and movements, but also because it emerged intact after 1945, with more than a third of the land mass of Asia, in the largest surviving empire in the world. The Soviet Union had supported revolutionary wars against the former empires. Its post-war advances in Eastern and Central Europe were augmented by further successes against capitalism and Western liberalism. The most spectacular was the revolution in China only four years after the end of the War. Although this was by no means a Soviet victory, it was seen as a defeat for residual foreign interests in Eastern Asia. It was both a restoration of much of the fallen Ching empire and a resurgence of Chinese national pride.[13] In addition, it also created, for a while, the spectre of a vast Sino-Soviet Communist Empire that could take over the rest of Asia.

It is a measure of the strength of anti-empire sentiments that both Soviet and Chinese leaders did their utmost to counter the impression that their countries were empires. They themselves mounted anti-empire campaigns to try to prove that they were liberators in the struggle against capitalist and "neo-colonial" empires.[14] In turn, they aroused the United States and its allies to launch counter-attacks against Soviet imperial behaviour within the USSR and among its satellite states, and against Chinese policies towards minority peoples along China's long land borders, notably those of Tibet. Most Asian nationalist leaders, however, were not taken in by the propaganda. They calculated their own enlightened self-interests carefully, and either aligned with the United States or the Soviet Union accordingly, or sought some independent "neutralist" way.[15] Their goal was largely to stay in power in order to complete the urgent developmental and nation-building tasks in their respective countries. In this, they were relieved that, by the late 1950s, the Soviet Union in Asia was contained by the self-reliant ambitions of the Chinese, who were themselves determined not to be dominated by any other power.

By that time, it had become clear that the Cold War between the USA and the USSR provided the overwhelming reality that determined most other developments in international politics. Even then, there had not been a uniform Asian response to this new reality. It was understood that this war was an extension of the European struggle after 1945, a possible hot war that had, through the intensifying nuclear arms race, paradoxically been cooled down by the recognition that the stakes had become dangerously high. Although it had gradually become clear that the unrelenting struggle for supremacy between the two superpowers was producing a strategic equilibrium, delicately called the central balance, which promised global stability, it did not seem that way to most Asian leaders.

In theory, neither superpower wanted to build empires and neither would allow the other to do so. In defence of the equilibrium achieved, both would work to prevent other lesser powers from seeking empires of their own. In reality, the Soviet Union was recognized as a restructured Tsarist Russia and, therefore, an empire in all but name. The United States was more difficult to describe, expanding from a former colony to become "The First New Nation", and achieving imperial power which it disclaimed. Nevertheless, it was the closest to inheriting the mantle and range of the British empire and was certainly regarded as controlling the largest "informal" global empire.[16]

Cold War rhetoric portrayed each of the superpowers as a liberating force. Together, the two provided the balanced security that would allow causes like social equality and justice, freedom and democracy, to prevail. But down-to-earth Asian nationalists fighting to build their nation states were wary of new kinds of empires that might arise in the name of progress and human salvation. They saw no secure protection from the two superpowers, especially in a world where many countries were seeking to become nuclear powers. There was no guarantee that, in the longer run, those other countries would not seek to build their own empires in their own region or neighbourhood.

Instead, they saw a nuclear arms race and the probable accumulation of ever greater power in a number of rich or large countries, including some in Asia. Most Asian countries, especially the smaller nation states, recognized that only a few could qualify, or would want, to join the "nuclear club": countries like China, Japan and India; others which felt directly threatened by their neighbours; and some of the belligerent nations of the Middle East.[17] Cold War politics had demonstrated that a sure way of achieving power status was by the possession of nuclear arms. The immediate past experience of the lesser new nations in Asia suggested that they had to learn to work together to extend the boundaries of nuclear-free zones and thus help prevent the emergence of new empires.

A good example of such a response to the regional instability caused by Cold War developments may be seen in the relations between China and the superpowers. When the newly unified mainland government of China became a nuclear power in the 1960s, it caused considerable alarm among its neighbours. Although no match for the superpowers, China was large and populous. It sought full independence from the superpowers, having fought against the United Nations forces under the leadership of the USA during the Korean War and thrown off Soviet tutelage by the late 1950s. It supported revolutionary wars, largely in Asia, but also in other parts of the Third World, against what it considered client states of the superpowers. It launched a war on the borders between India and the Tibetan highlands. When the Vietnam War drew both superpowers into the heart of Southeast Asia, China sought a major role for itself. Indeed, China became so active in world politics that both superpowers played on the fears of China's neighbours that it would once again become the dominant empire in Asia. Even fellow communists in Vietnam became worried by the threat of a revitalized China on its northern borders.[18]

With this background in mind, it is easy to understand why Asian nations were quick to learn from the European strategies for achieving peace and stability in response to the Cold War. In particular, the experience of regional security organizations, and even the idea of economic communities, was appealing. As a direct result, an organization like the Association of Southeast Asian Nations (ASEAN) became relatively successful. While it could no prevent instability in the region, it did keep alive the anti-empire alertness that each of its members had carried with it from an earlier period. This example shows that regional initiatives can both support local efforts to make peace and bring international involvement in to help ensure stability. ASEAN, of course, showed its sympathies mainly towards the USA and its allies during the Vietnam War. Yet the existence of ASEAN was acknowledged by both superpowers, and its relative cohesion helped the protagonists to delimit the areas of conflict. Insofar as the organizations firmly cooperated with one another, this contributed ultimately to the negotiations for an acceptable peace in the region.[19]

The Cold War may not have caused as much instability in other parts of Asia as it did in Eastern Asia. It certainly forced the superpowers to mix their roles from time to time, either aggravating conflict by their rivalries or containing wars that endangered global peace. In South Asia, for example, the Cold War allowed India and Pakistan, each looking to one of the superpowers, to build up their respective military strengths. But this was no guarantee of either peace or security when an opportunity arose for India to assist in Pakistan's dismemberment. At the same time, Cold War rivalry also helped preserve national boundaries, as it enabled the smaller and weakened Pakistan to help the USA check Soviet power in Afghanistan. Yet another example can be found in the potentially destabilizing acts of extensive arms sales by one power which were made to balance out over time by the other: while the Soviet Union carefully monitored the development of India's military capacity, the USA and its allies assured Pakistan of countervailing help.[20]

As for the Middle East, the record was less successful. On the surface, the superpowers saw to it that no power gained a dominant position. But the reality was much more complicated. On the one hand, it would appear that both of them armed the Middle Eastern protagonists, whether Arab–Israeli or Iraqi–Iranian, to fight proxy wars, indeed, increasingly dangerous wars which only the superpowers themselves could try to regulate. On the other, their respective clients also seemed able to dictate the terms of the conflicts they really wanted to fight.[21] This often left the superpowers helpless to control the conditions necessary for stability and peace in any single region.

The fact that Cold War rivalry has enabled anti-empire sentiments in Asia to survive and that no new empires have emerged during the Cold War years may be better appreciated today now that the central balance is gone and only one superpower holds sway. But that was not how most Asian countries saw those trying and eventful years. There is as yet no nostalgia for the Cold War among Asian leaders. It would be premature to draw any conclusions about the long-term role of the Cold War in ensuring peace, but these leaders are likely to agree that the superpowers had striven for stability and acted in support of widely-shared anti-empire ideals.

This brings me to the third shadow hanging over Asia, which was more immediate and real than the Cold War, that is, the external and internal challenges to the legitimacy of the new Asian nation states. The challenges had stemmed from conditions in Asia after the end of the Second World War, notably a China unified only to be divided again, a Korea restored to independence only to be divided again, and a host of newly emerging states spawned by European empires during the late 1940s and early 1950s. The various transfers of power, whether they were violent or not, by the Dutch, the French, and the British, to local nationalist leaders did not bring peace and stability to the former colonies. Not one single post-imperial country in Asia (this excludes both a severely damaged Japan and an unstable Thailand) was assured of the basic ingredients of nationhood – those of unity, cultural homogeneity and freedom from external interference. None could be confident that the departure of the imperial powers would strengthen the national economy, produce more jobs for their people, and enable the new states to better defend themselves.[22] Nor could they resist looking to Cold War rivalries to help them fight off the challenges to their legitimacy. This was true for them irrespective of size and location.

The fact was that the end of Great Power empires left little peace and even less stability. All that was assured was a chance for legitimacy as newly emerging nation states. There was the United Nations Organization, which each new state could join and so obtain a licence to practise nationhood. There were international financial and commercial institutions like the World Bank and the International Monetary Fund (IMF), and the General Agreement on Tariffs and Trade (GATT), from which support could be received to assist economic development. Other regional organizations were established for post-imperial Asia and Africa. But the reality was that issues of legitimacy went beyond that of recognition and identity of sovereign nation states.

Of increasing concern were questions of legitimacy of the government of each of these states, and questions of how the ruling party or elites came to power and maintained themselves in power. At the level where empires and anti-empires were on top of the diplomatic and strategic agenda, these questions were often ignored. As long as Asian leaders could point to the threat to the independence of their nations, they could emphasize their anti-empire concerns and ask that national unity be seen as a higher legitimacy needed to deal with a dangerous world. In time, however, as international or regional stability was more assured, such questions returned to the fore. Have the leaders delivered to the citizenry the promises of economic growth and well-being, of social justice, of law and order?

Asia provides many contrasts to these questions. The economic successes registered for Eastern Asia and the Pacific Rim countries have made these questions of internal legitimacy more urgent. New middle classes have arisen, with demands for political participation that could destabilize their countries if not met. Elsewhere, however, subsistence agriculture still prevails and more traditional threats of revolutionary upheavals remain. The leaders know that failure to contain such forces would not only unseat them but could also unleash disruptive movements that would invite future external interventions.[23] In the context of the Cold War, they had understood the rules of the game enough to defend national integrity. But, as the world adjusts to the absence of superpower balance, Asian leaders may find that issues of internal legitimacy will become more pressing and more directly relevant to future peace and stability in their respective neighbourhoods.

Some Speculations about the Future

The several ways that the Asian nations positioned themselves through the Cold War have left many legacies. Now that the Cold War is over, these countries will ponder on the dangers that had not been anticipated before. What follows is wholly speculative, but premised on the weakening of one former superpower in North-east and Central Asia and the decreasing role of the remaining superpower in the rest of Asia. It is widely acknowledged that the long struggle for ascendancy led both powers to suffer economically from over-extension of resources. The two regions that gained from that struggle are the battlegrounds in Western Europe and Eastern Asia, and it is unlikely now that there will ever be a single superpower empire. Nevertheless, insofar as parts of East Asia have grown rich and strong during the Cold War years, countries in Asia will remain sensitive to their unevenness in size and to the prospect of ambitious powers seeking to build empires in the future.

It is unlikely that a stable world order will replace the central balance of two superpowers in the near future. But there are legacies of the Cold War period which could provide strong economic foundations for a multipolar world. The massive growth of the international trading system has endorsed the principles of free trade and capitalist market economies, particularly for North America, Western Europe, and Eastern Asia. There are signs that this legacy of rapid economic growth will have major ramifications elsewhere in the world for decades to come. For Asians, the emergence of a new role in world politics has drawn attention to the importance of skilful management of an international trade that is knowledge-led and technology-driven. Rapid economic growth has not only highlighted the reality of global interdependence but also supports the optimistic view of the role of economic power as a guarantor of future stability. The efforts to strengthen and widen the scope of ASEAN co-operation and explore other possible regional structures in Eastern Asia, as well as the moves towards a larger Asia–Pacific economic grouping, all belong to the new diplomacy of economic power.[24] Together with the heroic attempts to keep alive the General Agreement on Tariffs and Trade, they promise to build an economic order that would make future empires and Cold Wars less feasible.

For years, strategists have predicted the coming of a multipolar world, possibly a world of four or five smaller superpowers. It now appears that we are about to have that multipolar world, with one or two of the centres in Asia. If this occurs, the historic positions of uneven-sized countries, notably that of China and India, together now with Japan and Indonesia, give every reason for the smaller Asian countries to be immediately more wary of the future aspirants to imperial power in the region. The multipolar world, if and when it eventually settles down to become the basis of a new world order, does not appear likely to be more peaceful or more stable than the central balance of two superpowers. What is certain is that, with more players of potential but varying economic and political power, it will be harder to predict if the world is really through with empires.

Looking around in Asia, no Southeast Asian, Australasian or Central Asian leader would rule out the possibility of new empires emanating out of China or Japan. Nor is Indian dominance, perhaps short of the trappings of empire, over other South Asian states an impossibility. To counter such developments, it would be unwise to depend on the fact that nation states have been legitimized, or to count on the defensive forces of nationalism. Nor is it enough merely to put up regional structures enunciating principles of cooperation. And, for all its well-intentioned efforts, it would be premature to depend on the United Nations and other similar international organizations to protect smaller countries against future empires.

In short, it would appear that it is premature to suppress anti-empire feelings and dismantle existing anti-empire structures in Asia. There are few signs that Asian governments are ready to give full attention to the kinds of legitimacy that stress the democratic and human rights of their peoples. As long as there is the conviction that potential empires in Asia have to be met by vigilant anti-empires, questions of internal legitimacy are likely to be subordinated to external issues of security and remain of low priority. What may make a difference to these deeply ingrained attitudes is that the new world order will lead to a reappraisal of the very nature of empires in a future age of extensive interlocking trade.

A reappraisal of the new dimensions of this trade may show that the world depends on, and is deeply committed to, the international interdependence that would accompany it, and would no longer tolerate the military supremacy of any one or more powers. In that context, Asian governments may be prepared to believe that the age of empires as we have known them is truly over. A new generation of leaders may agree to proclaim that their anti-empires have become obsolete. For that to happen, however, the whole world would have to believe that the five or more smaller superpowers in Asia, North America, and the United States of Europe have found, and would be content with, new and largely economic roles for themselves. It would also have to believe that they have, by so doing, ensured that the attention and energies that have been given to anti-empires for so many decades will thereafter be turned towards those organizations and institutions that can be said to be truly global.

Notes

1. The variations are many and refer to the realms of, for example, the *Huangdi* in China, the *Tenno* in Japan, the Great Khan in Central Asia, the Sultan or the Shah in the Middle East and Mughal India, and the Maharaja in India.
2. Anti-colonial and anti-imperialist writings abound, so much so that much of the literature has been linked with tiresome old slogans and self-seeking

excuses for failure among some nationalist leaders. This is unfortunate. It has led to a blurring of the distinction between old empire-bashing attitudes, which are certainly backward-looking and negative, and the clear-sighted and legitimate concerns that smaller countries have about the re-appearance of empires. The latter has led many modern national leaders to work closely with other leaders of post-imperial nations to stiffen the anti-empire networks within various international and regional networks, including trying to make the United Nations into an anti-empire organization. There is no denying the strength of feeling among these new nations and their success in using anti-empire rhetoric and shaping their own anti-empire agenda against the return to empires in any form, including any re-crudescence of traditional Asian empires.

3. The first two volumes of the series edited by Boyd C. Shafer, *Europe and the World in the Age of Expansion*, provide the most useful overview of the subject. They are Bailey W. Diffie and George D. Winius, *Foundations of the Portuguese Empire, 1415–1580* (Minneapolis: University of Minnesota Press 1977); and Holden Furber, *Rival Empires of Trade in the Orient, 1600–1800* (Minneapolis: University of Minnesota Press 1976). Although outdated and controversial, K.M. Pannikar, *Asia and Western Dominance* (London: George Allen & Unwin 1959), presents a forceful Asian view that still deserves to be read.

   Two books by Charles R. Boxer, *The Portuguese Seaborne Empire 1415–1825* and *The Dutch Seaborne Empire 1600–1800* (London: Hutchinson 1969 and 1965 respectively), provide excellent background reading.

4. Where Asia is concerned, the story begins with India, T.G.P. Spear, *India: A Modern History* (Ann Arbor: University of Michigan Press 1961). Further east, in South-east Asia, Nicholas Tarling ed., *The Cambridge History of Southeast Asia* (Cambridge: Cambridge University Press 1992), volume 2, essay by Nicholas Tarling, 'The Establishment of the Colonial Regimes'.

   The broader issues have been the subject of numerous studies. A basic overview is William H. McNeill, *The Rise of the West: A History of the Human Community* (Chicago: The University of Chicago Press 1963). Two others are more focused: E.J. Hobsbawm, *Industry and Empire: An Economic History of Britain since 1750* (London: Weidenfeld and Nicolson 1969) and V.G. Kiernan, *European Empires from Conquest to Collapse, 1815–1960* (London: Fontana Collins 1983). Also, Paul Kennedy, *The Rise and Fall of the Great Powers: Economic Change and Military Conflict from 1500 to 2000* (New York: Random House 1987) has an excellent chapter on the geopolitics of this period.

5. John K. Fairbank ed., *The Chinese World Order: Traditional China's Foreign Relations* (Cambridge, MA: Harvard University Press 1968).

6. William L. Langer, *The Diplomacy of Imperialism 1890–1902* (New York: Knopf 1951; second edition, 1965); C.J. Bartlett, *The Global Conflict, 1880–1970: The International Rivalry of the Great Powers* (London: Longman 1984). For the empire in the Philippines, Lewis E. Gleeck Jr, *The American Half-Century, 1898–1946* (Manila: Historical Conservation Society 1984).

7. J.R. Jones, *Britain and the World 1649–1815* (London: Brighton, Har-

vester Press 1980) and Ronald Hyam, *Britain's Imperial Century 1815–1914* (London: B.T. Batsford 1976). Providing a broader framework for comparison is Eric Hobsbawm, *The Age of Empire 1875–1914* (London: Weidenfeld and Nicolson 1987).

8. Chapter 13 of McNeill, *Rise of the West,* summarizes the main features of some of the technological and cultural transfers that occurred; also Raymond F. Betts, *Uncertain Dimensions: Western Overseas Empires in the Twentieth Century* (Minneapolis: University of Minnesota Press 1985).

9. W.G. Beasley, *Japanese Imperialism 1894–1945* (Oxford: Clarendon Press 1987).

10. John Gallagher, Gordon Johnson and Anil Seal eds., *Locality, Province and Nation* (Cambridge: Cambridge University Press, 1973) and D.A. Low ed., *Soundings in Modern South Asian History* (London: Weidenfeld and Nicolson 1968) contain excellent essays. For South-east Asia, several essays in Tarling, *The Cambridge History of Southeast Asia* (1992), vol. 2, examine some of the inner contradictions of empire. An earlier collection which is still useful is William L. Holland ed., *Asian Nationalism and the West* (New York: Macmillan 1953). Also W. David McIntyre, *The Commonwealth of Nations: Origins and Impact 1869–1971* (Minneapolis: University of Minnesota Press 1977).

11. J.A. Hobson, *Imperialism : A Study* (London: Allen & Unwin, 3rd edition, 1938); Roger Owen and Bob Sutcliffe eds., *Studies in the Theory of Imperialism* (London: Longman 1972). Also Raymond F. Betts, *The False Dawn: European Imperialism in the Nineteenth Century* (Minneapolis: University of Minnesota Press 1975).

12. McIntyre, *Commonwealth of Nations,* (Minneapolis: University of Minnesota Press 1977); Betts, *Uncertain Dimensions,* (Oxford: Oxford University Press 1985); Kiernan, *European Empires* from *Conquest to Collapse,* 1915–1960 (London: Fontana 1982); For a broader view of the process, Franz Ansprenger, *The Dissolution of the Colonial Empires* (London: Routledge 1989; original German edition, 1981). Two specialist studies are illuminating: Hue-tam Ho Tai, *Millenarianism and Peasant Politics in Vietnam* (Cambridge, MA: Harvard University Press 1983) and Ramon H. Myers and M.R. Peatte eds., *The Japanese Colonial Empire, 1895–1945* (Princeton: Princeton University Press 1984).

13. John K. Fairbank, *The Great Chinese Revolution, 1800–1985* (New York: Harper and Row 1986).

14. It is extraordinary how quickly terms like neocolonialism, frequently heard in the 1960s and 1970s, have dated; see R.L. Rothstein, *The Weak in the World of the Strong: The Developing Countries in the International System* (New York: Columbia University Press 1977); R.A. Mortimer, *The Third World Coalition in International Politics* (New York: Praeger 1980). A valuable study of this phase in Asian history is Geoffrey Jukes, *The Soviet Union in Asia* (Berkeley, CA: University of California Press 1973).

15. U.S. Bajpai ed., *Non-alignment, Perspectives and Prospects* (New Delhi: Lancer Publishers 1983); Lawrence W. Martin, *Neutralism and Nonalignment: the New States in World Affairs* (New York: Praeger 1962). For South-east Asia, Dick Wilson, *The Neutralisation of Southeast Asia* (New York: Praeger 1975).

16. Informal empire describes "that shadowy area in international relations

where two states of vastly unequal power were theoretically equal sovereign states, but where the stronger of the two nevertheless exercised more power over the weaker than was common within the European state system. Especially in the nineteenth century, European states often tried to exercise informal control overseas while avoiding the full responsibilities of formal annexation"; Philip Curtin, Steven Feierman, Leonard Thompson and Jan Vansina, *African History* (London: Longman 1978), pp. 354–357. The United States learnt from the British experience with considerable success.

17. M.H. Haykal, *The Sphinx and the Commissar: The Rise and Fall of Soviet Influence in the Middle East* (London: Collins 1978); and R.C. Thornton, *The Bear and the Dragon: Sino-Soviet Relations and the political Evolution of the Chinese People's Republic, 1949–1971* (New York: American-Asian Educational Exchange 1972).

18. Michael Yahuda, *China's Role in World Affairs* (London: Croom Helm 1978); Wang Gungwu, *China and the World since 1949: The Impact of Independence, Modernity and Revolution* (London: Macmillan 1977).

19. Michael Leifer, *ASEAN and the Security of Southeast Asia* (London: Routledge 1989); Alison Broinowski ed., *Understanding ASEAN* (London: Macmillan 1982); Charles E. Morrison and Astri Suhrke, *Strategies of Survival: The Foreign Policy Dilemmas of Smaller Asian States* (Brisbane: University of Queensland Press 1978); Ralph Pettman, *Small Power Politics and International Relations in Southeast Asia* (Sydney: Holt, Rinehart and Winston 1976).

20. Jukes, *Soviet Union in Asia,* (Sydney: Angus and Robertson 1973); R.H. Donaldson, *Soviet Policy toward India: Ideology and Strategy* (Cambridge, MA: Harvard University Press 1974); T.V. Paul, *Reaching for the Bomb: the Indo-Pak Nuclear Scenario* (New Delhi: Dialogus 1984); Surjit Mansingh, *India's Search for Power: Indira Gandhi's Foreign Policy, 1966–1982* (Beverly Hills, Calif.: Sage Publications 1984); S. Nihal Singh, *The Yogi and the Bear: the Story of Indo-Soviet Relations* (New Delhi: Allied Publishers 1986); Rajvir Singh, *U.S., Pakistan and India: Strategic Relations* (Allahabad: Chugh Publications 1985).

21. Yehuda Lukacs ed., *Documents on the Israeli-Palestinian Conflict 1967–1983* (Cambridge: Cambridge University Press 1984).

22. Gunnar Myrdal, *Asian Drama: An Inquiry into the Poverty of Nations* (New York: A Twentieth Century Fund Study, 3 vols. 1968); David J. Steinberg et al., *In Search of Southeast Asia: a Modern History* (New York: Praeger 1971); Tarling, *Cambridge History of Southeast Asia,* Volume 2, part two.

23. Richard Higgott and Richard Robison eds., *Southeast Asia: Essays in the Political Economy of Structural Change* (London: Routledge and Kegan Paul 1985); Chandran Jeshuron ed., *Government and Rebellions in Southeast Asia* (Singapore: Institute of Southeast Asian Studies 1986); Richard Robison, Kevin Hewison and Richard Higgott (eds.), *Southeast Asia in the 1980s; the Politics of Economic Crisis* (Sydney: Allen & Unwin 1987).

24. Peter Drysdale, *International Economic Pluralism: Economic Policy in East Asia and the Pacific* (Sydney: Allen & Unwin 1988); Richard H. Solomon ed., *The China Factor: Sino-American Relations and the Global Scene* (Englewood Cliffs, N.J.: Prentice-Hall 1981); Stuart Harris and

James Cotton eds., *The End of the Cold War in Northeast Asia* (Melbourne: Longman Cheshire 1991); Amitav Acharya, *A New Regional Order in Southeast Asia: ASEAN in the Post-Cold War Era* (London: Adelphi Paper 279, 1993).

13

The Superpowers in the Middle East: Cold War and Post-Cold-War Policies

Carol R. Saivetz

Scholars and casual observers would agree that the rigidly bipolar configuration of the post-World-War-II era has disappeared. Indeed, confrontation between the two superpowers eased even prior to the December 1991 unraveling of the Soviet Union, as a result of then Soviet president Mikhail S. Gorbachev's "new political thinking". The changes introduced into the Soviet world view and foreign policy[1] produced agreements on arms control and progress toward the settlement of numerous Third-World conflicts. These trends accelerated with the final collapse of the USSR.

It can also be argued, however, that the erosion of bipolarity may have simultaneously facilitated Iraq's attack on Kuwait in 1990 and may give rise to other such acts of aggression in the future. Put more generally: Does the end of the Cold War represent the end of systemic constraints on local conflicts? Does it enhance the prospects for international cooperation to stop a local challenger? This essay will offer some preliminary answers to these questions by examining Cold-War and post-Cold-War great power policies in the Middle East. As an area in which there was intense superpower rivalry and in which there is continuing US and Russian interest, the Middle East is an excellent case through which to investigate the impact of the end of the Cold War on regional conflicts.

Because of the inherent complexity of superpower involvement in the Middle East (and elsewhere in the Third World), it is useful to subdivide our discussion of the Middle East into two areas: the Arab–Israeli dispute and the politics of the (Persian) Gulf.[2] The contrasts between superpower involvement in the Arab–Israeli–Palestinian conflict and in the Gulf provide additional insights into the dynamics of that involvement and the issues of regional stability/instability and the legitimacy of outside interventions.

The first section of this essay will explore the politics of the Cold War era in an effort to highlight how the superpower competition both exacerbated and dampened the local conflicts. The second section will examine the Gulf War and the beginnings of the

Middle East peace process, with a view to assessing the impact of the erosion of bipolarity. It will explore the USA's policy of "cooperative hegemony" and the Soviet Union's foreign policy of decline. The last section of the essay will speculate on the future of these two subregions and the policies of the great powers toward them.

The Middle East during the Cold War

Generally, regional power imbalances and regional politics provided opportunities for superpower involvement; yet, that very involvement was complicated by the vicissitudes of patron-client relations. Nowhere was that clearer than in the Middle East where, between 1955 and 1989, the competition between the Soviet Union and the United States became increasingly intertwined with intra-Arab rivalries and with the Arab–Israeli–Palestinian conflict. At times the superpower rivalry exacerbated, if not fueled, the local conflicts, which were largely indigenous in origins. At other times, the two superpowers cooperated to manage the crises that their involvement had inflamed. This characterization seems particularly true with regard to the Arab–Israeli conflict, but much less so in the arena of the Gulf. In 1967, the USSR challenged the relative stability of the Arab-Israeli region by forwarding to Egyptian President Gamal Abd al-Nasser false reports of Israeli mobilization on the Syrian border. While at best, officials of the USSR were deliberately ambiguous, Nasser interpreted Soviet signals as a green light to demand the removal from the Sinai of the United Nations Emergency Forces (UNEF). It would seem that the USSR hoped to deflect Israeli attention from Syria; moreover, many argue that Moscow at no point wanted war and indeed hoped that Nasser could consolidate his gains short of war.[3]

Once war broke out, the superpowers worked to prevent any escalation of the conflict, including outside military intervention. When an Israeli victory seemed imminent, Moscow moved to impose a cease-fire, and when it appeared that Israeli troops might seize Damascus, Moscow severed diplomatic relations with Tel Aviv and sent a note to President Lyndon Johnson threatening military action. The Johnson Administration countered by sending US ships toward Syria. Tacit crisis management culminated in the US–Soviet summit held in Glassboro, New Jersey at which President Johnson and Soviet Premier Aleksey Kosygin hammered out the compromise that became United Nations (UN) resolution 242.

Yet, crisis management left the regional power balances in a state of disequilibrium: Moscow faced the unenviable task of rearming the Arabs so as to redress the immediate power imbalances in the region at the same time as the Kremlin needed to pursue a diplomatic process designed to regain the captured territories. In other words, Moscow – to regain its *own* stature in the region – had to bolster the military strength of its clients, while convincing the Arabs not to use that strength to recoup their losses from the 1967 war.

This policy has been characterized by George Breslauer as "collaborative competition".[4] Begun in the aftermath of the Six Day War, this policy persisted until Mikhail S. Gorbachev came to power in 1985. Ironically, this phrase would also seem apt for US policy in the Kissinger era. Breslauer argues that Moscow aided Egypt during the War of Attrition so as to create a military stalemate that would facilitate negotiations.[5] At the same time, under Henry Kissinger's direction, US policy shifted to a more unilateralist approach: It would seem that Kissinger wanted not cooperation, but simply to oust the USSR from its role in the Middle East.[6]

The events surrounding the 1973 war also illustrate both the competitive and collaborative aspects of superpower involvement in the Middle East.[7] At first, the USSR was unwilling to condone another Middle East war, leading Anwar Sadat to evict 20,000 Soviet troops from Egypt in 1972. By 1973, however, Moscow seemingly acquiesced and resumed arms deliveries to Cairo. During the war, Moscow sought a cease-fire while the Arabs were still winning, but Egypt proved unwilling to comply; the "victorious" cease-fire would have salvaged both Soviet and Arab prestige and would have avoided the potential for escalation. As the tide of battle turned against the Arabs, the Kremlin resupplied its clients during the war. At the same time, the US dragged its feet on replacing Israeli losses, a policy seemingly directed at preventing an Arab rout. In some respects this policy was a mirror image of the Soviet policy: Kissinger apparently felt that a settlement would be more possible if the Arabs did not lose;[8] or at the very least, a stalemate might prevent Soviet interventionary threats.

Tacit crisis management threatened to break down, however, as the two superpowers negotiated a cease-fire. When Israel violated the cease-fire resolution and moved to surround the Egyptian Third Army, the Soviet Union was forced to protect its client. Troops in the southern military region of the USSR were put on alert and Moscow proposed a joint interventionary force to the US. In a note to President Nixon, Leonid Brezhnev wrote:

> I will say it straight that if you find it impossible to act jointly with us in this matter, we should be faced with the necessity urgently to consider the question of taking appropriate steps unilaterally. We canot allow arbitrariness on the part of Israel.[9]

The US responded by putting its troops in Europe on a DEFCOM 3 alert and intensifying pressure on Israel to allow the resupply of the Third Army.

The experiences of the superpowers in both the 1967 and 1973 Middle East wars illustrate that Moscow's or Washington's activities did seriously impinge on the course of events in the Third World: Soviet provocational actions in the spring of 1967 clearly unleashed the rush of events that culminated in the defeat of the USSR's clients. By the same token, Sadat forced the hand of his patron to support, at least tacitly, his war objectives. However, once the wars had broken out, the superpowers collaborated to prevent escalation. What had to be taken into account were not only events in the region, but their implications for the superpowers. Thus, Moscow needed to make clear that it would not allow its client(s) to go down in humiliating defeat. In the words of Alexander George:

> Each superpower shall accept military intervention by the other superpower in a regional conflict if such intervention becomes necessary to prevent the overwhelming defeat of a regional ally: moreover, in order to remove the other superpower's incentive to intervene in such situation each superpower shall accept responsibility for pressuring its regional ally to stop short of inflicting such a defeat on its local opponent.[10]

According to this logic, Soviet threats to intervene were legitimate and designed to restore the *status quo*. It was a stable situation that contained the inherent recognition of the legitimacy of outside interventions, namely the right of the superpowers to protect their vested interests and to compete collaboratively within the region. Yet, the *status quo* was not a situation that held hope for conflict resolution.[11]

In many respects, the outbreak of the Iran–Iraq War and superpower behavior during that conflict stand in sharp contrast to the actions of both the US and the USSR in the Arab–Israeli nexus. The roles of the superpowers were not as clearly defined; nor did their involvement have the parallelism of the Arab-Israeli conflict. When the war erupted in September 1980, the Soviet Union had relations with both combatants and the US with neither. In spite of this asymmetry, both superpowers held strong views on how the war should end. Throughout the eight years of the conflict, neither superpower wanted either Iran or Iraq to win the war. The best possible resolution of the conflict would have been a mediated settlement that would include a return to the *status quo ante*. The least acceptable to the superpowers would have been an Iranian victory that would deepen the shadow cast by Islamic fundamentalism and would represent a major danger to the Gulf states. Moreover, an Iraqi defeat would cost the Soviets their standing (already damaged) as supporters of the Arab cause. By the same token, neither the USSR nor the US would have been pleased by an Iraqi victory. Baghdad, since the mid-seventies, had demonstrated its independence from Moscow and its desire to be a major radical (and anti-American) force both in the Gulf and in the Middle East as a whole.

Strikingly, despite the congruity in Soviet and American views about the war and its dangers, there was no superpower cooperation or crisis management. If anything, Moscow was in a much better position than the US to attempt to influence the outcome and to that end established itself as the sole outside balancer. At the outbreak of the war, when it appeared that Baghdad could win a quick, decisive victory, Moscow tilted toward Teheran by permitting Libya and Syria to transship military equipment to Teheran. At the same time, the USSR suspended arms shipments to Iraq, but allowed its East European allies to send Baghdad spare parts. The 1982 Iranian counter-attack and subsequent occupation of Iraqi territory prompted the USSR to resume arms deliveries to Iraq. This tilt toward Baghdad remained in place until mid-1987 when several forces combined to propel the Soviet Union into a pro-Iranian policy. First, Gorbachev's emphasis on *perestroika* meant that policies designed to bolster the ailing Soviet economy were pursued. By mid-1986, economic relations with Iran expanded to include an agreement to resume natural gas shipments to the USSR, the establishment of standing joint USSR–Iranian economic commissions, and ultimately the return of Soviet technical advisors to Iran. Second, in the summer of 1987, Moscow's view was that Iraq – with US assistance – was gaining the upper hand. Thus, the USSR voted for United Nations Security Council resolution 598 which called for a cease-fire in the Gulf, but refused to go along with Security Council efforts to punish Iran for not abiding by the resolution.

This very brief history of the superpowers and the Iran–Iraq War reveals the limited impact of bipolarity on Gulf politics. First, the

Khomeini revolution in Iran had nothing to do with superpower confrontation *per se*, but that event more than any other had a decisive impact on the region. It effectively eliminated the US as a player in the early stages of the Iran–Iraq War. Second, superpower competition did not deter the Iraqi attack on Iran. On the one hand, we could argue that Saddam Hussein might not have attacked had the US preserved a presence in Iran. With the rupture in the US-Iranian relationship, Saddam had reason not to anticipate a US response and not to expect Moscow to try to control the war. On the other hand, with the US position in the region damaged by the Khomeini revolution, Moscow was left to play its careful balancing game for its own reasons. Most significantly, the asymmetry between the superpowers' positions meant that there was nothing in the situation as it developed to trigger the crisis management mechanisms that operated in the Arab–Israeli dispute.

It was Kuwait that attempted to engage the superpowers more directly in the conflict so that they would indeed collaborate in crisis management. The Kuwaitis approached Moscow which agreed to lease three tankers; simultaneously, the US agreed to reflag 11 tankers and to escort those ships through the Gulf. Although the Kuwaiti request actually provided Moscow with an "invitation" to maintain a presence in the Gulf, it simultaneously legitimized American naval activity. Moscow could not condemn the reflagging operation *per se* without calling into question its own assistance to Kuwait. For all practical purposes, the Kuwaiti effort failed; the war ended only after the accidental shooting down of an Iranian civilian airliner in July 1988.

Moscow may have played a more direct role than the US in the region, but that involvement proved detrimental to the USSR in the long run. Moscow's balancing act may have prolonged the war, thereby enabling the US to enlarge its military and political presence in the region. It was this aspect of the war that apparently alarmed the Soviet Union the most. In a major address to a Foreign Ministry Conference in June 1988, Foreign Minister Eduard Shevardnadze complained bitterly that no one had alerted the Soviet leadership to the fact that the war would promote this US military build-up.[12] Thus, as in the Arab-Israeli dispute, decisions based on local calculations, clearly affected the superpower balance in the region.

Transition: The End of the Cold War

Our analysis of superpower policies in the Middle East during the Cold War was facilitated by the comparison between politics in the Arab–Israeli and Gulf areas. The comparison revealed the variations in superpower involvement in, and response to, the indigenous conflicts in the two subregions. However, in the post-1989 period, it is far more difficult to differentiate policies toward the two regions, as the Iraqi invasion of Kuwait had a direct impact on the rhythm of politics throughout the Middle East.

The sources of the attack on Kuwait lie primarily in the politics of the region. Given the weakened condition of Iran, both as a result of ten years of Islamic revolution and of the Iran–Iraq war, Iraq, which sought to control Gulf oil,[13] calculated that the time was propitious to act on its historic hegemonic ambitions. Iraq's move could also be explained by considerations of prestige:[14] Saddam Hussein may well have attacked Kuwait to redress the discrepancy between his perceptions of Iraq's capabilities and prestige and other states' assessments of Baghdad's power.

There was also an international, i.e. systemic, component in Saddam's calculations. As the preceding section indicated, the imperatives for crisis management derived from bipolarity; at the same time, failure to move beyond "collaborative competition" could be ascribed to "non-systemic elements such as the ideological differences between the superpowers and the effects of domestic politics and leaders' beliefs".[15] By de-ideologizing foreign policy and by facilitating cooperation between the Soviet Union and the West, Gorbachev, through "new political thinking" weakened the bipolar structure of the Cold War era: not only was the USSR engaged in conciliation with the US, but Moscow was also in the process of ending its support to radical regimes across the globe. It would seem that Saddam calculated that, given the lessening of Soviet support, the attack on Kuwait would not evoke US countermeasures. Further, had the old "rules of the game" prevailed, Moscow would have, at the least, attempted to rein in its client so to forestall any US reaction.[16]

But it is not enough to analyze Iraqi motivations and the regional systemic features that go a long way toward explaining why Iraq hoped to consolidate its gains in Kuwait. Nor is it enough to note that the move into Kuwait was obviously considered illegitimate by both regional and international actors. We need to analyze both Soviet/Russian and US responses to the ensuing crisis in order to understand the emerging dynamics of the post-Cold-War era. Moscow's policies in this period can be characterized as those of a collapsing superpower; Washington's in contrast may be seen as "cooperative hegemony".

On the day of the Iraqi invasion, an official Soviet spokesman called for the "urgent and unconditional withdrawal of Iraqi troops from Kuwaiti territory";[17] the next day, the USSR also announced that it had suspended arms shipments to Baghdad. At the September 9 Helsinki summit between Gorbachev and President George Bush, the two leaders indicated that if the Security Council resolutions passed to that point were not sufficient, then further action would be necessary. The question of Soviet participation in the military coalition being assembled by President Bush haunted Moscow's policy throughout the crisis. In a major address at the UN in late September 1990, Soviet Foreign Minister Eduard Shevardnadze soundly condemned Iraq for violating international law and claimed that the UN could "suppress acts of aggression". He called for the revitalization of the Security Council's Military Staff Committee to deal with the unfolding crisis and, most importantly, he offered to contribute Soviet troops to the Security Council.[18]

It should be noted that Moscow, if it was to uphold "new thinking", had no choice but to condemn the Iraqi invasion of Kuwait and to support US initiatives at the United Nations. Simultaneously, Kremlin decision-makers were constrained because of the large number of Soviet civilian and military personnel living in Iraq and because of pressure from conservatives not to abandon the long-term relationship with Iraq. Gorbachev, forced to mediate among several competing groups and views and unable to choose among them, pursued at least two policies simultaneously. While Soviet officials worked with the US and the Security Council, special envoy Yevgeni Primakov was dispatched to Baghdad on three separate occasions to see if face-saving measures for Saddam Hussein could be devised and war could be averted. Primakov traveled to Baghdad on October 4–5, and again on October 28–30.[19] Unable to convince Saddam to withdraw, the USSR – albeit reluctantly – voted for Security Council resolution 678, authorizing the use of "all necessary means" to liberate Kuwait. Once the Gulf War began on January 16/17, criticisms from Soviet conservatives and the military reached a crescendo. This set the stage for Primakov's third mediatory trip to Baghdad. After a month of intensive coalition bombing, Primakov returned to Baghdad to devise a final plan to avoid the total destruction of Iraq. Even though Soviet efforts resulted in a vaguely worded agreement that included an Iraqi withdrawal within 21 days in return for the annulment of the other Security Council resolutions,[20] the plan was ultimately rejected by President Bush and the ground war began on February 24. It is important to note why this last-ditch mediation effort was launched. It was in many respects a declaration of independence, the pursuit of a slightly differentiated foreign policy line. Primakov's mission and the Soviet mediation effort were clearly designed to enhance Soviet prestige and perhaps to guarantee the Soviet Union a future role in the region. If Moscow's efforts had led to a negotiated cease-fire and Iraqi withdrawal, then the USSR would have won accolades and world-wide gratitude; the Kremlin would also have shown that it was a responsible and trustworthy member of the international community. Further, if those negotiations had led to regional security arrangements in which the Soviet Union played a role, then Moscow's stake in the region would have been secured.

The USA's role during the crisis contrasted sharply with Moscow's. After some initial hesitation, Washington apparently became convinced – with some prompting from British Prime Minister Margaret Thatcher – that a forceful response to the Iraqi attack was necessary: On August 8, President Bush announced that 200,000 troops would be dispatched to the Gulf. That the US was determined to take the leadership role was clear; nonetheless, this turned out to be hegemony by a combination of "invitation",[21] "cooperation", and arm twisting.

At first, the Arab states were reluctant to work with the US. When the Arab League met within days of the attack to condemn Iraqi aggression, it cautioned against foreign intervention; the Gulf Cooperation Council (GCC) modified this statement somewhat by claiming that the warning against foreign troops did not apply to any UN-authorized activities. Although the Arab states were wary of cooperating too closely with the West, Saudi Arabia ultimately "requested" US protection. (Yet, into September, there were disagreements as to which country would make offensive military decisions and where B-52s could be based.) Subsequently, the United Arab Emirates (UAE) formally announced that it would permit Arab and *other* friendly forces on its territory. Clearly, the US military effort designed first to deter an Iraqi attack on Saudi Arabia and then to expel Iraqi troops from Kuwait would have been severely handicapped if the deployment of US troops had not been permitted by the Gulf states.

Beyond the formal invitation to protect Saudi Arabia, the cooperative and coercive aspects of US hegemony become clear. Once the decision had been made to send the first military contingents to Saudi Arabia, several other states volunteered to contribute forces. The size and composition of the multinational force grew incrementally; in all, thirty-two countries contributed to the war effort. Neither Germany nor Japan contributed directly to the military effort because of constitutional prohibitions. Equally important was the financial commitment of several Middle Eastern states, as well as of Germany and Japan. As early as the end of August 1990, it was estimated that Operation Desert Shield was costing approximately $46 million a day; in addition, the US acknowleged that it wanted contributions to offset the costs.[22] Within a month, the Gulf states had promised some $12 billion to Operation Desert Shield. In this same period, Treasury Secretary Brady traveled to England, France, Japan, and South Korea in search of financial contributions to the operations.

A combination of cooperation and arm twisting may also be seen in the orchestrated diplomatic effort to secure the necessary votes and support for the UN Security Council resolution that authorized the use of force against Iraq. The momentum toward war increased when President Bush announced on November 8 that the US would double the size of the force in the Gulf and on November 22, when President Bush made a highly publicized trip to spend Thanksgiving with the forces stationed in Saudi Arabia. Against this backdrop, James Baker traveled widely to garner the requisite backing, meeting for example in Geneva with the foreign ministers of Security Council members Ethiopia, Zaïre, and Ivory Coast, and in Paris with the Finnish and Romanian foreign ministers. Baker next met in Cairo with Egyptian President Hosni Mubarak who agreed to support the UN resolution and with the Chinese foreign minister, who acknowledged that China would not block it; President Bush met in Geneva with President Assad. On November 29, UNSC 678 passed by a vote of 12-2.

It is exceptionally difficult to ascertain the balance among invitation, cooperation, and arm twisting that went into mustering the forces and money for the Gulf War. Cooper, Higgott, and Nossal have suggested that a focus on the perceptions of the followers, rather than on US leadership, will provide a more nuanced picture of the exact nature of the American role during the Gulf crisis and war.[23] They argue that, with the exception of Great Britain, none of the coalition partners was wholehearted in its participation. France, for example, although it voted with the US in the Security Council, made a last ditch effort to avoid the war with a proposal that Iraq ultimately rejected. And Turkey, while it refused to contribute troops, did permit US forces to fly from NATO bases on its territory. Clearly, the costs of not participating would have been greater: Yemen, for example, lost US assistance in retaliation for its "no" vote in the Security Council. Thus, US leadership was achieved by subtle coercion and by economic and political payments. Nonetheless, it would seem that in spite of differences over the extent of outside commitments and the timing of the war, no state questioned the legitimacy of US hegemony.

This becomes evident, for example, in the way the Bush Administration treated the Soviet Union at several junctures during the fall. On the one hand, the Administration was sensitive to the opposition facing Gorbachev and Shevardnadze at home: Baker, therefore, acquiesced to Shevardnadze's wish to substitute "all necessary means" for "military force" in the wording of the final Security Council resolution. On the other hand, although Bush did not want to precipitate a major disagreement with Moscow, it was clear that he was not going to be deterred from confronting Saddam Hussein. Shevardnadze was not consulted when the decision to dispatch troops to the Gulf was taken.[24] Moreover, during the fall, when Primakov went to Washington to report on his meetings with Saddam, Bush reportedly told the special envoy that he (Bush) was not going to bargain with Saddam.[25] Finally, recognizing Gorbachev's dilemma, especially after Shevardnadze's resignation and the crackdowns in Lithuania and Latvia, the Bush Administration informed Gorbachev about the attack on Iraqi forces within an hour of its start.

In terms of costs to the US, weapons were promised to the Gulf states and Israel and, significantly, the US forgave Egypt's debt of $7.1 billion. Israel requested $1 billion in additional military aid and compensation for a proposed multi-billion dollar arms sale to Saudi Arabia. In many respects, the most serious cost may have been incurred in dealings with Syria. On September 13, Secretary of State Baker met with Syrian President Assad; and later in September, Syria, after 14 years of civil war, consolidated its military and political hold over Lebanon. It would seem fair to conclude that had Syria not backed the coalition effort, that if it had even just sat out the war, the US would not have so apparently condoned the bloody consolidation of Syrian power in Lebanon.

Ironically, although the US had rejected Saddam's linkage of the Gulf crisis with the Arab-Israeli dispute, the war and its aftermath indeed can be linked to the opening of the Middle East peace process. The Gulf War decisively demonstrated that a major Middle East conflict need not have Israel as its focal point: An Arab grouping had coalesced to challenge the Iraqi attack and Israel had, in effect, been a silent partner in that coalition. It should also be noted that the Arab component of the coalition joined states that had previously been opposed to each other. Conservative Gulf sheikhdoms joined with radical Arabs and both welcomed Egypt's reintegration into Middle East councils – despite the Egyptian–Israeli Peace Treaty. These realignments contributed to the possibility of an ongoing peace process.

The war also demonstrated that the West need not be seen as the perennial enemy and that a short-term Western presence need not be the catalyst for local instability. Western forces had come into the region – with the acquiescence of some of the Arab states – to reassert older established rules of the game and to protect their own economic interests. And although Saddam Hussein (and the PLO) tried to use the historic anti-Westernism of Islamic society, he failed because Iraq's attack on Kuwait threatened the other regional actors. As for the Soviet Union, the Gulf War demonstrated that Moscow would no longer support radical Arab causes unquestioningly and would cooperate with the US to restore the *status quo*. If, as has been argued above, bipolarity enhanced the prospects for crisis management, but ideological division prevented crisis avoidance or resolution, then the significant changes introduced by Gorbachev and the cooperation demonstrated during the Gulf War were auspicious for crisis resolution.

These alterations paved the way for the US, and ostensibly the USSR, to call for a regional peace conference to address the Arab-Israeli-Palestinian conflict. During two trips to the Middle East following the Gulf War, Baker secured tentative Israeli, Egyptian, and Syrian agreement to attend a jointly sponsored regional peace conference. The US established itself as a "facilitator" among the several participants to settle the kinds of procedural issues that could disrupt the process. As with Gulf War coalition-building, James Baker and other US envoys had to exercise leadership by a combination of invitation and subtle coercion. With hindsight, it is apparent that Moscow was at best a secondary player; nonetheless, the Kremlin, until the collapse of the Soviet Union, was looking to enhance its superpower status by acting as the "co-facilitator" of the process. The USSR's long-standing ties to several of the potential participants helped to push them to the negotiating table. In late

July at a summit in Moscow, Bush and Gorbachev announced that invitations to the conference would be sent out in October. The Madrid meetings began on October 30 1991.

Thus the ongoing Middle East peace process was an outgrowth of the defeat of Iraq, the changed Middle East balances that resulted from the war, and of the continuing weakness of the Soviet Union in the aftermath of the coup attempt. The crisis precipitated by the failed hardline coup in Moscow in August 1991 is beyond the scope of this essay; nonetheless, several preliminary points that relate to Soviet policy in the Middle East need to be made. It would seem fair to speculate that the military dissatisfaction with the conduct of Soviet foreign policy which was manifested during the fall of 1990 grew and may have been one of the factors contributing to the coup attempt. Furthermore, it has been reported that three of the coup plotters resented and feared that the USSR was becoming too dependent on the United States.[26] Questions about who was in charge in Moscow enhanced the US role as broker and probably also convinced the Syrians and the PLO to participate in the meetings. Moreover, the USSR re-established diplomatic relations with Israel as a *quid pro quo* for participation in the scheduled peace conference.[27]

Thus, by the end of 1991, many of the "classic" features of Middle East politics had disappeared.

The US, Russia, and Future Patterns in the Middle East

If there were any doubts that the Cold War was ending, they were dispelled by the dissolution of the Soviet Union and the emergence of 15 new states on the international scene. Although it is still far too early to ascertain the new configuration of world power, the impact of the Soviet collapse is unmistakable. The unraveling of the USSR has expanded the borders of the Middle East, as the Muslim republics of the former Soviet Union become incorporated into the Middle East state system. Within that newly defined system, threats to regional security abound, including ethnic conflicts and border disputes that are more volatile because of arms proliferation. Yet, with the disappearance of the USSR, these local conflicts will no longer be viewed as proxy wars for the superpowers. At the systemic level, Russia is seeking to re-establish itself in the "new world order" and to define the specifics of its foreign policy. Simultaneously, the United States has emerged as the single superpower with all the costs and responsibilities that that position entails.

The map of the Middle East has changed with the addition of the formerly Soviet Central Asian states. It seems to be assumed that, as Muslim states, Kazakhstan, Kirghizsan, Tajikistan, Turkmenistan, and Uzbekistan will become Middle East actors, or at the least, a bridge to the Middle East. Many Middle Eastern states, including Turkey, Iran, Oman, Saudi Arabia, Egypt, and Israel have been actively proffering various kinds of assistance in the hopes of influencing the future role these Soviet successor states will play in the Middle East. Although all these offers of aid are welcomed by the Central Asians, the involvement of Iran and Turkey particularly reflects a growing rivalry between them for a major role in the post-Gulf-War Middle East.

Teheran's activism in Central Asia may also be a manifestation of Iran's continuing competition with Iraq. With the defeat of Baghdad in the 1991 Gulf War, Iran has sought a new regional role. It has undertaken a massive arms build-up (see below) and hopes to establish itself as the center for economic expansion and cooperation. Additionally, Iran has openly discussed its religious agenda, namely the "right of the Muslim people of these republics to a political, economic and social system based on Islamic teachings...".[28] Turkey, too, is under pressure to carve out a new international role as NATO searches for a new raison d'être and as Ankara's relations with the European Community (EC) remain unclear. Given the EC's current limitations on Turkish goods, Ankara certainly views Central Asia as potentially a vast market for Turkish products. Further, although influence in Central Asia cannot substitute for membership in the EC, Turkey's presence there adds to Anakara's international stature. Turkey is also seen as a counter to Iranian Islamist influence in that it is a secular, but Muslim state, with ties to the West. Thus the competition between Turkey and Iran goes well beyond Kazakhstan, Kirghizstan, Tajikistan, Turkmenistan, and Uzbekistan: It includes the formation of rival blocs, each of which includes some of the Soviet successor states.

With the end of both the Cold War and the Gulf War, several forces are affecting regional politics, especially in the Gulf area. Even a partial list reveals multiple indigenous security threats. First, there are ethnic conflicts and irridentist movements that threaten not only the stability of individual states, but also relations between them. These would include: the Kurds in Turkey and Iraq; the Shi'a in southern Iraq; and the Azeris in northern Iran. If we accept the inclusion of the new Central Asian states in the Middle East, then

we must add the problems of the ethnic Russians in all these republics, and the Uzbeks in Tajikistan and the Tajiks in Uzbekistan,
among others. (This last potential conflict could ultimately draw in
Teheran because the Tajiks are ethnic Persians with links to Iran.)

Moreover, as long as the current leaders stay in power, historic
interstate rivalries will remain potentially explosive. The hegemonic
rivalry between Iran and Iraq would top this list. Both have sought
to bolster their arsenals, and Iran has staged raids across the Iraqi
border to attack the camps of Shi'a dissidents. Additionally, there is
the Syrian–Iraqi rivalry, and of course the Palestinian problem.
Border disputes, especially in the Gulf region, also represent a
potentially disruptive force and in some cases serve to reinforce the
historic rivalries. For example, even though the United Nations has
recently demarcated the border between Iraq and Kuwait, there are
no guarantees that Iraq will accept the loss of Umm Qasr and other
areas to Kuwait. Iran has long disputed the ownership of several
small islands in the Gulf and on September 10 1992 seized control
of three islands that it had administered jointly with the UAE. More
recently, Iran constructed eight missile launching pads on Abu
Musa.

Many of these problems are reinforced by regional arms races
and the proliferation of both conventional and "non-conventional"
weapons. During the Cold War, the Soviet–American competition
helped to fuel the Arab-Israeli arms race; but, the superpowers
worked to impose balanced limits between the combatants. By the
1980s, other suppliers – such as Brazil, West Germany, France, and
China – increased their shares of the arms market, making control
far more difficult. In the absence of the Soviet-American competition, it may well be that only the richer states will be able to purchase weapons or components and from a variety of suppliers.
Baghdad, despite the devastation of the Gulf War still possesses
350 planes and Iran has purchased MiG 29s and at least 20 new Su
24s, which will be added to the planes "acquired" from Iraq during
the Gulf War. Overall, it is estimated that Iran has spent over $2
billion on weapons acquisitions. Moreover, with the purchase of
two Kilo class submarines from Russia, Iran now possesses the only
submarines in the region. Syria too, even though it has been
involved in the peace process, has recently acquired MiG 29s,
T–72M1 tanks, radar jammers, and Korean Scud C missiles;[29] and
Libya is working on expanding its chemical weapons capabilities.

Although the above is certainly not a complete listing of the
Middle East arsenals, it does point to the proliferation of surface-to-

surface missiles. The Korean Scud D, for example, has a stated range of over 600 miles and can be modified to become nuclear-capable. To counter this and others, the US has sold Patriot missiles to Israel, Saudi Arabia, Kuwait, and possibly the UAE. Additionally, the US has sold F-15s to Saudi Arabia in the hopes of establishing a balance in the region. However, because of the costs of the Gulf War and the weakness in the international oil market, the oil-rich Gulf states find themselves forced to downsize their procurement plans. Simultaneously, several states have created indigenous arms industries, capable of manufacturing and also modifying missile and other technologies. Moreover, Israel has a known nuclear capabality, while Iran – not to mention Iraq – is seeking technology for the same purpose from North Korea and others.[30] All of these factors contribute to slippage in any attempt at an arms control regime for the Middle East.

In this context, it must be noted that many of the purchases mentioned above are from Russia. Within the past year, Russia has begun exporting its top-of-the-line military equipment, including Backfire bombers and antiship missiles, just to name a few. It has participated in airshows and in arms fairs to create markets for its equipment. Given the difficulties of converting military enterprises to civilian industry and fears of dramatic economic upheavals if many of these enterprises are permitted to close, Russia maintains that arms sales are an economic necessity. We have thus seen the submarine sale to Iran mentioned above, the aircraft sales to both Iran and Syria, and sales of combat vehicles to the UAE and perhaps Oman.[31] Weapons may also be coming from the other Soviet successor states. Kazakhstan, for example, has privatized some military enterprises and permitted them to negotiate international sales on their own. This is to say nothing of "private" deals or smuggling. Of concern in this regard are reports of uranium being smuggled out of several republics and destined, according to many sources, for the Middle East.

All of these regional forces are at play in a new international environment. At present, Russia's role is limited. In Russia, contradictory forces are operating to form what there is of Russian foreign policy. First, Russia and the other new states are so preoccupied with their domestic problems that they evidence little interest in the outside world. This was painfully clear when in January 1992, Russian President Boris Yeltsin did not bother to attend the opening round of the multilateral peace talks that were held in Moscow: According to official Russian statements, he was instead trying to resolve the dispute with Ukraine over the Black Sea Fleet. This simultaneously highlights a second force: What interest there is in foreign policy, at the moment, surrounds relations with the so-called "near-abroad." Each of the successor states is preoccupied with relations with the states of the former USSR, because dismantling the legacies of the Soviet Union is their primary economic and political task.

Third, resentment by many politicians and average citizens to the loss of superpower status may propel Russia into greater involvement with the outside world – especially in the Middle East, an area of historic Russian and Soviet interest. The question is what form that involvement would take. At one extreme of the political spectrum, there are those in the military and among the communists who pine for the old connections with long-time allies such as Iraq. Some even argue that Russia's economic woes could be solved by resuming arms shipments – for hard currency – to Baghdad. At the other extreme are those who advocate isolationism. In the middle range, many recognize that Russia cannot just withdraw from the outside world. In a document called the "Foreign Policy Concept of the Russian Federation", Russia's role in the Middle East is described as follows:

> Russia's attitude toward the region is detemined primarily by its geostrategic and geopolitical significance. ...
> The stabilization of the situation in the Middle East is among Russia's first-priority interests. Based on this, we should continue *active participation* in the settlement of the Arab-Israeli conflict. ...
> Russia must continue to occupy a decisive and principled position in regard to any cases of destabilization. ... Russia may help them [UNSC] to find fair and legal solutions to complex contradictions. ... [including] a security system in the zone of the Persian Gulf. ...[32]

The document goes on to outline the need to base this security system on the states in the region, that is to reduce any foreign presence; moreover, it is implicit that this system should include Iraq. Finally, the section on Middle Eastern policy includes support for the further development of relations with Israel. If we view this as a vision for the future, then Russia – even under a moderate/reformist regime – will eventually seek to regain a position as a major actor in the region.

Currently, precisely because the Soviet Union has collapsed, the US finds itself the major outside superpower capable of affecting the fortunes of the Middle East. At least for the foreseeable future, the region will remain an area of concern for the US. Even in the absence of the Soviet threat, Washington will not soon renounce its desire to protect the free flow of Gulf oil, nor will it allow historic ties with several states in the region to lapse. By the same token, the end of the Cold War has rendered the challenges facing the US far more difficult. In the Arab-Israeli conflict, the end of the ideological and geopolitical competition between the former Soviet Union and the US has certainly enhanced the prospects for, but not assured, a political settlement. In contrast, the end of the Cold War has not enhanced the stability of the Gulf region. There, Iran and Iraq both seem intent on challenging the current order; moreover, as noted above, there remain myriad ethnic and boundary disputes that are fueled by continuing arms races.

The US must, therefore, redefine and refine several aspects of its policy. In the context of the Arab–Israeli–Palestinian dispute, the dissolution of the USSR reduces the strategic importance of Israel to the US. The US has also learned that it must be more "evenhanded" so as to establish its credentials as an honest broker. Therefore, issues that could be overlooked in the past in the name of security will potentially be far more divisive in the future. For the Arabs, the process that began with Gorbachev's reassessment of Soviet support for radical Arab causes culminated in the complete loss of their outside patron. As a result, Syria and the PLO recognized the need to join the US-co-sponsored Middle East peace talks. These changes – as well as challenges to Yasir Arafat's PLO – in the Arab-Israeli arena produced the recent Israeli-PLO accord on mutual recognition and self-rule for the Gaza Strip and Jericho that was brokered by Norway. Yet, although the agreement had been facilitated by Norway, it was signed at the White House in a ceremony presided over by President Bill Clinton. Additionally, Washington has so far played a key role in raising funds to support infrastructure development in Gaza.

The US role in the Gulf, as the sole pre-eminent power, is at once more singular and more complex. In the words of Bernard Lewis: "[the] main aim of US policy is to prevent the emergence of a regional hegemony – of a single regional power that could dominate the area and thus establish monopolistic control of Middle Eastern oil."[33] Thus the US must decide on a blend of policies that will ensure the flow of Gulf oil and will maintain the relative stability of the area. So far, that policy has consisted of bilateral arrangements and elements of both the invitational and cooperative hegemony that were visible during the war. Within months of the war's end, GCC officials agreed to permit the storage of US military equipment in the region. Furthermore, in addition to the sale of the F-15s to Saudi Arabia, Washington has signed a 10 year security pact with Kuwait that includes US access to ports and, storage facilities, future Kuwaiti purchases of US equipment, and most significantly, joint training and military exercises. And, the cooperative aspects of the USA's role are visible in the enforcement of the United Nations resolutions with regard to Iraq.

Yet, the experience of cooperative hegemony would seem to indicate that while welcoming its pre-eminent role, the US has learned that there are limits to its leadership. These limitations are interrelated with the question of the legitimacy of that role and of the "rules" of the post-Cold-War era – as far as they have been defined. If we define legitimacy as the "acceptance of the framework of the international order by all major powers..."[34] then it is clear that cooperative hegemony promotes the legitimacy of US leadership. Washington seems to understand that it cannot intervene unilaterally and will most probably not seek a role that could be construed as "imperial".[35] At the time of writing, and despite the role played by Norway in the recent PLO–Israel accord, no state has seriously challenged the US role in promoting Middle East peace and, despite differences of opinion regarding goals and timing during Desert Storm, major US allies supported the coalition efforts. In the short run, therefore, the prospects for coordinated efforts – under US leadership – to ensure regional stability seem assured.

In the longer run, however, several forces may be at work to undermine US pre-eminence and perhaps the legitimacy of the current transitional order. Some observers would argue that the logic of international relations dictates that other powers will rise to challenge the US role.[36] It has also been suggested that the Arabs could well look to the EC in an effort to balance Washington's influence. Still others would urge the US not to fight to retain pre-eminence.[37] Given the economic stringencies at home, Washington must decide where and how to invest its money, military power, prestige. Finally, it should also be noted that the Middle East, as the Foreign Ministry document cited above suggests, will remain an area of interest for Russia. The end of the Cold War should not be taken to mean that Russian and US interests will always be parallel there.

These uncertainties raise serious questions about the longer-term future of the USA's cooperative hegemonic role in the Middle East: How far will the US be willing to go, for example, in protecting the Kurds and Shi'a of Iraq when Turkey and Saudi Arabia, each for its own reasons, do not want the dismemberment of Iraq? Should Arab-Israeli talks falter, would the US turn a blind eye to a future Arab-Israeli war as long as oil were flowing from the Gulf? Will the US seek to protect pro-Western governments? What can it do to protect them? For the moment, these questions remain unanswered.

To return to the questions posed at the outset, the impact of the end of the Cold War on Middle East politics remains unclear. On the one hand, local conflicts will no longer be viewed through the lens of superpower rivalry, and the probability of cooperation among outside forces has been enhanced. Moreover, the lessening of Arab-Israeli tensions that results from the PLO-Israel accord may, in the short run at least, make any US role in the region more acceptable – particularly to the Arab Gulf states. On the other hand, as noted above, with the collapse of the Soviet Union and the uncertain longevity of US cooperative hegemony, indigenous forces will play an increasingly predominant – and potentially destabilizing – role in the region.

Notes

1. See Carol R. Saivetz, "'New Thinking' and Soviet Third World Policy", *Current History*, October 1989.
2. Because of the dispute between Iran and the Gulf Arabs over the name of the (Persian) Gulf, this paper will use the term Gulf, rather than either Persian or Arabian Gulf.
3. Galia Golan, *Soviet Policies in the Middle East, from World War II to Gorbachev* (Cambridge: Cambridge University Press 1990), p. 63.
4. Breslauer, "Soviet Policy in the Middle East, 1967–1972," in Alexander George, *Managing U.S.–Soviet Rivalry, Problems of Crisis Prevention* (Boulder: Westview Press 1983) p. 75.
5. Ibid., p. 87.
6. George Breslauer argues that the Soviet Union wanted to bolster Egypt, while attempting to push negotiations forward (ibid., p. 75). His argument is seconded to some extent by Galia Golan.
7. The war itself occurred within sixteen months of the signing of the SALT I agreement and the Basic Principles Agreement (BPA). The latter was intended to codify superpower behavior and to institutionalize crisis management and prevention mechanisms. Article I of the BPA called for peaceful coexistence and article II required the superpowers to renounce efforts to obtain unilateral advantages from unfolding Third World con-

flicts. See the discussion in William Quandt, *Decade of Decision* (Berkeley: University of California Press 1977), the chapter on the 1973 war.

8. See discussion in Quandt, idem.

9. Golan, op. cit., p. 92 (see note 3).

10. "US-Soviet Efforts to Cooperate in Crisis Management and Crisis Avoidance," in Alexander L. George, Philip J. Farley, Alexander Dallin, *US-Soviet Security Cooperation Achievements, Failures and Lessons* (New York: Oxford University Press 1988), p. 584.

11. In a less optimistic interpretation, Janice Gross Stein questions when the norms for cooperation were triggered. She argues: "Only when the patron of the loser deliberately and self-consciously manipulated the risk of confrontation through threat of intervention, did the other patron exert sufficient pressure to force an end to the fighting." Janice Gross Stein, "Proxy Wars – How Superpowers End Them: the Diplomacy of War Termination in the Middle East," *International Journal* 35, No. 3 (Summer 1980) pp. 478–519. This quotation is from p. 496.

12. The transcript of the Foreign Ministry conference is contained in *International Affairs*, October 1988.

13. Laurie Mylroie, "Why Saddam Hussein Invaded Kuwait," *Orbis*, Winter 1993, p. 125.

14. Robert Gilpin, *War and Change in International Politics* (New York: Cambridge University Press 1981), p. 33.

15. Benjamin Miller, "A Theoretical Analysis of U.S.–Soviet Conflict Management in the Middle East," in Steven Spiegel, *Superpower Conflict Management in the Middle East* (Boulder: Westview Press 1992), pp. 71–72.

16. Robert Jervis, "The Future of World Politics, Will it Resemble the Past?" *International Security*, Vol. 16, No. 3 (Winter 1991/1992), p. 60.

17. TASS, 2 August, 1990, in FBIS SOV 90 150, 3 August 1990, p. 3.

18. Shevardnadze's speech at the UN, TASS, 25 September 1990, FBIS SOV 90 187, 26 September 1990, p. 4.

19. A good example is "The War Which Might Not Have Been," *Pravda*, 27 February 1991, pp. 1,7.

20. See TASS, 22 February 1991, FBIS SOV 91 037, 25 February 1991, p. 10.

21. The term is borrowed from Geir Lundestad, "Empire by Invitation? The US and Western Europe, 1945–1952," *Journal of Peace Research*, Vol. XXIII (1986).

22. To that end, Baker, in a return trip to the Gulf, secured Saudi promises for $500 million per month to support the US military effort and an additional $44 billion per year to aid economies hurt by upholding the Iraqi embargo. Additionally, the Kuwaiti Government-in-Exile offered $5 billion for the multinational effort ($2.5 billion earmarked for the US and an additional $2.5 billion to defray the costs of the boycott).

23. See Andrew Fenton Cooper, Richard A. Higgott, and Kim Richard Nossal, "Bound to Follow? Leadership and Followership in the Gulf Conflict", *Political Science Quarterly*, Vol. 106, No. 3 (Fall 1991), pp. 391–410.

24. Michael R. Beschloss and Strobe Talbott, *At the Highest Levels* (Boston: Little, Brown and Company 1993), p. 250.

25. Ibid., p. 277. In doing this, Bush apparently had the support of Shevard-

nadze. According to Talbott and Beschloss, Sergei Tarasenko, one of Shevardnadze's aides, cabled the State Department to say that Shevardnadze did not approve of Primakov's proposals. The inference drawn by Dennis Ross and Robert Zollick was that Washington should quash the proposals.

26. Stephen Kinzer, "Three in Coup Feared U.S. Dependency", *New York Times*, October 7, 1991, p. A7.

27. Historically, the USSR had claimed that it would re-establish diplomatic relations with Israel only *after* it would be included in a peace conference. Israel, for its part, stated repeatedly that it would agree to Soviet participation in an international conference only *after* diplomatic relations were restored.

28. Voice of the Islamic Republic, 25 August 1992, FBIS NES 92 166, 26 August 1992, pp. 52–53.

29. Scotty Fisher, "New Threats, New World Order Alter Israel's View of Mideast Security Realities", *Armed Forces Journal International*, February 1993, p. 30.

30. See Clyde Haberman, "Israel Seeks to Keep North Korea From Aiding Iran", *New York Times*, 20 June 1993, p. 6.

31. "Russia Strives to Make its Mark", *Jane's Defence Weekly*, 13 February 1993.

32. FBIS USR 93 037, 25 March 1993.

33. Bernard Lewis, "Rethinking the Middle East", *Foreign Affairs*, Vol. 71, No. 4 (Fall 1992), p. 111.

34. Henry Kissinger, *A World Restored*, as cited in Gilpin, *War and Change in World Politics,* p. 12.

35. Bernard Lewis argues that America is disinclined to play the imperial role because it is incompatible with democracy and with US public opinion. See his arguments in "Rethinking the Middle East", op. cit., (see note 33).

36. Christopher Layne, "The Unipolar Illusion, Why Great New Powers Will Arise", *International Security*, Vol. 17, No. 4 (Spring 1993).

37. See, for example, the arguments in Robert Jervis, "International Primacy, Is the Game Worth the Candle?" *International Security*, Vol. 17, No. 4 (Spring, 1993).

Part IV

Are Democratic States Always Peaceful Towards One Another?

14

The Voice of the People:
Political Theorists on the International
Implications of Democracy[1]

Michael W. Doyle

There appears to be a growing impression that step by step with the increase in domestic civil rights and popular self-government, the prospects for international peace improve. The spread of popular government and the growth of civil society in Eastern Europe and (with fits and starts) the former Soviet Union seem to many thus not only to herald but also to cause the radical reduction of international tensions in Europe and the wider world.

In the popular press, the notion seemed so widespread that *The Economist* (ever a dasher of cold water on popular optimisms) felt that the spirit of the day called for a rebuttal.[2] Prominent political leaders have clearly contributed to this perception. For example, in a speech before the British parliament in June of 1982, President Reagan proclaimed that governments founded on a respect for individual liberty exercise "restraint" and "peaceful intentions" in their foreign policy. (He then announced a "crusade for freedom" and a "campaign for democratic development".)[3] President Bush, similarly, on 1 October 1990, in an address before the United Nations General Assembly, declared: "Calls for democracy and human rights are being reborn everywhere. And these calls are an expression of support for the values enshrined in the Charter. They encourage our hopes for a more stable, more peaceful, more prosperous world."[4] In his 1991 UN Address ("Pax Universalis", 23 September 1991) he stated equally unequivocally: "As democracy flourishes, so does the opportunity for a third historical breakthrough: international cooperation."[5]

The Cold War is over. President Yeltsin has explicitly declared that he (also the Russians?) no longer regards the United States as an enemy and no longer targets missiles in our direction.[6] President Bush celebrated victory – by "the Grace of God" – in the 1992 State of the Union Address in the name of the "G.I. Joes and Janes" and even more nameless US taxpayers to whom he wished to credit the demise of communism, which "died this year".[7] President

Clinton embraced the Russian leader at the recent Vancouver Summit in the Spring of 1993 and, together with the other members of the G–7, reaffirmed a commitment to the financial backing of Russian democracy while, more generally, defining the United States's strategy as one of enlarging the community of democratic nations.

These pronouncements of our time also find roots in classical democratic theory. The American revolutionary, Thomas Paine, in 1791 proclaimed: "Monarchical sovereignty, the enemy of mankind, and the source of misery, is abolished; and sovereignty is restored to its natural and original place, the nation. ... Were this the case throughout Europe, the cause of war would be taken away."[8] Democratic pacifism, according to Paine and other and later democrats, rests on the view that the aggressive instincts of authoritarian leaders and totalitarian ruling parties make for war. Democratic states, founded on such individual rights as equality before the law, free speech and other civil liberties, private property, and elected representation are fundamentally against war. When the citizens who bear the burdens of war elect their governments, wars become impossible. Furthermore, citizens appreciate that the benefits of trade can be enjoyed only under conditions of peace. Thus the very existence of free-market democracies, such as the USA, Japan, and our European allies and now possibly Hungary, Czech republic, Poland, and, perhaps, a democratic Russia makes for peace. Some contemporary scholarship provides evidence to support these claims in which free and democratic, "libertarian" states are seen to be inherently peaceful.[9]

Nonetheless, there are good reasons for us to be skeptical of this association between peace, tolerance, restraint, on the one hand, and democracy, on the other. Both in classical theory and in historical practice four major associations have been claimed for popular government, and only one of them promises the modern assured association of peace and democracy that the politicians and much of the public seem to expect.

The first claim, ranked by longevity, is that of democratic *imperialism*, that democracies are an effective, perhaps even the best means to launch imperial aggression. This is the view of Thucydides, which influenced classical political thought up to and including Machiavelli.

The second is that democracy should be associated with effective defence in all directions, a policy of *isolationism* within a pervasive and generalized state of war. Democratic government requires of its international relations independence, above all else. This is Rousseau's vision.

The third asserts that democracies are shaped by *internationalism* – peaceful, but as Paine too may be implying, not necessarily in the relations with non-democracies.[10] This is also Immanuel Kant's vision.

And only the fourth, the most modern, makes the optimistic claim – *pacifism* – that is now so popular.

I would like to explore the arguments underlying these radically different visions of the effects of popular government and try to sort out the reasons for their differences. I do so partly in the hope that in understanding these different visions of popular government and its effects, we will have the analytic tools that will help us better anticipate what sort of world we seem to be moving towards.

Democratic Imperialism

Thucydides's view of the effects of democracy on relations between states (*poleis*) serves as a valuable counterpoint to the modern impression. Rather than peace, rather than restraint, power and imperial growth, excess and factionalism were the traits that he saw associated with democracy. This association leaves us with two puzzles. The larger one is of course why do we see democracy as peace-loving when he saw it as empire-making, and this I postpone to the conclusion. The smaller puzzle, Thucydides's own dilemma, is how an institution so useful in making an empire could be so prone to destroying it.

Democracy meant that power was in the hands not of the minority but of the "whole people". Citizens enjoyed equality before the law, a political career open to talents, and a special freedom and tolerance in private matters.[11] In actual practice, of course, Athens was a society that rested on commerce and small agriculture but that also exploited slave labor in silver mines at Laurium and in domestic service. For the 40,000–50,000 male citizens, democratic self-rule was real; the assembly and its democratically elected Council of 500 being the dominant voice in the legislative affairs of the state, just as the ten democratically elected *strategoi* were in military and executive affairs.

For Thucydides, states are driven by "honor, security and self-interest" (I:76). States cannot escape from constant danger because "when tremendous dangers are involved no one can be blamed for looking to his own interest" (I:76). Since weakness always means subjection, only independent strength guarantees independent security; so states must look to their own relative power.

For Thucydides and other Athenians, the most straightforward connection between democracy and power lies in the importance of naval power. When naval power relies upon oared galleys, a navy of free rowers is inherently superior to a navy of slave rowers, since in the heat of battle the former can be called upon to defend their ship. And, as Pseudo-Xenophon noted: "...the poorer classes and the demos rightly possess more authority than the well-born and the rich because it is the demos that rows the ships and keeps the city powerful."[12]

A second democratic source of power is simply the resources released when the citizens have a stake in the survival and success of the state. Rather than spending resources in coercing the citizenry, the state can draw upon citizens' resources for what are regarded as public purposes (Thucydides I:17). A free society, furthermore, is a society in which deliberation in public can guide and, through the exercise of reason, improve public policy.

Third, and in addition to providing the institutional framework that allows Athens to draw upon the resources of the mass of its citizens, democratic institutions also provide a large part of its motive force, both material and ideal. As Pericles so eloquently explained in his "Funeral Oration" for the Athenian war-dead, a democratic polity is the necessary expression of a free society, and only in a free society are the creative energies of the populace allowed full play to develop. A free society allows an "adventurous spirit" to rule, producing a willingness to take risks, to increase production, and to trade far and wide. By the 440's, moreover, paid jury duty provided valuable sources of additional income to approximately half of the citizenry.[13] Colonial settlement on the confiscated lands of recalcitrant "allies" offered a livelihood to smaller numbers. Of the 1000 talents of annual state revenue in 431, 600 were derived from imperial taxation, fees, and tariffs.[14] Equally important (according to Pericles) is the authority public magistrates derive from the Athenian respect for law (II:37). Moreover, the freedom of Athens produces a willingness to take risks, a confidence in an ability to overcome dangers; and these contributed to the Athenian patriotism that underlay the empire (II:39–40).

And fourth, together those domestic traits make Athens an attractive center for all the Ionian peoples and offer the material basis that permits Athens to "make friends by doing good to others" (I:40). They sought access to the economy Athens controlled. The masses sought association with the Athenian demos; indeed they could be counted on as allies in many cases against their own oligarchic rulers. Athenian liberality, together with manifest productivity of its economy and cultural vitality of its society, also produces the international "popularity" that made association with the Athenian polis, even in its imperial form, attractive to the masses throughout much of the Greek world.[15] (The demos of Mytilene, for example, resisted the efforts of the oligarchic faction to liberate Mytilene from the Athenian empire; so that when the oligarchy mistakenly armed them, they surrendered the city to Athens, III:27.)

Democracy, however, is also a source of eventual weakness, over-extension, and self-destruction. Indeed, it is here, in Thucydides's history of the Peloponnesian War, in which democracy first acquired its reputation for such disastrous factionalism that, more than two thousand years later, the American authors of the *Federalist Papers* still felt it necessary to try to rebut the charge.[16] Athenian democracy fractured under stress. The great plague of 430 undermined trust (those first to help others became the most likely to be infected, II:51). Afterwards the patriotic respect for the laws and for caution, courage, and brilliance that had led the citizens to follow the wise strategy of attrition prescribed by Pericles (who embodied all three virtues) broke down into passion, suspicion, and self-interest. The citizens let themselves be led by lesser men who had one but not the rest of his virtues – they followed the merely cautious (Nicias), or merely courageous (Cleon), or merely brilliant (Alcibiades).[17] Each of these leaders and the policies of appeasement, brutality, and adventurousness they advocated became the public policy of a majority of the democratic citizenry. Nowhere better than in the debate over whether to send an expedition to conquer hitherto neutral Sicily do the effects of factionalism emerge. Thucydides sums up the debate and fateful decision in this way:

> There was a passion for the enterprise which affected everyone alike. The older men thought they would either conquer the places against which they were sailing or, in any case, with such a large force, could come to no harm; the young had a longing for the sights and experiences of distant places, and were confident that they would return safely; the general masses and the average soldier himself saw the prospect of getting pay for the time being and of adding to the empire so as to secure permanent paid employment in the future. The result of this excessive enthusiasm of the majority was that the few who actually were

opposed to the expedition were afraid of being thought unpatri-
otic if they voted against it, and therefore kept quiet (VI:24).

Athenian democracy, rather than inhibiting, thus contributed to war.
In a world that required that states look to their relative power in
order to maintain security, democracy was valued because it
enhanced state power and, in particular, helped establish imperial
power. But more than simply adding to resources and influence, it
also, as a tragic by-product, shaped and reshaped public goals and
visions. Both directly and indirectly democracy engendered sup-
plementary reasons for expansion – to maintain employment, to
enhance glory, to stir up adventures, to expand commerce, to
educate other peoples in democratic civilization. These new goals –
each chosen by a temporary majority – led to unnecessary wars
which then undermined the security of the state. That was and is the
democratic tragedy of which Thucydides warned us.

Democratic Isolationism

Everywhere he turned, Rousseau saw oppression and corruption.
Nonetheless, he thinks human beings are by nature good and that
they can find a just freedom in (and only in) a social contract governed by self-determining free citizens. But even those just societies
were surrounded by an exceptionally dangerous state of war, some
of whose danger was produced by just those optimistic features of
trust and solidarity carried on to the battlefield.[18]

Like Thucydides and Machiavelli (and indeed all realists),
Rousseau finds the international condition among states to be a
state of war. It is characterized by "social misery".[19] In the natural
condition of mankind before the institution of states, there are many
quarrels and fights, but war is a social creation of states, an act
expressing an intention to destroy or weaken an enemy state and the
"state of war" is characterized by the continuing intention of poli-
cide, temporarily lacking the act.

The state of war, moreover, is inherently unjust. Justice calls for
a union of force and law, with force controlled by law. In most
(corrupt) states men suffer the worst of both worlds because we
suffer the evils of two conditions: "so long as the prince is regarded
as absolutely uncontrolled, it is force alone which speaks to the
subject under the name of law and to the foreigner under the name
of reason of state: so taking from the latter the power and from the
former the very will, to offer resistance. ... force reigns under the

empty name of justice."[20] But even if we had a just state internally, international politics would remain the mere exercise of force without the control of law, for international law is a mere "illusion" – for want of any global sanction to make it an effective replacement for the exercise of force.

Describing the condition of all states in an anarchic international system, Rousseau appears to be a strikingly structural interpreter of world politics.[21] But Rousseau differs from structuralists in his route to these conclusions, and, in the end, he leaves a more varied set of possibilities open to the political struggle of rulers and also of citizens. He seeks to go beyond the condition of a corrupt Europe and examines ideal democracy together with two partly-imagined, partly-real partial escapes – an isolated "Corsica" and a defensively constituted "Poland". But no escape from war is reliable, not even democracy.

Rousseau develops the foundations of international politics in a grand derivation from the state of nature. Rather than the tamer of natural man, Rousseau portrays the typical state as his ultimate oppressor. In the original state of nature, stripped of all the attributes of civilization, man is a gentle animal, according to Rousseau. He is naturally equal and his social relations are completely casual and neither cooperative nor warlike. "I see him satisfying his hunger at the first oak, and slaking his thirst at the first brook; finding his bed at the foot of the tree which afforded him a repast; and with that all his wants supplied."[22] Lacking in language he has few thoughts. Reason guides his pursuit of simple wants. He experiences few fears, which include fear of pain and cold, but not of death. He readily expresses his natural compassion for the sufferings of others.

Soon, scarcity arises as the numbers of men increase. This leads to a second state of nature, which is both progressive and regressive. It is progressive because increased interdependence leads to stable relationships, the first "expansion of the human heart". Families are organized and love comes to characterize human relations within them. Language evolves and reason develops as careful calculation rewards its practitioners with increased material benefits. Here we develop what we think of as specifically human consciousness beyond that which we share with the animals.

At the same time, scarcity is the origin of property, possession, rivalry, pride, hatred, and jealousies. Individualism and familism replace natural happiness. Cooperation becomes inherently problematic. We become "stag hunters", who lacking in trust and motivated by self-interest, abandon the common prey for the individual target of the hare.[23] Pride becomes the source of contentious comparisons. Metallurgy and agriculture create extensive mastery of nature, more intensive social dependence, and fiercer competition.

The more skilful at these more productive technologies became the rich, the less skilful became the poor. Inequality breeds more inequality. Deceit and pretension come to characterize human relationships. The poor then react and try to steal from the rich; the rich to oppress and protect themselves from the poor.

Then the rich decide to form a "social contract". In order to protect their property, they trick the poor into accepting a legal equality of rights in property that in effect secures their unequal superiority in possessions and influence. Armed with the power of the state, the rich and the domestically powerful pursue their particular interests at home and abroad. They create more violence and mayhem among states in pursuit of their wealth and prestige than had ever characterized the state of nature. Conflict now occurs between organized armies and not individual quarrelers.[24]

The typical foreign relations of Europe are the foreign relations of these corrupt states, as described by the Abbé de St. Pierre (whose peace plan Rousseau examines). The balance of power can mitigate international tyranny, but it does so through the threat of war. Therefore, says St. Pierre, sovereigns need to combine their separate and fundamental interests in security and subordinate their private interests to an organized league of collective security.

In his critique of St. Pierre's *Peace Project*, Rousseau shows how peace is impossible for them. This is because (1) monarchs prefer their apparent interest (prestige and relative superiority) to their real interests in security. And, even if the monarchs were sensible, (2) their ministers of state are the very individuals who gain from the existence of wars. They are hardly likely to abolish the wars which are their greatest source of profit and influence (p. 101). And (3), even if both monarchs and ministers become committed to rational, national cooperation, how would one ensure that all states came to the same realization at once, except through force. And Rousseau concludes by asking: Should peace then be more desired or feared?[25]

Having dismissed international organization as a route to peace, Rousseau considers the route to peace through domestic political revolution – through democracy. He does so in three ways.

First, Rousseau imagines the hypothetical creation of a just Social Contract that would liberate citizens from their subjection and inequality. Sometime early in its history, before corruption had become deeply ingrained in the character and the institutions of a people, a great moral Legislator might be inspired to break their chains and set them on the path to self-government.

Each citizen would be asked to pledge all, not to a corrupt monarch or his ministers, but to each other. Sovereignty would be made secure at home, since no one could justly challenge the authority of the laws and the citizens would escape from the strife of the state of nature. Each citizen would also become both equal to all others and free. Inalienable, indivisible, infallible as an expression of the true interests of the people as a whole, and therefore all encompassing, the people assembled would decide laws applying to all on an equal basis, absolutely, and thus constitute the General Will. The General Will would thus be inherently general (meaning national, or coextensive with the polity) and rational – it was the people rightly understanding their long-term general interests.[26]

Unlike the corrupted monarchies St. Pierre tried to save, the Social Contract would pursue no whims or private interests that would lead the state into possibly frequent battles. Wars would only be fought for national purposes that expressed the long-term rational interests of the people. Wars would only be fought if necessary; but, if fought, they would be unrestrained in their degree of violence except by the natural sympathies that were part of the natural human condition. Soldiers would volunteer for any war the Social Contract required and fight until the death. And wars would only be fought among states – among the soldiers who fight for states, not against non-combatants.

But would wars be necessary in a state of war inhabited by just, rational Social Contracts directed only by the General Will? Would the compassion of the original state of nature translate into a pacific General Will or would the spirit of jealousies (the family rivalries) of the late state of nature translate into a jealously patriotic General Will?

Quite probably, the latter, Rousseau seems to say. For Rousseau notes that even if the ministers St. Pierre describes were not privately interested in war, the very independence of states precludes a stable solution to international cooperation. Disappointment breeds rivalry, and particular national advantages, even considered from the purest standpoint of rational long-run national interest, can clash. When the expected costs of war now are exceeded by the expected costs of the insecurity or material loss that would follow from not having a particular strategic pass or river under national control or from not having control of a particular natural resource, then there is nothing in the General Will that would preclude a war.[27]

Although we cannot imagine national reform achieving global peace, Rousseau suggests it might allow particular states to mitigate or even escape, at least for a while, the general state of war.

Second, Rousseau thus explores a model for an isolationist peace. Corsica is his model of the small, undeveloped society (an eighteenth-century version of the exemplary role played by Tanzania, Albania, or Burma in our times?). The Genoese blockaded the island, devastated the coasts, slaughtered the native nobility. This tragedy represents a fortunate opportunity for authentic reform. From devastation, a wise Corsican leadership can establish a society and republic of free farmers and small manufacturers, restricting trade with the outside world to the barest essentials. As a new "Sparta," it could cultivate its virtue with its small farms tilled by robust soldiers.[28] Here, while rural simplicity persists, "Everyone will make a living, and no one will grow rich."[29] Enjoying isolation and guaranteed by the unity a similarity of social circumstances brings, Corsica would present little temptation to and great resistance against any great power seeking a colonial conquest.[30] The Corsicans would gain security in their time, until the increase in population creates a need for extensive manufactures and commerce, and with them an end to virtue, simplicity, and the self-dependence that might have for a time made Corsica strong and safe in the surrounding state of war.

Third, Rousseau examines the establishment of non-provocative defence. Not all eighteenth-century states were of Corsican dimensions or potential democratic virtue. For the larger, more developed (more corrupted) states, Rousseau offers the example of Poland (an eighteenth century Egypt, Brazil or India, perhaps). Introducing rustic equality and democratic virtue (not to speak of island isolation) is out of the question in a traditional society dominated by aristocratic landowners, afflicted with the odd domestic disability of the anarchic Polish diet and its *liberum veto*, and surrounded by imperialistic great powers.

Instead, Rousseau recommends a step by step progressive reform creating as a surrogate for Corsica's island isolation, a non-provocative defence of Polish independence. By cultivating education, cultural festivals, and a political system rewarding patriotic participation in public life, the Polish nationalists can make Poland indigestible for any foreign conqueror.[31] Combining patriotism, confederalism, central sovereignty, and a militia army, Rousseau hopes that Poland's enemies will find her neither an offensive threat nor an easy prey to invasion. Beyond that, and especially during the vulnerable period when it begins to undertake the reforms it needs, Poland can rely on the balance of power, the natural support of Turkey, which is Russia's and Austria's rival to the south.

Reforms alter the state of war – mitigate its particular effects for particular states. The rational prudence of the democratic General Will removes that aspect of conflict and war caused by monarchical and ministerial caprice. Isolation contains interdependence. Non-provocative defences assuage conflicts caused by fear of pre-emptive attack and deter attacks prompted by the likely success of easy conquest.

Each democratic reform reduces the danger. None of them removes states from the state of war.

Liberal Internationalism

Liberal democratic internationalists who have wanted to claim that "free states" are different from other states relax two of the assumptions Rousseau makes. Liberals retain the assumption of the state as the essential, stable, and institutionalized unit of decision. But they relax the assumption that states are single rational egoistic calculators in favor of a view that sees states as complex representative institutions – liberal republics or constitutional democracies. At the same time, they relax the assumption that states are motivated by security defined in terms of power, material interests, and prestige in favor of the assumption that constitutional democracies are motivated as well by the value of cosmopolitan individual freedom.

In Immanuel Kant's philosophy of liberal internationalism these two innovations work together and have significant effects on world politics. In *Perpetual Peace*,[32] Kant shows how liberal republics lead to a dichotomous international politics: peaceful relations – a "pacific union" among similarly liberal states – and a "state of war" between liberals and non-liberals.

First, republican governments, he argues, tame the aggressive interests of absolutist monarchies and ingrain the habit of respect for individual rights. Wars then appear as the direct charges on the people's welfare that he and the other liberals thought them to be. Yet these domestic republican restraints do not end war. They did not for Thucydides or Rousseau. If they did, liberal states would not be warlike, which is far from the case. They do introduce republican caution, Kant's "hesitation," in place of monarchical caprice. Liberal wars are only fought for popular, liberal purposes. The historical liberal legacy is laden with popular wars fought to promote freedom, protect private property or support liberal allies against non-liberal enemies.[33]

Second, in order to see how the pacific union removes the occasion of wars among liberal states and not wars between liberal and non-liberal states, we need to shift our attention from constitutional law to international law, Kant's second source. Complementing the constitutional guarantee of caution, international law adds a second source – a guarantee of respect. The separation of nations is reinforced by the development of separate languages and religions. These further guarantee a world of separate states – an essential condition needed to avoid a "global, soul-less despotism". Yet, at the same time, they also morally integrate liberal states "as culture grows and men gradually move towards greater agreement over their principles, they lead to mutual understanding and peace" (PP, p. 114). As republics emerge (the first source) and as culture progresses, an understanding of the legitimate rights of all citizens and of all republics comes into play; and this, now that caution characterizes policy, sets up the moral foundations for the liberal peace. Correspondingly, international law highlights the importance of Kantian publicity. Domestically, publicity helps ensure that the officials of republics act according to the principles they profess to hold just and according to the interests of the electors they claim to represent. Internationally, free speech and the effective communication of accurate conceptions of the political life of foreign peoples is essential to establish and preserve the understanding on which the guarantee of respect depends.

Domestically just republics, which rest on consent, then presume foreign republics to be also consensual, just, and therefore deserving of accommodation. The experience of cooperation helps engender further cooperative behavior when the consequences of state policy are unclear but (potentially) mutually beneficial. At the same time, liberal states assume that non-liberal states, which do not rest on free consent, are not just. Because non-liberal governments are perceived to be in a state of aggression with their own people, their foreign relations become for liberal governments deeply suspect. In short, fellow liberals benefit from a presumption of amity; non-liberals suffer from a presumption of enmity. Both presumptions may be accurate. Each, however, may also be self-fulfilling.

Democratic liberals do not need to assume either that public opinion rules foreign policy or that the entire governmental elite is liberal. It can assume that the elite typically manages public affairs but that potentially non-liberal members of the elite have reason to doubt that anti-liberal policies would be electorally sustained and endorsed by the majority of the democratic public.

Lastly, cosmopolitan law adds material incentives to moral commitments. The cosmopolitan right to hospitality permits the "spirit of commerce" sooner or later to take hold of every nation, thus creating incentives for states to promote peace and to try to avert war. Liberal economic theory holds that these cosmopolitan ties derive from a cooperative international division of labor and free trade according to comparative advantage. Each economy is said to be better off than it would have been under autarchy; each thus acquires an incentive to avoid policies that would lead the other to break these economic ties. Since keeping open markets rests upon the assumption that the next set of transactions will also be determined by prices rather than coercion, a sense of mutual security is vital to avoid security-motivated searches for economic autarchy. Thus, avoiding a challenge to another liberal state's security or even enhancing each other's security by means of alliance naturally follows economic interdependence.

A further cosmopolitan source of liberal peace is that the international market removes difficult decisions of production and distribution from the direct sphere of state policy. A foreign state thus does not appear directly responsible for these outcomes; states can stand aside from, and to some degree above, these contentious market rivalries and be ready to step in to resolve crises. The interdependence of commerce and the international contacts of state officials help create cross-cutting transnational ties that serve as lobbies for mutual accommodation. According to modern liberal scholars, international financiers and transnational and transgovernmental organizations create interests in favor of accommodation. Moreover, their variety has ensured that no single conflict sours an entire relationship by setting off a spiral of reciprocated retaliation. Conversely, a sense of suspicion, such as that characterizing relations between liberal and non-liberal governments, can lead to restrictions on the range of contacts between societies. And this can increase the prospect that a single conflict will determine an entire relationship.

No single constitutional, international or cosmopolitan source is alone sufficient. Kantian theory is neither solely institutional nor solely ideological, nor solely economic. But together (and only together) the three specific strands of liberal institutions, liberal ideas, and the transnational ties that follow from them plausibly connect the characteristics of liberal polities and economies with sustained liberal peace.[34] But in their relations with non-liberal states, liberal states have not escaped from the insecurity caused by anarchy in the world political system considered as a whole.[35] Moreover, the very constitutional restraint, international respect for individual rights, and shared commercial interests that establish grounds for peace among liberal states establish grounds for additional conflict in relations between liberal and non-liberal societies.

Democratic Pacifism

The modern thesis that democracies are inherently peaceful has received an eloquent and scholarly restatement in the engagingly provocative *Retreat From Doomsday: The Obsolescence of Major War* by John Mueller.[36] Mueller marshals extensive evidence to demonstrate that major war has gradually moved "toward terminal disrepute because of its perceived repulsiveness and futility" (Mueller, 1989, p. 4). Both the psychic and physical costs of war have made it obsolete. Like duelling and slavery, it has become socially and morally repulsive. Like pyramid building, it has become too costly. It no longer seems worth it.

Schumpeter's "Sociology of Imperialisms", offers considerable evidence to support this view while it develops a comprehensive analysis of the sources that underlie the forces of democratic pacifism. Published in 1919 as a refutation of Lenin's *Imperialism*, Schumpeter's essay made a coherent and sustained argument concerning the pacifying (in the sense of non-aggressive) effects of liberal institutions and principles.[37] Unlike some of the earlier liberal theorists, who focused on a single feature, such as trade,[38] or failed to examine critically the arguments they were advancing, Schumpeter saw the interaction of capitalism and democracy as the foundation of liberal pacifism and he tested his arguments in a sociology of historical imperialisms.

Schumpeter defined "imperialism" as "an objectless disposition on the part of a state to unlimited forcible expansion" (p. 6). Excluding imperialisms that were mere "catchwords" and object-ful imperialisms (e.g. defensive), he traced the roots of objectless imperialism to three sources, each an atavism. Modern imperialism resulted from the combined impact of a "war machine", warlike instincts, and export monopolism.

Once necessary, the war machine later developed a life of its own and took control of a state's foreign policy. "Created by the wars that required it, the machine now created the wars it required" (p. 25). And so, Schumpeter tells us, the army of ancient Egypt, created to drive the Hyksos out of Egypt, took over the state and pursued militaristic imperialism. Like the later armies of the courts of absolutist Europe, it fought wars for the sake of glory and booty, for the sake of warriors and monarches – wars *gratia* warriors.

A warlike disposition, elsewhere called "instinctual elements of bloody primitivism", is the natural ideology of a war machine. It also exists independently; the Persians, he says, were a warrior nation from the outset (pp. 25–32).

Under modern capitalism, export monopolists, the third source of modern imperialism, push for imperialist expansion as a way to expand their closed markets. But the absolute monarchies were the last clear-cut imperialisms. Nineteenth century imperialisms merely represent the vestiges of the imperialisms created by Louis XIV and Catherine the Great. Thus the export monopolists are an atavism of the absolute monarchies, for they depend completely on the tariffs imposed by the monarchs and their militaristic successors for revenue (pp. 82–83). Without tariffs, monopolies would be eliminated by foreign competition.

Modern (nineteenth-century) imperialism, therefore, rests on an atavistic war machine, militaristic attitudes left over from the days of monarchical wars, and export monopolism, which is nothing more than the economic residue of monarchical finance. In the modern era, imperialists gratify their private interests. From the national perspective, their imperialistic wars are objectless.

Schumpeter's theme now emerges. Capitalism and democracy are forces for peace. Indeed, they are antithetical to imperialism. And the further (to Schumpeter) development of capitalism and democracy means that imperialism will inevitably disappear.

Capitalism produces an unwarlike disposition; its populace is "democratized, individualized, rationalized" (p. 68). The people's (daily) energies are daily absorbed in production. The disciplines of industry and the market train people in "economic rationalism"; the instability of industrial life necessitates calculation. Capitalism also "individualizes"; "subjective opportunities" replace the "immutable factors" of traditional, hierarchical society. Rational individuals demand democratic governance.

And democratic capitalism leads to peace. As evidence, Schumpeter claims that (1) throughout the capitalist world an opposition has arisen to "war, expansion, cabinet diplomacy"; (2) contemporary capitalism is associated with peace parties; and (3) the industrial worker of capitalism is "vigorously anti-imperialist". In addition, (4) the capitalist world has developed the means of preventing war, such as the Hague Court; and (5) the least feudal, most capitalist society – the United States – has demonstrated the least imperialistic tendencies (pp. 95–96). (The US left over half of Mexico unconquered in the war of 1846–48.)

His explanation for liberal pacifism was quite simple. Only war profiteers and military aristocrats gain from wars. No democracy would pursue a minority interest and tolerate the high costs of imperialism. When free trade prevails, "no class" gains from forcible expansion: "foreign raw materials and food stuffs are as accessible to each nation as though they were in its own territory. Where the cultural backwardness of a region makes normal economic intercourse dependent on colonization, it does not matter, assuming free trade, which of the 'civilized' nations undertakes the task of colonization" (pp. 75–76).

Later in his career, in *Capitalism, Socialism, and Democracy*, Schumpeter developed a much more sophisticated model of capitalist political economy and he acknowledged that "almost purely bourgeois commonwealths were often aggressive when it seemed to pay – like the Athenian or the Venetian commonwealths."[39] But he stuck to his (pacifistic) guns, restating the modern view that capitalist democracy "steadily tells ... against the use of military force and for peaceful arrangements, even when the balance of pecuniary advantage is clearly on the side of war which, under modern circumstances, is not in general very likely" (p.128).[40]

Comparisons

Thucydides, Rousseau, Kant, and Schumpeter are each advocates (and theorists) of popular, or democratic, or representative republican government. Yet they expect democratic foreign relations to be (variously) imperialist, isolationist, internationalist, and pacific. How can we explain their differences and understand the multiple legacies of democratic foreign affairs?

The pattern of expected foreign relations of democratic states that they offer us can be seen in the following table:

Foreign Relations of Democratic States

with/	Peace	War	Imperialism
Democracies	S,K	R,T	T
Non-Democracies	S	R,T,K	T,K

(Where S=Schumpeter; K=Kant; T=Thucydides; and R=Rousseau)

Thucydides's democratic imperialism, Rousseau's democratic isolationism, Kant's liberal internationalism, and Schumpeter's liberal pacifism rest on fundamentally different views on the nature of man, the state, and international relations.

Let us examine the theorists pairwise.

Schumpeter and Kant. Schumpeter's man is rationalized, individualized, and democratized. He is also homogenized, pursuing material interests "monistically". Since his material interests lie in peaceful trade, he and the democratic state that he and his fellow citizens control are pacifistic. Schumpeter's "materialistic monism" leaves little room for non-economic objectives, whether espoused by states or individuals. His states, moreover, are the same. The political life of individuals seems to have been homogenized at the same time as the individuals were "rationalized, individualized, and democratized". Citizens, capitalists and workers, rural and urban, seek material welfare. Schumpeter presumes that no one seems to want to rule. He also presumes that no one is prepared to take those measures (such as stirring up foreign quarrels to preserve a domestic ruling coalition) that enhance one's political power, despite detrimental effects on mass welfare. Just as ideal domestic politics are homogenized, so world politics, too, is homogenized. Materially monistic and democratically capitalist, all states evolve toward free trade and liberty together. Countries differently constituted seem to disappear from Schumpeter's analysis. "Civilized nations" govern "culturally backward regions."

Unlike Schumpeter's capitalist democracies, Kant's constitutional democracies – including our own – remain in a state of war with non-republics. Liberal republics see themselves as threatened by aggression from non-republics that are not constrained by representation. Liberal politicians often fail in their categorical moral duties and stir up foreign quarrels with non-liberal states as a way of enhancing their own domestic power. And even though wars often cost more than the economic return they generate, liberal republics also are prepared to protect and promote – sometimes forcibly – democracy, private property, and the rights of individuals overseas against non-republics, which, because they do not authentically represent the rights of individuals, have no rights to non-interference. These wars may liberate oppressed individuals overseas; they also can generate enormous suffering.

Thucydides and Rousseau. Thucydides's citizens (unlike Schumpeter's) are splendidly diverse in their goals, both at home and abroad. Their characters are shaped in varying proportions by courage, ambition, fear, profit, caution, glory, and patriotism. Although they are equal before the law and all citizens have a right to vote, their circumstances greatly differ, divided as they are among rich and poor, urban and rural. Internationally, their states are driven by fear, honor, and self-advantage. States too are radically unequal in size, resources, and power. Such a people and such a state find imperialism useful, feasible, and valued. In a dangerous world, empire adds to the security, profit, and glory of the powerful majority, even if not of all the citizens. The demos makes naval power effective and cheap.

Rousseau's citizens of the Social Contract, too, are equal, rational, and free. But, going beyond legal equality, social and economic equality distinguish them from Thucydides's Athenians. Particular "wills" such as the ones that drove the Athenians to Sicily would yield to the General Will – the rational, national, general interest – which Thucydides (Pericles) had defined as precluding further imperial expansion. The exploitation of non-citizens in the empire (the source of so much national revenue) also would be unacceptable in a Rousseauian republic that demanded that all men be free, ruling and being ruled on an equal basis. This obviously precludes slavery. It also requires that every other form of political rule that did not give an equal voice to all affected had to be excluded from a free democracy, which is why Rousseau's democracy had to be small. Nor, lastly, would Rousseau allow the extensive commerce that made empire both valued and feasible. The Rousseauian democracy was free, independent, and isolationist.

Rousseau and Kant. Kant's citizens, like Rousseau's, are free, politically equal, and rational. The Kantian state thus is governed publicly according to law, as a republic. Kant's constitutional democracy thus also (logically) solves the problem of governing equals. But his citizens are different in two respects. They retain their individuality, whether they are the "rational devils" he says that we egoists often find ourselves to be or the ethical agents, treating other individuals as ends rather than as means, that we can and should become. And they retain their diversity in economic and social circumstance.

Like Rousseau's direct democracy, Kant's constitutional democracy exercises democratic caution in the interest of the majority. But unlike Rousseau's General Will, Kant's republics are capable of appreciating the moral equality of all individuals. The Rousseauian citizen cedes all rights to his fellow citizens, retaining only the right to equal consideration. In order to be completely self-determining, Rousseau requires that there be no limit but equality on the sovereignty and authority of the General Will. The resulting communitarianism is intense – every aspect of culture, morality, and social life is subject to the creation and the re-creation of the national citizenry. The tendency to enhance domestic consciousness through external hostility and what Rousseau calls *amour propre* would be correspondingly high. Just as individuality disappears into collective consciousness, so too does an appreciation for the international rights of foreign republics.[41] These international rights of republics derive from our ability to reconstruct in our imagination the act of representation of foreign individuals, who are our moral equals. Kant appears to think that the General Will, which Rousseau thinks can be realized only within the community, can be intuited by each individual as the Categorical Imperative. Rousseau's democracy – for the sake of intensifying national identity – limits our identification to fellow citizens.

This imaginative act of Kantian cosmopolitan identification benefits from the institutional process of republican government. Constitutionally divided powers among the executive, legislature, and the judiciary require public deliberation and thereby mitigate the effect of particular passions or hasty judgment. Rousseau's direct democracy appears to slight the value of republican delay.

Moreover, for the sake of equality and autonomy, Rousseau's democracy precludes the private ties of commerce and social interaction across borders that lead to both domestic diversity and transnational solidarity. These material ties sustain the transnational, or cosmopolitan, identity of individuals with each other that serves as the foundation of international respect, which in turn is the source of the spirit of international law that requires tolerance and peace among fellow constitutional democracies (while exacerbating conflict between constitutional democracies and all other states).

Rousseau shares with Kant democratic rationality. Rousseau, however, excludes both the moral individualism and the social pluralism that provide the foundations for Kant's "international" and "cosmopolitan" laws, and thereby precludes the liberal peace.

Comparing Thucydides and Rousseau, on the one hand, Kant and Schumpeter, on the other, we can say that whatever the differences in their special views of man and the nature of domestic politics, the first two agree that the polis or state either does or should command all force and command all loyalty. Differences among actual states and personal values are then contained by their similar degree of national authority. There is thus no room for the individualism and domestic diversity that Kant finds is at the root of the transnational loyalties and transnational interests that make a democratic peace. Nor is there room for the simple transnational materialism Schumpeter sees as governing the interests of pacific democratic majorities. The democracies of Thucydides and Rousseau remain in a state of war.

Present Implications

To the extent that these theoretical distinctions tap the actual range of diversity in the development of contemporary democracies, they offer us some useful warnings about the international implications of the current trend toward democratization.[42]

Although majority rule may be a necessary condition of a state of peace, it is not a sufficient condition. Rousseau's portrait of the search for autarchy and national identity presupposes a continuing state of war with all outside polities; it undermines democratic peace. Thucydides's picture of democratic imperialism illustrates the impact of unrestrained passions and material interests.

In order to establish peace among themselves, democracies can follow Kant's route, defining individual rights in such a way that the cosmopolitan rights of all mankind are entailed in the moral foundations of the rights of domestic citizens. And then they must allow the material ties of transnational society to flourish among themselves. Or, attempting to guarantee an indiscriminate global peace, they can follow Schumpeter's prescription, relying upon the supposedly pacifying culture of capitalism and the material interests of free trade underlying it.

What are the implications for world politics today of these moral and political choices? Real states are always more complicated than theoretical models. But unlike even just thirty years ago, today we see few, if any, states aspiring to revolutionary Rousseauian democracy (Iran might come closest). We find many more in the Balkans and around the Black Sea and elsewhere that Thucydides would easily recognize, practising imperialism subject to supposedly democratic plebiscite in pursuit of limitless security, nationalist honor and crude self-interest.

The dominant forms of contemporary democracy, fortunately, appear to be liberal and capitalist, Kantian and Schumpeterian. They share pluralist and republican polities; capitalist and market economies; materialist and rationalist cultures, with a commitment to human rights. The long record of liberal internationalism – both liberal solidarity with fellow liberals and liberal imperialism toward non-liberals – decides in favor of the Kantian roots of rights married to markets. On the other hand, recent mood swings toward complacency, "donor fatigue" and over-burdened United Nations peace-keeping – as the scramble for profit displaces Cold War internationalism – may highlight and draw upon the material sources of Schumpeterian pacifist isolationism.

In either case, liberal democracy accounts for, and claims credit for, extraordinary international feats. To a record of two centuries of peace among liberal democracies, it adds an extraordinary geostrategic triumph: the solidarity of the Free World during the Cold War, America's long undefended democratic borders with Canada and Mexico, the reconciliation of the democratic states of Europe in the post-war period, and the successful assimilation of the defeated Axis powers, Germany and Japan and Italy, into the liberal order of the "Free World". And just as Britain peacefully ceded international hegemony to the United States in the middle twentieth century, liberal internationalism promises a peaceful transition if the United State's decline leads to another liberal transition – to a united Europe or possibly Japan.

Yet the history of liberal internationalism and the political foundations of the liberal peace give us three warnings about – or typical failures of – liberal internationalism.

The first is complaisance – let us call it the "1921–1931 Problem". Where liberal internationalism among liberal states has been deficient is in preserving its basic preconditions under changing international circumstances, and particularly in supporting the liberal character of its constituent states.

It has failed on occasion, as it did in regard to Germany in the 1920s, to provide adequate international economic support for liberal regimes whose market foundations were in crisis. It failed in the 1930s to provide military aid or political mediation to Spain, which was challenged by an armed minority, or to Czechoslovakia, which was caught in a dilemma of preserving national security or acknowledging the claims (fostered by Hitler's Germany) of the Sudeten minority to self-determination.

Far-sighted and constitutive measures have only been provided by the liberal international order when one liberal state stood pre-eminent among the rest, prepared and able to take measures, as did the United States following World War II, to sustain economically and politically the foundations of liberal society beyond its borders. Then measures such as the British Loan, the Marshall Plan, NATO, GATT, the IMF, and the liberalization of Germany and Japan helped construct buttresses for the international liberal order.[43]

Thus, the decline of US hegemonic leadership may pose dangers for the liberal world. The danger is not that today's liberal states will permit their economic competition to spiral into war nor that a world economic crisis is now likely, but that the societies of the liberal world will no longer be able to provide the mutual assistance they might require to sustain liberal domestic orders if they were to be faced with mounting economic crises.

The most pressing danger of complaisance today is how to support Russia and its democratic neighbors in the Commonwealth of Independent States – what is left of a shaky union of quasi-independent and hopefully still democratizing republics in the middle of Eurasia.

Isolationists decry both the involvement and the cost. But neither liberal principles nor liberal interests allow the luxury of non-involvement. Even in the isolationist aftermath of World War One, providing humanitarian aid to the Russians, financial support for Germany, and policing the Caribbean seemed to be an automatic part of the liberal project.

Even if liberal principles did not call for universalism, liberal interests now do. Trade and investments reach across the world. The oil on which the US and its closest economic partners in Europe and Japan rely still depends on Middle East supplies, as the crisis in the Gulf reminded us. The cost, moreover, of the forty-five year Cold War has to be calculated in trillions.[44] The possible failure of democratization in Russia would place thousands of nuclear weapons in the hands of the "fascist situation" of which Ambassador Robert Strauss warned.[45] A renewed Cold War, next with Russian Fascism, has to be the largest, even if far from the most likely, threat to the security liberal democracies now enjoy.

The second danger lies in imprudent crusading – the problem of liberal imperialism to which liberal powers, including the United States, have repeatedly succumbed. Here liberals need to avoid the tendency to engage in crusades that are costly and counter-productive – both morally and materially. Neither villages nor countries can be destroyed in order to be saved. Nor should we assume that every realization of fundamental human rights requires the duplication of "Kansas City".

The third danger is vehement paranoia – what might be called the "1901–1911 Problem", the escalation of hostilities that preceded World War I. In relations with powerful non-liberal states, liberal states have often missed opportunities to pursue the negotiation of arms reduction and arms control when it has been in the mutual strategic interest and failed to construct wider schemes of accommodation that are needed to supplement arms control. Prior to the outbreak of World War I, this is the charge that Lord Sanderson leveled against Sir Eyre Crowe in Sanderson's response to Crowe's famous memorandum on the state of British relations with Germany.[46] Sanderson pointed out that Crowe interpreted German demands to participate in the settlement of international disputes and to have a "place in the sun" (colonies), of a size not too dissimilar to that enjoyed by the other great powers, as evidence of a fundamental aggressiveness driving toward world domination. Crowe may well have perceived an essential feature of Wilhelmine Germany, and Sanderson's attempt to place Germany in the context of other rising powers (bumptious but not aggressively pursuing world domination) may have been naive. But the interesting thing to note is less the conclusions reached than Crowe's chain of argument and evidence. He rejects continued accommodation (appeasement) with Germany not because he shows that Germany was more bumptious than France and not because he shows that Germany had greater potential as a world hegemon than the United States (which he does not even consider in this connection). Instead he is (legitimately) perplexed by the real uncertainty of German foreign policy and by its "erratic, domineering, and often frankly aggressive spirit" which accords with the well-known personal characteristics of "the present Ruler of Germany".

In this context, contemporary Japan is another Germany. Germany was a *Rechtstaat* at home, capitalist, and semi-individualist in culture. Its foreign policy, however, had not been placed under the control of representative government. So, too, Japan is less than a complete liberal republic. It is democratic, but, until the 1993 victory of Prime Minister Hosokawa's movement, hegemonically under the sway of the Liberal Democratic Party. It is capitalist – though very well organized from the top both privately and publicly. It is egalitarian – but not individualist in culture (though here we can also note signs of change with the new spirit of fledgling Japanese consumerism). If we add a history of US racism toward the Japanese and Japanese racist chauvinism toward foreigners, we have a dangerous combination.

In short, there is plenty of room for the sort of spiralling misperception and rivalry that characterized the pre-war Anglo–German antagonism. We will need institutions and multifaceted contacts to offset the economic tensions that are likely to be an increasingly important part of the relationship.

The liberal world has entered a nearly unprecedented condition of security and it appears to be significantly linked to the surge of democracy world-wide. But that good fortune is neither guaranteed to persist nor will it necessarily involve peace.

Even if the Iraq War is unlikely to be repeated soon, "Grenada" and "Panama" are likely to arise frequently in the new world order we are entering, If we want to avoid them becoming revivals of destructive imperialism, we will need to have the institutions of multilateral security, whether in the UN or regional organizations, ready to provide guidance and multilateral restraint.

Moreover, it is very much in our hands whether the 1990s do in fact become another "1930s", brief moments before the collapse of collective security into complaisance (as occurred in the Manchurian Incident of 1931) and then war. Another cold war with a Russia after a next, perhaps successful, authoritarian coup could re-enact the European crisis of liberal democracy that began with the Reichstag Fire of 1933.

Or instead, will the 1990s become a pre-World-War-I style rivalry spiralling into extensive hostility. Will the US–Japanese relationship follow on the model of the pre-World-War-I antagonism between Germany and Britain?

Either alone or both together could radically alter our pacific prospects and make whatever investments in institution-building and development aid we now consider expensive seem cheap in retrospect.

Notes

1. I would like to thank the members of the 1993 Tromsø Colloquium sponsored by the Nobel Institute and Ms. Hongying Wang for their critical comments and Ms. June Garson and Ms. Philomena Fischer for secretarial support. I also benefited from discussions of this paper in seminars held at the New York University Law School chaired by Lea Brilmayer and at Yale Law School chaired by Paul Kahn.
2. See *The Economist*, 1 September 1990.
3. President Ronald Reagan, "Address to Parliament", *The New York Times*, 9 June 1982.
4. He earlier announced as a "plain truth: the day of the dictator is over. The people's right to democracy must not be denied." See *Department of State Bulletin*, June 1989.
5. President Bush's first two examples were individual enterprise and international trade; he then justified the large cuts in US tactical nuclear forces by the decline in hostility that stemmed from the survival of democratic forces in the USSR after the 1991 coup.
6. Like so many of Mr. Yeltsin's good intentions, practice falls short. Russian rocket forces still have US targets coded into their missiles. See "60 Minutes", Sunday, 31 October 1993. One can assume that US targeting has exhibited an equal bureaucratic inertia.
7. See *The New York Times*, 29 January 1992.
8. Thomas Paine, *The Rights of Man*, in Eric Foner, ed., *Complete Writings*, I, (New York: The Citadel press 1945) p. 342.
9. See Schumpeter, Rummel (note 34), and Mueller (note 36).
10. Paine's own remark as well as his militant role in the American and French revolutions leaves us with an interesting ambiguity. Monarchs engage in war amongst themselves, Paine notes; but is war between monarchs and democracies the product of the monarchs attacking the democracies or the democratic nations attacking the "miserable and inimical" monarchs?
11. Thucydides, *The Peloponnesian War*, translated by Rex Warner, introduction by M.I. Finley (Harmondsworth: Penguin 1972) Book I: Paragraph 37 (i.e. in following citations, I:37).
12. Pseudo-Xenophon, *Constitution of Athens* I:2.
13. N.G.L. Hammond, *A History of Greece* (Oxford: Clarendon Press, 3rd ed. 1986) p.301.
14. *Ibid.*, Hammond, p. 347.
15. But for a thorough treatment see the debate on this issue between Ste Croix and Bradeen in *Historia*, in 1954 and 1960. For current scholarship on the international implications of Thucydides's history see Richard Ned Lebow and Barry Strauss, eds., *Hegemonic Rivalry* (Oxford: Westview 1991).
16. In "Federalist No. 10."
17. John Finley's *Thucydides* (Cambridge: Harvard University Press 1942) suggests this interpretation.
18. He is a realist who sees equally important causes of the state of war in the structure of the system, the nature of mankind, and the varying domestic structure of states. In Kenneth Waltz's terms, Images One, Two, and Three are operating together and with equal significance (see Kenneth Waltz, *Man, the State and War* (New York: Columbia University Press 1954)).

For this point and many others, see Stanley Hoffmann's classic essay on Rousseau in *The State of War* (New York: Praeger 1965).

19. J.J. Rousseau, "Fragment on War," *A Lasting Peace* (London: Constable 1917), p. 128.
20. *Ibid.*, p. 127 in the "Fragment on War."
21. See for example, Harry Hinsley, *Power and the Pursuit of Peace* (Cambridge, 1963) chap. 3. For this author's discussion of the varieties of realism see "Thucydidean Realism", *Review of International Studies* (1990).
22. J.J. Rousseau, "Second Discourse", in *The Social Contract and the Discourses* (New York: Dutton 1950), p. 200.
23. *Ibid.*, "Second Discourse", p. 238.
24. *Ibid.*, "Second Discourse", p. 252.
25. See "St Pierre's Project" and Rousseau's "Judgment of St. Pierre's Project" in *A Lasting Peace*, above (note 19).
26. *Ibid.*, "Social Contract", pp. 28–29.
27. Rousseau, if this is correct, would not agree with A.J.P. Taylor's statement,"That if every state followed its own interest, all would be peaceful and secure" (Taylor, *Struggle for Mastery in Europe*, Oxford University Press 1971), p. xx).
28. Judith Shklar, *Ordinary Vices* (Cambridge: Harvard University Press 1985), pp. 28–29.
29. J.J. Rousseau, "Corsica," in Frederick Watkins ed., *Political Writings*, (Edinburgh, Nelson 1986), p. 308.
30. *Ibid.* Valuable contextual remarks on Rousseau can be found in Torbjorn Knutsen, *A History of International Relations Theory* (Manchester: Manchester University Press 1992) chap. 5, and Grace Roosevelt, *Reading Rousseau in the Nuclear Age* (Philadelphia Temple University Press 1990).
31. J.J. Rousseau, "Poland", in Watkins (1986), pp. 169–181, 183. (See note 21.)
32. Immanuel Kant, "Perpetual Peace" (1795), in Hans Reiss, ed., *Kant's Political Writings* (Cambridge: Cambridge University Press 1970), pp. 93–130.
33. Kant regards these wars as unjust and warns liberals of their susceptibility to them (*Perpetual Peace*, in 1970, p.106). At the same time, he argues that each nation "can and ought to" demand that its neighboring nations enter into the pacific union of liberal states (PP, p. 102).
34. The evidence for the existence and significance of a pacific union is discussed in Doyle ("Kant, Liberal Legacies and International Affairs", Part 1, *Philosophy and Public Affairs*, 12, 1983a, pp. 205–235). For a careful statistical treatment see Zeev Maoz and Bruce Russett, "Alliance, Contiguity and Wealth: Is the Lack of Conflict Among Democracies a Statistical Artifact?", *International Interactions* 17, 3, pp. 245–267. Clarence Streit (*Union Now*, New York: Harpers 1938, pp. 88, 90–92) seems to have been the first to point out (in contemporary foreign relations) the empirical tendency of democracies to maintain peace among themselves, and he made this the foundation of his proposal for a (non-Kantian) federal union of the fifteen leading democracies of the 1930s. D.V. Babst ("A Force for Peace", *Industrial Research*, 14, April 1972, pp. 55–58) performed a quantitative study of this phenomenon of "democratic peace". And R. J. Rummel did a similar study of "libertarianism" (in the sense of *laisser-faire*)

focusing on the postwar period ("Libertarianism and International Violence", *Journal of Conflict Resolution*, 27, 1983, pp. 27–71). I use liberal in a wider (Kantian) sense in my discussion of this issue (1983a). In that essay, I survey the period from 1790 to the present, and find no war among liberal states. Babst did make a preliminary test of the significance of the distribution of alliance partners in World War I. He found that the possibility that the actual distribution of alliance partners could have occurred by chance was less than 1% (p.56). But this assumes that there was an equal possibility that any two nations could have gone to war with each other; and this is a strong assumption. Rummel has a further discussion of significance as it applies to his libertarian thesis. Recent work has extended these arguments into considerations of strategies of international reform (e.g. James Lee Ray, *Democracies and International Conflict*, Columbia: University of South Carolina Press 1994), patterns of evolution in the international system by George Modelski (and see Charles Kegley, "The Long Postwar Peace During the Cold War", *Jerusalem Journal of International Relations* 14 December 1992, pp. 1–18), and implications for the categorization of contemporary international theory (Joseph Nye, "Neorealism and Neoliberalism", *World Politics* 1988).

35. For evidence, please see Doyle ("Kant, Liberal Legacies and Foreign Affairs", Part 2, *Philosophy and Public Affairs* 12, Fall 1983, pp.323-53). Although there are serious studies that show that Marxist regimes have higher military spending per capita than non-Marxist regimes, this should not be interpreted as a sign of the inherent aggressiveness of authoritarian or totalitarian governments or – with even greater enthusiasm – the inherent and global peacefulness of liberal regimes. Stanislav Andreski ("On the Peaceful Disposition of Military Dictatorships", *Journal of Strategic Studies*, 3, 1980, pp. 3–10), for example, argues that (purely) military dictatorships, due to their domestic fragility, have little incentive to engage in foreign military adventures. And according to Walter Clemens ("The Superpowers and the Third World", in Charles Kegley and Patrick McGowan, eds., *Foreign Policy:USA/USSR*, 1982, pp. 117–118) the United States intervened in the Third World more than twice as often in the period 1946-1976 as the Soviet Union did in 1946–1979. Relatedly, Posen and VanEvera found ("Overarming and Underwhelming", *Foreign Policy* 40, 1980, p. 105) that the United States devoted one quarter and the Soviet Union one tenth of their defence budgets to forces designed for Third World interventions (where responding to perceived threats would presumably have a less than purely defensive character).

36. *Retreat from Doomsday* (New York: Basic Books 1989). This is also the view of Rummel (1983) discussed above and for a discussion of other aspects of "commercial liberalism" see Robert Keohane *After Hegemony*, (Princeton: Princeton University Press 1984), pp. 22–24.

37. Joseph Schumpeter, *Imperialism and Social Classes* (New York: World 1955).

38. Montesquieu, *Spirit of the Laws*, I, Bk 20, chap. 1.

39. Joseph Schumpeter, *Capitalism, Socialism and Democracy* (1950), pp. 127–128.

40. He notes that testing this proposition is likely to be very difficult, requiring "detailed historical analysis". But the bourgeois attitude toward the mili-

tary, the spirit and manner by which bourgeois societies wage war, and the readiness with which they submit to military rule during a prolonged war are "conclusive in themselves" (1950, p. 129).

41. Drawing on historical evidence of the early twentieth century Stephen VanEvera ("Primed for Peace", *International Security*, 15, 3 Winter 1990–91) reaches a similar conclusion about the dangers of militaristic nationalism. The comparison detailed here, however, suggests an even wider indictment of the danger of nationalism among democracies.

42. A lively and informative debate, much of it published in *International Security*, has considered the relevance of Realist and Democratic Liberal categories as metaphors with which to interpret the recent revolutionary changes in the international politics of Eastern Europe and the Soviet Union. See, in particular, John Mearsheimer's criticism of liberalism ("Back to the Future", *International Security*, 15, 1, Summer 1990); Jack Snyder's discussion of policy paths ("Avoiding Anarchy in the New Europe", *International Security*, 14, 4, Spring 1990); and Daniel Deudney and John Ikenberry's survey of external influences on Soviet behavior (*Review of International Studies*, 1991).

43. Charles Kindleberger, *The World in Depression* (Berkeley: University of California Press 1973); Robert Gilpin, *U.S. Power and the Multinational Corporation* (New York: Basic Books 1975); and Fred Hirsch and Michael Doyle, "Politicization in the World Economy" in Hirsch, Doyle and Edward Morse, *Alternatives to Monetary Disorder* (New York: Council on Foreign Relations/McGraw Hill, 1977).

44. Greg Treverton in *Rethinking America's Security* estimates $11 trillion.

45. See *The New York Times*, 20 November 1991.

46. Memoranda by Mr. Eyre Crowe, 1 January 1907, and by Lord Sanderson, 25 February 1907, in G.P. Gooch et al., eds.. *British Documents on the Origins of the War, 1898–1914*, 3 (London: HMSO 1928), pp. 397–431.

Part V

Peace, Stability, and Legitimacy: Some Speculations about the Future

15

The Cycle of Great Powers: Has it Finally Been Broken?

Robert Gilpin

Every age must live amidst the rubble of vanished great powers and the imperial structures that they have usually created. The dynamics of international affairs can, in fact, be told largely in terms of the rise and fall of successive dominant powers and their empires.[1] As the terms "Pax Romana" and "Pax Britannica" suggest, these hierarchical structures at their maturity gave order and stability to particular ages. Sooner or later, however, an imperial structure fragments from within or is destroyed by rising powers on its periphery. With the decline and eventual collapse of imperial edifices, subordinate peoples may enjoy once again self-determination and the right to express themselves. The price paid for regained freedom, however, has frequently been political instability and inter-group conflict that ceases only with the emergence of a new imperial rule or an equilibrium among the contending forces. In time the cycle of rise, maturity, and decline recommences and runs its full course.

Our own age is especially strewn with the debris of former great powers. Perhaps never before in the history of the world has the human race been confronted with a similar set of challenges arising from such historical legacies. From the First World War onward, the world has witnessed the successive collapse of one empire after another; efforts to find a permanent and peaceful solution to the accumulating consequences have failed. Instead, one ruin has been piled upon another like the layers of prior civilizations discovered in archeological digs. On almost every continent, the collapse and receding of former great powers and their spheres of influence have left behind ethnic rivalries and political instabilities. In the Balkans, the Middle East, and the Eastern Mediterranean, the international community has yet to deal effectively with the consequences of the disintegration of the Ottoman Empire earlier in this century. In Eastern Europe, the end of Soviet domination has raised again the specter of the nationalistic conflicts that had attended the collapse of the Habsburg Empire as a result of World War I. Throughout

Asia, Africa, and South America, the end of what the political geographer Halford MacKinder called "the Columbian Epoch" has left a legacy of stunted political and economic entities.[2] Perhaps only in north-east Asia, as witnessed by the rapid development of Japan's former colonies Taiwan and South Korea, has Karl Marx's prophecy been fulfilled that capitalist imperialism was a progressive force for economic development.

The contemporary world is experiencing those political phenomena that have historically accompanied the decline of great powers and the weakening of the international order that they created. Conflicts among formerly repressed peoples have reasserted themselves; in the Balkans and around the periphery of the former Soviet Union, ethnic groups that only yesterday lived together in peace under imperial rule or whose security was guaranteed by other great powers, are now slaughtering one another; while the horrors of "ethnic cleansing" taking place in former Yugoslavia are not historically unprecedented, especially in Eastern Europe, humankind did believe that it had progressed beyond such primitivism. In addition, the collapse of imperial structures and the drawing of new political boundaries have divided formerly united peoples and given rise to irredentist movements; in some cases, as in the fragmented Soviet empire, the former oppressors have become the newly oppressed, or at least harbor fears of political reprisals. And, furthermore, more and more powers are seeking to fill the vacuum left by the retreat of the old order; China, Iran, Germany, Japan, Serbia, and Turkey, among other contenders, are rapidly expanding their influence into the former domains of Soviet and American primacy. Thus, the cycle of the rise and fall of great powers, it would appear, continues unabated.

Optimism and Pessimism, Idealism and Realism

This sober assessment is strongly challenged by many analysts who find encouraging signs in contemporary developments. Many scholars argue that Western imperialism itself has left a legacy of powerful concepts of liberal democracy and national self-determination that not only have served to undermine Western domination but also have made new empires exceedingly difficult to create.[3] In Europe itself, which has been the seedbed of so much conflict in the modern world, many analysts reason that, with the crucial exception of the Balkans, the traditional sources of enmity and conflict have disappeared.[4] In fact, it is argued, the troubles in

Yugoslavia, in the Middle East, and elsewhere are but transitory throwbacks to anachronistic modes of political behavior that the human race is outgrowing. International politics, it is alleged, is experiencing a beneficial transformation with the spread of both liberal democracy and the market system of economic organization. In fact, this argument runs, the contemporary era is witnessing the first true metamorphosis in human affairs and, at long last, the cycle of the rise and decline of great powers with its unfortunate consequences has been broken. In its place, it is argued, a more humane, beneficent, and stable global order is taking shape.

The proponents of the belief that the world is undergoing an historic and benevolent transformation point to several developments to substantiate their position. The first argument is that, on a cost/benefit calculation, war no longer pays; the advent of nuclear weapons and other means of mass destruction has outmoded war as a means of settling international disputes.[5] The second argument is that the increasing economic integration of the globe, especially the increasing importance of transnational corporations, has created common economic interests across national boundaries and transnational corporate alliances that transcend the traditional parochialism of nation states and ethnic nationalism; with the defeat of communism, the Second Great Age of Capitalism is taking shape and leading to the creation of a liberal, multilateral global economy in which every society can benefit through peaceful commerce. The third argument is that with the triumph and spread of democracy throughout the world, nations will pursue more peaceful foreign policies; the fundamental premise of this argument is that democratic societies do not fight with one another. Humankind, it might be said, is now passing through the trauma of the end of the modern, imperial age into a post-modern, post-imperial age that will be more peaceful and more just.

In effect, many observers believe that Immanuel Kant's prediction of a more benign and humane world is at long last being fulfilled. In his *Perpetual Peace* and his *Universal History*, Kant foresaw the ultimate triumph of Reason and the liberal values of eighteenth-century Enlightenment.[6] The success of liberalism and its associated values such as freedom, individualism, and democracy, Kant believed, would bring about a transformation of international politics and human affairs in general.[7] Applied to international affairs, liberalism has been interpreted to mean the self-determination of all peoples, the settlement of all disputes by peaceful means, and a world economy based on open markets. Thus, an international order founded on liberal principles would benefit all nations politically and economically and would thereby automatically bring to an end the destructive cycle of imperial orders.

According to Kant, several natural mechanisms and objective historical laws would ensure this political transformation. In particular, three inevitable developments, he argued, would eventually pacify the human race. First would be the institution of republican government; with the displacement of authoritarian governments by the rule of the people, nations would become more pacific because, as many argue in the contemporary era, "democracies do not fight".[8] Secondly, as the republican form of government spreads from one society to another so that more and more became republican or democratic, this development would lead to an ever-widening "zone of peace" or "pacific union" among the democracies. And thirdly, the spread of commerce would create bonds of mutual interest among states; international commerce and mutual economic gain would become a force for world peace. In summary, according to Kant, Nature's plan is to create a political constitution that is perfect both at the national and international levels.

Perhaps this Kantian faith in the automatic workings of moral progress and the ultimate triumph of liberal values *is* being fulfilled with the defeat of authoritarian communism and the triumph of democratic capitalism. Yet, the disturbing events of the post-Cold-War era may be more endemic to the human condition than a mere aberration of the moment that will pass as Nature's plan manifests itself. Perhaps political conflict, as realist theorists such as Thomas Hobbes and Hans Morgenthau believe, is an inherent feature of human affairs rather than a primitive, historical stage out of which humankind is about to emerge. As one of America's Founding Fathers, James Madison, believed, power – even in the hands of democrats – can be abused and must always be balanced by countervailing power.[9] Yet, even such thoughts as these need not lead to despair and resignation over the prospects for liberal values in a less than perfect world.

In contrast to the Kantian belief in inevitable progress toward a liberal order, one can juxtapose the British historian E.H. Carr's conception of liberalism's place in human affairs. In his *The Twenty Years' Crisis, 1919–1939: An Introduction to the Study of International Relations* (1951), Carr argued that the success of liberalism (or what he called Idealism) and its values is always contingent.[10] Carr argued that the emergence and survival of a liberal and stable international order, such as the nineteenth-century Pax Britannica or the post-World-War-II era of Western domination, were dependent upon favorable economic, political, and technological factors. When these favorable circumstances have disappeared, as began to happen in the closing decades of the nineteenth century and may again be occurring in the closing decades of the present century, the ascendancy of liberal values such as the belief in peace and free trade has been undermined and human affairs have reverted to their more basic Hobbesian character. For liberalism to succeed, Carr argued, it must be joined with power. Or, in his formulation, idealism and realism must go together.

What Carr's realist interpretation of liberal eras suggests is that a stable and liberal international order must be based on a strong political, economic, and ethical foundation. For idealism and realism to become united, there are certain prerequisites. First of all, there must be an international *distribution* of economic, political, and military power generally favoring the liberal economic and political status quo; in other words, societies favoring liberal values must be in the ascendancy. Secondly, the major powers in the international system must accept the *legitimacy* of the existing liberal economic and political status quo; this requirement means that no powerful state, in the words of former American Secretary of State Henry Kissinger, "like Germany after the Treaty of Versailles ... expresses its dissatisfaction in a revolutionary foreign policy".[11] And, thirdly, the liberal international economic and political order must be governed by a set of generally accepted rules or international *institutions*; these norms and institutions must meet the interests and moral commitments of at least the dominant powers. Until and unless all three of these prerequisites are met, the prospects for a stable and liberal international order are quite limited.

This essay will address the issue of international order in the post-Cold-War era from this "realist" perspective and will discuss the prospects for a more benign, legitimate, and stable international order. With the defeat of fascism in World War Two and of Soviet Communism in the Cold War, is the world undergoing an uneasy yet steady transformation toward a liberal international order? Or, with the absolute decline of the Soviet Union and the relative decline of the United States, are we witnessing once again the cycle of great powers out of which will eventually emerge a new imperial order (or orders) based on the interests of new great powers? The discussion begins necessarily with the decaying postwar international order.

The Cold War International Order

Throughout most of the post-war era the prerequisites of a stable and liberal international order generally did exist. The most important feature of this post-war order was, of course, the dominant position of the United States with its commitment to the political status quo, to an open liberal multilateral world economy, and, despite backsliding, to human rights. The principal American violation of its commitment to liberal values was the Vietnam War, in which the United States, as Raymond Aron cogently argued, shifted from being an "imperial" to becoming an "imperialistic" power.[12] The bipolar stalemate of the superpowers and the clearly defined spheres of influence following the Yalta Agreement, at least in Western Europe, helped stabilize the global situation. The recent tragic events in the Balkans and the acceleration of the proliferation of nuclear weapons no doubt have caused some observers to accept the judgment of Kenneth Waltz that a bipolar international system is superior to its alternatives.[13] More and more people are looking back with nostalgia to the Cold War and asking whether the world was not better off when the stalemate between the two superpowers contributed to international stability.

While the Soviet Union and many Third World nations challenged the predominance of the Western powers and the legitimacy of the world capitalist system, for the first time in the history of the world the major capitalist powers were in essential agreement on the legitimacy of a liberal world economy and the primacy of political cooperation against what they perceived to be the communist and the occasional Third World threat. Despite American rhetoric and Soviet blustering to the contrary, the Soviet Union, with a few major exceptions such as its sponsorship of the Korean War, the placement of offensive missiles in Cuba, and its ill-fated aggression in Afghanistan, took no major direct actions to overthrow the international status quo order and in some ways could be judged a conservative power seeking to retain its gains from World War Two. The third great power, China, following the consolidation of its traditional territories, with the exception of Taiwan, was also more interested in preserving than changing the international status quo. In brief, no major power was sufficiently unhappy with the legitimacy of the international status quo to challenge it through the use of military force.

In the international economic sphere, the principles of a liberal, multilateral world economic regime were embodied in the norms and institutions of the Bretton Woods system. Under American leadership and with the cooperation of the other capitalist powers, the International Monetary Found (IMF), the General Agreement on Tariffs and Trade (GATT), and the World Bank managed the international economy. In contrast to the latter decades of the nineteenth century and the inter-war years, an international effort was made to subject the economic behavior of states to internationally agreed-upon rules. The result was the creation of a highly interdependent world economy that gave the world the most prosperous period in its history. However, the distribution of the gains between North and South was highly uneven and gave rise to profound issues of distributive justice. The belief that the international economic system was unjust and illegitimate led in the mid-1970s to the unsuccessful efforts by developing countries to create a New International Economic Order.

In broad historical terms, the Cold War international political order was a relatively stable one. There were of course a number of very destructive, limited wars, and the nuclear arms race was exceedingly dangerous as well as costly. Nevertheless, the international order was effectively preserved through the system of bipolar mutual deterrence and the conservative foreign policies of the two superpowers. With good reason, John Lewis Gaddis has characterized the Cold War era as "the long peace".[14] The great powers themselves never fought one another directly even though they did employ proxies and, on at least one occasion, were at the brink of nuclear war. In other respects, too, the post-war era was a remarkable and praiseworthy one. It witnessed the reconciliation of France and Germany, thereby laying the basis for a peaceful Western Europe and the beginnings of the effort to create a politically unified European Community. The two superpowers, for their own not necessarily noble reasons, encouraged the dismantling of the overseas European empires and thus assisted in ending three centuries of European domination over non-Western peoples. The United States put the concept of human rights and the Soviet Union put the concept of economic rights on the international agenda for the first time. The open and liberal international economy facilitated the economic development of those nations, particularly in East Asia, that were able to take advantage of the opportunity. These economic and political achievements were of historic significance.

In retrospect, as Samuel Huntington has observed, the outstanding feature of the Cold War era was the economic and political expansion of the United States. American influence expanded into

Western Europe, the Middle East, and Asia until this expansion came to an end in the bloody jungles of Vietnam. On the whole, in my judgment, American liberal imperialism in the Third World was a disaster. But this is not Huntington's point. Huntington's important observation on the most defining characteristic of the post-war era is best made by Huntington himself:

By the year 2000 it should be clear retrospectively that the dominant feature of international politics during the thirty years after World War II was neither the East-West confrontation between the US and the Sino-Soviet bloc nor the North-South conflict between the developed and the underdeveloped countries. Instead, the crucial relationship was that between the United States and Western Europe and the dominant feature of international politics during this period was the expansion of the power of the United States. A crucial feature of this expansion was the extension of American power into the vacuums which were left with the decline of the European influence in Asia, Africa, and even Latin America. ... Where possible of course, the Soviet Union, and later China, tried to move into these vacuums (e.g., the Soviet Union and the Middle East, 1945–1948; China and southeast Asia today). But also almost without exception, the U.S. rather than the communist powers has played the dominant role in replacing European influence. The decline of Europe and the expansion of American influence (political, economic, and military) have gone hand-in-hand. The relation between these changes has attracted relatively little attention because: (a) the European powers have generally declined gracefully and there has been a minimum of overt conflict between the U.S. and Europe; and (b) the shift in U.S.–European power relations has been legitimated by the common need to prevent Soviet or Chinese influence from replacing European influence. Americans have devoted much attention in recent years to the expansion of communism (which has, in fact, expanded very little since 1949), and in the process they have tended to ignore the expansion of the United States influence and presence throughout much of the world in terms of aid, investment, bases, trade patterns, deployment, and commitments. Future historians will, I think, view the Soviet Union, China, and the United States as expansionist powers during this period, but they will view the U.S. as a highly successful expansionist power and the other two as frustrated expansionist powers.[15]

As I shall note below, one of the outstanding features of the post-Cold-War world is the reassertion of Japanese and European (German?) influence with the collapse of the Soviet empire and the recession of American power.

In summary, the postwar international order succeeded in that it managed to avoid the nuclear disaster that everyone feared. The years from 1950 to 1973 were the most prosperous in world history. A number of developing societies, especially in East Asia, were able to begin the long ascent from historic poverty. But the era was neither a just nor, for most of the human race, a legitimate one. On the contrary, the international order served principally the interests of the great powers and their allies. Despite pretenses to the contrary, too little was done to assist ex-colonial peoples. The American doctrine of human rights was too frequently ignored when the objectionable behavior of America's own allies and/or of the United States itself was involved. The Soviet Union under Stalin rivaled history's worst despotisms, and his successors prior to Mikhail Gorbachev were not much better. One could easily continue this litany of international wrongs. Whatever one thinks of this era in human history, however, it is over. With the sudden collapse of the Soviet Union and its empire, one must be concerned about the nature of the emergent international order. While there is some loose talk about the United States as "the one and only" superpower capable of creating a new world order in its own image, it is already quite obvious that this formulation is highly over-simplified, to say the least. A new order is surely forming, but what kind of order will it be?

The Post-Cold-War International Disorder

Today, in the post-Cold-War era, despite the triumph of democracy, the three prerequisites of a liberal and stable world order do not yet exist. Many commentators, in fact, note that the collapse of the Soviet Union and the end of the Cold War have actually considerably increased international instability. Global recession and monetary upheavals have significantly weakened the postwar movement toward a unified, multilateral global economy. The Yugoslav crisis could not have happened, or rather would not have been *allowed* to happen, during the Cold War. At that time co-operation among the major capitalist economies would have stabilized the world economy and tacit American–Soviet cooperation would have prevented the intra-Yugoslav conflicts from reaching the level that they have reached in 1993. Today, weapons of mass destruction are spreading to more and more developing nations. Throughout the world the overall decline of the Soviet Union and the economic decline of the United States have greatly undermined the post-war international balance of military and economic power. In the contemporary era, the balance among these declining powers and rising powers such as Japan, Germany, and China is in flux. While there are grounds for both optimism and pessimism, the fluidity of power relations casts global affairs into a state of considerable uncertainty. In Western Europe, there is still some basis for cautious optimism. The reconciliation of France and Germany ends an enmity that has been at the root of the two great European wars of this century. Germany, which was bypassed by the liberal ideals of the Enlightenment, has been transformed into a democratic society.[16] In the early post-war period the occupying powers destroyed the Bismarckian pact of "iron and rye" that had been a source of German bellicosity. Great Britain, which has historically stood aloof from the continent, has joined the continental nations in their remarkable effort to create a European economic and political community. Never before in modern history could serious claims be made, as many now assert, that a war among the nations of Western Europe has become an impossibility.[17]

Yet, one can not be completely sanguine about the European situation. First, there is the vital question of whether or not the West Europeans will extend the benefits of their new order to their East European neighbors and what will result if such action is not taken. In addition to the fate of the East Europeans and the Balkans, the German Question still exists. The German Question lies at the very heart of modern European history, and, as Henry Kissinger once observed, comes in two basic forms.[18] The Germans may be too weak, as was the situation during the Thirty Years War; in this case, they become the prey of their neighbors. Or else the Germans are too strong, and they prey on these same neighbors. During the Cold War, most Europeans and many Germans began to believe that, with the division of Germany into two parts and with each part in the sphere of influence of one or another of the superpowers, the German Question had at long last been settled. The unification of Germany raises the German problem once again. German society, as suggested above, has most certainly changed, and German leaders want the new Germany integrated into and bound by a larger European political and economic entity. However, the belief of Germans and others that the Europeanization of Germany is necessary to avoid another attempt on the part of Germany to Germanize Europe suggests continued worries over the German problem. Many Europeans continue to fear a united Germany. For the moment, it can be said that the effort of Germany and its neighbors to bind Germany into a stable and legitimate European political order is a truly unprecedented development in international affairs.

Then, there is also the Russian Question. The collapse of the Soviet empire and, subsequently, of the Soviet Union itself, was a unique event. In contrast to other empires, its collapse was not accompanied by a devastating war. As a result, the institutions of the Soviet empire – the monolithic Party, the huge military machine, and the intelligence apparatus – remain largely intact, albeit greatly reduced and partially disorganized. These instruments of power could be revived and exploited by a resurgent, nationalistic ruling clique that wanted to restore Russian influence in the world. It is wrong, therefore, to dismiss Russia as a great power as many contemporary observers do. Russia has indeed lost its East European empire, has been reduced considerably in size, and must share the Eurasian heartland with a possibly nuclear-armed Ukraine. In geopolitical terms, the rimlands of Eurasia have triumphed over the heartland. Yet, it is a very serious mistake to discount Russia. While Russia may not now be, and perhaps never was, a superpower equal to the United States, Russia continues to be a great and imposing power.

Despite its troubles of the moment, Russia may, in fact, have gained some advantages for the long term. It has shed the economic burdens of empire and ideology that shackled its economy and diplomacy. When Russia reappears on the world scene, which it surely will, it will have some important strategic options due to its central position on the Eurasian landmass; it could choose to play those options. Already, it should be noted, Russia is claiming a special regional role for itself in the troubled former border lands of the Soviet Union.[19] If one is tempted to dismiss Russia, one has only to ask how very different the conduct and outcome of the Gulf War would have been if the Soviet military rather than President Gorbachev had determined Soviet policy! Russia has been a great power for over two centuries and has vital interests in Eastern Europe, the Middle East, and East Asia. It is highly unlikely that either a democratic or an authoritarian Russia will neglect these long established interests.

At the other end of the Eurasian peninsula, developments are transforming East and South-east Asia. Although the region has become the most economically dynamic in the world, the end of the Cold War and the steady retreat of American power from the region are undermining what has been a relatively stable political order since the end of the Vietnam War. Foundations of a stable and legitimate post-Cold-War international order have not yet been established in this region, and in fact, the Cold War in Asia is not really over. The division of the Korean peninsula into two hostile and possibly nuclear-armed nations is far from resolved. Japan and Russia have failed to settle the issue of the Northern Islands, with the consequence that Japan is reluctant to assist the struggling democracy of post-Soviet Russia. China still claims Taiwan and other neighboring islands. In South-east Asia, the Cambodian issue is far from settled and Vietnam's neighbors still regard that Leninist state with considerable suspicion. Asia is, in fact, experiencing an unprecedented arms race as rival regional powers anticipate the retreat of American and Soviet power.

Asia also has its Japan and China Questions. Japan appears to be overturning its "peace constitution", which among other restrictions, prohibited the dispatching abroad of Japanese troops. And China, for the first time since the Ming Dynasty, is building a "blue water" navy and is rapidly modernizing its military. Japan now has the world's second most important economy, and China has become the fastest growing economy in the world. If Chinese economic growth continues at its present rate and the country does not fragment, China will one day be the world's largest economy. For the short term, however, the foremost issue in East Asia is that of Japanese economic expansionism. Under Japanese leadership, the East and South-east Asian economies are rapidly being integrated into a new East Asian Co-prosperity Sphere which, this time around, is true to its name. If these developments continue, the redistribution of economic and military power toward East Asia could constitute a political and military challenge to the rest of the world. Over the long term, however, the most critical issues facing Asia and the world are how the Chinese will choose to use their rapidly growing economic and military power, and whether China and Japan will become partners or regional rivals.

In addition to the above issues is the American Question. Although many celebrate the United States as the only remaining superpower, American economic power continues to decline relative to America's major economic competitors. While America's overall productivity is higher than that of its major rivals, the growth rate has slackened considerably. The continuing failure to resolve the federal budget deficit is causing the nation's foreign debt to increase and burden the economy. Although American international competitiveness has revived in recent years, the nation's trade and payments deficits continue to be huge. These signs of economic decline and their manifestations in reduced living standards and higher unemployment cause one to inquire what America's response will be to its diminished position. Will it find the will and the leadership to resolve these difficulties? Or will it adopt reckless policies of trade protection and the like that will harm not only itself but the rest of the world?

Thus far, I have dealt with the political and economic problems that must be faced in the post-Cold-War world. There is yet another important development with threatening implications for world order in the revival of the force of religion in human affairs. The end of the East–West ideological struggle threatens to give way to renewed religious conflicts. If such religious strife were to become prevalent, international politics could revert to the type of religious and ideological conflicts that the Treaty of Westphalia (1648) and the doctrine of national sovereignty sought to eliminate from international affairs. Since that time the guiding principle of modern statecraft has been that only the security interests of states are the legitimate concerns of international relations. No longer would such domestic issues as religion or ideology, which are not easily subject to compromise, be the concern of international diplomacy.

From the perspective of this principle of legitimacy, the unraveling of former Yugoslavia and its consequences are especially dismaying. As Wolfgang Danspeckgruber, my Princeton University colleague, has observed, the internecine conflict in the Balkans is at once a struggle for control of the land and a clash among rival religions. The former Yugoslavia is the confluence of the three great imperial religions that have struggled for pre-eminence in that part of the world for centuries: Eastern Orthodoxy, Roman Catholicism, and Islam. Other religious conflicts are exacerbating international politics around the Eurasian periphery. In the Middle East the struggle between Israel and its Arab neighbors is exacerbated by fundamentalists on both sides. On a wider canvas, Sunni versus Shia, Hindu versus Muslim, and similar conflicts abound. But the development that could become of overriding importance is the revival of Islam as a political force. While the rise of Islamic fundamentalism is misunderstood in many quarters and is greatly exaggerated as a threat to Western civilization, the return of Islam to the political stage is an event of great historic moment. Despite the seriousness of these developments, however, it is unlikely that the world is reverting to the type of inter-civilizational conflicts that characterized international affairs prior to the rise of the modern state system.

As many commentators have observed, we now live in a truly global international system. Modern technologies and the end of the Cold War have united the world. Another effort is being made to make the United Nations an effective instrument of universal peace. Trade and investment are integrating the world economically, even though the movement toward an interdependent world economy has slowed in recent years and economic regionalism in Western Europe, North America, and East Asia has become more important. Nations are learning that they must cooperate to solve global ecological and other problems. Despite these hopeful and promising developments, however, it is unrealistic to argue that international affairs have been or are being fundamentally transformed by economic, technological, and other developments. Carr, not Kant, I believe, will have the last word on this matter.

Some have argued that war is no longer a rational instrument of national policy. Yet, if the world is witnessing "the end of war", as many contend, why are so many of these same individuals concerned about the continuing proliferation of nuclear weapons? The proliferation of nuclear and other weapons of mass destruction is of overwhelming significance. The confrontation in the Gulf would have been very different indeed if Saddam Hussein had been more patient and had waited to absorb Kuwait *after* he had acquired a rudimentary nuclear arsenal. Under such circumstances, it is very doubtful whether the United States and its United Nations allies would have challenged his aggression; he surely would have fulfilled his ambition of becoming the master of the Gulf and its riches. Even though nuclear weapons have made war exceptionally risky, they have also become the great equalizer and, under some circumstances, could be a destabilizing factor in international affairs. The strategy of nuclear "brinkmanship" and the manipulation of the nuclear threat are potentially very dangerous instruments of statecraft. As more and more nuclear powers come into existence, the danger of miscalculation and accidental nuclear war increases. The proliferation of nuclear weapons and other advanced technologies to poor and desperate nations with burgeoning populations that might desire to overturn what they consider to be an illegitimate status quo is a novel and threatening development. In no part of the world is this possibility more ominous than in the contemporary Middle East. War may indeed be irrational and increasingly so, but it is still very much a factor in international affairs.

A second argument is that the nation state and the control of territory are anachronistic. The state, it is argued, is buffeted from the outside by transnational economic and other forces and from the inside by sub-national groupings seeking self-determination. There is obviously considerable truth to this argument. Yet, despite the growth of economic interdependence and the linking of all peoples through modern communications, we still live in a world where an individual's prosperity and good fortune are tied to his/her nationality. And when poor refugees from Mexico, Eastern Europe, or China seek to cross national boundaries in order to share the prosperity, more and more frequently they are being denied entry; the control of territory by states is still very much a feature of political and economic life. The territorial state, which arose in the early modern period, came into existence because it served important political, economic, and emotional needs. The modern state displaced earlier forms of political organization such as tribes and multiethnic empires because it provided personal security and promoted economic development; with the rise of the nation states in the nineteenth century, the nation state has also given individuals a sense of personal identification. While Americans and West Europeans may find the nation state a less useful means to achieve their goals than in the past, most of mankind still looks to the nation state as its salvation. Consider the plight of the Kurd or the Palestinian who has been bereft of his or her own state! In effect, what is taking place as empires and great powers recede, as in the case of the Soviet empire today, is a continuation, albeit on a world-wide scale, of the process of state-creation that began in Western Europe over three centuries ago. From this perspective, the rise of sub-national identities and demands for ethnic self-determination are merely another manifestation of this universal process of state-creation. What is unique and particularly frightening about our own age is that this process and the recurrent phenomena associated with it have been greatly exacerbated by ultra-nationalism, weapons of mass destruction, and population pressures.

A third argument is that the world, especially with the collapse of communism, has at long last become economically and technologically unified. While this point too has merit, it must be noted that the world is still far from being unified politically. In fact, the international community lacks an adequate institutional framework within which its pressing political, ecological, and other issues may be resolved. The presently available alternatives leave much to be desired. For many observers, the United Nations, following its success in the Gulf War, has become the instrument of choice as the most appropriate foundation for building a new world. But the unique circumstances surrounding this rare success of the principle of collective security must be appreciated; since the end of the Gulf War, the criss-crossing interests and resultant stalemates that have traditionally afflicted the United Nations have already reappeared, as one witnesses in Yugoslavia. Other analysts propose that the Conference on Security and Cooperation in Europe, which was so instrumental in ending the Cold War in Europe, be universalized as an instrument of world order. Yet the principle of unanimity on which this body must function limits its usefulness greatly. Others recommend a return to the model of "the concert of Europe", perhaps by extending NATO membership to Russia and thus creating a "security community" encompassing the Great Powers. Or, maybe the so-called G–7 (composed of the advanced industrial powers) should run the world.[20] Proposals such as the above, which revive at the global level the European concept of rule by a concert of the Great Powers, would be deeply resented by those Asian and Third World powers that are most dissatisfied with the international status quo. The proposals for Great Power rule also assume that the Great Powers are more united on the new world order than is indeed the case.

Conclusion

In this final decade of the twentieth century, the stability and legitimacy of the international status quo are under serious challenge. Although the major industrial countries, with some minor exceptions, may be content with the distribution of global wealth and the existing territorial division of the globe, many ethnic groups and organized states reject both the legitimacy of the international economy and existing political boundaries. Emerging powers are asserting themselves; they possess the potential to threaten the international order. Even among the leading industrial economies, some states believe that they do not have a "say" in international affairs commensurate with their newly gained economic and political power. Both Japan and Germany, for example, have requested permanent seats in the Security Council of the United Nations and enhanced roles in the Bretton Woods institutions. Of longer term significance, a majority of the world's population lives in dire poverty and regards the economic status quo as unjust. Previous efforts of Third World states to create a New International Economic Order were thwarted; yet their hope for a greater influence in global economic and political matters has certainly not disappeared. The combination of mass poverty and overpopulation with the spread of nuclear weapons suggests that more and more nations will have both the incentive and the capability to challenge militarily what they consider to be an unjust and illegitimate order. In brief, the international community must not only work toward the solution of these problems but must also create a new set of norms and institutions, or at least modify existing ones, in ways that reflect post-Cold War political and economic realities and, thereby, increase the stability as well as the legitimacy of the system. In the meanwhile, it would be a mistake to assume that the cycle of great powers with its attendant consequences has been broken.

Notes

1. Paul Kennedy, *The Rise and Fall of the Great Powers: Economic Change and Military Conflict from 1500 to 2000.* (New York: Random House 1987).
2. Halford J. MacKinder, "The Geographical Pivot of History". Reprinted in *Democratic Ideals and Reality.* (New York: W.W. Norton 1962), p. 241.
3. Malcolm Yapp, "The Legacy of Empire in Western Asia", *Asian Affairs.* Vol. XXIII (old series, Vol. 79), Part III. (October 1992), pp. 259–270.
4. Stephen Van Evera, "Primed for Peace, Europe After the Cold War", *International Security*, Vol. 15, No. 3 (Winter 1990), pp. 7–57.
5. John E. Mueller, *Retreat from Doomsday: The Obsolescence of Major War* (New York: Basic Books 1989).
6. Both Kant's *Perpetual Peace: A Philosophical Sketch* (1795) and *Idea for a Universal History with a Cosmopolitan Purpose* (1784) can be found in Hans Reiss, ed., *Kant's Political Writings.* Trans H.B. Nisbet. (Cambridge University Press 1970).
7. The definition of "liberalism" as the belief that society is composed of rational individuals capable of choosing for themselves is adapted from a comment by Professor William McNeill at the conference on which this volume is based.
8. The revival of interest in Kantian liberalism among scholars of international relations and others is due largely to Michael Doyle's three excellent articles: "Kant, Liberal Legacies, and Foreign Affairs", *Philosophy and Public Affairs.* Vol. 12, No. 3 (Summer 1993), Part I, pp. 205–235, and Vol 12, No. 4 (Fall 1993), Part 2, pp. 323-353; and "Liberalism and World Politics", *American Political Science Review.* Vol. 80, No. 4 (December 1986), pp. 1151–1169.

9. Doyle, *ibid.*, makes the especially interesting point that, while liberal states may not fight among themselves, they are frequently bellicose toward non-liberal states.

10. 2nd ed., London: Macmillian 1951.

11. Henry A. Kissinger, *A World Restored – Metternich, Castlereagh, and the Problems of Peace, 1812–22* (Boston: Houghton Mifflin 1957), pp. 1–2.

12. Raymond Aron, *The Imperial Republic: The United States and the World, 1945–1973*. Trans. by Frank Jellinek. (Englewood Cliffs, New Jersey: Prentice Hall 1974).

13. Kenneth N. Waltz, *Theory of International Politics*. (Reading, Massachusetts: Addison-Wesley 1979).

14. John Gaddis, *The Long Peace: Inquiries into the History of the Cold War*. (New York: Oxford University Press 1987).

15. Samuel Huntington, "Political Development and the Decline of the American System of World Order". (Toward the Year: 2000: Work in Progress. *Daedalus* 1967), pp. 927–28.

16. The bypassing of Germany by the Enlightenment is the argument of Gordon Craig, *Germany, 1866–1945* (New York: Oxford University Press 1978). The postwar transformation of German society is discussed by Peter Katzenstein, "Taming of Power: German Unification, 1989–1990", in Meredith Woo-Cumings and Michael Loriaux. eds., *Past as Prelude: History in the Making of a New World Order* (Boulder: Westview Press 1993), pp. 59–81.

17. A contrary, less optimistic opinion is that of John J. Mearsheimer, "Back to the Future: Instability in Europe After the Cold War", *International Security*. Vol. 15, No, 1 (Summer 1990), pp. 5–56.

18. Henry A. Kissinger, *The Necessity for Choice: Prospects of American Foreign Policy* (New York: Harper and Brother 1961).

19. *The New York Times,* 1 March 1993, p. A7.

20. A sampling of proposals for a global concert of the great powers is the following: Coral Bell, "Why Russia Should Join NATO: From Containment to Concert", *The National Interest*. No. 22 (Winter 1990/91), pp. 37–47; Charles A. Kupchan and Clifford A. Kupchan, "Concerts, Collective Security, and the Future of Europe", *International Security*. Vol. 16. No. 1 (Summer 1991), pp. 114–161; and Richard Burt, "More Power to the Powerful", *The New York Times*, 14 May 1993, p. A31.

16

Peace, Stability, and Legitimacy, 1990–2025/2050

Immanuel Wallerstein

The period from 1990 to 2025/2050 will most likely be short on peace, short on stability, and short on legitimacy. In part, this is because of the decline of the United States as the hegemonic power of the world-system. But in even larger part, it is because of the crisis in the world-system as a world-system.

Hegemony in the world-system means by definition that there is one power in a geopolitical position to impose a stable concatenation of the social distribution of power. This implies a period of "peace", meaning primarily the absence of military struggle – not all military struggle, but military struggle among great powers. Such a period of hegemony requires, and at the same time engenders, "legitimacy", if by that is meant the feeling by major political actors (including amorphous groups such as "populations" of the various states) either that the social order is one of which they approve or that the world ("history") is moving steadily and rapidly in a direction they would approve.

Such periods of real hegemony – wherein the ability of the hegemonic power to impose its will and its "order" on other major powers is without serious challenge – have been relatively short in the history of the modern world-system. In my view, there have been only three: those of the United Provinces in the mid-seventeenth century, of the United Kingdom in the mid-nineteenth, and of the United States in the mid-twentieth. Their hegemonies, defined in this way, lasted about 25–50 years in each case.[1]

And when such periods have ended, that is, when the erstwhile hegemonic power became once again simply one major power among others (even if it continued to be for some time the strongest among them militarily), then quite obviously there ensued less stability, and correlatively less legitimacy. This implies less peace. In this sense the present period following US hegemony is essentially no different from that which followed British hegemony in the mid-nineteenth century or Dutch in the mid-seventeenth.

But if this were all there were to describing the period

1990–2025, or 1990–2050, or 1990–?, then it would scarcely be worth discussing except as a matter of the technical management of a shaky world order (which is how too many politicians, diplomats, scholars, and journalists have indeed been discussing it).

There is however more, probably much more, to the dynamic of the coming half-century or so of great world disorder into which we have entered. The geopolitical realities of the interstate system do not rest exclusively, even primarily, on the military *rapport de forces* among that privileged subset of sovereign states we call great powers, that is, those states which are large enough and wealthy enough to have the necessary revenue base to develop a serious military capability.

First of all, only some states are wealthy enough to have such a tax base, such wealth being more the source than the consequence of their military strength, though of course the process is one of circular reinforcement. And the wealth of these states relative to other states is a function both of their size and of the axial division of labor in the capitalist world-economy.

The capitalist world-economy is a system that involves a hierarchical inequality of distribution based on the concentration of certain kinds of production (relatively monopolized, and therefore high profit, production) in certain limited zones, which thereupon and thereby become the loci of the greatest accumulation of capital. This concentration enables the reinforcement of the state structures, which in turn seek to guarantee the survival of the relative monopolies. But because monopolies are inherently fragile, there has been a constant, discontinuous, and limited but significant relocation of these centers of concentration all through the history of the modern world-system.

The mechanisms of change are the cyclical rhythms, of which two are most consequential. The Kondratieff cycles are circa 50–60 years in length. Their A-periods essentially reflect the length of time particular significant economic monopolies can be protected; their B-periods are the periods of geographical relocation of those kinds of production whose monopolies have been exhausted, as well as the period of struggle for control of the prospective new monopolies. The longer hegemonic cycles involve a struggle between *two* major states to become the successor to the previous hegemonic power by becoming the primary locus of the accumulation of capital. This is a long process which eventually involves having the military strength to win a "thirty years' war". Once a new hegemony is instituted, its maintenance requires heavy costs, which eventually and inevitably lead to a relative decline of the current hegemonic power and a new struggle for successor hegemony.

This mode of a slow but certain repeated restructuring and recentering of the capitalist world-economy has been very efficacious. The rise and decline of great powers has been more or less the same kind of process as the rise and decline of enterprises. The monopolies hold for a long while but are ultimately undermined by the very measures taken to sustain them. The subsequent "bankruptcies" have been cleansing mechanisms, ridding the system of those whose dynamism is spent and replacing them with fresher blood. Through it all, the basic structures of the system have remained the same. Each monopoly of power held for a while but, just like economic monopolies, was undermined by the very measures taken to sustain it.

All systems (physical, biological, and social) depend on such cyclical rhythms to restore a minimal equilibrium. The capitalist world-economy has shown itself to be a hardy variety of historical system and has flourished rather exuberantly for some 500 years now, which for an historical system is a long time. But systems have secular trends as well as cyclical rhythms, and the secular trends always exacerbate the contradictions (which all systems contain). There comes a point when the contradictions become so acute that they lead to larger and larger fluctuations, which in the language of the new science, means the onset of chaos (the sharp diminution of that which can be explained by deterministic equations), which in turn leads to bifurcations, whose occurrence is certain but whose shape is inherently unpredictable, and out of which a new systemic order emerges.

The question is whether the historical system in which we are living, the capitalist world-economy, has entered or is entering into such a time of "chaos". I propose to weigh the arguments in this regard, offer some guesses about the forms such "chaos" might take, and discuss what courses of action are open to us.

Time Frames and Great Powers

I propose not to discuss at length the elements that I consider to be the "normal" reflections of a Kondratieff B-phase or of a hegemonic B-phase; I will merely summarize them very briefly.[2] I should however make clear that, although a hegemonic cycle is much longer than a Kondratieff cycle, the inflection point of a hegemonic cycle coincides with that of a (but not of course of every) Kondratieff cycle. In this case, that point was circa 1967–73.

The phenomena that are symptomatic of a normal Kondratieff B-phase are: the slowdown of growth in production, and probably a decline in per capita world production; rise in rates of active waged work unemployment; relative shift of loci of profits from profits from productive activity to gains from financial manipulations; rise of state indebtedness; relocation of "older" industries to lower wage zones; rise in military expenditures, whose justification is not really military in nature but rather that of countercyclical demand creation; falling real wages in the formal economy; expansion of the informal economy; decline in low-cost food production; increased "illegalization" of interzonal migration.

The phenomena that are symptomatic of the beginning of hege-monic decline are: increased economic strength of "allied" major powers; currency instability; decline of authority in world financial markets with the rise of new loci of decision-making; fiscal crises of the hegemonic state; decline of organizing (and stabilizing) world political polarization and tension (in this case, the Cold War); decline of popular willingness to invest lives in the maintenance of hegemonic power.

All this, as I have said, seems to me to have been "normal" and historically expectable. What should now happen, in the "normal" cyclical process, is the rise of replacement structures. We should enter, within 5-10 years, a new Kondratieff A-phase, based on new monopolized leading products, concentrated in new locations. Japan is the most obvious locus, Western Europe the second, the United States the third (but what may prove to be a "poor third").

We should also now see a new competition for hegemony begin. As the US position crumbles, slowly but visibly, two successor applicants should flex their muscles. In the current situation, they could only be Japan and the European Community. Following the pattern of the two previous successions – England vs France to succeed to the Dutch; and the US vs Germany to succeed to Great Britain – we should in theory expect, not immediately but over the next 50–75 years, that the sea/air power, Japan, would transform the previous hegemonic power, the US, into its junior partner, and begin to compete with the land-based power, the EC. Their struggle should culminate in a "thirty years' (world) war" and the putative triumph of Japan.

I should say right off that I do not expect this to happen, or rather not quite. I think both processes of reorganization – that of the world-wide system of production and that of the distribution world-wide of state power – have already begun, and in the direction of the "traditional" (or "normal" or previous) pattern. But I expect the process to be interrupted or diverted because of the entry into the picture of new processes or vectors.

To analyze this clearly, I think we need three separate time frames: the next few years; the following 25–30 years; the period after that.

The situation in which we find ourselves today (say since 1991 until say 1995/7/9) is quite "normal". It is not yet one that I would call "chaotic"; rather it is the final acute sub-phase (or the culminating moment) of the current Kondratieff B-phase – comparable to 1932–39, or 1893–97, or 1842–49, or 1786–92, or.... The world-wide rates of unemployment are high, rates of profit low. There is great financial instability, reflecting acute and justified nervousness in the financial market about short-run fluctuations. Increased social unrest reflects the political inability of governments to offer plausible short-run solutions and therefore to recreate a sense of security. Scapegoating within states and beggaring-thy-neighbor among states become more politically attractive in a situation where the usual adjustment remedies seem to provide in fact little instant alleviation of pain.

In the course of this process, a large number of individual enterprises are reducing their activity or are being restructured or are going bankrupt, in many cases never to reopen. Particular groups of workers and particular entrepreneurs will thereby lose out permanently. While all states will suffer, the degree of suffering will vary enormously. At the end of the process, some states will have risen and others fallen in comparative economic strength.

At such moments, great powers are often paralyzed militarily because of a combination of internal political instability, financial difficulties (and therefore reluctance to bear military costs), and concentration on immediate economic dilemmas which leads to popular isolationism. The world's response to the warfare attendant upon the collapse of Yugoslavia is a typical instance of such paralysis. And this, I insist, is "normal" – that is, part of the expectable patterns of the operation of the capitalist world-economy.

Normally, we should thereafter come into a time of recovery. Following the shakedown of the waste (both of luxury consumerism and ecological carelessness) and inefficiencies (whether log-rolling or featherbedding or bureaucratic rigidities) there should come a new dynamic thrust, lean and mean, of new monopolized leading industries and newly created segments of world purchasers to augment the total effective demand – in short, renewed expansion of the world-economy en route to a new era of "prosperity".

The three nodes, as already suggested and as is widely acknowledged, will be the US, Western Europe, and Japan. The first ten years or so of this next Kondratieff A-phase will no doubt see an acute competition between the three centers to gain the edge for their particular product variation. As Brian Arthur has been showing in his writings, which particular variant wins out has little or nothing to do with technical efficiency, and everything to do with power.[3] To power one might add persuasion except that in this situation persuasion in turn is largely a function of power.

The power of which we are speaking is primarily economic power, but backed by state power. Of course, this constitutes a self-reinforcing cycle. For a little power leads to a little persuasion which creates more power, and so on. It is a matter of one country propelling itself into the lead and running with it. At some point, a threshold is passed. The "Beta" products lose out, and there are "VHS" monopolies. My bet is simple: Japan will have more VHS's than the EC, and US entrepreneurs will make deals with Japanese entrepreneurs to get a cut of the pie.

What the US entrepreneurs will get out of such arrangements, as they fully commit themselves in the years between, say, 2000 and 2010, is quite obvious – not being left out altogether. What Japan will get out of it is equally obvious, three things especially: (1) if the US is a partner, it is not a competitor; (2) the US will still be the strongest military power, and Japan for many reasons (recent history and its impact on internal politics and regional diplomacy plus the economic advantages of low military expenditure) will prefer to rely on a US military shield for a while yet; (3) the US still has the best R & D structure in the world-economy, even if its advantage here too will eventually disappear, and Japanese enterprises will reduce costs by taking advantage of this structure.

Faced with this grand economic alliance, the EC members will put aside all their minor quarrels, if they have not long since done so. The EC will probably by then have incorporated the EFTA countries, but *not* the countries of East-central Europe (except perhaps in a limited free-trade area, possibly akin to the prospective relation of Mexico to the US in NAFTA).

Europe (that is, the EC) will constitute a second economic megalith and a serious competitor to the Japan–US condominium. The rest of the world will relate to the two zones of this bipolar world in multiple ways. From the viewpoint of the economic centers of power, there will be three crucial considerations about how important these other countries are: the degree to which their industries will be essential to or optimal for the operation of the key commodity chains; the degree to which particular countries will be essential to or optimal for the maintenance of adequate effective demand for the most profitable sectors of production; the degree to which particular countries will serve strategic needs (geomilitary location and/or power, key raw materials, etc.).

The two countries not yet significantly or sufficiently integrated into the two networks in creation, but which it will be essential to include for all three of the above reasons will be China for the Japan–US condominium and Russia for the EC. In order for these two countries to be well integrated they will have to maintain (in the case of Russia, first achieve) a certain level of internal stability and legitimacy. Whether they can do so, and perhaps be helped to do so by interested parties, is still an open question, but I believe the odds to be moderately favorable.

Peace and Prosperity Again?

Suppose this picture is correct: the emergence of a bipolar world-economy with China part of the Japan–US pole and Russia part of the Europe pole. Suppose also that there is a new, even very large, expansion of the world-economy from say 2000–2025 or so on the basis of new monopolized leading industries. What can we then expect? Would we have in effect a repeat of the period 1945–1967/73, the "*trente glorieuses*" of world-wide prosperity, relative peace, and above all, high optimism for the future? I do not think so.

There will be several differences that are evident. The first and most obvious to me is that we shall be in a bipolar rather than a unipolar world-system. To categorize the world-system between 1945 and 1990 as unipolar is not a view that is widely shared. It goes against the auto-designation of the world as one of a "cold war" between two superpowers. But since this "cold war" was based on an arrangement between the two antagonists that the geopolitical balance would be essentially frozen, and since (despite all the public declarations of conflict) this geopolitical freeze was never significantly violated by either of the two antagonists, I prefer to think of it as a choreographed (and hence extremely limited) conflict. In reality, it was US decision-makers who were calling the shots, and their Soviet counterparts must have felt the weight of this reality time and time again.

By contrast, in the years 2000–2025, I do not expect that we will be able to say that either Japan–US or the EC will "call the shots". Their economic and geopolitical real power will be too balanced. In so elementary and unimportant a matter as votes in interstate agencies, there will be no automatic, or even easy, majority. To be sure, there may be very few ideological elements to this competition. The base may be almost exclusively that of material self-interest. This will not necessarily make the conflict less acute; indeed, it will be harder to patch it over with mere symbols. As the conflict becomes less political in form, it may become more mafioso in form.

The second major difference derives from the fact that the world investment effort may be concentrated in China and Russia during the years 2000–2025 to a degree comparable to the concentration of investment in Western Europe and Japan in the years 1945–67/73. But this will mean that the amount that is left over for the rest of the world must be different in 2000–2025 than in 1945–67/73. In 1945–67/73, virtually the only "old" area where there was continued investment was the US. In 2000–2030, continued investment will have to cover the US. Western Europe, and Japan (and indeed a few other areas such as Korea and Canada as well). The question therefore is, after one has invested in the "old" areas plus the "new" ones, how much would remain (even in small doses) for the rest of the world, and the answer will surely be much less than in the period 1945–67/73.

This in turn will translate into a situation quite different for countries in the "South" (however defined). Whereas, in 1945–67/73, the South did benefit from the expansion of the world-economy, at least from its crumbs, in 2000–2030 it risks not getting even crumbs. Indeed, the current disinvestment (of the Kondratieff B-phase) in *most* parts of the South may be continued rather than reversed in the A-period ahead. Yet the economic demands of the South will not be less but more. For one thing, the awareness of the prosperity of the core zones and the degree of the North–South gap is far greater today than it was 50 years ago.

The third difference has to do with demography. World population continues for the time being to follow the same basic pattern it has been in for some two centuries now. On the one hand, there is world-wide growth. It is fueled primarily by the fact that, for the poorer five-sixths of the world's population, death rates have been declining (for technological reasons) while birth rates have not been, or not as much (because of the absence of sufficient socio-economic incentive). On the other hand, the percentage of world population of the wealthy regions of the world has been going down, despite the fact that the decline in their death rate has been far sharper than that of the less wealthy regions because of the still greater lowering of their birth rate (primarily as a way of optimizing the socio-economic position of middle-class families).

This combination has created a demographic gap parallelling (perhaps exceeding) the economic North-South gap. This gap was to be sure there already in 1945–67/73. But it was less great then because of the still persisting cultural barriers in the North to limiting the birth rate. These barriers have now been largely swept aside, precisely during the 1945–67/73 period. The world demographic figures of 2000–2025 will reflect this far more acute disparity in social practices.

The response we can expect is truly massive pressure for migration from South to North. The push will clearly be there, not only from those prepared to take low-paid urban employment but *a fortiori* from the significantly growing numbers of educated persons from the South. A bigger pull than before will also be there, precisely because of the bipolar split in the core zones, and the consequent acute pressure this will cause for employers to reduce labor costs by employing migrants (not only as low-skilled personnel but just as much as middle-level cadres).

There will of course be, as there already is, an acute social reaction within the North – a call for more repressive legislation to limit entry and to limit the socio-political rights of those who do enter. The result may be the worst of all de facto compromises: an inability to prevent effectively the entry of migrants combined with the capability to ensure second-class political status for them. This would imply that by 2025 or so, in North America, the EC, and (even) Japan, the population socially defined as being of "Southern" origin may well range from 25-50 percent, and much higher in certain sub-regions and within large urban centers. But since many (perhaps most) of these persons will not have voting rights (and perhaps only limited access at best to social welfare provisions), there will be a high correlation of those occupying the lowest-paid urban jobs (and urbanization will by then have reached new heights) with those who are being denied political (and social) rights. It was this kind of situation in Great Britain and France in the first half of the nineteenth century which led to well-founded fears that the so-called dangerous classes would pull the house down. At that time, the industrialized countries invented the liberal state to overcome just this danger, granting suffrage and offering the welfare state to appease the plebeians. In 2030, Western Europe/North America/Japan may find themselves in the same position as Great Britain and France in 1830. "The second time as farce"?

The fourth difference will have to do with the situation of the middle strata in the core zones. These were the great beneficiaries of the period 1945–67/73. Their numbers increased dramatically, both absolutely and relatively. Their standard of living went up dramatically as well. And the percentage of posts defined as being "middle stratum" went up sharply as well. They became a major pillar of stability of the political systems, and it was a very large pillar indeed. Furthermore the skilled workers, the economic stratum below them, came to dream of nothing more than to become part of these middle strata – via union-backed wage increases, higher education for their children, and government-aided improvement in living conditions.

Of course, the overall price for this expansion was a significant rise in costs of production, a secular inflation, and a serious squeeze on the accumulation of capital. The present Kondratieff B-phase is consequently spawning acute worries about "competitivity" and about the fiscal burdens of the state. This worry will not diminish, but indeed increase, in an A-phase in which there are two acutely competing poles of growth. What one can expect therefore is a persistent effort to reduce, absolutely and relatively, the numbers of middle strata in the production processes (including the service industries). There will also be a continuation of the present attempt to reduce state budgets, an attempt which ultimately will threaten most of all these middle strata.

The political fallout of this cutback on middle strata will be very heavy. Educated, used to comfort, middle strata threatened with being *déclassé* will not passively accept such a retrogression of status and income. We have already seen them show their teeth during the worldwide revolution of 1968. To pacify them at that time, economic concessions were made in the period 1970–85 for which these countries are paying the price now, and these concessions will be difficult to renew, or if renewed will affect the economic struggle between the EC and Japan–US. In any case, the capitalist world-economy will be faced with an immediate dilemma of either limiting capital accumulation or suffering the politico-economic revolt of erstwhile middle strata. It will be a bitter choice.

The fifth difference will be in the ecological constraints. Capitalist entrepreneurs have been living off the externalization of costs from the beginnings of this historical system. One major externalized cost has been the cost of renewing the ecological base of an ever-expanding global production. Since entrepreneurs did not renew the ecological base and there was also no (world) government ready to impose taxation sufficient for this purpose, the ecological base of the world-economy has been steadily reduced. The last and largest expansion of the world-economy, from 1945–67/73, used up the remaining margin, which is what has given rise to the green movements and the planetary concern for the environment.

The expansion of 2000–2025 will therefore lack the necessary ecological base. One of three outcomes are possible. The expansion will be aborted, with the attendant political collapse of the world-system. The ecological base will be depleted more than it is physically possible for the earth to sustain, with attendant catastrophes such as global warming. Or the social costs of cleaning-up, limitation of use, and regeneration will be accepted seriously.

If we assume that the third, and functionally least immediately damaging of the three, is the collective path chosen, it would create an immediate strain on the operations of the world-system. Either the clean-up would be done at the expense of the South, and thereby make still more acute the North–South disparity, providing a very clearly-focused source of North-South tension, or the costs would be disproportionately assumed by the North, which would necessarily involve a reduction of the North's level of prosperity. Furthermore, whichever path is taken, serious action on the environment will inevitably reduce the margin of global profit (despite the fact that environmental clean-up will itself become a source of capital accumulation). Given this second consideration, and given a context of acute competition between Japan–US and the EC, we may expect considerable cheating and therefore inefficacy in the process of regeneration, in which case we are back to either the first or the second outcome.

The sixth difference will be in the reaching of two asymptotes in the secular trends of the world-system: geographical expansion, and de-ruralization. The capitalist world-economy had already in theory expanded to include the entire globe by 1900. This was, however, true primarily of the reach of the interstate system. It became true of the reach of the production networks of the commodity chains only in the period 1945–67/73. It is, however, now true of both. The capitalist world-economy has equally been undergoing a process of de-ruralization (sometimes called, less exactly, proletarianization) for 400 years, and for the last 200 with increasing speed. The years 1945–67/73 saw a spectacular jump in this process – Western Europe, North America, and Japan becoming fully deruralized and the South partially but significantly so. It is probable this process will be completed in the period 2000–2025.

The ability of the capitalist world-economy to expand into new geographical zones has historically been a crucial element in maintaining the rate of profit and hence the accumulation of capital. It has been the essential counter to the creeping rise in the cost of labor which the combined growth in both political and workplace power of the working classes has entailed. An inability to recruit new working strata which had not yet acquired either the political or the workplace power to increase the part of the surplus-value they could retain would lead to the same kind of squeeze on the accumulation of capital that is being caused by ecological exhaustion. Once geographical limits are reached and populations are de-ruralized, the difficulties entailed by the political process of cost reduction becomes so great that savings cannot really be achieved. Real costs of production must rise globally and therefore profits must decline.

There is a seventh difference between the coming Kondratieff A-period and the last one, which has to do with the social structure and the political climate of the countries of the South. Since 1945, the proportion of the middle strata in the South has risen significantly – no hard task, since it was extraordinarily small up to then. Even if it rose only from 5 percent to 10 percent of the population, it means that it has doubled in proportion and, given the population increase, quadrupled or sextupled in absolute numbers. And since these are proportions of 50–75 percent of the world population, we are talking of a very large group. The cost of keeping them at the consumption level to which they feel minimally entitled will be impressively high.

In addition, these middle strata, or local cadres, were by and large quite busy/preoccupied in the period 1945–67/73 with "decolonization". This was obviously true of all those living in those parts of the South which were colonies as of 1945 (almost the whole of Africa, South and South-east Asia, the Caribbean, and miscellaneous other areas). It was also almost as true of those living in the "semi-colonies" (China, parts of the Middle East, Latin America, Eastern Europe) where various forms of "revolutionary" activity comparable in psychic tonality to decolonization were occurring. It is not necessary here to evaluate the quality or the existential meaning of all these movements. It is enough to observe two characteristics of these movements. They consumed the energies of large numbers of people, and especially of the middle strata. And they were suffused with political optimism which took a particular form, best summed up in the pithy saying of Kwame Nkrumah: "Seek ye first the political kingdom, and all things shall be added unto you". In practice this meant that the middle strata of the South (and the potential middle strata) were ready to be somewhat patient about their weak economic status, since they felt sure that if during a first 30-year period or so they (the middle strata of the South) could achieve political power, then in the subsequent 30-year period they or their children would find their economic reward.

In the period 2000–2025. not only will there be no "decolonization" to preoccupy these cadres and keep them optimistic, but their economic situation will almost certainly become worse, for the various reasons adduced above (concentration on China/Russia, expansion of numbers of cadres in the South, worldwide effort to cutback on middle strata). Some of these may escape, that is migrate, to the North. This will only make the plight of those who remain more bitter.

The eighth and ultimately most serious difference between the last and the next Kondratieff A-phase is purely political: the rise of democratization and the decline of liberalism. For it must be remembered that democracy and liberalism are not twins, but for the most part opposites. Liberalism was invented to counter democracy. The problem that gave birth to liberalism was how to contain the dangerous classes, first within the core, then within the world-system as a whole. The liberal solution was to grant limited access to political power and limited sharing of the economic surplus-value, both at levels that would not threaten the process of the ceaseless accumulation of capital and the state-system that sustained it.

The basic theme of the liberal state nationally and the liberal interstate system world-wide has been rational reformism, primarily via the state. The formula of the liberal state, as it was developed in the core states in the nineteenth century – universal suffrage plus the welfare state – worked marvelously well. When a comparable formula was applied in the twentieth century to the interstate system in the form of the self-determination of nations and the economic development of underdeveloped nations, it stumbled over the inability to create a welfare state at the world-level (as advocated, for example, by the Brandt Commission). For this could not be done without impinging on the basic process of the capital accumulation of capital. The reason was rather simple. The formula applied within core states depended for its success on a hidden variable: the economic exploitation of the South, combined with anti-South racism. At the world level, this variable did not and logically could not exist.[4]

The consequences for the political climate are clear. The years 1945–67/73 were the apogee of global liberal reformism: decolonization, economic development, and above all optimism about the future prevailed everywhere – West, East, and South. However, in the subsequent Kondratieff B-phase, with decolonization completed, the expected economic development became in most areas a faint memory, and optimism dissolved. Furthermore, for all the reasons we have already discussed, we do not expect economic development to return to the fore in the South in the coming A-period and we believe optimism has thus been fatally undermined.

At the same time, the pressure for democratization has been steadily growing. Democracy is basically anti-authority and anti-authoritarian. It is the demand for an equal say in the political process at all levels and equal participation in the socio-economic reward system. The greatest constraint on this thrust has been liberalism, with its promise of inevitable steady betterment via rational reform. To democracy's demand for equality now, liberalism offered hope deferred. This has been a theme not merely of the enlightened (and more powerful) half of the world Establishment but even of the traditional anti-systemic movements (the "Old Left"). The pillar of liberalism was the hope it offered. To the degree that the dream withers (like "a raisin in the sun"), liberalism as an ideology collapses, and the dangerous classes become dangerous once more.

The Onset of "Chaos"

This then is where we seem to be heading in the next A-period, circa 2000–2025. Although it may appear to be a spectacularly expansive period in some ways, it will be very sour in others. This is why I expect little peace, little stability, and little legitimacy. The result will be the onset of "chaos", which is merely the widening of the normal fluctuations in the system, with cumulative effect.

I will suggest a series of things which will probably occur, none of them being new phenomena. What may be different will be the inability to limit their thrusts and thus bring the system back to some kind of equilibrium. The question is the degree to which this lack of ability to limit the thrusts will prevail.

1) The ability of the states to maintain internal order will probably decline. The degree of internal order is always fluctuating, and B-periods are notoriously moments of difficulty, but for the system as a whole, and over 400–500 years, internal order has been steadily increasing. We may call this the phenomenon of the rise of "stateness".

Of course, over the last 100 years, the imperial structures *within* the capitalist world-economy (Great Britain, Austria–Hungary, most recently the USSR/Russia) have all disintegrated. But the thing to notice is rather the historic construction of states, which created their citizenry out of all those located within their boundaries. Such was metropolitan Great Britain and France, the United States and Finland, Brazil and India. And such also was Lebanon and Somalia, Yugoslavia and Czechoslovakia. The break-up or collapse of the latter is quite different from the break-up of the "empires".

One may dismiss the breakdown of stateness in the peripheral zone as either expectable or geopolitically insignificant. But it goes against the secular trend, and the breakdown of order in too many states creates a serious strain on the functioning of the interstate system. It is, however, the prospect of the weakening of stateness in the core zones that is most threatening. And the undoing of the liberal institutional compromise which we have argued is occurring suggests that this is happening. The states are deluged with demands both for security and welfare which they are politically unable to meet. The result is the steady privatization of security and welfare which moves us in a direction out of which we had been moving for 500 years.

2) The interstate system has also been growing more structured and regulated for several hundred years, from Westphalia to the Concert of Nations to the UN and its family. There has been a tacit assumption that we have been easing ourselves into a functional world government. In a spirit of euphoria, Bush proclaimed its imminence as a "new world order", which met with a cynical reception. The threat to "stateness" and the disappearance of reformist optimism have on the contrary shaken an interstate system whose foundations were always relatively weak.

Nuclear proliferation is now as inevitable and will be as rapid as expanded South–North migration. Per se, it is not catastrophic. Medium-size powers are probably no less "trustworthy" than big ones. Indeed they may be all the more prudent in that they may fear retaliation even more. Still, to the extent that stateness declines and technology advances, the creeping escalation of local tactical nuclear warfare may be difficult to contain.

As ideology recedes as the explanation of interstate conflicts, the "neutrality" of a weak confederal United Nations becomes ever more suspect. The ability of the UN to "peace-keep", limited as it is, may decline rather than increase in such an atmosphere. The call for "humanitarian interference" may come to be seen as merely the twenty-first century version of nineteenth-century Western imperialism, which also affected civilizational justifications. Might there be secessions, multiple secessions, from the nominally universal structures (following the line North Korea has suggested *vis-à-vis* the IAEA)? Might we see the construction of rival organizations? It is not to be ruled out.

3) If the states (and the interstate system) come to be seen as losing efficacy, where will people turn to for protection? The answer is already clear – to "groups". The groups can have many labels – ethnic/religious/linguistic groups, gender or sexual preference groups, "minorities" of multiple characterizations. This too is nothing new. What is new is the degree to which such groups are seen as an *alternative* to "citizenship" and participation in a "state" that by definition houses many groups (even if unequally ranked).

It is a matter of trust. Whom shall we trust in a disorderly world, in a world of great economic uncertainty and disparity, in a world where the future is not at all guaranteed? Yesterday, the majority answered the states. This is what we mean by legitimacy, if not of the states that existed in the present, then at least of those states we could expect to create (post-reform) in the near future! States had an expansive, developmental image; groups have a defensive, fearful image.

At the same time, and this is precisely the rub, these same "groups" are also the product of the phenomenon of democratization, of the sense that the states have failed because liberal reform was a mirage, since the "universalism" of the states involved in practice forgetting or repressing many of the weaker strata. Thus the "groups" are products not only of intensified fear and disappointments but also of egalitarian consciousness-raising, and thus are a very powerful rallying point. It is hard to imagine that their political role will soon diminish. But given their self-contradictory structure (egalitarian but inward-looking) the amplification of this role may be consequently quite "chaotic".

4) How then will we dampen the spread of South–South wars, "minority"–"minority" conflicts in the North, that are one kind of derivation of such "groupism"? And who is in the moral, or military, position to do such dampening? Who is ready to invest their resources in it, especially given the projection of an intensified and roughly-balanced North–North competition (Japan–US vs EC)? Here and there, some efforts will be made. But for the most part, the world will look on, as it did in the Iran–Iraq war and as it is doing in former Yugoslavia or in the Caucasus, or indeed in the ghettos of the US. This will be all the more true as the number of simultaneous South–South conflicts grows.

Even more serious, who will limit North–South little wars, not only initiated, but deliberately initiated, not by the North but by the South, as part of a long-term strategy of military confrontation? The Gulf War was the beginning, not the end, of this process. The United States won the war, it is said. But at what price? At the price of revealing its financial dependence on others to pay for even little wars? At the price of setting itself a very limited objective, that is, one far less than unconditional surrender? At the price of having the Pentagon discuss a future world military strategy of "win, hold, win"?

President Bush and the US military gambled that they could get their limited victory without much expenditure of lives (or money). The gamble worked, but it may seem wise to the Pentagon not to push one's luck. Once again, it is hard to see how the US, or even the combined military of the North, could handle several Persian Gulf "crises" at the same time. And, given the pattern of the world-economy and that of the evolving world social structure I have postulated for 2000–2025, who would be so bold as to argue that such multiple simultaneous Persian Gulf "crises" will not occur?

5) There is one last factor of "chaos" we should not underestimate – a new Black Death. The etiology of the AIDS pandemic remains a subject of great controversy. No matter, since it may have launched a process. AIDS has promoted a revival of a new deadly TB whose spread will now be autonomous. What is next? This disease-spread not only reverses a long-term pattern of the capitalist world-economy (parallel to reversing the pattern of the growth of stateness and the strengthening of the interstate system) but it contributes to the further breakdown of stateness both by adding to the burdens of the state machinery and by stimulating an atmosphere of mutual intolerance, and this breakdown in turn feeds the spread of the new diseases.

The key thing to understand is that it cannot be predicted which variables the spread of pandemic diseases affect more: It reduces food consumers but also food producers. It reduces the number of potential migrants, but it increases labor shortages and need for migration. In every case, which more? We shall not know until it is over. This is simply one more instance of the indeterminacy of the outcome of bifurcations.

Hierarchy and Privilege versus Democracy and Equality

This, then, is the picture of the second time frame, the entry into a period of chaos. There is a third time frame, the outcome, the new order that is created. Here one can be most brief because it is the most uncertain. A chaotic situation is, in a seeming paradox, that most sensitive to deliberate human intervention. It is during periods of chaos, as opposed to periods of relative order (relatively determined order), that human intervention makes a significant difference.

Are there any potential intervenors of systemic, constructive vision? I see two. There are the visionaries of restored hierarchy and privilege, the keepers of the eternal flame of aristocracy. Individually powerful persons but lacking any collective structure – the "executive committee of the ruling class" has never held a meeting – they act (if not conjointly, then in tandem) during systemic crises because they perceive everything to be "out of control". At that point, they proceed on the Lampedusan principle: "everything must change in order that nothing change". What they will invent and offer the world is hard to know, but I have confidence in their intelligence and perspicacity. Some new historical system will be offered, and they may be able to push the world in its direction.

Against them are the visionaries of democracy/equality (a couple I believe to be inseparable). They emerged in the period 1789–1989 in the form of the anti-systemic movements (the three varieties of "Old Left"), and their organizational history was that of a gigantic tactical success and an equally gigantic strategic failure. In the long run, these movements served more to sustain than to undermine the system.

The question-mark is whether a new family of anti-systemic movements will now emerge, with a new strategy, one strong enough and supple enough to have a major impact in the period

2000–2025, such that the outcome will not be Lampedusan. They may fail to emerge at all, or to survive, or to be supple enough to win out.

After the bifurcation, after say 2050 or 2075, we can thus be sure of only a few things. We shall no longer be living in a capitalist world-economy. We shall be living instead in some new order or orders, some new historical system or systems. And therefore we shall probably know once again relative peace, stability, and legitimacy. But will it be a better peace, stability, and legitimacy than we have hitherto known, or a worse one? That is both unknowable and up to us.

Notes

1. See "The Three Instances of Hegemony in the History of the Capitalist World-Economy" in Immanuel Wallerstein, *The Politics of the World-Economy: The States, the Movements, and the Civilizations* (Cambridge: Cambridge University Press 1984), pp. 37–46.
2. Each of the points here summarized briefly has been elaborated at greater length in many essays written over the past 15 years, a good collection of which is included in my *Geopolitics and Geoculture: Essays in a Changing World-System* (Cambridge: Cambridge University Press 1991).
3. See *inter alia* W. Brian Arthur, "Competing Technologies, Increasing Returns, and Lock-in by Historical Events", *Economic Journal*, XLIX, No. 394, March 1989, pp. 116–131; and W. Brian Arthur, Yu. M. Ermoliev & M. Kaniovski, "Path-Dependent Processes and the Emergence of Macro-Structure", *European Journal of Operations Research*, XXX, 1987, pp. 292–303.
4. A more detailed exposition of this effort and its failure is expounded in two of my recent essays: "The Concept of National Development, 1917–1989: Elegy and Requiem", in *Re-examining Democracy: Essays in Honor of Seymour Martin Lipset* (Newbury Park: Sage 1992), pp. 79–88; "The Collapse of Liberalism", in R. Miliband & L. Panitch, eds., *Socialist Register 1992: New World Order?* (London: Merlin 1992), pp. 96–110.

17

Peace, Legitimacy, and the Post-Cold-War World: Where Do We Go From Here?

John Lewis Gaddis

The events of the past year have been disillusioning in the extreme for those who thought that the end of the Cold War would allow the angelic nature of mankind at last to manifest itself in the conduct of world affairs. The international community has failed, most miserably, to settle a brutal civil war in former Yugoslavia, one made all the more appalling by the revelation that it is still possible for Europeans to want to kill other Europeans. Violence reminiscent of fascism appears on the rise elsewhere in Europe even as European leaders avert their eyes from it, preferring instead to concentrate on implementing the Maastricht treaty, a document so arcane in its provisions and so vague in its promised benefits that several of its most important national sponsors do not dare let their own people vote on it. The Marxist–Leninist world has found as much pain as exhilaration in the transition to freedom, democracy, and capitalism; meanwhile large portions of what we used to call the "third world" continue to sink more deeply into conditions of overpopulation, undernourishment, and the resulting predictable discontent. The one remaining superpower, the United States, seems only a shadow of its former self, having demonstrated not only uncertainty over *where* it wants to lead the rest of the world – there is nothing new in that – but also over *whether* it wants to continue to do so.[1] That, for many American allies and some erstwhile adversaries as well, may be the most unsettling thing of all.

In fact, the situation is not all this bad. We should not let our disappointment over the fact that the end of the Cold War did not change human nature cause us to lose sight of what we have accomplished over the past five years, which is to build the most promising basis for a peaceful and equitable international order that we have had in this century. The threat of a superpower nuclear war no longer looms over us, and although the danger of nuclear use has by no means gone away, the scale of the worst-case catastrophe this could now involve is so much smaller than that of the best-case results of what a Soviet–American nuclear war would have produced that it pales by comparison. Indeed, the prospect of any great-power war breaking out for any reason is sufficiently remote to be almost unthinkable:[2] Regional and civil wars are no less dreadful for those who have to endure them, but they are distinctly preferable to world wars for the world as a whole. Democracy and capitalism have spread more widely than ever before; communications link the most remote regions more closely than would have been conceivable a few years ago; and even allowing for situations like that in former Yugoslavia, it is probably fair to say that human rights on a global basis are more widely respected now than they have ever been. Nor is it written anywhere on tablets of stone that Americans *always* have to lead on *every* issue. So before we get too depressed about the current state of affairs, we ought to ask the question: would we like to have the Cold War – or indeed any other period in the modern history of international relations – back again? What we have achieved is by no means perfect; but it is progress, and we should not lose sight of that fact.

Nevertheless, acknowledging progress does not relieve us of the obligation to examine our current difficulties and to try to devise means of alleviating them. It is not enough simply to stumble from crisis to crisis, relieved that the Cold War is over but disappointed at how disorderly its aftermath is turning out to be. We need an analytical framework within which to understand these events; only then can a coherent strategy for coping with them emerge. Such frameworks and strategies are not impossible to achieve: the concept of containment provided such an approach for the West during the Cold War, one whose fundamental assumptions and anticipated results have now been amply vindicated. We have no equivalent geopolitical vision for the post-Cold-War world, however, and it is high time we came up with one. It is, in effect, 1947 all over again.

The Triumph of Self-Determination and Economic Integration?

Let us begin, at least, with a preliminary diagnosis. One of the causes of our post-Cold-War malaise lies, it seems to me, in a tendency to accord praiseworthy ideas excessive deference. Philosophers since Plato have known of the gap that exists between principles and realities, and the practice of statecraft ever since – to say nothing of the conduct of life – has revolved around the need to bridge that gap. The history of the Soviet Union itself, and indeed of the entire Marxist world, reflected the practical difficulties that can arise from the literal application of abstract principles;[3] nor have the Western democracies entirely avoided these difficulties themselves during the course of this century.[4]

Somehow, though, the abruptness with which the Cold War ended, together with the astonishingly peaceful manner in which that happened, gave rise to the curious notion that ideas had triumphed over history, which is the messy process by which ideas get put into imperfect practice. It should have been a hint of trouble ahead that the intellectual community took as seriously as it did Francis Fukuyama's article from the summer of 1989 entitled "The End of History", for if that odd literary effort implied anything at all, it was that we had reached the stage at which concepts like democracy and capitalism could be literally implemented, and that therefore the processes of history – by which Fukuyama meant the compromises that had to be made in translating ideas into reality – had come to an end.[5]

History, of course, did not end, but Fukuyama's article did anticipate a kind of thinking that would become widespread over the next several years. Most Westerners had assumed that the Soviet Union would fight to the death – and perhaps to the death of everyone else as well – before it would allow its empire in Eastern Europe to collapse, or Germany to reunify, or its own status as a state to pass into history. When all of these things did happen with virtually no blood shed, a kind of euphoria set in, based on the belief that we had entered a new era in which the gap between the articulation of principles and their effective implementation had been significantly narrowed.

This post-Cold-War euphoria took two forms. In the political realm, it encouraged the belief that the old liberal vision of a world in which people could choose their own forms of government was not only desirable but feasible as the basis upon which to build a new international order. Self-determination, it now appeared, was a good thing in principle *and* an achievable thing in practice. A renewed and intensified commitment to this idea would produce a more peaceful world with greater respect for human rights than had been possible during the Cold War, or for that matter, in all the international systems that had preceded it.

In the economic realm, post-Cold-War euphoria celebrated the apparent vindication of market capitalism, the absence of which had undermined Marxist regimes throughout the world. This idea, too, was rooted in the liberal tradition; unlike the principle of political self-determination, though, its plausibility had already been demonstrated during the Cold War through the creation of a tripartite economic relationship between the United States, Western Europe, and Japan that had significantly reduced barriers to international trade and investment and thereby produced, or so it was argued, unparalleled material prosperity.[6] Given the eagerness with which citizens of the former communist world seemed to want to have these benefits extended to them, it was only natural to come to see global economic integration as well as not only admirable in principle but achievable in practice.

Accordingly, although more by emotion than by calculation, the triumphant Western democracies fell into a pattern of regarding political self-determination and economic integration no longer as distant goals, but rather as priorities for immediate action. One could see this in the shift that gradually took place in attitudes toward the break-up of the Soviet Union: the initial view had been that only the Baltic States and perhaps Armenia, Azerbaijan, and Georgia would constitute viable sovereignties; but after the August coup in Moscow, the West reconciled itself to the independence and official recognition, as well, of Ukraine and Belarus, and by the end of the year to that of all the remaining non-Russian republics.[7] Meanwhile, the reunification of Germany and the prospect of having to deal with an expansion of capitalism into Eastern Europe accelerated the movement toward economic integration that was already well under way in the European Community, with the result that the Maastricht Treaty was signed in the same month, December 1991, that the Soviet Union at last fell apart.[8] The year 1992, it was widely expected, would be the *annus mirabilis* in which a new world order based upon the principles of political self-determination and economic integration would finally emerge.

Instead it is no exaggeration to say, quoting a prominent personage, that 1992 turned out to be an *annus horribilis* for both of these principles. Having witnessed how peacefully the Soviet Union had disintegrated, the international community almost automatically – even absent-mindedly – extended diplomatic recognition to the constituent republics of Yugoslavia, despite clear evidence that the break-up of that country was not going to proceed with anything like the ease or the relative peacefulness with which the former Soviet Union had ceased to exist.[9] As a consequence, the international community soon had a bloody three-way civil war on its hands in Bosnia-Hercegovina, with no idea of how to resolve it.[10] Similarly, although fortunately at far less human cost, the architects of Maastricht found themselves unexpectedly in trouble with their own citizens as they attempted to explain the lengthy and complicated document they had negotiated. By the end of the year, the vision of an integrated European economy with a common currency and no barriers to flows of commerce, capital, and labor looked more distant than it had for a long time; and at the same time protectionist pressures were on the rise in the country that had done the most to create an open world economy during the preceding half century, the United States itself. Neither political self-determination nor economic integration, it appeared, were going to be as easy to accomplish as the prophets of the new world order had expected – to say nothing of those who believed that history had come to an end.

So what was going on here? How was it that so many high hopes were dashed so quickly? How had so many bright people underestimated the difficulties they would confront in seeking so literal an implementation of ideas which, while praiseworthy in principle, had hitherto had little practical application? Part of the problem, obviously, was simply wishful thinking. The end of the Cold War had forced a suspension of belief in some of the most fundamental assumptions upon which our understanding of international relations had rested for some four decades;[11] hence it ought not to have been surprising that an equivalent suspension of belief in the existence of practical difficulties regarding integration and self-determination should also have arisen.

But that is only an immediate explanation for what happened. A deeper and more serious cause may lie in our failure to establish whether the principles of political self-determination and economic integration are always and in every situation compatible with one another. Just because ideals share the quality of being admirable does not mean that they will complement each other when put into practice. Indeed, if there is any pattern that emerges from the first years of the post-Cold-War era, it is that the things one does to achieve political autonomy and economic prosperity are not necessarily the same.

Are Self-Determination and Economic Integration Contradictory?

The ideas of political self-determination and economic integration do not seem, at first glance, to be contradictory. Were not both of them rooted in the American federal constitution of 1787, which sought to establish individual rights within a kind of common market? Did they not form the basis of the liberal tradition in Britain during much of the nineteenth century, with its emphasis on representative government and free trade? Was it not Woodrow Wilson himself who most explicitly linked political self-determination with economic integration in his famous Fourteen Points speech in 1918, a linkage that Franklin D. Roosevelt and Winston Churchill then reiterated in the Atlantic Charter of 1941? And was not the whole idea of the Marshall Plan and NATO one of simultaneously containing the Soviet Union while rehabilitating Europe, thereby achieving the twin goals of democracy and prosperity at the same time? It is not at all clear, from a conventional historical perspective, that these two principles do clash; and if that is indeed the case, then we can simply chalk our current difficulties up to a combination of bad luck and occasional mismanagement, while looking to the future with an optimism worthy of Fukuyama.

But there are other ways to read history that are not quite so encouraging. Consider the American Revolution itself, in which the colonists found their right to determine their own political future at odds with their economic interests, which were to remain a part of the British empire. Consider how much self-determination the expansion of capitalism during the nineteenth century actually allowed: Marx did have some basis, after all, for complaining about the effects of industrialization upon human liberty. Consider the difficulties that arose, in Eastern and Central Europe after World War I, in attempting to implement Wilson's vision of a simultaneously democratic and prosperous world: it became all too clear at the Paris Peace Conference and afterwards that economic and political logic did not always correspond. Consider how delicate a compromise the Atlantic Charter really was, because of the tension lying beneath the surface of Anglo-American relations over the future of the British empire and how the principle of self-determination was going to affect it.[12] And consider how far the Cold War world really was from reflecting Wilson's vision: it may tell us something about the contradictions inherent in the ideas of political self-determination and economic integration that the Cold War geopolitical settlement – which wound up insulating about a third of the world from the workings of both of these principles – lasted more than twice as long as the one Wilson so carefully and conscientiously designed.[13]

So we may be in the presence here of one of those fundamental fault-lines in human history: a deep zone of strain that has existed for a long time without our noticing it, because other more striking features of the geopolitical landscape – a great depression, two world wars, the Cold War – have covered it up. But as those features have eroded away, underlying tectonic configurations have become clearer, and the tremors that routinely take place along the self-determination/integration fault-line have become more difficult to ignore. We are, by this logic, simply getting back to normal.

Precisely what is it, though, about political self-determination and economic integration that is, or may be, contradictory? The proverbial woman from Mars, looking at this subject for the first time, might point out that the principle of self-determination would appear to call for breaking up large concentrations of power – like the British empire for the Americans, or the Soviet Union and its empire for those who were subjected to it – thereby bringing the control of government and politics closer to home. Democracy works, in other words, through the diffusion of power, by shifting it from the few to the many. But the principle of economic integration would appear to require individuals and even states to relinquish power, insofar as it involves the right to control their economic lives. They must give up the authority to set prices, divide markets, determine interest rates, establish tariffs, and regulate working conditions by assigning these tasks to international market forces, or to international institutions, or failing that, to some international hegemon capable of providing the order the world economy requires if it is to function.[14] Prosperity occurs, or so it is claimed, when power is shifted from the many to the few.

Now obviously this is oversimplified. Martians, like most outsiders, tend not to be aware of the subtleties and nuances that complicate life; and certainly it would be difficult to sustain the argument that political self-determination and economic integration are contradictory in all respects. The prosperity that comes from economic integration, for example, may well encourage democracy: that form of government does not easily coexist with chronic poverty. It may also be that a certain amount of democracy is required if an entrepreneurial spirit is to emerge in a post-industrial age: innovation does not flourish in rigid, hierarchically-organized systems. Economists would insist that the very genius of market capitalism is that it diffuses power among millions of producers and consumers; political scientists would point out that self-determination increases the number, if not always the influence, of sovereign states.

But it is also true that an uncompromising commitment to self-determination would produce anarchy by creating hundreds if not thousands of individual sovereignties; and an uncompromising commitment to economic integration would produce absurdity by leaving states with no authority at all over the conditions in which their own citizens live. There is, thus, an optimum point somewhere short of anarchy and absurdity with respect to how far one can apply each of these principles. Much of the difficulty we have run into in the post-Cold-War era appears to result from the fact that we have yet to find it.

Self-Determination and Stability

Certainly the principle of self-determination has never been applied consistently for any length of time. After a brief period of experimentation with self-determination in the form of the Articles of Confederation, the United States adopted a federal constitution that created a republic, not a democracy, with the right of the people to control their own government carefully restricted within it. To be sure, Washington paid lip-service to the idea during the European revolutions of 1848, when it lacked the means of providing any other kind of support; but the true American attitude toward self-determination became clear only in 1861–65, when the United States shed more blood than in all their other wars put together to deny that right to a portion of its own citizenry.

Woodrow Wilson's endorsement of self-determination during World War I was motivated as much by the immediate desire to undermine Germany's ally, the multi-national Austro–Hungarian empire, and by the need to counter the ideological appeal of the Bolshevik Revolution, as by any belief that it could be literally implemented. He quickly compromised to meet the demands of allies and to ensure the viability of the new states that were being created in Eastern and Central Europe, even though this meant leaving that part of the world full of disgruntled people whose hopes for political autonomy had been raised but not fulfilled. Much the same thing happened in Asia and the Middle East, where Wilson's rhetoric set off waves of nationalist expectations ranging from those of Jews and Arabs in Palestine to those of Ho Chi Minh in Indochina, none of which Wilson had any serious intention of trying to meet.[15]

Despite Roosevelt's and Churchill's renewed commitment to self-determination in the Atlantic Charter of 1941, the settlement of the next world war wound up being based on its wholesale denial. No one gave the unfortunate people of Eastern Europe an opportunity to vote on whether they wanted to be included within a Soviet sphere of influence, and although American influence was extended, for the most part, with the consent of those who became subject to it,[16] no votes were taken either on such arrangements as the partitions of Germany, Korea, Indochina, and even China itself if one counts Taiwan, as one should, as part of that country. Self-determination was hardly the animating principle of either super-power's policies during the Cold War, and yet that conflict gave rise to a remarkably stable and long-lasting international order: that fact alone ought to give us pause before we too readily assume a direct relationship between self-determination and international stability.

So just what is the nature of that relationship? Wilson would have argued, and may even have believed, that if people are free to choose their own forms of government, they will have little reason to want to overthrow theirs or anyone else's, and that the causes of war and revolution will therefore drop away. There are, it would appear, several difficulties with this proposition:

(1) What is the particular identity that justifies having a state? No one would take the idea of self-determination so far as to extend sovereignty to every individual; but the concept clearly does not confine itself either, at the other end of the spectrum, only to those states that already exist. Otherwise one could never have justified recognizing the successor states of the Austro–Hungarian, Russian, and Ottoman empires after World War I, or, for that matter, of the former Soviet Union and Yugoslavia today. None of the possible bases for state identity – language, religion, ethnicity, geography, ideology – command universal assent, as the history of places like Palestine, Tibet, Cyprus, Northern Ireland, and Québec amply testify. No sooner had the former Soviet republics proclaimed their own independence in 1991 than challenges arose to many of them from groups within their own borders, groups that would never have entertained seriously the notion of having their own state as long as a super-state ruled over them. As Wilson discovered after World War I, the very proclamation of the principle of self-deter-mination can create new expressions of national consciousness even as it legitimizes the expressions of older ones, and it is not at all clear where that process finally stops.[17]

(2) If identity provides no universally applicable basis for state-hood, what about viability? One thing that has limited the practice of self-determination in the past has been concern that the new state would lack the capacity to defend itself, or to sustain its population. The need for defensible borders and the requirement of reasonably self-sufficient economies led Wilson to tolerate departures from

self-determination in such countries as Czechoslovakia and Poland after World War I. But today the international community frowns, much more than it did in Wilson's days, on the idea that new states should fortify themselves against attack, or wall themselves off from international markets. The issue of viability, which once constrained the making of states, therefore carries less weight now; and yet the international recognition of Bosnia-Hercegovina provides a tragic example of what can happen when these old criteria of viability are neglected.

(3) What is likely to be the relationship of the new state to its neighbors? Is it not unrealistic to expect that the creation of such states will sweep away old antagonisms? What is the basis for the belief that if people have the right to choose, they will always choose peace? What is to prevent a people from deciding, by perfectly democratic means, that they hate rather than love their neighbors, and want to "cleanse" their surroundings of them? Aggression and civil violence are not always instigated, in all situations, by authoritarian leaders. They may arise spontaneously from the people, and the creation of a new state, especially if it involves displacing the citizens of an old one, can very much encourage these tendencies.

(4) How does the new state fit into the international community of which it is a part? What happens in the wider world obviously affects the security of individual states; but what if the formation of new states unsettles previously stable arrangements in world politics? It is not at all clear that a proliferation of sovereignties provides any guarantee of a more orderly world: it may do just the opposite. In the absence of empires and with the decline of superpowers, however, who speaks for the interests of the international system as a whole?[18]

We have given insufficient attention to the question of how far the principle of self-determination should proceed in the post-Cold-War world, or to what the alternatives to it might be if we should decide that it has gone too far. We have tended, unthinkingly, to equate self-determination with peace and order; and we have failed to recognize – or to recall from lessons of the past – just how much violence and disorder an excessively literal application of this principle can bring about. We need, in short, to return self-determination to its historical context, which means recognizing that it is a contingent and not an absolute principle; that it will not work for all people in all situations; and that some compromises – perhaps many – may have to be made in applying it.

Integration, Stability, and Prosperity

What about the principle, then, of economic integration? The fundamental premise here, of course, goes back to Adam Smith: that if barriers to flows of commerce and investment are removed, each nation will concentrate on producing what it makes best and all will benefit accordingly. Attempts to manage exchanges of goods and services, whether through mercantilism, protectionism, or other less overt means, only perpetuate inefficiencies; the wider and more open the market-place the more efficiently the economy operates. As in the case of self-determination, though, there is reason to question whether this principle really works that way in practice, for several reasons:

(1) Our historical experience with economic integration is more limited than most people realize. There has never been a true free trade regime, in which commodities, capital, and labor crossed international boundaries with no restrictions at all. Trade has flowed freely within regional markets, but almost always under the auspices of an imperial or quasi-imperial structure that was never intended to distribute benefits impartially. The closest the world has come to an economic integration that linked sovereign states were the systems of *relative* free trade presided over by Great Britain during most of the nineteenth century and by the United States during the decades that followed World War II. But these too were empires of a sort, and although the states that participated in them probably did benefit from doing so, the hegemons who ran them did so disproportionately. The European Community purports to seek economic integration in the absence of a dominant hegemon, but its membership is much more restricted than was that of earlier British and American hegemonic systems; it originated early in the Cold War under the sponsorship of the Americans,[19] and even today it is hardly a relationship among equals. The belief that all nations will prosper to the same extent from economic integration remains, therefore, unconfirmed.

(2) Until quite recently, problems of transportation and communication precluded the development of global markets in any event. Distance imposed a kind of compartmentalization that limited the extent to which economies could integrate, even if the governments under whose authority they operated would have been willing for them to do so. It is only within the past two decades that reductions in the cost of shipping commodities and even more striking cuts in the cost of transmitting information have made possible markets

that are truly worldwide for an impressive range of goods and services. But this is a very different environment from the one in which Adam Smith formulated his ideas, and it is not at all clear how well they will hold up in it.

(3) When inefficient enterprises failed in the old system of regional markets, those who worked in them could either shift to other occupations at home, or seek wider opportunities abroad. An eighteenth century English shepherd thrown off land that had been enclosed to improve agricultural productivity could go to work in a nearby coal mine or in one of the new factories that coal-fired steam power was making possible; there was also the option of emigrating to the United States or other relatively unpopulated regions where the language and culture were similar and demands for labor seemed insatiable.[20] With today's multinational corporations, though, the opening of a new factory in Mexico or China can cause workers in Liverpool or Akron to lose their jobs. Differences in language and culture impose few barriers to switching investments as needed to maximize profits; but switching workers to wherever new jobs may be – or even retraining them for alternative jobs at home – is another matter entirely. Both emigration and re-education[21] are likely now to require cultural transformations, something that was not always true in earlier days when smaller and less integrated markets existed.[22]

(4) The trend toward global economic integration, therefore, is generating social pressures that are not easily relieved. Displaced workers continue to look to their governments either for new jobs or for unemployment relief; but when the country itself is losing out to more competitive economies elsewhere, the resources available to provide such benefits dwindle accordingly. There is, as yet, no global social safety-net. Meanwhile, the existence of an international labor market is shifting the racial, religious, and linguistic composition of many societies, a situation very few nations have handled without significant social disruption.[23] And even where immigration is not a major issue, integration tends to threaten those cherished peculiarities that define national character, however illogical these may be from a purely economic perspective.[24] There is such a thing as preserving the right to eccentricity, and people do not easily part with it.

The role of the state is not, and has never been, simply that of facilitating the operations of the market. It is rather that of enhancing the overall well-being of its citizens, both from an economic and a non-economic perspective. Market systems alone, whatever their other virtues, do not accomplish this. It follows that any government that defines its responsibilities solely or even primarily in economic terms is apt to find its political base increasingly fragile: people normally do not vote the way economists think. It should be no surprise, therefore, that the Maastricht Treaty has met with a less than enthusiastic reception within the European Community, or that the North American Free Trade Agreement is not proving easy to sell in the United States. Both of these accords may well go into effect in the end. But the questions they have raised will not disappear; indeed they are likely to become more serious with the passage of time, especially as economic integration is extended more widely to parts of the world where the problem of disproportionate benefits could become even greater.

Legitimacy and Literal-Mindedness

All of this is only to say that the closer one comes to a literal application of the principle of economic integration, as is the case with the principle of political self-determination, the nearer one gets to an unworkable situation in which the authority of the state as we have known it is undermined. Legitimacy rests, after all, upon the willingness of citizens to entrust states with the responsibility of safeguarding and advancing their own interests. Regimes that fail to perform that task sooner or later lose that legitimacy: that is what has just happened to most of those that followed the Marxist–Leninist path. But oppression and incompetence are not the only conditions that can erode official authority: it can also be compromised if the standards we expect from states, and from those who lead them, are set too high.

It is commonplace these days to deplore the absence of effective leadership: nowhere in the post-Cold-War world, it sometimes seems, is there a politician who commands respect. What is the likelihood, though, that so many countries would have chosen ineffective leaders at just the same time? Statistical odds alone make such a triumph of mediocrity seem improbable. The real crisis of leadership today may well result from our current habit of expecting political self-determination and economic integration at the same time. In our euphoria over how the Cold War ended, we may have established standards that no state, or coalition of states, can hope to achieve. It would hardly be surprising, under such circumstances, if the reputations of all states and of all leaders were to suffer as a result.

Some people, of course, might see this as a good thing. There is a tendency, especially in intellectual and academic circles, to distrust all power; governments and governors are, by definition, its most visible repositories. They are by no means the only ones, though: indeed the case has been made for years that power is shifting from states to transnational interest groups, whether of a corporate, professional, social or religious character.[25] Not even the survival of states as we know them can be taken for granted: states have not always existed in their present forms, and they may not do so in the future. But it is difficult to know, right now, just what we would replace states with if the need to do so should ever arise. Because the new centers of power for the most part lack the mechanisms of accountability that most states have evolved over time, it would seem imprudent to allow challenges to state authority, whether from the integration of the market-place or the fragmentation of defunct empires, to proceed too far. And yet that is the direction toward which our current literal-mindedness with regard to economic integration and political self-determination would appear to point us.

This literal-mindedness is, in part, an artifact of the Cold War and how it ended. That conflict provided an unusually receptive climate for economic integration, especially in Europe, because the Americans decided early on to encourage that tendency as one of several paths to containment. It was only natural that a strategy promising wealth as well as security, backed by the most powerful nation in the world at the time, should have made substantial progress, even in the face of old nationalist rivalries. Similarly, the events of 1989–91 made the process of political self-determination look far easier than anyone had previously thought it could be, and that too contributed to a certain literal-mindedness. What may be happening now is that the particular conditions that favored economic integration and political self-determination are beginning to pass from the scene; but our intellectual habits have yet to accommodate themselves to this development.

Another reason for our present literal-mindedness may have to do with the extent to which we compartmentalize categories in our minds, thereby failing to see their interrelationships.[26] How many people who have been enthusiastic about self-determination in Eastern Europe and the former Soviet Union have thought through what the economic prospects of these new countries are likely to be? How many of those who have worked over the years for economic integration have considered what the domestic political reaction to that process may entail? The architects of Maastricht might have done better to shift their attention from the chimeras of common currencies and an agreed-upon definition of "subsidiarity" to the more pressing matters of how one might ensure the success of democracy and capitalism in Eastern Europe and the former Soviet Union. Proponents of German reunification certainly did not give sufficient attention to what the economic and social implications of that action might be for Germany itself and for the rest of the European Community. It is a rare leader these days who can think *simultaneously* about economics and politics, and yet in the real world these subjects coexist, overlap, and interact with one another all the time.

One of the reasons Western strategy worked during the Cold War was precisely that it was not bound by past experience and it was not compartmentalized: the founders of the Marshall Plan, NATO, and the European Community were able to put their immediate past behind them and think creatively about the *interconnections* of politics, economics, and Cold War strategy. One reason the Soviet Union lost the Cold War was that the thinking of its leaders became excessively mono-dimensional, focusing too narrowly on military considerations at the expense of everything else. But how well are we doing today in thinking ahead multi-dimensionally, and how well are we training the coming generation to do so? The trends, I think, are not encouraging.

Strategies and Conclusions

Where, then, do we go from here? How are we to devise strategies for coping with the post-Cold-War world? We should, first of all, not be shy about asking what might seem to be naive questions. What, precisely, do we gain by pushing simultaneously, or even separately, for economic integration and political self-determination? If the answer to this question turns out to be an ideological one – that these things are inherently good in themselves, and that no further benefits need be specified – then that ought to be a signal that pontification, but not thought, has taken place. Truly praiseworthy concepts do not require ideologies to justify them.

Second, we need to give greater attention to the interrelationships among phenomena. Life and politics, unfortunately, do not organize themselves in the way that universities, think tanks, and government agencies tend to. Unless we can change the way we train people to think – unless we can make them see that the real world is multi-faceted and therefore multi-disciplinary – then we are hardly likely to prepare them adequately for the complexities they will have to think about.

Third, we need to revive the art of thinking in contingent, not absolute, terms. We need to recognize that history has not ended, which means that principles will have to be compromised, as they have always been. Ideologies most often fail, not because they have adjusted their principles to fit reality, but because they have attempted to turn those principles, without adjustment, into official policies. We need to be careful not to make the mistake of transforming good ideas like economic integration and political self-determination into inflexible dogmas, however "politically correct" it may be to do so.

Fourth, we need to recognize that although authoritarian empires have collapsed, the need for some authority still remains. Neither prosperity nor democracy will flourish under conditions of anarchy; we badly need to find some center of authority, whether at the national or international level, that can restore at least some of the order the old Cold War system, for all its faults, did provide.[27]

Finally, and related to the above, we need to determine whether the post-Cold-War world is mature enough to construct a generally-accepted framework of order without having to have some hegemon impose it. Europeans invited the United States to play that hegemonic role after both of the great world wars of this century: obviously it did so with far greater skill, imagination, and success following the second of these than after the first. Today, in the wake of the debacle over Bosnia and the muddle over Maastricht, a third invitation is being extended to the Americans to lead once again, but there are no signs as yet that Washington has either the will or the necessary wisdom to accept it. One of the most creative uses of our present adversity, I think, could be to find an acceptable multilateral alternative.

The end of the Cold War presents us with an unprecedented opportunity to build a new kind of international order, free of great power wars hot and cold, from which we should be able to approach more closely than ever before the ancient goals of justice, prosperity, and liberty. We will not construct that world, though, by insisting on perfectionism. The conduct of statecraft will always involve the compromising of principles, something the most skilful practitioners of statecraft have known all along. If we insist on treating all such compromises as cynicism, if we prefer ideological purity at the expense of practical accomplishment, then we are sure to undermine whatever legitimacy the new international order has attained by overcommitting it before it is even fully in place. Millennial thinking is the last thing we need, now that the millennium is finally upon us.

Notes

1. The Clinton Administration's hasty disavowal of the so-called Tarnoff doctrine has by no means refuted the accuracy of the observations the new Under-Secretary of State is alleged to have made.
2. See John Mueller, *Retreat from Doomsday: The Obsolescence of Major War* (New York: Basic Books 1989).
3. For more on this, see John Lewis Gaddis, "The Tragedy of Cold War History", *Diplomatic History*, XVII (Winter, 1993), pp. 11–12.
4. A point made years ago with great force and some justification in George F. Kennan, *American Diplomacy: 1900–1950* (Chicago: University of Chicago Press 1951).
5. Francis Fukuyama, "The End of History?" *The National Interest*, #16 (Summer, 1989), pp. 3–18.
6. Robert Gilpin, *The Political Economy of International Relations* (Princeton: Princeton University Press 1987), provides an excellent description of this system.
7. Note the speed with which the Bush Administration abandoned the premises of the President's own speech of 1 August 1991, in Kiev, in which he had warned against "suicidal nationalism based on ethnic hatred". [*The Economist Yearbook: 1991 in Review* (London: Economist Books 1992), p. 91.]
8. *Ibid.*, pp. 95, 106–7.
9. See, for an example of such warnings, Misha Glenny, *The Rebirth of History: Eastern Europe in the Age of Democracy* (London: Penguin Books 1990), pp. 118–42.
10 Secretary of State Warren Christopher has now acknowledged that "there were serious mistakes made in the whole process of recognition of the former Yugoslav states of Croatia and Slovenia", and has charged that "the Germans bear a particular responsibility in persuading their colleagues and the European Community" to follow this course, which in turn provoked the outbreak of civil war in Bosnia. [*International Herald Tribune*, June 19–20, 1993]. Needless to say, the German government does not agree with this assessment.
11. John Lewis Gaddis, "International Relations Theory and the End of the Cold War", *International Security*, XVII (Winter, 1992/93), pp. 5–58.
12. See David Reynolds, *The Creation of the Anglo-American Alliance, 1937–1941: A Study in Competitive Co-operation* (Chapel Hill: University of North Carolina Press 1982), especially pp. 286–94.
13. I have discussed this point at greater length in John Lewis Gaddis, *The*

Long Peace: Inquiries into the History of the Cold War (New York: Oxford University Press 1987), pp. 215–45.

14. See Gilpin, *The Political Economy of International Relations*, pp. 72–73; also Robert O. Keohane and Joseph S. Nye, *Power and Interdependence: World Politics in Transition* (Boston: Little, Brown 1977), pp. 42–46.

15. The best discussion is N. Gordon Levin, *Woodrow Wilson and World Politics: America's Response to War and Revolution* (New York: Oxford University Press 1968), especially pp. 236–51.

16. See Geir Lundestad, "Empire by Invitation? The United States and Western Europe, 1945–1952", *Journal of Peace Research*, XXIII (September, 1969), pp. 263–77.

17. Thomas J. Knock, *To End All Wars: Woodrow Wilson and the Quest for a New World Order* (New York: Oxford University Press 1992), pp. 248–50.

18. Certainly not the United Nations, which has yet to demonstrate a capacity to act coherently with respect to designing a stable international system.

19. John W. Young, *Cold War Europe, 1945–1989: A Political History* (London: Edward Arnold 1991), pp. 29–30.

20. Paul Kennedy provides a fine discussion of the importance of both technological innovation and overseas emigration in averting a nineteenth century Malthusian crisis in Great Britain in *Preparing for the Twenty-First Century* (London: Harper Collins 1993), pp. 3–10.

21. I have in mind here the fact that job retraining today – even in many low-paying service industries – requires learning to use computers and their associated technology, a feat that, for a pre-computer generation, may approximate the difficulty of having to learn a foreign language in middle age.

22. Kennedy has pointed out yet another difficulty: that whereas "earlier migration went from the technologically advanced societies into the less advanced societies, contemporary migrations chiefly move from less developed societies toward Europe, North America, and Australasia". [*Preparing for the Twenty-First Century*, p. 42.]

23. Although nations like the United States, Canada, and Australia, perhaps because their entire history is one of immigration, seem to handle the problem better than most.

24. For example, the French insistence that the national interest requires subsidizing small farmers, the equivalent British belief about coal-miners, and the German love affair with the *Deutschmark*. There are innumerable other examples.

25. The classic argument, of course, is Keohane and Nye, *Power and Interdependence*. But see also, for a more recent discussion, James N. Rosenau, *Turbulence in World Politics: A Theory of Continuity and Change* (Princeton: Princeton University Press 1990).

26. It would be interesting to consider to what extent this tendency reflects the trend toward professionalization, both within academia and government. The professionalization of disciplines, however praiseworthy it might be, is more likely to produce a contraction rather than an expansion of vision.

27. In this connection, see William H. McNeill's characteristically insightful essay, in this volume, which suggests the durability of polyethnic empires.

Part VI

Conclusions

18

Conclusions

Paul Kennedy

Almost one hundred years ago, the Great Powers of Europe were deeply concerned about the likely "fall" of one of their number, and about the related issues of "peace, stability, and legitimacy". The declining Great Power was, of course, the Ottoman Empire, often cruelly referred to by contemporaries as "the sick man of Europe". Its relative power had deteriorated throughout the nineteenth century, even as that of other states (Russia, Britain, Germany, Italy) had grown. Its internal condition, always rather weak, was exacerbated by economic stagnation, a feckless and incompetent government, and the continued challenge of ethnic minorities and subject peoples to Ottoman rule. In 1894 Sultan Abdul Hamid II recommenced the persecution of his Armenian subjects, causing such moral repulsion among at least British public opinion that Lord Salisbury's government in London was forced to consider some form of intervention; but that idea in turn alarmed other governments and simply heightened the controversy.[1]

It is easy to see how the possible collapse of the Ottoman Empire a century ago provoked examination of the related but sometimes contradictory issues of peace, stability, and legitimacy. During the preceding decades, the Great Powers had several times (1876–78, 1885–87) come close to war over the future of the Ottoman Empire and associated Balkans issues, so it was natural to apprehend that the first casualty of the Ottoman Empire's collapse would be *peace*. None of the Great Powers actively sought war over this issue; but virtually all of them were willing to risk hostilities to prevent a rival gaining too much from the Empire's demise. Moreover, because two of the interested parties, Britain and Russia, were *global* Great Powers, the conflict would not be a merely local event but would instead stretch from the North Sea to East Asia.

It went without saying, therefore, that the fall of the Ottoman Empire had the potential to produce great and perhaps unimaginable instabilities. As things stood, Europe enjoyed a "balance" of power between the Triple (Germany; Austria–Hungary; Italy) and

Dual (Russia; France) alliances, with Britain uncommitted by treaty but inclining towards the former. If the disintegration of the Ottoman Empire led to Russian control of the Straits and south-east Balkans, the implications for Austria–Hungary – the next candidate to be "sick man of Europe"– were ominous. If, however, Russia's foes gained Constantinople, the Tsarist regime would confront massive internal dislocations, especially in southern grain-exporting regions. Failure abroad, nineteenth-century autocrats recognized, increased the prospects of instability at home,[2] a fact that would become even more clear in 1905/06. Yet, was the continued existence of the Ottoman Empire really a factor for stability, when its internal rule provoked repeated uprisings by minorities whose plight attracted the sympathies (and potential intervention) of external supporters?

Finally, was not the real source of the crisis the fact that the Ottoman Empire's legitimacy was being called into question? The underlying principles of the post-1814 Concert of Europe rested upon the assumption of non-interference in the internal affairs of the Powers; while cooperation to preserve international stability was a sought-after common good, that purpose was assumed regardless of the internal conditions of the member-states, which after all ranged from Republican France to Tsarist Russia. This was why, for example, the Western-European nations had not interfered in Russia's further suppression of Polish liberties in 1863, although liberal public opinion was much angered by the reported outrages. Nonetheless, however respected this policy of non-interference – and conservative regimes, hostile to the agitations of their own ethnic minorities, were generally the firmest in respecting it – it might perhaps have its limits if the brutalities were too great; and the slaughter of Armenians in downtown Constantinople, appalling the Western embassies, came close to that watershed.

Furthermore, by the close of the nineteenth century the statesmen of Europe had to pay attention to the growing influence of public opinion. The spread of the middle class and the rising rates of literacy, *plus* extensions of the franchise, interacted with the emergence of mass-circulation newspapers whose editors were interested in foreign and imperial affairs.[3] First-hand and blood-curdling accounts of slaughters, wired via Reuters or Havas by a journalistic witness in time to be read over breakfast, were circumventing government control of information from abroad and provoking what the "old diplomacy" abhorred – a heated public debate precisely about the internal affairs of another state. The classic case here had been Gladstone's 1876 crusade against the "Bulgarian atrocities", which threw Disraeli's cabinet into acute confusion over its Turkey policy and caused great concern in every foreign office of Europe for its implications;[4] and in some respects the 1894–95 Armenian crisis was a replay of that earlier event. Obviously, the more a free press and parliamentary democracy in any country prevailed, the greater the prospect of public opinion influencing official policy; even the autocratic regime of Tsar Nicholas II was increasingly sensitive to public pressures about the internal conditions of Turkey.[5]

Falls, "Overstretch", and the Sources of Power

As it turned out, deterred by the opposition of the other Great Powers and then the reluctance of most of his cabinet to risk war, Salisbury was unable to go ahead with measures to punish the Turks, and the crisis slowly subsided. However unpleasant the Sultan's regime, peace and stability were more powerful than the question of legitimacy.

This century-old incident is extremely useful for our purposes because it both contains all of the complex issues addressed by this book *and* demonstrates their interconnectedness. Like the other case-studies in the story of *The Rise and Fall of the Great Powers*,[6] the condition of the Ottoman Empire possessed certain basic characteristics. To begin with, the process of rise and fall was usually an elaborate and (more especially) a lengthy one, lasting generations or even centuries rather than decades: few Great Powers expanded and collapsed as swiftly as the Third Reich, although even that story of Nazi imperialism might be viewed as a particularly nasty and extreme phase in the longer evolution of Germany's power-relationships with its neighbors.[7] Generally, the downward part of the cycle did not follow a smooth, unbroken trajectory but tended instead to contain periods of setback, crisis, and earnest debate, interspersed with other periods when a collapse seemed less likely, perhaps even with times when revival and renewal looked possible. Some powers declined, revived, and declined again.[8] As Professor Samuel Huntington observed, with respect to the late-1980s debate about the "relative decline" of the United States, this was not the first time such a controversy over America's future had occurred.[9] Perhaps all this is simply the consequence of the fact that Great Powers (and especially Number One powers), having acquired so much territory and influence, take a lengthy time to cede the accumulated layers. But even if that is the historical record, will it be true in the future, when the pace of technological and scientific change is faster, ideas and news travel so much more quickly, and the pressures upon statesmen to take decisive actions are more intense?

The *causes* of a Great Power's fall, and the manifestations of that collapse, offer a much more variegated picture. No doubt all of them decline because of "overstretch", which merely means that there exists a mismatch between a Great Power's obligations and its capabilities, between its desired policies and its actual resources. But there is a significant difference between Great Powers that collapse at the end of a protracted military struggle, like the Austro–Hungarian Empire in 1918, and those that, while weakened and buffeted by wars, fade away more gradually, like Spain in the eighteenth century and Britain in the twentieth. We know *when* the Third Reich fell; but the point at which Britain was no longer a Great Power is much less clear: did it occur at the Suez crisis (1956), or when India gained its independence (1947), or had its loss of real *independence of action* – one way of defining a Great Power – actually taken place during the Second World War itself, as the Empire grew ever more reliant upon its American ally?[10]

This raises the further complication of how power is measured, and what the different sources and components of power are. More traditional accounts prefer to point to the evidence of "hard", tangible assets: military strength, manifested in success during wartime and substantial armed forces available in peacetime to defend national interests and deter aggressors; plus economic strength, meaning large productive facilities, a broad technological base, and considerable financial assets, all of which could be drawn upon to sustain the front-line fleets, armies, and air forces.[11] In that respect, the better the symbiosis between the military and the economic arms of power – which would always be relative to the circumstances of the time, and therefore subject to change – the more likely would be the prolongation of a Great Power's tenure. Of the nations examined here, Britain and the United States were both able to develop mutually-reinforcing elements of naval/military and manufacturing/financial power to sustain their international position for generation after generation. By contrast, other nations were often more one-sided in the sources of their Great-Power status. For example, during much of the eighteenth century, the Dutch Republic was probably the leading financial and commercial nation in the world, but Amsterdam's bankers alone could not tilt the balances against French land power and British sea power. More obviously, the Austro-Hungarian Empire in 1914, and even more Japan in the 1930s and the USSR in the 1980s, possessed very considerable military forces, but the latter rested upon such inadequate or inefficiently used economic foundations that the military machine could not sustain itself – indeed, the military "top-heaviness" to some degree exacerbated the relative economic weakness.

More recently, the elements of "soft" (non-military) power have been introduced into this debate: the influence of cultural images, the important role of ideas, the ability of a dominant culture to transmit messages to societies on the other side of the Earth, the global reach of multinational corporations, it is argued, all possess at least the potential *to affect outcomes,* which is one very general definition of "power".[12] This argument is attractive initially, and may have something in it; but it is often much more difficult to measure the influence of "soft" power than that of military force. Does the global reach of, say, Hollywood movies in today's world enhance American power – or is the effect a mixed one, provoking resentments (e.g., in France, Malaysia, Singapore, Islamic societies) as much as admiration and emulation? Is this an argument that is used as a form of psychological consolation by elites aware that their nation's relative strategic and economic power has declined, as in Paris's determined efforts to project French culture and language into (say) East-Central Europe or, more notoriously, the claim of British statesmen in the late-1940s and early-1950s that their country could at least still exert influence by "playing Greece to America's Rome", an assumption which received a rude shock during the Suez crisis when the *real* foundations of national power were demonstrated.[13]

Instinctively, then, today's realists feel that facts like the size of the US federal deficit, the new position of Germany in Europe, or the possibility of regime failure in Russia, have more to tell us about *power* than Coca-Cola sales in Brazil or the number of people playing cricket in the former British Empire. Perhaps the most sensible compromise here is to require evidence of where "soft power" (or, for that matter, any type of power) has actually worked – as, for example, in the role of the Catholic Church in weakening the legitimacy of the Communist regime in Poland, thereby providing an ironic riposte to Stalin's quip about "how many battalions has the Pope?" When claims are made about a nation's cultural or ideological power but the evidence of its influence upon policy is not given or remains only circumstantial, we should remain skeptical.

Falls, Peace, and Stability

That the rise and fall of Great Powers interacts with issues of peace and stability is close to being a truism. In strict logic, the long-term processes behind a country's relative rise – the growth of its population, the development of its industry and commerce, the enhancement of its resources – are not inherently prejudicial to peace; and there are distinguished contemporary scholars who point to "the rise of the trading states" and posit the question of whether a nation can become a Great Power economically *without* building up its military strength to alter the strategic balances.[14] Perhaps that will be true in the future, given the existence of nuclear weapons and the globalization of world production and finance, both of which are held to reduce the arguments in favor of nations going to war. But the historical record points to an intimate connection between "rise and fall" and "peace and war". In the mercantilist era, where commercial expansion was attended and most usually *achieved* by trade wars, it was virtually impossible to separate the economic from the military dimensions of policy: profit and power went hand in hand, mutually reinforcing the rising states and working to the disadvantage of those that were relatively losing (or never possessed) wealth and might.[15] In any case, no Great Power's rise was unattended by war, although there obviously was a difference between, say, Russia and Germany's expansion *through* wars and the growth of American power in the twentieth century, which was *accompanied* by wars but, at least outside its own hemisphere, not driven by a desire for territorial gain. Even the Habsburg Empire, initially cobbled together more through marriage than wars, was involved in conflict after conflict as its relative power in Europe grew. The lack of a global sovereign, and the competitive instincts of nation states as their relative influence waxes and wanes, give reinforcement to the arguments of today's Realist school that it would be unwise to assume a lasting Great-Power peace in the decades ahead.

The issue of stability also forms an inextricable part of the dynamic of rise and fall, albeit in many different, often contradictory ways. Each Great Power strove to create internal stability, which was manifested in various expressions of authority – laws, customs, taxes, uniforms, flags, and so on. There was usually an "imperial" language (French in West Africa, English in the Indian sub-continent, Russian in central Asia) which took precedence over the myriad of indigenous tongues. There were also attempts to recruit locals into the imperial service, and to find what Ronald Robinson termed "collaborators" among elite groups, to allow for a more efficacious rule. Although there might be occasional turbulences and revolts (the Indian Mutiny, or the Hungarian uprising of 1956), peace and stability were general characteristics within the Great Powers' *imperium* and were in fact claimed as rationales for the rule, as a form of public good: hence the use of such terms as the *Pax Britannica* or *Pax Sovietica*. To be sure, there are different types of peace, and many members of an imperial society probably found it less "peaceful" than those enjoying real power. But whenever arguments were advanced for the liberalization of European minorities, or the decolonization of India and Africa, the counter-argument most favored by conservatives was that such moves would create instabilities and local conflicts as successor groups battled for control. Great-Power rule, it was claimed, was the antidote to anarchy.

On the whole, the conservatives' argument has been correct. There are of course examples of a peaceful transfer of power, whether it was in Africa in the early 1960s or East-central Europe (though not Romania) in 1989. But the fact that Great Powers usually ruled over an ethnically heterogeneous collection of peoples; that internal transfers or migrations of populations had occurred during the long period of imperial rule, creating minorities within minorities; that many internal borders had been drawn to reflect administrative convenience, *not* the actual location of ethnic groups; and that, with a few exceptions, the empire had not prepared its subjects for self-rule, had often fiercely opposed it, and only conceded independence in the turmoil of its own collapse, all produced conditions which made for subsequent local conflicts and wars. In that respect, the present convulsions in former Soviet republics are analogous to, say, the communal strife in the Indian sub-continent in 1947.

Legitimacy: Past and Future

Of all the elements covered in these investigations, that of "legitimacy" is clearly the trickiest. In many instances, far from existing in harmony with peace and stability, legitimacy was in tension with them – as, for example, in the pro-Soviet regimes imposed by Stalin across East-central Europe. The matter is contentious because it requires an answer to the basic question "legitimate to whom?" or "legitimate for whom?" To the many Armenians, Kurds and other non-Turkish peoples struggling to be free from Abd al-Hamid II's rule in 1894, the argument that the Ottoman regime had to be preserved for the sake of international peace and stability was unconvincing, because in their view (and in the view of their Western-liberal sympathizers) the very regime itself was illegitimate.

Questioning the legitimacy of a Great Power's authority – was British rule in Ireland, or Habsburg rule in the Czech lands, legitimate? – has been the characteristic of any group claiming to speak and act for the subject people in question. Historically, the disagreement was settled by *force majeure*: if the rebellious elements were not strong enough, the Great Power's rule was maintained – regardless of whether or not the suppressed minorities deemed it illegitimate. Moreover, because international law traditionally recognized only nation states as legitimate entities and the latter generally opposed interference in a country's internal affairs (out of fear that others would do the same to them), independence movements rarely received full backing even from foreign governments sympathetic to their cause, lest that be regarded as a hostile act. Thus, the Soviet Union may have denounced capitalist-dominated regimes as illegitimate in that they did not represent the working classes, but Moscow never openly interfered when, say, there was a general strike in Britain or France; and in much the same way the West may have regarded recent Communist governments in Eastern Europe as illegitimately forced upon their citizens, but did not seek to subvert them, indeed, maintained diplomatic relations with them!

This issue of legitimacy is likely to grow in significance as the twenty-first century unfolds, and for two reasons. The first is that, eschewing the traditional diplomatic habit of non-interference, international organizations and public opinion are increasingly raising the issue of human rights *within* states. Motivated first by a reaction to the horrors of National Socialism, and then sustained by fresh examples of internal atrocities in the post-1945 decades, the argument that regimes should be measured according to their respect for human rights and the rule of law promises repeated controversy in the future; this is so because it both challenges the non-interference tradition *and* it provokes debate over the ideological and cultural norms employed in judging a country's internal practices. The first, the contradiction between respecting nation states as sovereign and insisting upon universal human rights codes, has already been reflected in ambiguous references in recent publications from the UN Secretary-General's office.[16] And the second issue, of *"whose* definition of human rights should prevail?"*, engendered very strong debate as recently as the June 1993 conference in Vienna on international human rights, where various Asian and African spokesmen denounced what they saw as a Western attempt to impose its mores upon the rest of the world. With a modern communications revolution bringing gruesome details of human rights abuses and atrocities to international opinion in a much more direct and vivid way than was possible a century ago, this tension is unlikely to go away.

The second reason why legitimacy issues will impact upon foreign affairs is the growing call that the *world order itself* is not legitimate, especially at the economic level. Since the richer one-quarter of the nations of the globe possess three-quarters of its wealth and consume three-quarters of its resources, does that not call for readjustment if one is really concerned about long-term peace and stability? How can prosperous but blinkered Western states criticize the legitimacy of the *internal* arrangements of an African or Asian nation, the argument goes, when the *international* distribution of power and wealth is so distorted that it cannot be regarded as legitimate? After all, did not the Universal Declaration of Human Rights, adopted by the UN General Assembly in 1948, call for the right to "an existence worthy of human dignity" and to "a social and international order" as well as to more traditional constitutional rights to peaceful assembly, free elections, secret votes, and so on? With US Congressmen denouncing Developing World regimes for not operating like a New England town assembly, and African and East Asian politicians calling for a new international economic order to replace the present "unfair" one, the issue of how to measure *what* is legitimate will rumble on.

Whether or not Great Powers in the future would rise and fall according to a historical pattern – a matter already of much academic interest[17] – it is clear that peace, stability and legitimacy will continue to occupy a central role in world affairs. Indeed, it may be that the forces for global change bearing down upon all societies, rich and poor alike, will intensify the debate upon such problems. On one side of the planet, in the laboratories and research institutes of developed nations, new technologies are transforming the way we manufacture, assemble, process, trade, and communicate. The internationalization of industry, distribution, services, and capital-flows is intensifying. National currencies are now dwarfed by the sheer volume of daily foreign-exchange dealings. Companies are breaking free of their national or regional roots to become true multinationals, driven by market forces to switch production and investment from one place to another, to replace assembly-workers with machines, to reduce labor costs. On the other side of the globe, rapid population growth occurs in virtually all poorer, resource-depleted societies. The pressure upon environments is intensifying, the pace of internal migration from the countryside to vast shanty-cities grows greater, and the social and political order – already weakened by ethnic and religious strife – is in some states visibly buckling. We now live in a world whose total population rises by 95 million annually *without* an equivalent increase in jobs, and in which for the first time in history billions of people, poor as well as rich, can see on television how "the other half" lives. We are badly damaging our ecosystems, global and local, with consequences (many scientists believe) of the utmost gravity to humankind's future.

These world-transcending technological, demographic, and environmental tendencies are important to the future story of rising and falling Great Powers because they present potential *new* threats to stability – one of our key themes – and also because they add to the debate about "what is real peace?" "What is legitimate?" Is it, for example, "legitimate" to drain water from millennia-old aquifers under the Middle East sands during the next couple of decades precisely when the human population in that region is forecast to double? Can we expect real "peace" in Central American countries where most of the territory is owned by a small number of families and millions of peasants are driven to eke out a living on marginal lands, with corresponding impacts upon the environment? Are the actions of 200,000 traders and speculators, linked by satellite and computers to a global trading network, "legitimate" when they combine to weaken a nation's currency value? Will fast-growing populations in the developing world, desperately needing to invest in healthcare for children, women's education, basic infrastructure, skill training, and so on, achieve internal "stability" if they follow World Bank advice to slash government spending?

It is difficult to produce a neat conclusion from these trends because too much is going on and different observers notice different parts of the complex dynamics of global change. But if we bring together our understanding of the historical process of the rise and fall of Great Powers, and join it to an appreciation of the newer, fast-moving, interacting forces for change, we may have reason to be concerned about the future of world peace, stability, and legitimacy. Truly, as the Chinese curse puts it, we are fated to live in interesting times.

Notes

1. John A.S. Grenville, *Lord Salisbury and Foreign Policy: The Close of the Nineteenth Century* (London: The Athlone Press 1964), chapter II.
2. See Dietrich Geyer, *Russian Imperialism: The Interaction of Domestic and Foreign Policy 1860–1914* (New Haven: Yale University Press 1987), *passim*.
3. Paul M. Kennedy, *The Rise of the Anglo-German Antagonism 1860–1914* (London/Boston: Allen & Unwin 1980), chapters 5 and 18.
4. R.T. Shannon, *Gladstone and the Bulgarian Agitation 1876* (London: Thomas Nelson 1963), *passim*.
5. Martyna Fox, *The Eastern Question in Russian Politics: Interplay of Diplomacy, Opinion and Interest, 1905–1917*. (Ph.D. dissertation, Yale University, New Haven, 1993).
6. Kennedy, *The Rise and Fall of the Great Powers: Economic Change and Military Conflict from 1500 to 2000* (New York: Random House 1987), *passim*.
7. David Calleo, *The German Problem Reconsidered* (Cambridge: Cambridge University Press 1978).
8. John Gallagher, *The Decline, Revival, and Fall of the British Empire* (New York: Cambridge University Press 1982), *passim*.
9. Samuel Huntington, "The United States – Decline or Renewal?", *Foreign Affairs*, vol. 67 (Winter 1988–89), pp. 76–96.
10. Corelli Barnett, *The Collapse of British Power* (New York: Morrow 1972), p. 593.
11. Kennedy, *The Rise and Fall of the Great Powers*, passim (see note 6).
12. Joseph S. Nye, *Bound to Lead* (New York: Basic Books 1990), especially chapter 6.
13. Diane B. Kunz, *The Economic Diplomacy of the Suez Crisis* (Chapel Hill, NC/London: The University of North Carolina Press 1991.)
14. Richard Rosecrance, *The Rise of the Trading States* (New York: Basic Books 1985).
15. See Charles Henry Wilson, *Profit and Power: A Study of England and the Dutch Wars* (New York: Longmans, Grien 1957), *passim*.
16. Boutros Boutros-Ghali, *An Agenda for Peace* (New York: United Nations 1992), pp. 9–10.
17. Christopher Layne, "The Unipolar Illusion: Why New Great Powers Will Arise", *International Security*, vol. 17, no. 4 (Spring 1993), pp. 5–51 – plus the additional comments by Robert Lewis and Samuel Huntington in the same issue.

19

The Fall of Empires:
Peace, Stability, and Legitimacy

Geir Lundestad

> *"There is nothing more contrary to nature than the attempt to hold in obedience distant provinces."*
> Edward Gibbon

In this essay I shall present my own views on the overall relationship between the fall of great powers and peace, stability, and legitimacy. My conclusions are considerably influenced by the content of the other contributions in this book, but I make no effort to strike a balance between the many different and complex interpretations expressed here.

The essay distinguishes between great powers and empires. Most great powers expanded by taking control over territories outside their own core areas. They became empires. These empires generally provided stability compared with the previous order, but over time the traditional legitimacy – international, national, and local - on which empires rested was undermined. In the end the empires collapsed. The successor states that arose were often based on ethnic self-determination and in this sense they were more legitimate than the old empires, but the new order also tended to be less stable than the old one. Thus, the conclusion is that there appears to be a tension between peace and stability on the one hand and modern legitimacy on the other.

Great Powers and Empires

The rise and fall of great powers was in part related to war. Nothing has contributed more to swift and comprehensive change in great power configurations in the twentieth century than the two world wars. It may be argued that most of the sweeping changes caused by the world wars would have happened sooner or later even without the wars, but, as a minimum, the wars greatly accelerated the fall of certain states and the rise of others. In part the fall of great powers was related to the economic, military, and technological changes on which Paul Kennedy focuses so heavily in his celebrated *The Rise and Fall of the Great Powers*.[1]

Practically all great powers developed empires in the sense that they came to control territories outside their core areas. The falling away of these "distant provinces" represented a crucial part of the decline of most great powers, a part largely ignored by Kennedy in *Rise and Fall*.

Empires rise, and then they fall. The traditional empires are all gone, including the British, the French, the Ottoman, the Austro-Hungarian. Now the Soviet empire is gone as well. The only remaining question marks concern the United States and even more China, which, in different ways, some have argued, still control imperial structures. When we say that empires fall, we primarily mean that the "distant provinces" fall away. The outlying areas of the empires could be vast. In 1909 the population of the British empire was 7.7 times greater that that of Britain itself, the area ratio was 1:94.[2] While the "distant provinces" fall away, the core areas usually remain intact. The larger the core area, the better a great power is generally able to retain its position. This is the main reason why the many comparisons between late nineteenth/early twentieth century Britain and late twentieth century United States are really misleading. Britain had a rather limited geographical core, the United States has a much larger one. Thus, the twentieth century has to a large extent been dominated by the United States and Russia/the Soviet Union with their vast cores, as Torqueville and others before him had predicted.[3] Germany had to give up its hopes for *Lebensraum*, but with its core largely intact, it has been able to stage two comebacks as a great power, Japan one.

In most cases the geographical line of division between the core and the more distant lands seemed obvious, although complications could certainly arise. At the turn of the century, British politicians, with Joseph Chamberlain in the lead, hoped that imperial federation and customs union could compensate for Britain's rather limited base.[4] The French, and the Portuguese as well, tried to do away with the formal separation between home land and colonies. These efforts all failed. However, the fall of the Soviet Union has illustrated better than anything the lack of absolute lines of division between core and "distant provinces". Not only did the outer empire in Eastern Europe fall away, but the Soviet Union itself collapsed into 15 independent states.

In this sense the United States seems rather unique. What distinguishes it from a traditional empire is the fact that the semi-distant lands, most of which were conquered from Mexico in the 1830s–1850s, have been so successfully integrated into the larger unit. The more distant lands on many continents, while being strongly influenced by the US, virtually all maintained their independence. Today the United States is one of the few very large states whose territorial integrity is accepted by virtually all of its citizens. Russia may well be reduced in size, India's break-up has been predicted since its creation, China's historically remarkable unity is threatened, despite its population being 94 percent Han (Tibet, Inner Mongolia, possibly Sinkiang), even democratic market-oriented Canada is in trouble.

Old and New Forms of Legitimacy

The falling away of the "distant provinces" was related to deep moral-political changes leading to a gradually disappearing legitimacy for imperial rule as such. In the final analysis empires rested on force, but the use of such force became increasingly difficult. Little by little imperial rule came to break with accepted norms at three basic levels: the international (the world community), the national (in the home country), and the local (in the colonies or provinces).[5] In other words, imperial rule lost its "legitimacy".

Legitimacy is here defined as a certain state of affairs being perceived as "in accordance with established rules, principles, or standards", in other words that this state of affairs "can be justified".[6] The traditional basis of legitimacy for imperial rule was dynastic. The ruler had the right to conquer whatever territory he was able to conquer and this territory could then be passed on to his heirs, more or less in the same way other forms of property were passed on to the next generation. Early on emperors came to desire some form of religious blessing for their rule, since this could strengthen their position. Imperial rulers could even find it opportune to mobilize popular, or national, sentiment, but this, again, was not something they had to do. This traditional world was one of subjects, not citizens.[7]

In this century the Austro-Hungarian empire, for instance, reflected the dynastic principle. Many pragmatic reasons, particularly of a security and an economic nature, existed for the continuation of Habsburg rule, but these did not in any way constitute the basis of imperial rule as such.[8]

Traditional forms of legitimacy have lingered on to this very day, but with the French Revolution the basis for legitimacy began to change. More and more, rule, including imperial rule, had to be justified with reference to what it did for the citizens. Modern, as opposed to earlier empires, had to provide some sort of popular justification for the rule even over "distant provinces".

As William McNeill argues in his contribution in this book, "the norm for civilized governance was laminated polyethnic empire". But this norm gradually changed to that of the nation state. The national doctrine came in two basic versions, the French and the German. In the French version it meant popular sovereignty and constitutional rule within a more or less given territory, almost regardless of the ethnic and cultural background of the various groups living inside this territory. (In France this background was relatively homogeneous anyway.) The French revolutionary case itself illustrated that the justification could be different from the "real" reasons for imperial rule. France expanded far beyond its traditional borders of the Atlantic, the Rhine, the Alps, and the Pyrénées without showing too much concern for the actual support it enjoyed in the various areas.

The German version emphasized the connection between the right of self-determination and cultural and ethnic unity, in the sense that the various cultural and ethnic groups had this right of self-determination. The problem was that in Central and Eastern Europe the various peoples lived side by side and not in nicely separated areas. The German version, too, was undoubtedly biased in favor of more traditional interests as the rather comprehensive definitions of German territory from 1848 onwards showed. Some groups were quite simply seen as more equal than others. Nevertheless, nationalism – in whatever version – presented a dramatic challenge to any form of imperial rule.

From Europe the concept of the nation state gradually spread to the rest of the world, and then normally in the French version since the alternative, the German model, could easily have led to chaos in the form of a very high number of states with endless quarrels over borders. This change of norms from empire to nation states, this erosion of the basis of imperial legitimacy, came to mean the end of imperial rule.

Imperial Rule and International and National Legitimacy

In Western Europe the process of formation of nation states was largely complete with the unification of Germany in 1870–71. (Norway, Ireland, and Iceland followed later.) In the eastern part the Ottoman empire was at this time continuing its disintegration. As Istvan Deak shows in his essay, until the First World War Austria–Hungary was holding up well, although Vienna's fear of a break-up was an important part of the origins of the war itself. The nationality question came out of control only in 1917–18. As late as January 1918, in his Fourteen Points, President Wilson still favored "the freest opportunity of autonomous development" for the peoples of Austria–Hungary, only later amended to read "complete independence for the people of Austria–Hungary". Similarly, only in early 1918 did even the South Slavs and the Czechs give up reform of the empire into a multinational federation for full independence.[9]

After the First World War, national self-determination became the norm, the legitimate standard, in all of Europe. Even where this norm was violated in practice, as in the Soviet Union, it was accepted in theory. The appeasement policy of the 1930s was in part based on the difficulty of opposing the right of Germans to join the mother country. In another way, however, Germany under Hitler presented an extreme version of imperial legitimacy in that here the *Lebensraum* ideology reflected the total victory of home country considerations over any attempt whatsoever to achieve suppport in "non-Aryan" areas.

Outside of Europe and the Americas, despite the successes of different kinds of nationalisms in Japan and in China, the system of imperial rule generally remained strong until the Second World War. In the inter-war period the primary colonial powers, Britain and France, dominated the League of Nations, and the main revisionist states, Germany, Italy, and Japan, were not opposed to imperial rule as such. Rather they wanted to create empires of their own.

Only after the Second World War, with the domination of the two anti-colonial powers, the United States and the Soviet Union, and with the increase in the number of new states, did imperial rule lose its legitimacy at the international level.[10] But by then imperial rule was also losing its legitimacy both at the national level in the home country and at the local level in the colonies.

The starting point for imperial rule was for it to have legitimacy in the home area. The basis for this legitimacy varied. The British, like other colonial powers, were long convinced that they brought progress and civilization to the backward areas of the world. This view was summed up by one Victorian administrator of India, Fitzjames Stephen, in the following rather typical way:

> The essential parts of European civilization are peace, order, the
> supremacy of law, the prevention of crime, the redress of wrong,
> the enforcement of contracts, the development and concentration
> of the military force of the state, the construction of public
> works, the collection and expenditure of the revenue required for
> these objects in such a way as to promote to the utmost the pub-
> lic interest, interfering as little as possible with the comfort or
> wealth of the inhabitants, and improvement of the people.[11]

In the Soviet case, domestic, as well as foreign, legitimacy was
grounded primarily in the Marxist–Leninist ideology. Through the
class struggle, history marched inevitably from feudalism to capitalism and on to socialism and communism. In Eastern Europe this
march of history was expressed in the form of the establishment of
the people's democracies.[12] Although Communism had only minority support in Eastern Europe, its expansion there and later in China
made even many non-Communists around the world feel that
Communism might well come to represent the wave of the future.

Since the United States did not see itself as having any empire, it
did not have to provide justifications of this sort. Most Americans
agreed that the United States had to take on the global role it did
after 1945 "to protect democracy against the totalitarian evil of
Communism". The underlying assumption was that Washington did
not do this primarily for its own sake, but for the sake of the many
states threatened by Soviet Communism. If the Americans were not
wanted, they would go home.

While British rule over the colonies was frequently imposed,
although often in combination with cooperative arrangements, and
Soviet rule over Eastern Europe was largely imposed, the American
position in Western Europe in the first years after the Second World
War can be called an informal "empire by invitation".[13] There is
little doubt why the Europeans issued their invitations: Economic
invitations were issued because only the United States could provide substantial economic assistance for Europe's war-ravaged
economies. Politico-military invitations were issued because only
the United States could provide credible guarantees against the
Soviet–Communist threat. Moreover, the United States possessed
more "soft power" than any other state, in the form of the attrac-
tiveness of its ideology, culture, and institutions.[14]

Most imperial powers lost the *will* to maintain their empires
before they lost the *power* to do so, although the two were of course
closely related. Portugal, the weakest of them all, maintained its

empire the longest. It collapsed only in 1974–75 with the introduction of democratic rule. Much of the explanation for the loss of will was found in the erosion of old-fashioned imperial legitimacy. In Britain many different forces undermined this kind of legitimacy: the spread of democracy, which brought new forces to power and made it increasingly difficult to deny democratic rule to the colonies, the concentration on expanding the social welfare of the home country, the many different effects of the First and particularly the Second World War, from the destruction of racist social Darwinist thinking to the emphasis on democracy in the fight against fascism, evolving concepts of interest and security that undermined the imperial rationale, etc.

Ultimately imperial rule rested on force, but it became increasingly difficult to use this force. The tolerance level for the use of force varied from imperial capital to imperial capital. It also changed over time. The Indian mutiny of 1857–58 was suppressed with considerable ferocity. The ferocity did not weaken the legitimacy in Britain of imperial rule, it rather strengthened it: The "bettering" of the Indian would take even longer than had been expected. The much more limited Amritsar massacre of 1919, however, led to a certain immediate outburst of patriotic feeling in some British quarters, but soon had quite the opposite effect.[15] In 1945 the new Viceroy, Lord Wavell, commented on "the weakness and weariness of the instrument still at our disposal in the shape of the British element in the Indian Civil Service". The massive use of force was now quite simply out of the question, also for an emotional old imperialist such as Winston Churchill.[16] Even after the Second World War, France, on the other hand, accepted quite massive use of force, as evidenced by the wars in Indochina and in Algeria, but in the end the moral-political crisis over Algeria led to the fall of the Fourth Republic.

In the Soviet case, at least in hindsight, we can see that Moscow's will to use force had been eroding even before Mikhail Gorbachev took over in 1985. In 1953 in East Germany and in 1956 in Hungary the Red Army intervened alone, in 1968 in Czechoslovakia Moscow wanted and got the formal support of its Warsaw Pact allies (with the exception of Romania), and in 1980–81 in Poland the task of suppression was left to the Polish forces alone.[17] In 1988–89 Soviet physical power remained intact, but not the will to use this power.

At the very moment when the Soviet Union had finally become the equal of the United States in some important respects, the entire system imploded. As Vladislav Zubok in particular shows, a high degree of external legitimacy could not compensate for the slow erosion in domestic legitimacy which in turn was related to faltering economic growth, increasingly serious nationality, health, and environmental problems, rife corruption, etc. Gorbachev knew the system had to be reformed but had only the vaguest ideas what the reforms ought to lead to; he gave up the old basis of Communist legitimacy, however weak, without understanding the need to establish a new one. He was clear on one point, however: force would not be used on a major scale. With popular support for Communist rule dwindling both in Eastern Europe and in the Soviet Union, this meant the end of Soviet rule.[18]

The growing legitimacy problems of imperial rule made the imperial power take on a substantial and, generally, an increasing share of the total expenses involved in maintaining the empire. The subsidies which imperial capitals often came to supply to the provinces represented an attempt to stop the erosion of imperial legitimacy. Yet, the growing costs in turn undermined domestic support for the continuation of imperial rule. A vicious circle was created.

In the British case, the best studies available indicate that while the absolute expenses involved in running the empire were small, the British level of taxation in the late nineteenth–early twentieth century years was higher than in its industrial competitors. Taxes in the dependent Empire, on the other hand, were 20 to 40 percent lower than in other "underdeveloped" areas. In India, where the British pressed the hardest for self-financing, taxes were actually lower than in the Princely States. For the state the trend was clear: the colonies cost more and more. The profits that British individuals and companies, as opposed to the British state, made, were also generally higher before 1885 than after.[19]

In the Austro-Hungarian case, after the *Ausgleich* of 1867 the distribution of common expenses between Austria and Hungary were renegotiated every ten years. Here the Austrians were actually able to reduce their share somewhat, but after 1907 they still paid 63.6 and the Hungarians 36.4 percent of common expenses. (In 1900 the population relationship was 55.7 percent for Austria and 41.0 percent for Hungary.) But in this case Vienna paid a heavy price for such economic concessions in the form of increasing Hungarian political autonomy.[20]

Even in the Soviet case, where the element of consent on the part of the governed was smaller than in the other empires we are dealing with, similar developments can be seen. In the early years after

1945 the Soviet Union was taking substantial resources out of Eastern Europe, not only from the defeated Axis countries, but also from the Allied states. In one particularly striking example, in 1945–46 the Soviet Union paid only one-tenth of world market prices for Polish coal deliveries.[21] In 1956 the Polish Communists for the first time protested against such deliveries of coal to the Soviet Union. In the 1970s, the relationship was reversed. Now the Soviet Union was subsidizing oil and gas deliveries to Eastern Europe, and in return the Eastern Europeans often paid with rather shoddy industrial goods which could not be exported to Western markets. As one study of energy supplies within the Soviet bloc concludes, "The Soviet insistence, in 1968, on maintaining limits on East European autonomy also entailed accepting the responsibility for the cost of making compliance possible".[22] Within the Warsaw Pact the highest defense expenditures had to be borne by the Soviet side, despite the Soviet economy clearly being weaker than that of several of the Eastern European countries.[23]

Related mechanisms can be detected also within the loosest of all imperial structures, the American one. After 1945 the United States was clearly the world's economic leader. This status undoubtedly involved economic benefits, but it also involved great expenses varying from the more than 100 billion dollars provided in credits and grants in the years from 1945 to 1965 to the many concessions made within GATT in general and *vis-à-vis* the Japanese in particular.[24]

In NATO, the United States paid much more for defense than did its allies. And *American* troops, not the troops of the "vassals", were deployed to suffer the heaviest initial casualties in case of war, a rather special arrangement in historical terms.[25] In an effort to reduce its expenditures and bring back the troops, the United States promoted European integration. Such a structure in which the imperial center did not even participate was a historical novelty. Thus, Vienna worked hard to centralize decision-making within the Habsburg empire, London was always at the center of any Commonwealth arrangement, and Moscow came out against federative plans for Eastern Europe.[26]

Even the British and the Americans undoubtedly set up their international orders with their own advantage in mind, but we know the outcome: under these very orders, Britain came to be surpassed economically by several other powers, while the United States soon entered a period of relative decline economically both *vis-à-vis* Western Europe and Japan.

Imperial Legitimacy in the "distant provinces"

The legitimacy of imperial rule was only decided in the home country. The attitudes of the "distant provinces" were even more important, in part because they had such a decisive impact on attitudes in the home country. Independence was something the "distant provinces" seized.

After the initial period of establishing control, colonial rule generally functioned well and met little opposition. Thus, in the 1920s and 1930s, the British empire was generally quieter than it had ever been before. As long as the "provinces" accepted the white colonialists' right to rule, few problems existed. But once black and yellow people rejected white supremacy, imperial rule rested rather, directly on force. After the Second World War the days when "every white skin automatically extracted a salute" were gone. Many different factors led to such rejection: Western Enlightenment values, often imbibed by the local elites in their education first in the metropole and later in the colonies themselves, the experiences of colonial troops in the two world wars, the rise of Marxism–Leninism and of the Soviet Union, and, probably most important, Japan's victories in the early phase of the Second World War, etc. [27]

In the inter-war period, in addition to the Middle East and Ireland, there was one exception to the imperial calm, India. The Indian Congress Party changed from being the debate forum for a narrow upper class, which it had been in the initial years after its founding in 1885, to a well-organized mass movement bent on full independence after 1919. Gandhi's leadership transformed the policies of the Congress as well as its support in the villages. To a large extent Gandhi was able to set the political agenda which eventually lead to independence. In 1945–46, India's towns and villages had slipped beyond British control. The armed forces were on the verge of mutiny. Wavell reported that India had become ungovernable.

Once the gates had been opened in India, it proved difficult to close them elsewhere. This was not realized by contemporary politicians, as witnessed in a war-time statement by Herbert Morrison, Labour's deputy leader, that giving independence to the African colonies would be "like giving a child of ten a latch-key, a bank account, and a shot-gun". The demonstrations/riots in Accra in the Gold Coast from 28 February to 4 March 1948 led to 29 dead and 237 injured. Earlier these events would hardly have qualified as a major crisis, but now they led directly to Ghana's independence nine years later.[28] As A.D. Low has argued, "It is not fanciful to assert that many of the critical battles for British colonial Africa were fought, not on the banks of the Volta, the Niger, or the Zambesi, but on the Ganges."[29] The imperial rationale had been undermined, a pattern had been set, and quickly decolonization accelerated to a process of almost incredible speed.

It is difficult to escape the conclusion that empires contain within them the seeds of their destruction. It is simply impossible to run a vast empire entirely from the imperial center, and once lower units are formed it appears that sooner or later they almost inevitably will compete with the imperial center.[30] This proved to be the case with the colonies, where the units were, to a large extent, artificial creations. It was even more difficult to hold historic states with well-developed identities in place. In this perspective the surprise is not that the Austro-Hungarian empire collapsed, but that it functioned so well for as long as it did. In part this was the result of playing the "historic" nationalities, Germans, Magyars, and Poles, against the "non-historic" Slovenes, Croats, Romanians, Ukrainians, etc. (with the Czechs having features of both).[31]

The fall of the Soviet empire resulted in great part from the implosion of the imperial center. But the basis for Soviet rule was never solid in that most East Europeans were not only hostile to Moscow, but also considered themselves culturally superior to the Russians – not a very good foundation for an empire (unless the superior subjects held a privileged position as the Greeks did in the Roman empire and the British liked to think they did in the American one).

After the *Gleichschaltung* of the Stalin years, the history of Eastern Europe after 1953 is the history of the evolution of national forms of Communism where the limits of what Moscow was obliged to permit were constantly stretched. The interventions of 1953, 1956, and 1968 only temporarily interrupted this process. Even without the imperial implosion, it seems likely that sooner rather than later the development of these national forms would have broken not only the Soviet mould, as Yugoslavia, Albania, and Romania had already done, but even the Communist one, as Poland and Hungary were getting close to doing in the 1980s.[32]

One is tempted to draw a similar, although admittedly quite speculative conclusion about the long-term outcome of a victory in Europe for Hitler-Germany. As Wolfgang Mommsen suggests, it is unlikely that German supremacy over such a vast and culturally strong area would have lasted, based as it was on *Lebensraum* and racial hierarchy thinking, elements that strongly limited local support in most parts of Europe.

There may be elements which hold empires together for shorter or longer periods, such as geographic conditions, economic complementarity or ideological bonds. Common defense needs perhaps represent the strongest of all such bonds, but these needs fluctuate with the outside threat. Practically all of Austria–Hungary could unite against the Turkish advance, and the Germans and the Magyars could unite against the Russian–Slavic threat, but with millions of Slavs within the empire even the Russian–Slavic threat divided it.[33] Yet, in the long run the unifying elements all seem to lose out to the desire for independence.

The post-1945 American "empire" was built very much on the Soviet–Communist threat. With the collapse of the Soviet Union, history would seem to suggest that a gradual but comprehensive redefinition of relations between the United States, Western Europe, and Japan is likely to take place. Although it is a vast exaggeration to talk about the "fall" of the United States, there is actually near unanimity among scholars that the American position has declined, particularly on the economic side, compared with the situation in the first twenty years after the Second World War.[34] On the Western side the consequences of the collapse of the Soviet Union and the decline even of the United States are already apparent in the difficulties formerly American-led organizations such as NATO and GATT are experiencing.

Pax Imperialis?

What then of the relationship between legitimacy and stability? While rivalry between great powers often results in war, and disagreement over the borders of their respective spheres may be a more specific source of tension (for instance the many conflicts over Belgium, Poland, the Yugoslav area, Afghanistan, and Korea), it is often assumed that great powers promote peace at least *within* their imperial borders. When they collapse, on the other hand, this will increase the local level of conflict.

This observation seems to hold true in most cases. Thus, Britain was generally able to maintain order within its huge empire, encompassing at its apogee about 25 percent of the world's population and 22 percent of its territory. In Africa, not only imperial, but also African historians argue that colonialism brought about a greater degree of peace and stability. The African-dominated *UNESCO General History of Africa* concludes that "not even the anti-colonial and Marxist schools would deny the fact that after the colonial occupation ... most parts of Africa especially from the end of the First World War onwards enjoyed a great degree of continuous peace and security".[35] In India British rule may well have prevented a "Balkanization" on the ruins of the Moghul empire. The British were able to control vast territories with few forces. 75 000 British troops, supported by 150 000 Indian troops, controlled a population of about 300 million.[36]

Austria-Hungary's stability was celebrated in the famous 1848 dictum of the Czech historian and politician Frantisek Palacky: "If Austria did not exist, it would be necessary to invent her", a dictum which found echo not only among contemporary statesmen, but also among later historians.[37] Finally, in Eastern Europe in the years from 1945 to 1989 the Soviet Union was able to maintain an even more stable structure than had Austria–Hungary.

Some qualifications are in order, however. Pax Britannica, like other orders, did not mean that there was peace everywhere. In such a vast empire smaller wars were almost always taking place somewhere. In fact, "there was not a single year in Queen Victoria's long reign in which somewhere in the world her soldiers were not fighting for her and for her empire".[38]

More specifically two observations should be made. First, the initial period, when imperial control was established, was seldom peaceful and frequently led to great losses of life among the local populations, much smaller among the imperial troops. In Africa the worst example was probably the Congo where the population may have been halved in three to four decades (famine and disease undoubtedly contributed greatly to this tragic outcome).[39] The establishment of Habsburg control in Central Europe and Soviet control over Eastern Europe was so closely related to wars with outside powers, the Ottoman empire and Nazi Germany respectively, that it is virtually impossible to separate the two.

Second, as we have seen, empires collapsed in great part because of local resistance. The British yielded early and were therefore able to give up power largely peacefully. India had been the prime target of colonialism; in 1946–47 it set the stage again by gaining its freedom. (An earlier model was of course found in the independence of first the United States and then of Latin America.) The French experience in the bloody wars of Indochina and Algeria illustrated what could take place if an attempt was made to hang on to power in the face of great opposition. Thus, the peace and stability of great power rule was often limited to the long years in the middle of its rule, less to its beginning and its end.

Stability and Legitimacy

Thus, whether we are talking about the Pax Britannica, the Pax Sovietica, or other orders, compared with what preceded and what followed, the imperial orders generally represented stability. The stability of the long middle period of the Pax Britannica was replaced by local wars, for instance between India and Pakistan or in the Middle East. As Carol Saivetz shows in her contribution, the Cold War sometimes enhanced the level of conflict, but often it served to contain violence. It is unlikely that the post-Cold War order will be any more stable than that of the Cold War. In Europe, where the two superpowers had the strongest influence, the end of the Cold War has clearly led to a higher rather than a lower level of violence.[40]

When the ethnic nation states were formed, the expectation had been that this would lead to a more peaceful world. As J.G. Herder expressed it in the 1780s: "Cabinets may deceive each other; political machines may exert pressure on each other until one is shattered. Fatherlands do not march against each other in this way; they live quietly side by side and help each other like families."[41]

Herder's conclusion was much too simplistic. The complicated, not to say tense relationship between stability and legitimacy, and then legitimacy in the sense of ethnic-national independence, is seen in Asia and Africa, but is best illustrated in Central and Eastern Europe. The long period of peace from 1815 to 1859 rested upon Austrian control over, or suppression of, Italy. Italy could only be united after the French had helped defeat the Austrians in 1859. German national aspirations could only be fulfilled after three wars, against Denmark, Austria, and France. From 1870 to 1914 the Austro-Hungarian order was remarkably stable and, one might add, rather flexible. But, at least in modern national(ist) terms, it was based on the suppression of the national rights of most groups other than the Hungarians and, to a lesser extent, the Germans.

The inter-war order was more legitimate than the Austro-Hungarian one in the sense that many large ethnic groups finally acquired their own states, but it was also rather unstable. The new states quarreled over borders and population rights. In Eastern Europe no order could be fully legitimate, and the right of Germans to join the mother country was only the most explosive of the many unresolved issues.[42]

The Soviet empire represented the most clear-cut example of the tension between stability and legitimacy. Despite the Red Army's interventions, on the whole the Soviet order was remarkably stable, and "the long peace" in Europe was based on Soviet domination of the Eastern half.[43] But this most stable of orders was also the least legitimate of orders. When the Pax Sovietica collapsed, a host of ethnic-national questions sprang to the surface. The new post-Cold-War order was clearly more legitimate than the Soviet one, but it was definitely also less stable.[44]

One should hasten to add that neither the Austro-Hungarian nor the Soviet empire was able to solve the ethnic-national questions which represented such a problem from a legitimacy point of view. At best they simply postponed them, at worst they aggravated them. The latter was almost certainly the effect of the Soviet empire. In reaction against the oppressive uniformity and the extreme degree of centralization, once the various ethnic-national forces finally had a chance to express themselves, they tended to go to the extreme.[45]

Most of us probably find a positive message in the fact that the "distant provinces" became independent states. But, as John Gaddis shows in his contribution, this process now raises serious questions. About 3500 groups define themselves as "nations". This means that so far only about 5 percent of them have achieved statehood.[46] How many states will there "eventually" be and how will the creation of the new states affect peace and stability?

In this overall perspective, the attempt to form new and larger units out of smaller ones is dramatic. The history of the United States is interesting, but so special that few conclusions can probably be drawn on the basis of the American experience. The European Community has been able to combine geographic widening from 6 to 12 members with a deepening of the content from a common market to some sort of rudimentary economic federation. In view of three major wars between France and Germany in 70 years, this level of integration is remarkable indeed, but outside "the four freedoms" the emphasis is still more on the national than on the joint European level. The EC budget still makes up only 1.4 percent of the total EC gross national product, compared to more than 20 percent for the federal budget in the U.S.

How does the tension between stability and ethnic-national legitimacy stand in relation to Immanuel Kant's well-known argument about the peaceful nature of democracies as presented in its modern version by Michael Doyle?[47] In his original study Doyle was not able to find a single example of a democracy going to war against another democracy (as opposed to going to war against a dictatorship or conducting colonial wars).

It should be emphasized that the establishment of ethnic-national states, which is the dimension of legitimacy focused upon here, does not necessarily mean the introduction of democracy, as we have seen in many countries in Asia and Africa after the collapse of colonialism and in many parts of the old Soviet Union after its implosion. Furthermore, few states are ethnically homogeneous, and sometimes the legitimacy problems of the old empire are simply transferred to the new states. (For instance, from Austria–Hungary to Yugoslavia, to Bosnia-Hercegovina, and to the various parts of Bosnia.)

There is probably much to the argument of the peaceful nature of democracies, but the kind of absolute correlation established by Doyle depends in part on strict definitions of democracy which exclude some difficult cases. Historically, the American civil war, the Spanish-American war, the Boer war, and the enthusiasm for war in most great powers in 1914 – all of these defined out by Doyle – would tend to make one skeptical about the existence of any absolute relationship between democracy and peace. More recently the wars between Israel and Lebanon, Greece and Turkey, India and Pakistan all raise similar questions, although it is striking that really substantial clashes have occurred only when one or both of these parties have had non-democratic governments.[48]

Today, as we see in Serbia, Croatia, and Bosnia and in Armenia and Azerbaijan, there seems to be no lack of popular support for war against another government with popular support, although, again, they may not necessarily be defined as full democracies. As is evident from Doyle's own essay in the present book, these examples have also made Doyle himself question his earlier conclusions somewhat. Furthermore, the spread of democracy will probably underline the fact that the zone of peace through North America, Western Europe, and Australia–New Zealand has depended on other factors than the form of government alone. Yet, to the extent it continues to hold up, Kant–Doyle's argument should give reason for some optimism, since there have never been as many democracies in the world as there are today.[49]

It would be nice if, in life as in politics, all good things went together. Unfortunately, often they do not, as I have tried to show in this analysis of the complex relationship between the fall of great powers and peace, stability, and legitimacy.

Notes

1. Paul Kennedy, *The Rise and Fall of the Great Powers. Economic Change and Military Conflict from 1500 to 2000* (New York: Random House 1987).

2. *The Penguin Atlas of World History. Volume Two: From the French Revolution to the Present* (Penguin Books 1978), p. 102. Geir Lundestad, *The American "Empire" and Other Studies of US Foreign Policy in a Comparative Perspective* (Oxford–Oslo: Oxford University Press–Norwegian University Press 1990), p. 55.

3. Theodore Draper, *Present History: On Nuclear War, Detente, and Other Controversies* (New York: Vintage Books 1984), pp. 323–351.

4. Bernard Porter, *The Lion's Share. A Short History of British Imperialism 1850–1983* (London: Longman 1984), pp. 129–139. Aaron L. Friedberg, *The Weary Titan. Britain and the Experience of Relative Decline, 1895–1905* (Princeton: Princeton University Press 1988), pp. 49–51, 83–88.

5. This section is in part inspired by Wm. Roger Louis and Ronald Robinson, "The United States and the Liquidation of the British Empire in Tropical Africa, 1941–1951", in Prosser Gifford and Wm. Roger Louis, eds., *The Transfer of Power in Africa. Decolonization 1940–1960* (New Haven: Yale University Press 1982), pp. 31–56.

6. *The Random House College Dictionary* (New York: Random House, 1984), p. 765. *The Advanced Learner's Dictionary of Current English* (London: Oxford University Press 1967), p. 558.

7. For some interesting comments on early legitimacy, see James Mayall, *Nationalism and International Society* (Cambridge: Cambridge University Press 1990), pp. 26–32.

8. Among the many histories of Austria–Hungary I have relied most upon Robert A. Kann, *A History of the Habsburg Empire 1526–1918* (Berkeley: University of California Press 1974); Stanley R. Williamson, Jr., *Austria–Hungary and the Origins of the First World War* (London: Macmillan 1991); F.R. Bridge, *The Habsburg Monarchy among the Great Powers 1815–1918* (New York: Berg 1990); Alan Sked, *The Decline and Fall of the Habsburg Empire 1815–1918* (London: Longman 1989); Adam Wandruszka und Peter Urbanitsch, eds., *Die Habsburgermonarchie 1848–1918. Band VI: Die Habsburgermonarchie im System der Internationalen Beziehungen* (Wien: Verlag der Österreichischen Akademie der Wissenschaften 1989); Istvan Deak, *Beyond Nationalism: A Social and Political History of the Habsburg Officer Corps, 1848–1918* (Oxford: Oxford University Press 1990).

9. Kann, *A History of the Habsburg Empire 1526–1918*, pp. 487–520 (see note 8). See also Istvan Deak's contribution in the present book.

10. For a fine short analysis of this process, see Hedley Bull, "The Emergence of a Universal International Society", in Hedley Bull and Adam Watson, eds., *The Expansion of International Society* (Oxford: Clarendon Press 1984), pp. 117–126.

11. Quoted from J.M. Roberts, *The Triumph of the West* (London: BBC 1985), p.318. See also Porter, *The Lion's Share*, pp. 134–138 (see note 4).

12. See for instance *Soviet Foreign Policy. Volume II: 1945–1980* (Moscow: Progress Publishers 1981), pp. 16–17.

13. Lundestad, *The American "Empire"*, pp. 37–39, 54–62 (see note 2).
14. "Soft power" is Joseph Nye's concept. See his, *Bound to Lead. The Changing Nature of American Power* (New York: Basic Books 1990) particularly pp. 31–35.
15. For brief accounts of the Indian mutiny and Amritsar, see Porter, *The Lion's Share*, pp. 28–47, 251–254 (see note 4).
16. The Wavell quote is from P.J. Cain and A.G. Hopkins, *British Imperialism. Crisis and Deconstruction 1914–1990* (London: Longman 1993), p. 195. The most recent appraisal of Churchill is Robert Blake and Wm. Roger Louis, eds., *Churchill. A Major New Assessment of his Life in Peace and War* (Oxford: Oxford University Press 1993). See particularly the chapters by Ronald Hyam, "Churchill and the Empire", pp. 167–85 and by Sarvepalli Gopal, "Churchill and India", pp. 457–71. For India in general, see for instance Percival Spear, *A History of India* (Penguin Books 1965). Useful, as always, is also Porter, *The Lion's Share*, particularly pp. 254, 289 (see note 4).
17. Timothy Garton Ash, *The Uses of Adversity* (Cambridge: Granta Books 1989), pp. 222–23.
18. Mikhail Gorbachev, *Perestroika: New Thinking for Our Country and the World* (New York: Harper & Row 1987); Adam B. Ulam, *The Communists. The Story of Power and Lost Illusions 1948–1991* (New York: Scribner 1992). John Miller, *Mikhail Gorbachev and the End of Soviet Power* (New York: St. Martin 1993); Jeffrey Gedmin, *The Hidden Hand. Gorbachev and the Collapse of East Germany* (Washington, D.C.: AEI Press 1992).
19. Lance E. Davis and Robert A. Huttenbach, *Mammon and the Pursuit of Empire. The Political Economy of British Imperialism, 1860–1912* (Cambridge: Cambridge University Press 1986), pp. 315–16. Patrick K. O'Brien, "The Costs and Benefits of British Imperialism 1846–1914", *Past & Present*, No. 120, August 1988, pp. 163–200 and No. 125, November 1989, pp. 192–199;. D.K. Fieldhouse, *The Colonial Empires. A Comparative Survey from the Eighteenth Century* (London: Macmillan), pp. 380–394.
20. Williamson, *Austria–Hungary and the Origins of the First World War*, pp. 13.-15; Kann, *A History of the Habsburg Empire 1526-1918*, p. 605; Sked, *The Decline and Fall of the Habsburg Empire*, p. 233 (see note 8).
21. Hugh Seton-Watson, *From Lenin to Khrushchev. The History of World Communism* (New York: Praeger 1968), p. 255.
22. William M. Reisinger, *Energy and the Soviet Bloc. Alliance Politics after Stalin* (Ithaca: Cornell University Press 1992), p. 112.
23. Daniel N. Nelson and Joseph Lepgold, "Alliances and Burden-sharing: A NATO-Warsaw Pact Comparison", *Defense Analysis* Volume 2, No. 3, pp. 205–224, particularly p. 220.
24. Charles P. Kindleberger, "Hierarchy versus Inertial Cooperation", *International Organization*, Volume 40, Autumn 1986, particularly p. 841; Lundestad, *The American "Empire"*, pp. 37–39, 63–65 (see note 2). See also Alfred E. Eckes, "Trading American Interests", *Foreign Affairs*, 1992:4, pp. 135–154.
25. Ernest May, "The American Commitment to Germany, 1949–1955" in Lawrence S. Kaplan, ed., *American Historians and the Atlantic Alliance*

(Kent: Kent State University Press 1991), p. 76.

26. For an interesting paper on the Soviet case, see Leonid Gibianski, "The Formation of the Model of "The Socialist Camp" and the Soviet-Yugoslav Conflict in 1948", Paper presented at the conference The Soviet Union in Eastern Europe, 1945–1989, arranged by the Norwegian Nobel Institute, 28 February-1 March 1992.

27. For a stimulating treatment of the racial aspect, see R.J. Vincent, "Racial Equality", in Bull and Watson, *The Expansion of International Society*, pp. 239–54 (see note 10). See also Cain and Hopkins, *British Imperialism 1914–1990*, pp. 195–96 (see note 16).

28. The Morrison quotation is from Colin Cross, *The Fall of the British Empire* (London: Paladin, 1970), pp. 270–71. For the Accra riots, see also *ibid.*, pp. 278–79 and John D. Hargreaves, "Toward the Transfer of Power in British West Africa", in Gifford and Louis, *The Transfer of Power in Africa*, pp. 135–36 (see note 5).

29. D.A. Low, "The Asian Mirror to Tropical Africa's Independence" in Gifford and Louis, *The Transfer of Power in Africa*, p. 3 (see note 5).

30. Alexander J. Motyl, "From Imperial Decay to Imperial Collapse: The Fall of the Soviet Empire in Comparative Perspective" in Richard L. Rudolph and David F. Good, eds., *Nationalism and Empire. The Habsburg Empire and the Soviet Union* (New York: St. Martin 1992), pp. 15–43.

31. John-Paul Himka, "Nationality Problems in the Habsburg Monarchy and the Soviet Union: The Perspective of History" in Rudolph and Good, *Nationalism and Empire*, p. 82 in particular (see note 30).

32. Ash, *The Uses of Adversity* and *We the people: The Revolution of '89 Witnessed in Warsaw, Budapest, Berlin & Prague* (Cambridge: Granta Books, 1990). See also Richard Pipes, *The Vanished Specter of Communism*, Norwegian Nobel Institute Spring Lecture 1993 (Oxford: Oxford University Press 1994), pp. 52–67.

33. Kann, *A History of the Habsburg Empire*, pp. 25–27, 337–38, 607–08 (see note 8).

34. Lundestad, *The American "Empire"*, pp. 85–87 (see note 2). In her contribution in the present book Susan Strange might seem to go against this consensus. But I would argue that her emphasis on the change in American diplomacy from benign to malign hegemony and to unilateralism is actually another way of saying that the American position has declined.

35. A. Adu Boahen, "Colonialism in Africa: its Impact and Significance", in A. Adu Boahen, *Africa under Colonial Domination 1880–1935*, UNESCO General History of Africa, Volume VII (London: Heineman 1985), p. 785. For a somewhat different emphasis, see J.F. Ade Ajayi's contribution in the present volume. This more negative view should, however, be compared with his own more standard chapters in Ajayi, ed., *Africa in the Nineteenth Century until the 1880s*, UNESCO General History of Africa, Volume VI (London: Heineman 1989), particularly pp. 5, 788–89, 791.

36. Friedberg, *The Weary Titan*, pp. 220–21 (see note 4); Fieldhouse, *The Colonial Empires*, pp. 277–78 (see note 19).

37. Bridge, *The Habsburg Monarchy among the Great Powers*, p. 41. See also the references under note 8.

38. Byron Farwell, *Queen Victoria's Little Wars* (New York: Norton 1972), p. 1.

39. Boahen, "Colonialism in Africa", p. 785 (see note 35); John Lonsdale,

"The European Scramble and Conquest in African History" in Roland Oliver and G.N. Sanderson, eds., *The Cambridge History of Africa. Volume 6 from 1870 to 1905* (Cambridge: Cambridge University Press 1985), pp. 680–766, particularly p. 748.

40. For the many conflicts after 1945, see for instance Patrick Brogan, *The Fighting Never Stopped. A Comprehensive Guide to World Conflict Since 1945* (New York: Vintage Books 1990). For a strong, probably too strong indictment of the colonial heritage, see Basil Davidson, *The Black Man's Burden. Africa and the Curse of the Nation-State* (London: Currey 1992). I have speculated on the stability of the Cold War and the post-Cold-War orders in my "The End of the Cold War, the New Role for Europe, and the Decline of the United States" in Michael Hogan, ed., *The End of the Cold War. Its Meaning and Implications* (Cambridge: Cambridge University Press 1992), pp. 195–206 and in "Beyond the Cold War: New and Old Dimensions in International Relations" in Geir Lundestad and Odd Arne Westad eds., *Beyond the Cold War: New Dimensions in International Relations* (Oslo: Scandinavian University Press 1993), pp. 245–57.

41. The Herder quotation is from M.S. Anderson, *The Rise of Modern Diplomacy 1450–1919* (London: Longman 1993), p. 196. For a modern argument along similar lines, see Michael Walzer, "The Reform of the International System" in Øyvind Østerud, ed., *Studies of War and Peace* (Oslo: Norwegian University Press 1986), pp. 227–250.

42. My thinking on this point has been influenced by Michael Howard, "The Causes of War" in Østerud, *Studies of War and Peace*, particularly pp. 26–27.

43. John Gaddis, *The Long Peace. Inquiries into the History of the Cold War* (Oxford: Oxford University Press 1987), pp. 215–45.

44. The most pessimistic analysis of the new situation is found in John Mearsheimer, "Back to the Future: Instability in Europe after the Cold War", *International Security*, 15:1, Summer 1990, pp. 5–56.

45. For an interesting statement on this point, see Vaclav Havel, "The Post-Communist Nightmare", *New York Review of Books*, 27 May 1993, pp. 8–10.

46. Eugene Robinson, "Experts Fear Rise in Bosnia-Type Ethnic Conflicts as Peoples Fight for Identity", *International Herald Tribune*, 20 August, 1992, p. 5.

47. Michael Doyle, "Kant, Liberal Legacies, and Foreign Affairs", *Philosophy and Public Affairs* 12, Summer/Fall 1983, pp. 205–35, 323–35. See also Nils Petter Gleditsch, "Democracy and Peace", *Journal of Peace Research*, 29:4, November 1992, pp. 369–76.

48. Bruce Russett, *Grasping the Democratic Peace. Principles for a Post-Cold War World* (Princeton: Princeton University Press 1993), particularly pp. 16–21.

49. Samuel P. Huntington, *The Third Wave: Democratization in the Late Twentieth Century* (Norman: University of Oklahoma Press 1991).

Index